Making the American Self

℘☞ Daniel Walker Howe

Making the American Self

Jonathan Edwards to Abraham Lincoln

OXFORD
UNIVERSITY PRESS

2009

OXFORD

UNIVERSITY PRESS

Oxford University Press, Inc., publishes works that further
Oxford University's objective of excellence
in research, scholarship, and education.

Oxford   New York
Auckland   Cape Town   Dar es Salaam   Hong Kong   Karachi
Kuala Lumpur   Madrid   Melbourne   Mexico City   Nairobi
New Delhi   Shanghai   Taipei   Toronto

With offices in
Argentina   Austria   Brazil   Chile   Czech Republic   France   Greece
Guatemala   Hungary   Italy   Japan   Poland   Portugal   Singapore
South Korea   Switzerland   Thailand   Turkey   Ukraine   Vietnam

First published by Harvard University Press, 1997
First issued as an Oxford University Press paperback, 2009
198 Madison Avenue, New York, NY 10016

www.oup.com

Oxford is a registered trademark of Oxford University Press

Library of Congress Cataloging-in-Publication Data
Howe, Daniel Walker.
Making the American self : Jonathan Edwards to Abraham Lincoln
/ Daniel Walker Howe.
p.   cm.
"First published by Harvard University Press, 1997."
Includes bibliographical references and index.
ISBN 978-0-19-538789-6 (pbk.)
1. National characteristics, American.
2. Identity (Psychology)—United States.
3. United States—Intellectual life—1783–1865.   I. Title.
E169.1.H769 2009
973—dc22   2009000982

9 8 7 6 5 4 3 2 1

Printed in the United States of America
on acid-free paper

For Sandra

Contents

Self-culture is possible, not only because we can enter into and search ourselves. We have a still nobler power, that of acting on, determining, and forming ourselves. This is a fearful as well as glorious endowment.

—William Ellery Channing, *Self-Culture,* 1838

Introduction

Once upon a time Americans spoke very freely about the importance of constructing oneself properly. They encouraged people, especially the young, to "self-improvement" and "self-culture," to "make something of themselves." As examples for imitation, they pointed to individuals they called "self-made men." Today the language for speaking about the self has changed enormously, and it is not even clear to us what was meant by the old-fashioned terminology.

This is a book about ideas Americans once had concerning the proper construction of the self. It treats the period from the early 1700s to the later 1800s, a span of about a century and a half. It is a book of intellectual history, that is, it tries to explain ideas expressed in the past—their *content,* relationship to each other and to earlier ideas people knew about—and their *context,* including the lives of the people who expressed them and their audiences. For the most part, it deals with what David A. Hollinger has called "the discourse of intellectuals."[1] The people I place in the foreground were not only literate and intelligent but also (to varying degrees) original thinkers. They were engaged in a common discussion ("discourse") lasting across several generations about the composition of human nature, the motivation of human behavior, and what can be done about the social problems these create. Thoughtful people could participate in such a discussion because they shared a common model of what human nature was like and how human selves should be constructed. Not until the final section of the book, however, do we encounter subjects who thought of themselves as something like intellectuals in our sense—that is, as members of a distinct social group especially concerned with ideas and social criticism. The word was seldom used in this sense before the late nineteenth century: our usage of it presupposes both the bifurcation of culture into high and popular, and the evolution of the concept of alienation by Romantics, Marxists, and others.[2] It will become clear that I believe the sources I use discuss issues relevant to the experience of a wide range of Americans. The practice of self-construction was not peculiar to intellectuals as a social group (or even to people of intelligence, which was and is a much larger group).

Some of the people examined here were well known and influential in their time; at least one of them (Thoreau) was not. They were chosen because I felt that they understood the issues of this particular discussion well and could help illuminate them for us in our own time. Their writings do not fall into any single literary or professional *genre* recognized today, or even in their own time. I hope that the very diversity of source material—public and private, political, psychological, polemical, philosophical, theological, even advice to parents—illustrates the pervasiveness of the model of human nature under examination.

Because the book is organized around illustrative examples, it is far from comprehensive, much less exhaustive, in its coverage. In my opening chapter I present the contrasting views of two colonial Americans, Jonathan Edwards and Benjamin Franklin, who illustrate respectively the traditional distrust of individual autonomy and the new enthusiasm for it. Edwards and Franklin agreed, however, in their assessment of human nature and the difficulties it put in the way of a virtuous life. In the next chapters I describe the origins of the eighteenth-century model of human nature that Edwards and Franklin shared with so many others, and then demonstrate how that model was applied by Thomas Jefferson and the framers of the American Constitution. Moving to the nineteenth century, I address the increasingly wide practice of self-construction and the appearance of the cult of the self-made man, illustrated by Abraham Lincoln and Frederick Douglass. I discuss the efforts to shape the selves of others made by some of the great nineteenth-century reformers. In the final section of the book I turn to the New England Romantics, who were probably the Americans of their time most deeply committed to the process of self-construction. Margaret Fuller and Henry David Thoreau were powerfully innovative thinkers who went far beyond the bounds of conventional attitudes in their reflections upon self-construction.

In this book, my hope has been to shed a series of spotlights on a theme that has hitherto not been well understood. But in offering this selection of subjects, I have left out many other possibilities. I have not treated Southern planters other than Jefferson and Madison, although the plantation aristocracy was deeply committed to the practice of self-construction. I have not treated charlatans or tricksters, although examples ranging from P. T. Barnum to Brer Rabbit come readily to mind. I have not treated parodies or critiques of self-construction, although Melville's *The Confidence Man* could have lent itself to that purpose. Thus there will be plenty of opportunity for more work along the lines suggested here.

During the generation after the Second World War, American scholars tended to overestimate what intellectual history could accomplish. Since the inevitable disillusionment set in, they have tended to underestimate it. This book is written in the belief, chastened and modest, that intellectual history does have something to offer to our general understanding of the past, helping illuminate its politics, literature, religion, and social life. For that reason, I think of it as a contribution to interdisciplinary American Studies.

?• THE CONSTRUCTION OF THE SELF

What do I mean by a "self"? The literary scholar Stephen Greenblatt offers a good definition: "a sense of personal order, a characteristic mode of address to the world, a structure of bounded desires."[3] Clearly, consciousness and agency are essential characteristics of the self and implied in this definition. Of the attributes specifically mentioned by Greenblatt, I have been mostly concerned with the last, "a structure of bounded desires." Much of this book is about what motivates people, and how their desires can be kept within bounds that are acceptable to others, or to God. Those Americans whom we shall examine believed that if we kept our desires within certain bounds, we would be doing the best thing for ourselves as well.

Being a historian, not a political scientist, sociologist, psychoanalyst, or literary critic, I have taken a rather empirical approach to the subject of self-construction, and may therefore be accused of having neglected theory. The theorist of the self whom I have found the most relevant and rewarding for my own work is the philosopher Charles Taylor. The account given in this book may even be conceived as taking place within a corner, so to speak, of his large volume on *Sources of the Self: The Making of the Modern Identity.*[4] But the present book contains scarcely any explicit discussion of his work, or that of other eminent theorists of the self such as Anna Freud, Michel Foucault, Jürgen Habermas, Colin Campbell, Marcel Mauss, or Ervin Goffman, though perhaps it may be found to address their ideas by implication.

In another sense, however, this book *is* theoretical. The nature of the sources I have used led me to deal more with ideas *about* self-construction than with its *practice.* The distinction is not a sharp one, since self-construction is to a large extent accomplished verbally. A writer or speaker discussing how the self should be constructed is not only drawing upon personal experience but is also to some extent engaged in a conscious performance, that is, in an act of self-construction.

The prevailing attitude toward self-construction of the thinkers we shall examine in this book was that individuals are valuable in their own right and that they should develop their full potential while exercising self-control. They postulated not only the existence of a self as the consequence of an individual's personal and social history, but also the capacity of the individual for critical reflection upon that self, with the power to modify it through conscious effort. Such a view of the self and its potential raised important political questions, and these will be of direct concern in what follows. How should the institutions of government be structured to maximize opportunity for self-fulfillment? What kinds of educational opportunities and practices are implicit in this vision of the self? Is self-development a right or a duty? To what extent should society intervene to help the disadvantaged develop their potential? Can the proper fulfillment of some individuals be accomplished without the exploitation of others—for example, slaves or women? Classical political theory, though devoting much attention to the proper fulfillment of the self, had taken it for granted that some persons would be excluded from participation in this process and even sacrificed to the development of others. In American history, a major source of conflict can be found in efforts to apply the doctrine of self-development to people previously excluded from it. Although the conception of the autonomous self as here examined originated in the Enlightenment, explicit expansion of its relevance to include African-Americans and women was almost entirely deferred to the age of the American Romantics. This is one of the reasons why I shall be interested in the transition from the Enlightenment to Romanticism in relation to the construction of the self.

Much of the recent scholarly writing on the subject of self-construction treats the enterprise as essentially pathological.[5] For this reason, I feel compelled to state openly that I consider the opportunity to make one's own identity a healthy kind of autonomy. Just because self-construction was once available only to the elite does not mean that it is undesirable or an unworthy goal. On the contrary, many good things—such as enough food to eat, the right to political expression, or access to beautiful objects—have been monopolized by elites in various times and places, and we rejoice when they become more widely available.

It also seems important to explain at the outset that I have not found the kind of individualism that concerns me here to be at polar opposition to a strong sense of community, so that to emphasize one necessarily involves moving away from the other. On the contrary, the quest for a personal identity can entail joining a new community, and projects of self-discipline or self-improvement can be undertaken collectively as well as individually. The rise of individualism in the antebellum period, which I trace, was in fact accompanied by a growing nationalism. I also hope to show that individualism does not necessarily mean hedonism, narcissism, or irresponsibility, but that it is fully compatible with a strong sense of moral order.

?❧ THE BALANCED CHARACTER

During the period treated by this book, the dominant model for what was considered a wisely constructed self was that of the "balanced character." This ideal self was understood within the paradigm (to use an overworked term in what nevertheless still seems a valid sense) of faculty psychology. The psychology of the age taught that human nature could be analyzed in terms of certain components, such as the "understanding" (powers of awareness, including both sensation and reflection) and the "will" (powers of action or motivation). Among the powers of the will could be distinguished a variety of human motives, typically arranged in a hierarchically defined sequence of "faculties." The moral and rational powers (because they partook of the divine nature) had precedence over emotional and instinctive impulses (animal powers). Last of all came the mechanical reflexes (vegetative powers), over which there was no conscious control. Those powers that were under some degree of conscious control could be cultivated or restrained by the exercise of will. In this book I discuss faculty psychology as a historical phenomenon and am not directly concerned with its validity as a model for understanding human nature. We are prone to patronize the past and assume that the ideas of a former age are false. Lest the reader jump to this easy conclusion, I will mention a well-argued recent study presenting a version of faculty psychology not dissimilar to that we shall be examining: Robert H. Frank's *Passions within Reason.* The author weighs the power of the passions, assesses their social function, and discusses how they can be enlisted in the service of reason—all of which are issues that the subjects of this book addressed.[6]

The faculty psychology of the eighteenth and nineteenth centuries was considered a science in the sense of being governed by fixed laws, but not in our sense of being value-free. On the contrary, it was avowedly concerned not only with the way human beings behaved but also with the way they should behave. All human faculties had legitimate objectives entitled to fulfillment, but the proper balance among them was difficult to attain. Left to themselves, some of the lower powers might wreak havoc. An unregulated faculty—whether pride, licentiousness, or some other appetite or emotion—was called a passion. The good life required continual self-discipline, as one sought to "suppress his passions" or "cultivate and improve his virtues." The animal powers present in everyone were "captives impatient of every subjection, and ready every moment to mutiny."[7] Despite these difficulties, however, some people managed to construct a balanced character. To have done so was to have achieved the proper development or control of each of the faculties of one's nature—and in particular, to have achieved the supremacy of reason over passion.

The ideal of the balanced (that is, properly proportioned) character was important not only to discussions of private life but also to discussions of public life. Faculty psychology provided a language for the discussion of public issues that was fully comparable in importance to the language of the covenant or the language of classical republicanism.[8] The analogy between the construction of individual character and the construction of the commonwealth permeated much of public discourse, from Washington's Farewell Address to Lincoln's Gettysburg Address (to choose famous examples). Nations, like individuals, had to work to maintain the supremacy of reason over passion, and the deliberate sense of the common good over demagogy, fanaticism, and faction. The close affinity between the individual/psychological and the public/political use of the balanced ideal can be illustrated in the description of George Washington by the Jacksonian historian George Bancroft:

> His faculties were so well balanced and combined, that his constitution, free from excess, was tempered evenly with all the elements of activity, and his mind resembled a well ordered commonwealth; his passions, which had the intensest vigor, owned allegiance to reason; and with all the fiery quickness of his spirit, his impetuous and massive will was held in check by consummate judgment. He had in his composition a calm, which gave him in moments of highest excitement the power of self-control, and enabled him to excel in patience, even when he had most cause for disgust.[9]

This paradigm of human faculties, together with its moral imperative for self-control and its analogy for the body politic, was maintained by a wide range of contemporary cultural supports, including classical learning, Renaissance humanism, Christian theology, Enlightenment science, and Scottish-American moral philosophy.

In the development of Western political thought, the control of passion by reason has been an issue of critical importance. Stephen Holmes's *Passions and Constraint* shows how the creation of free political institutions required that people control such strong passions as tribal hatred or the resentment of social slights by the exercise of sober rationality. As Holmes demonstrates, early liberal thinkers—from Adam Smith to John Stuart Mill—did not imagine that people were governed by calculated self-interest; on the contrary, they complained that people were enslaved by their passions, from which bondage only a combination of conscience, prudence, and wise institutions could deliver them. "Most human behavior was understood to spring from unthinking habit or irrational passions. Rational choice of action was exceptional." From this point of view, to bring people to a rational appreciation of their long-term interest would be a substantial achievement, a precondition for modernity. "The principal aim of [early] liberals who wrote favorably of self-interest was to bridle destructive and self-destructive passions, to reduce the social prestige of mindless male violence, to induce people, so far as possible, to act rationally, instead of hot-bloodedly or deferentially." Modern political thought developed out of the assumptions of faculty psychology and its imperative to subordinate passion to reason. Writing as a political scientist and legal philosopher, Holmes argues that this imperative was well justified.[10]

Originally, the model of the balanced character was considered applicable in full only to elite males. One of the major themes of our account will be the progressive democratization of the model, as it is extended to include poor men, women, and people of color. Inevitably, the ideal itself is adapted and transformed in the course of this process. The democratization begins as early as the first chapter, with Benjamin Franklin's application of the precepts of gentlemanly self-control to artisans and tradesmen in the colonies. And as we shall see, Scottish moral philosophy, which was the formal, academic embodiment of the paradigm of balanced faculties, similarly begins as the expression of a particular elite perspective and broadens its appeal over the next several generations.

Two historical dynamics largely explain the widening appeal of the balanced character as an ideal for self-construction. The first of these was the international evangelical revival affecting the Protestant world. Americans spoke of the First and Second Great Awakenings, in the eighteenth and nineteenth centuries respectively, to refer to their aspects of this revival.[11] The call of the preacher for people to make "a decision for Christ," to be "born again" in Christ, was the first form of conscious self-reconstruction that many Americans encountered, and it remained an important and peculiarly dramatic one. Although some evangelicals viewed the ideal of the balanced character as a rival to their own ideals of self-discipline, many others came to embrace it. Even the famous revival preacher Jonathan Edwards subscribed to the model of the balanced, controlled character, as we shall see. Particularly after John Witherspoon had adapted the Scottish school of philosophy to the requirements of Calvinist orthodoxy, evangelical Christians became powerful propagators of both the balanced character ideal and the faculty paradigm that explained it.

The second historical dynamic broadening the appeal of the balanced character was the spread of commerce and commercial relationships, sometimes called "the market revolution." This term can be misleading in implying a change that is sudden and violent and imposed upon people against their opposition. In many parts of America the market revolution was experienced as a gradual expansion of economic opportunities, as resourceful farm families found new ways of supplementing their income.[12] The balanced character was an asset when it came to making one's way in the new commercial economy. Along with new income came new ways of spending it, the chance to exercise taste. Commercial relationships led people to encounter strangers more often than subsistence husbandry did, and a new form of polite culture developed to regulate dealings with strangers. In the exercise of middle-class tastes and middle-class politeness, balance and control were also valuable qualities. The cultivation of the balanced, controlled character proved advantageous to the members of the new middle class not only in their capacity as producers, but also in their capacity as consumers and social beings.

This book tells part of the story of the acceptance of what can be called "individualism," that is, the belief that ordinary men and women have a dignity and value in their own right, and that they are sufficiently trustworthy to be allowed a measure of autonomy in their lives. The right to self-construction is the right to decide what kind of person one wishes to be and also the right to fulfill one's potential. It is therefore related to the right to choose one's religion, occupation, or political preference. It is essentially what Thomas Jefferson meant by the right to the "pursuit of happiness." When the people discussed in this book spoke of "self-government," they meant it in both a political and a psychological sense, and they believed that the two senses went together. Only people who could govern themselves psychologically— that is, who could rationally control their own impulses—would be capable of governing themselves politically.[13] Because the two ideals of self-government—political and psychological—were linked in this way, it was logical that when one of them was democratized, the other would be also.

The people who are treated in this book believed that there was more to self-government than self-control; they also believed in self-development. Indeed, there were those (Abraham Lincoln was one) who argued that the very purpose of political freedom was to enable people to develop their faculties, to "improve themselves" or "make something of themselves" (expressions that were common in Lincoln's America). More often than not, efforts to promote the ideal of the balanced character went hand in hand with efforts to suppress violence and cruelty, to promote education, to reform inhumane institutions and customs.[14]

The subjects of this book believed that restraint or discipline was important for the responsible exercise of autonomy: the distinction between liberty and license was meaningful to them.[15] The inevitable conjunction of voluntarism with discipline will be a recurrent theme in our story. But in the last analysis there is a difference between self-control and restraint imposed by one's superiors. The history of the construction of the self in the period covered here is fundamentally a history of human empowerment, not of covert repression. If the promise of human empowerment has not yet been fully realized, that does not imply no progress has ever been made.

֎ REPUBLICANISM AND LIBERALISM

Historical scholarship in the past generation has devoted considerable attention to the contrast between classical republican and liberal philosophies of government.[16] What is called the republican outlook has been traced from the ancient city-states through the Renaissance city-states to English republican theorists of the Puritan Interregnum and thence to America.[17] The liberal outlook is much newer, originating in the Enlightenment, where it is particularly identified with the writings of John Locke and Adam Smith.[18]

Both philosophies played a significant role in shaping early American political consciousness and institutions. Historians have worked to sort out their relative importance and the process by which liberalism eventually replaced republicanism. In doing so, however, they have sometimes tended to confuse matters rather than clarify them, partly because historians tend, as a consequence of their own analyses, to differentiate republicanism and liberalism too sharply. The fact is that most Americans who wrote about politics in the preindustrial period subscribed to both republican and liberal ideas and drew upon them both freely when they wanted to make a point. The distinction between the two philosophies is more one of our making than of theirs. To them, what was important was that their political ideas, republican and liberal alike, were true. The pedigree of the principles, showing how and by whom their truth had first been perceived, was a secondary matter.[19]

The most important theoretical difference between republicanism and liberalism as these are conventionally presented relates to the concept of the common good. Republicanism teaches that there is such a thing as the common good, which can be discovered by inquirers of wisdom and virtue. Republicanism therefore argues that free government can work only when the electorate is educated and public-spirited enough to discern and act on the common good. On the other hand, it is often said that liberalism teaches that there is no such thing as a common good, only individual preferences. And indeed it is essential, if a liberal government is to work, that diversity of viewpoints be accepted as legitimate (through a combination of institutional restraints and attitudes of tolerance) and that people advance their respective preferences through legal means.[20]

The American thinkers whom we shall be examining endorsed, as good liberals would, individual rights and limited government. Yet they did not abandon the notion of a common good and continued to attach importance to it. They tended to define their common good in a way compatible with their liberalism, as that social state most conducive to individual self-development. Put another way, the common good was thought to be that state of society and institutions which would produce individuals with balanced characters; fittingly enough, then, the constitution of the polity itself should also be balanced.

In his fine study of *Liberal Virtues,* Stephen Macedo has shown that liberal political philosophy is in principle every bit as concerned with the virtuous character development of the citizen as is classical republicanism. Both philosophies require citizens who will take an interest in public affairs, and liberalism requires in addition that citizens practice the virtues of tolerance and open-mindedness. People have to be moral agents to count as "free" in a liberal sense, which necessitates their developing a "capacity for critical thought and autonomous choice." Some people, unfortunately, "lack the discipline to resist desires and inclinations for the sake of valued long-term projects and commitments." To achieve the capacity for autonomy, one must "actively shape not simply one's actions, but one's character itself." Macedo concludes that there is an "ideal liberal personality" which is characterized by "reflective self-awareness, active self-control, an openness to change, and critical support for the public morality."[21]

What Macedo has shown to be true in principle, this book argues was true in fact. The conscious construction of the autonomous self was not merely *compatible* with American institutions, not only *logically required* by them, but was in historical fact *practiced* by Americans, and for the reasons Macedo gives. The thinkers described in this book believed that, to the extent individuals exercised self-control, they were making free institutions—liberal, republican, and democratic—possible. And as the scope of American democracy widened, so too did the practice of self-construction.

The concept of virtue which was most influential in American thinking was not limited in reference to political or social life but also applied to private life and character. All of these thinkers considered virtue to be something objective, not merely subjective, although they offered varying definitions of it. Virtue was the subject of the study of moral philosophy, which included political philosophy (and indeed all the rest of what we would call social science) within its broad domain. This concept of virtue was not derived directly from classical or neoclassical sources but from Christianity and the Enlightenment, particularly from the Christian moral philosophers of the Scottish Enlightenment such as Francis Hutcheson and Thomas Reid. The good life consisted of the pursuit of virtue in both a public and a private sense. Virtue, as early Americans understood it, was compatible with both community spirit and defense of self-interest, and with both republican and liberal political principles.[22]

How early American political thinkers drew upon both republican and liberal ideas will become clearer after we examine the faculty paradigm of human nature as they understood it. In the prevailing model of faculty psychology, most fully articulated by moral philosophers working in the Scottish-American tradition, there were two faculties of the will acknowledged as rational: conscience (the moral sense) and prudence (the sense of self-preservation). Conscience was a guide to virtue; prudence a guide to self-interest. All acknowledged that in a properly balanced character, these would be the number one and number two motives, respectively; they would control the actions of the individual, and to them the various emotions and appetites of human nature would be subordinated. When the model was applied by analogy to the body politic, the common good was discerned by men of wisdom and virtue; enlightened self-interest by men of prudence.

Unfortunately (and there will be a lot to say about this difficulty) the strength of the faculties of the will varied *inversely* to their rank in the sequence of rightful precedence. Although conscience was rightfully supreme, it was notoriously the weakest of motives; the emotions (passions) were the strongest, with prudence somewhere in between. It was therefore essential to devise means to strengthen the conscience in the interest of preserving society—that is, in the interest of the common good. One way of doing so was to enlist the power of prudence on the side of conscience, as illustrated in Poor Richard's famous maxim, "Honesty is the best policy"—that is, a commitment to the truth is not only moral but also prudentially advantageous.

When we turn from the construction of a balanced character to the construction of a balanced polity, this technique opens the door for supplementing republican motives with liberal ones. What the wise and virtuous citizen, dedicated to the common weal, might do out of principle, a prudent one might do out of enlightened self-interest. This, as we shall see, was the argument of *The Federalist.* Liberalism, far from being a threatening rival to republicanism, became in fact its welcome ally in the task of making free government work. Within the framework of faculty psychology, prudential motives could gradually come to be of increasing importance without overtly disturbing the paradigm. Conversely, as we shall see, classical republican devices like balanced government could become the welcome ally of liberal principles like personal autonomy, private property, and government by consent.

A superb example of the synthesis of liberalism with classical republicanism through faculty psychology is *Cato's Letters,* a seminal text of eighteenth-century Anglo-American political thought written by John Trenchard and Thomas Gordon, which appeared in England weekly from 1720 to 1723 and was later published in book form.[23] Cato (the collective pseudonymous author) brilliantly denounces the financial scandals and political corruption of Sir Robert Walpole's government from a Radical Whig point of view. Especially in the early letters, Cato makes extensive use of classical allusions and defends such classical republican principles as balanced government. Much of Cato's satire takes the form of relating examples from ancient history which contemporaries could recognize as his code for discussing the events and personalities of his own time. Cato repeatedly quotes Machiavelli favorably and endorses his Renaissance neoclassical humanist principle that free institutions require a vigilant and engaged public opinion, which Cato calls "public virtue."[24] He sees this popular virtue as threatened by corruption within the government, brought about by venal favor-seekers and speculators typified by the men responsible for the disastrous South Sea Bubble.[25] Like others in the Radical Whig tradition, Cato warns against the dangers of a standing army, preferring to entrust the protection of a free people to a militia of armed and virtuous citizenry.[26] His invocation of the authority of the seventeenth-century patriot Algernon Sidney requires a subsequent disclaimer that he does not share Sidney's notoriously antimonarchical, prorepublican views.[27]

Yet, as the letters continue, it becomes clear that Cato's classical and neoclassical vocabulary, for all its rhetorical usefulness, has been put to Lockean liberal purposes. Cato considers that the only legitimate basis of government is popular consent; the divine right of kings he dismisses with contempt. Governments rightfully possess only delegated powers "conveyed by the society to their public representative." Free governments are characterized by "checks and restraints appointed and expressed in the constitution itself." When a magistrate "exceeds his commission," his acts are "void."[28] Besides citing Locke explicitly, Cato also makes use of his ideas of the state of nature, natural rights, and government as existing for the protection of natural rights. The right of revolution is defended by invoking the law of nature.[29] Cato is not troubled by any logical contradiction between liberal individualism and republican communitarianism. "What is the public, but the collective body of private men, as every private man is a member of the public? And as the whole ought to be concerned for every private individual, it is the duty of every individual to be concerned for the whole, in which he himself is included."[30]

Knitting together Cato's combination of liberalism with classical republicanism is his extensive use of faculty psychology. Only through a sound understanding of individual psychology can a sound political theory be created, Cato insists.[31] Human nature is a mixture of good and bad motives, he explains, but of these the selfish passions are the strongest. "The world is governed by men, and men by their passions."[32] Republican vigilance and liberal limitations on government are both required to keep the governors from exceeding the bounds of reason and justice. Without such constraints, rulers will indulge their passions and substitute personal will for law. "As long as the passions of men govern them, [rulers] will always govern by their passions, and their passions will always increase with their power."[33] Unfortunately, those in high places are often motivated by "unsocial passions" that spread to the rest of the people, who are not immune to them. For example, corrupt office-holders and financiers have recently played upon the passions of the British public, encouraging "avarice and ambition" and producing an orgy of speculation leading to the South Sea Bubble and its collapse. "This shows the little power that reason and truth have over the passions of men, when they run high."[34]

The solution to the problem does not lie in vain attempts to change human nature or stamp out its vices; that way lie fanaticism and oppression. To control the selfish passions we must instead trust institutional checks and balances, elections to remind rulers that they hold power only as "a trust," and a vigilant and free press.[35] A wise statecraft will enlist human nature to control human nature. "Unlimited power is so wild and monstrous a thing, that however natural it be to desire it, it is as natural to oppose it."[36]

Although he disapproves of the schemes of dishonest speculators, Cato wholeheartedly endorses honest industry and trade and welcomes the widespread prosperity to which they lead.[37] He sees increasing economic wealth as driving the progress of civilization, beginning with the "rough and unhewn virtue" of tribal society and developing through the "domestic arts and sciences" to its climax in the commercial society of his own time, with its "politeness and speculative knowledge."[38] Government can encourage economic progress by keeping taxes low and securing the rights of property. Cato's faith in progress will be typical of the thinkers we shall treat, and they will express it on both an individual and a collective level, through self-reform and improvement as much as through social reform and improvement.[39]

Whether one operated from republican or liberal premises or from a combination of both (as Cato and most of the reflective Americans of colonial and early national times did), the maintenance of proper balance of character and the general subordination of passion to reason was essential. Only a moral actor could be a republican citizen; only a prudent one could be a liberal citizen. In either system, the passions posed a political danger. As liberalism gradually replaced republicanism in American political thought, the paradigm of the balanced character remained as strong as ever—and indeed came to be applied more widely than ever: to all men, not just to the elite citizenry envisioned by classical republicanism. The success of the liberal democratic experiment depended as much upon the development of strong, virtuous individual character as it did upon wise institutions. An intellectual historian of nineteenth-century Britain has expressed it clearly: "The stronger the voluntary exercise of morality on the part of each individual—the more internalised that morality—the weaker need be the external, coercive instruments of the state. For the Victorians, morality served as a substitute for law, just as law was a substitute for force."[40]

The Victorians, both American and British, looked upon good manners as an ally in their struggle to foster individual morality as a bulwark of free government. Manners and morals went together. Indeed, a concern with the importance of manners to the public virtue of the commonwealth long antedated the Victorians; it goes back at least as far as *The Spectator* of Joseph Addison and Richard Steele (1711–1713). In the 1720s *Cato's Letters* endorsed "good breeding" as manifesting a sincere concern for others, and, as we shall see, a long American tradition followed, according a high estimate to the value of good manners.[41] A code of polite conduct was part of the elaborate set of inducements and sanctions—which also included religion, education, enlightened self-interest, and of course the law itself—upon which virtue was believed to depend. For the most part, the subjects of this book took polite culture seriously. One of the problems of writing about politeness historically is that we no longer take it as seriously as they did, and so we have difficulty understanding their attitude toward it. As they used it, the idea of politeness included not only outward behavior but also inward qualities of mental cultivation and good taste.[42] Thus it was an aspect of self-development considerably more important than learning table etiquette.

This book, like much other scholarship in the past generation, contradicts the thesis of Daniel Boorstin that Americans were immune to European ideologies.[43] In fact, we shall see how Americans participated in discourse with other thinkers throughout the Western world. Yet, although it is clear that Americans were more ideologically aware than Boorstin supposed, they still appear a practical people, as he insisted they were and are. Americans have internalized, supplemented, synthesized, and adapted European ideas concerning both human nature and the nature of society. While not claiming that Americans were unique (or exceptional), I would defend the legitimacy of writing a book on the subject of the construction of the self *in America*. The opportunity for self-construction, though far from universal, has been more widespread in the United States than elsewhere, and the discussion of it has occupied a particularly prominent place in American attempts at national self-definition. It is invoked in the Declaration of Independence as the right to the pursuit of happiness. Thus it is related not only to our individual but also to our collective project of self-construction.

PART I

Virtue and Passion in the American Enlightenment

Benjamin Franklin, Jonathan Edwards, and the Problem of Human Nature

"Reason should govern Passion, but instead of that, you see, it is often subservient to it." So ran the conventional wisdom of the eighteenth century, in this case stated by Sir Richard Steele in *The Spectator*. Throughout the eighteenth century, the Western world typically thought of human nature in terms of a model of faculties or powers. The "active powers," which collectively composed the "will," supplied the motives prompting human action. The most common version of eighteenth-century faculty psychology arranged these powers in a hierarchical sequence. First in order of precedence came the rational faculties of the will: conscience (or the moral sense) and prudence (or self-interest). Below them were the emotional springs of action, called either by the approving term "affections" or the more derogatory word "passions," as the context might dictate. Still further down were mechanical impulses like reflexes, not subject to conscious control at all. The hierarchical structure of human nature, explained a later number of *The Spectator*, corresponded to humanity's intermediate position in the great chain of being, partly divine, partly animal.[1]

The model just described provided the basis for much of the philosophy, psychology, and literature of the eighteenth century. It was treated as the common sense of the matter by an age that idealized common sense. Embodied early in the century in such authoritative literary works as *The Spectator* and Alexander Pope's poetic *Essay on*

Man, it was codified late in the century by the Scottish moral philosopher Thomas Reid. John Locke had worked within it, for the most part, in his writings on human understanding and education; Francis Hutcheson and David Hume challenged it by proposing to treat conscience as an emotional, rather than a rational, faculty.

Eighteenth-century faculty psychology was both descriptive and normative; that is, it was not only a psychology but also an ethic. By right, conscience should govern the commonwealth of the mind, but in practice, the passions were often too strong for it. As we have indicated, passion was considered the strongest faculty of the will, conscience the weakest, with prudential reason somewhere in between. The psychological fact, countless writers warned, was that the motivating power of the faculties varied in inverse proportion to their rightful precedence. This discrepancy between psychological fact and ethical imperative may be termed the problem of human nature. It is no exaggeration to call it *the* central problem of eighteenth-century moral philosophy.

The two greatest intellectuals of colonial British America were Benjamin Franklin and the Calvinist theologian Jonathan Edwards; each addressed, in his own way, the problem of human nature as their generation defined it. Both men were avid readers of *The Spectator* in their youth and were thoroughly conversant with its model of human nature.[2] Both were informed participants in the world of eighteenth-century moral philosophy; Franklin knew many of its leading figures personally. Franklin and Edwards were in agreement on the seriousness of the problem. "All things in the soul of man should be under the government of reason, which is the highest faculty," Edwards instructed his congregation; but "men's passions sometimes rise so high that they are, as it were, drunk with passion. Their passion deprives them very much of the use of reason." Franklin's *Poor Richard's Almanac* taught its readers the same lesson: "He is a governor that governs his passions, and is a servant that serves them." "If passion drives, let reason hold the reins."[3] While agreeing on the nature of the problem posed by their community of discourse, Franklin and Edwards display for us, in the solutions they offered to it, differences of fundamental importance.

ৡ BENJAMIN FRANKLIN

Benjamin Franklin (1706–1790) is, of course, one of the most famous exemplars of self-construction who ever lived. He rose from obscurity to wealth, influence, and immense international popularity and fame. In old age he composed an *Autobiography* that is one of the classic "how-to" books, a manual full of lessons drawn from his own life—frequently from his own mistakes—on how to develop virtuous habits, how to fashion one's image, how to win friends and influence people. Franklin played many parts in the long drama of his career: businessman, scientist, lobbyist, legislator, colonial bureaucrat, republican diplomat, statesman, sage. The more we know about him, the more we are struck with the ironies of his self-created identities. Franklin boasted of his spartan thrift in youth, but relished the good life in maturity. A sophisticated cosmpolite, he cultivated an image of transparent simplicity. Full of advice on the importance of making friends, in real life he made plenty of enemies too.[4] As an American emissary in Paris, he found it convenient to be mistaken for a Quaker because of their reputation for honesty. He achieved a remarkable self-detachment, best manifested in his ability to laugh at himself. He made no secret of his sexual indiscretions. Franklin adopted so many different identities in the course of his elaborate self-constructions that some commentators have despised him as a hypocrite, while others have despaired of ever knowing who the real Franklin was; indeed, whether there was a real person at all or just a series of guises.[5]

Why did Franklin engage in this lifelong process of identity formation and urge it so upon others? Self-construction, as Franklin practiced it, was not undertaken merely for the sake of expediency but also as a matter of high principle. Why did he believe it was so important to recreate a self (or selves) by conscious plan? To answer that question, let us examine first his estimate of human nature, and then the various methods by which he sought to improve on that nature. In doing so, we shall take Franklin seriously, as a thinker concerned with serious issues. That he was also an ambitious man, capable of being manipulative, may be readily acknowledged.

"Men I find a sort of beings very badly constructed," Franklin wrote Joseph Priestley, his friend and fellow scientist, moral philosopher, and reformer. "They are generally more easily provoked than reconciled, more disposed to do mischief to each other than to make reparation, and much more easily deceived than undeceived." Franklin found human motivation a complex mixture, but he had no doubt that the baser impulses were the more powerful. For this reason, he felt Hobbes's depiction of the state of nature "somewhat nearer the truth than that which makes the state of nature a state of love."[6] Some of

Franklin's satires on human motives have a bite worthy of Jonathan Swift.[7] Characteristically, however, Franklin's low estimate of human nature did not lead him to express any personal *Angst*. In the Will he drew up in 1750, he thanked God for giving him "a mind with moderate passions."[8]

As a good eighteenth-century scientist, Franklin celebrated the rational order of the physical universe. (In a religious service he composed in 1728 he prescribed the reading of lessons; not from Scripture, however, but from John Ray's *The Wisdom of God in Creation* [1691] and other authoritative works of Enlightenment natural theology.)[9] Franklin took this rational order as a norm to apply to human affairs, both social and individual. In a properly ordered society, there would be no conflict between individual and community; each existed to serve the other. A person with a properly balanced individual nature would live a socially useful life. "Wise and good men are, in my opinion, the strength of the state," Franklin wrote the American philosopher Samuel Johnson; but neither is there any cause to doubt that he shared the assumption of the Declaration of Independence (which, of course, he helped Jefferson draft) that the state exists to serve wise and good men. The moral faculty, for Franklin, was the rational power that perceived the appropriateness and utility of actions in promoting both individual and collective happiness. "Virtue and sense are one," declared Poor Richard.[10] We may be confident that Franklin would have approved the teaching of his Scottish contemporary Francis Hutcheson: "That action is best which procures the greatest happiness for the greatest numbers."[11]

Just as external nature could be made to yield the secrets of its divine order to scientific research, so, Franklin was convinced, there could be a science of human nature, that is, of morality. Like all good science (in Franklin's view), moral science would have practical application to human affairs. This was by no means an eccentric opinion in the eighteenth century. Individual and social morality were governed by analogous principles: "No longer virtuous, no longer free, is a maxim as true with regard to a private person as a commonwealth." The danger to the individual posed by a usurping vice or passion was the same as that of a demagogue or tyrant to the state.[12]

The order of the external universe, though a model to be imitated, did not provide Franklin much encouragement for human moral strivings. The philosophical system that commended itself to Franklin's science and logic was deterministic deism. Yet deism, with its remote artificer-god, provided no basis for such human needs as prayer, special providence, or moral incentives. As he observed in his *Autobiography*, "I began to suspect that this doctrine, though it might be true, was not very useful." Having reached this conclusion, Franklin abandoned deist system-making and devoted himself instead to inquiries with practical application.[13] To his good friend George Whitefield he confided, "I rather suspect, from certain circumstances, that though the general government of the universe is well administered, our particular little affairs are perhaps below notice, and left to take the chance of human prudence or imprudence, as either may happen to be uppermost. It is, however, an uncomfortable thought, and I leave it." (After receiving the letter, the great envangelist wrote across the margin: "Uncomfortable indeed! And, blessed be God, unscriptural.")[14] Franklin's preoccupation with temporal goals, with human happiness rather than metaphysical values, should not be attributed to mere crassness of temperament. It followed from his conviction that the universe was ultimately indifferent, and that it was up to human beings to shape themselves and their destiny as best they could.

The most obvious alternative to deism was Christianity, in which Franklin had been reared by his Calvinist parents. The Christian religion seemed well suited to the needs of humanity, Franklin thought, provided it could be purged of intolerance and obsession with unanswerable theological conundrums. Like many subsequent Americans, he found refuge in the Anglican communion from the preoccupation with theology characteristic of the Reformed tradition. Anglicanism was traditionally concerned with issues of comprehensiveness and liturgy, both of which interested Franklin. It is a common mistake to suppose that Franklin involved himself with religion *solely* as a matter of social ethics; he also regarded worship and prayer as natural human impulses requiring expression. As the object of prayer, Franklin hypothesized a finite God, possessing passions, because he felt only such a divine being would be responsive to the worship of human beings.[15]

Like Locke, whom he followed in so many things, Franklin believed that the core of Christian belief consisted of a few short affirmations. Beyond that, religions justified themselves by their contribution to temporal human welfare, and should be judged accordingly. In a paper prepared in 1732, Franklin undertook to formulate a religious position that would be "a powerful regulator of our actions, give us peace and tranquillity within our own minds, and render us benevolent, useful, and beneficial to others."[16] He defended his Enlightenment version of Christianity against Calvinists on the one hand and deists on the other, and labored to see it taught in schools.[17]

In a vivid letter to an unknown deist, sometimes thought to be Thomas Paine, Franklin refused to discuss the truth of his correspondent's philosophy and strongly urged him not to publish it. Undermining respect for religion would not be socially beneficial, he explained.

> You yourself may find it easy to live a virtuous life without the assistance afforded by religion, you having a clear perception of the advantages of virtue and the disadvantages of vice, and possessing a strength of resolution sufficient to enable you to resist common temptations. But think how great a proportion of mankind consists of weak and ignorant men and women, and of inexperienced and inconsiderate youth of both sexes, who have need of the motives of religion to restrain them from vice, to support their virtue, and retain them in the practice of it till it becomes *habitual,* which is the great point for its security.[18]

It is clear in this passage that Franklin did not consider the Christian religion to be based on reason; on the contrary, he thought of Christian faith as an alternative to reason. ("The way to see Faith is to shut the eye of Reason," ran one of his aphorisms.) Encouraging religion was a concession to the strength of the nonrational component in human nature, especially appropriate for people in whom the rational faculty was undeveloped.[19]

Franklin's insistence upon discussing the issue entirely in terms of practical consequences became more and more typical of his attitude toward religion with the passage of time. In youth he had satirized Cotton Mather; later, however, he paid respectful homage to that Puritan patriarch for promoting philanthropic enterprises. "Opinions should be judged of by their influences and effects," he wrote to his parents.[20] A variety of different religions might all be deserving of support provided they all promoted socially beneficial virtues. Accordingly, Franklin contributed money to the Philadelphia congregations of several denominations (including the synogogue), while maintaining his family membership in Episcopal Christ Church.[21]

Organized religion was not the only form of association on behalf of virtue that Franklin endorsed. He formed a club in Philadelphia called the Junto, hoping that it would become the nucleus of an international United Party of Virtue. Junto members read and discussed good books, debated important topics, and enjoyed good fellowship. The association was envisioned as existing partly for self-improvement, partly for mutual aid of the members (in the form of business contacts as well as charity), and partly to exert virtuous leadership in the community. Had it developed in accordance with Franklin's vision, it might have become a kind of secular church of the Enlightenment. Only later did Franklin affiliate with an identifiable political party in Pennsylvania (the Quaker or Assembly party); during the years when the Junto was active, its founder probably thought of it as a nonpartisan political force sustaining reason and public virtue above the factionalism of ethnic or interest groups. Franklin apparently got the idea for the Junto from Mather's benevolent societies and the fictional club described in *The Spectator.* Evangelical Societies for the Reformation of Manners were common in early-eighteenth-century England and a favorite cause among Low Church Anglicans. However, the Masonic movement had already preempted the role Franklin envisioned for his order. When the Masons established a lodge in Philadelphia, Franklin joined it, and the Junto was gradually eclipsed.[22]

But Franklin's best known and most characteristic device for strengthening the conscience in its struggle to maintain supremacy over the baser motives was his invocation of prudential self-interest on the side of virtue. The prudential aphorisms of Poor Richard constituted Franklin's famous application of a general principle of eighteenth-century moral philosophy. According to this principle, conscience could compensate for its weakness by enlisting the motivating power of stronger faculties to do its bidding. For example, the love of fame—the "ruling passion of the noblest minds," according to Alexander Hamilton—could lead political men to serve the public interest when altruism alone might fail.[23] Franklin too relied on the love of fame this way; indeed, he regarded it as an enlightened form of prudence, akin to our concern with material well-being, rather than as a passion.

Even before Franklin, the Anglican Bishop Joseph Butler (1692–1752) had taught that the conscience could enlist the aid of prudence to help it control the passions.[24] By the latter part of the century this had become a standard technique for strengthening the motive to virtue in human behavior. Together, virtue and prudential self-interest made an effective combination in Franklin's scheme. The happiness of the greatest number, after all, was made up of many individual happinesses. If individuals could be persuaded to pursue their enlightened self-interest, this would be a large step in the right direction.[25] If they could be shown that their self-interest, properly understood, lay in hard work, honesty, thrift, and humility, the congruence between collective and individual welfare would be all the greater. Through publications like *Poor Richard's Almanac*, Franklin popularized *The Spectator's* gentlemanly precepts of self-construction among the common people of the colonies. To fashion the self the right way would help the average individual and society as well.

Franklin's invocation of prudence was part of a widespread upward revaluation of the faculty during the eighteenth century. At the beginning of the period, self-interest had generally been considered one of the passions, but by the end, moral philosophers had definitely promoted it to the rank of a rational faculty.[26] A key to this development lay in drawing a distinction between self-interest and pride. Pride, Franklin maintained, was very different from self-interest and could even blind a person to his true self-interest. While self-interest was rational, pride was a passion.[27]

Religion of course had its own form of prudential incentive: a heavenly reward. This incentive found a prominent advocate during the eighteenth century in Archdeacon William Paley (1743–1805), who made it central to his system of moral philosophy, called "theological utilitarianism." Franklin did not ignore this motive to virtue,[28] but he devoted much more attention to tangible temporal rewards. By doing so he included in his audience those for whom religion had lost its appeal. Virtue, he argued—in both his own voice and that of Poor Richard, his most famous *persona*—was a good bargain. A virtuous way of life—honest industry, rational foresight, restraint of the passions —was "the Way to Wealth."[29]

For a person who is usually associated with the work ethic, Franklin had surprisingly little to say about the intrinsic satisfactions of work. In fact, the joy of work for its own sake did not fit into his theoretical model of human motivation. He himself, after all, quit work at the age of forty-two, once he had acquired a sufficient fortune. The remainder of his life he devoted to science and public service—gentlemanly pursuits which, in the eighteenth century, did not count as work.

In 1730 Franklin printed in the *Philadelphia Gazette* two "Dialogues between Philocles and Horatio" treating the proper role of prudential self-interest. For a long time it was assumed that Franklin had composed the dialogues himself; thanks to Alfred Owen Aldridge, we now know that he reprinted them from the *London Journal* of the year before. But we may take it that Franklin did so because they set forth so well the view to which he subscribed. That Franklin picked up on the dialogues illustrates his involvement with the central issues of eighteenth-century moral philosophy. In the first dialogue, Philocles explains to the naive young Horatio that self-love has two versions: self-indulgence and enlightened self-interest. The former is short-term and passionate; the latter, long-term and rational. Horatio is persuaded to subordinate his passions to prudential reason for the sake of greater happiness. In the second dialogue, Philocles argues that the highest happiness lies in a life of benevolent virtue, the pleasure of which can never cloy. The conventional hierarchy of the faculties—moral sense, prudence, passion—has been legitimated. Nothing is said about the satisfactions of work.[30] Though Franklin devoted much of his energy to reinforcing the lesson of Philocles's first dialogue, he seldom recurred to the subject of the second, which would interest Jonathan Edwards.

A discipline closely related to moral philosophy in the eighteenth century was rhetoric. There was a widespread desire to reformulate the ancient rules of rhetoric so as to take advantage of the principles of eighteenth-century moral philosophy and, in particular, those of faculty psychology.[31] Franklin was a careful rhetorical craftsman, a pioneer in the all-important art of persuasive argumentation. Analyses of his writings on public issues and private morality reveal a strategy of invoking a mixture of various faculties on behalf of his case. Typically, his rhetorical stance is "to speak not simply as an individual promoting a private scheme, but rather as a representative of a group of rational, fair-minded, public-spirited men who strive to improve their community." While presenting himself as altruistic, Franklin addresses his audience's faculty of prudence and makes his appeal to their enlightened self-interest.[32] This is a rhetorical strategy that Publius, the pseudonymous author of *The Federalist Papers,* would bring to perfection.

Despite all the care with which he crafted his appeals, no one could be more aware than Franklin himself of the likelihood that they would fail. Human nature being what it was, exhortations to virtue, even when coupled with prudential incentives, were seldom efficacious. Poor Richard admitted that hardly anyone could really live by his precepts:

> Who is wise? He that learns from everyone.
> Who is powerful? He that governs his passions.
> Who is rich? He that is content.
> Who is that? Nobody.

At the conclusion of "The Way to Wealth," Franklin's valedictory summation of Poor Richard's precepts, he notes, "the people heard it, and approved the doctrine, and immediately practiced the contrary, just as if it had been a common sermon."[33]

The problem was one of human nature, not one of knowledge. "Men do not generally err in their conduct so much through ignorance of their duty, as through inattention to their own faults, or through strong passions or bad habits." More succinctly: "Inclination was sometimes too strong for Reason."[34] What was needed, Franklin recognized, was a practical regimen, an applied "science of virtue" or "art of virtue" (he used both terms). The importance of such a program he outlined in a dialogue he wrote for discussion at a meeting of the Junto. In it, Socrates persuades Crito that an applied science of virtue was the most important of all branches of learning.[35] As Franklin explained years later to his friend, the Scottish moral philosopher Lord Kames,

> Most people have naturally some virtues, but none have naturally all the virtues. To acquire those that are wanting, and secure what we acquire as well as those we have naturally, is the subject of an art. It is as properly an art as painting, navigation, or architecture. If a man would become a painter . . . he must be taught the principles of the art, be shown all the methods of working, and how to acquire the habits of using properly all the instruments. . . . My art of virtue has also its instruments and teaches the manner of using them.

Faith in Christ works as the requisite instrument for some people, Franklin acknowledged, though not for all. His own program would benefit everyone, including those with weak faith or none. The program involved systematic practice in a rotating sequence of individual virtues, and Franklin followed it himself over a period of many years.[36]

A modern scholar has noticed similarities between Franklin's program and the Puritan process called "preparation for grace."[37] But

Franklin's "art of virtue" was intended to operate naturally, not super-naturally, and to be suitable for all, not only the elect. The virtue it produced was an end in itself, not a manifestation of divine grace—or even of good intentions. The goal, in fact, was for virtuous behavior to become automatic, a conditioned reflex.[38] Ideally, it should be like the "mechanical powers": those unthinking reactions not subject to conscious will, humbler than the passions but the strongest of all the springs of action, being irresistible. The perfect person was one whose "knee-jerk" reactions were morally correct. "The strongest of our natural passions are seldom perceived by us; a choleric man does not always discover when he is angry, nor an envious man when he is invidious." Unreflective habit, an even stronger force than passion, could master it where reflective reason might not.[39]

For Franklin, the passions were to be denied only to the extent that they sacrificed long-term or general welfare. Like work, self-denial was not an end in itself. The end was happiness, that is, individual and collective well-being. "A sound mind and a healthy body, a sufficiency of the necessaries and conveniences of life, together with the favor of God and the love of mankind," was Franklin's definition of happiness.[40] Self-denial, like work, was only justified in terms of its results. Franklin wrote an essay to prove the point in 1735. Acting contrary to one's inclinations was not the essence of virtue, he argued. "Temperance, justice, charity etc. are virtues, whether practiced with or against our inclinations." A person who automatically acted right was to be preferred to one who pondered over it. "The most perfect virtue is above all temptation." Worst of all, in Franklin's eyes, was asceticism practiced for its own sake. "He who does a foolish, indecent, or wicked thing, merely because 'tis contrary to his inclination (like some mad enthusiasts I have read of, who ran about naked, under the notion of taking up the Cross) is not practicing the reasonable science of virtue, but is a lunatic."[41] Like the authors of *Cato's Letters*, Franklin was not interested in denying or supressing any aspect of human nature but only in controlling and manipulating them all in the interest of general happiness.

Clearly, Franklin was interested in virtuous behavior (that is, behavior productive of human happiness) regardless of the motive or source from which it stemmed. Christian love, voluntary associations like the Junto, prudential calculation, or ingrained habit—whatever worked would do. He concentrated his efforts on the young because it was during their time of life that habits, the most promising of the "instruments" of virtue, were most effectively formed.[42] In the last analysis, Franklin was more interested in "merit" than in "virtue." "True merit" he defined as "an inclination joined with an ability to serve mankind, one's country, friends, and family." Virtue might only be a matter of intention, but *merit* joined this with ability, a behavioral test that took account of acquired skills and habits.[43]

Franklin never wrote the definitive handbook he projected on "the art of virtue." Instead, he left his (incomplete) *Autobiography,* in which his own life story is related as a sequence of parables, each with its moral lesson. The book shows how to shape one's personality through fostering some impulses and restraining others. The rhetorical posture of the detached, self-controlled observer, like the postulated model of human faculties, is quintessential eighteenth-century moral philosophy and can be traced back to *The Spectator.* Overall, the lesson is that by shaping and controlling one's self, one can shape and control one's destiny, even in an uncaring world. Self-discipline is the key to success. The author Franklin is necessarily detached from the character Franklin in the book, since the character is meant to stand for Everyman, to be a model for universal imitation. (The postulated universal desire for success is part of the security for the system. A person who has constructed himself in accordance with Franklin's maxims will be of use to society because he will want a good reputation, and the way to gain that is by being useful to others.)

Franklin would have found the opposition between public and private virtue, supposedly characteristic of eighteenth-century American republicans, quite incomprehensible. For him, there was no conflict between virtue and commerce, or between the individual and the collective welfare. The prudential virtues that made one a good tradesman or a good housewife also characterized the good citizen.[44] Indeed, his *Autobiography* points out, the good reputation that one earns by private virtue can be put to use in politics. Far from there being a conflict between virtue and self-interest, self-interest should be a motive to virtue and virtue should be practically useful.[45]

It is a cliché, though not less true for being such, that Franklin was more interested in means than ends, in practice than theory. This does not mean he was unsophisticated; the choice was quite deliberate on his part. He accepted the prevailing model of the human faculties and addressed himself with shrewdness to the practical problems that model posed. He assumed that the autonomous, rational self would be socially useful and that society would appropriately reward, with fame, those who served it. He devoted little thought to the nature of virtue in and of itself. Once, when Franklin was planning the agenda for coming Junto meetings, he considered discussing "whether men ought to be denominated good or ill men from their actions or their inclinations." But then he crossed it off the list.[46] Very likely the question seemed too abstract to be interesting. It seemed quite otherwise to Jonathan Edwards.

❧ JONATHAN EDWARDS

Precocious Yale student, village pastor, revival preacher, missionary to the Indians, and finally president of Princeton University (then called the College of New Jersey), Jonathan Edwards (1703–1758) is remembered as the last and greatest of American Puritan evangelists and theologians. For the past generation, scholars have been engaged in a process of recovering and appreciating his impressive intellectual accomplishments. Edwards's philosophy restated the Protestant faith for the age of the Enlightenment. Like Benjamin Franklin, he was deeply concerned with the problem of human nature and with identifying the proper remedy for its deficiencies.

Unlike the cosmopolitan Franklin, Edwards never travelled outside the American colonies and spent most of his life in tiny villages. Yet Edwards worked in a transatlantic intellectual context every bit as much as Franklin did. As Norman Fiering has demonstrated, "Edwards's treatises on the will, on the affections, and on virtue are not readily classifiable in twentieth-century categories, but they can be comfortably fitted into the context of eighteenth-century moral philosophy debates."[47] These debates were predicated on a common model of the human faculties. The influential scholar of Puritan thought, Perry Miller, misled many a subsequent inquirer with his careless assertion that Edwards and Locke both discarded the model of faculty psychology.[48] In fact, Edwards argued within the terms of the prevailing dual system of faculties: the understanding, which consisted of the powers of perception, and the will, which consisted of the powers motivating action. "Knowledge of ourselves consists chiefly in right apprehensions concerning those two chief faculties of our nature, the understanding and the will. Both are very important: yet the science of the latter must be confessed to be of greatest moment; inasmuch as all virtue and religion have their seat more immediately in the will, consisting more especially in right acts and habits of this faculty."[49]

Edwards's use of the model and vocabulary of faculty psychology was encouraged by his admiration for the Platonic tradition, particularly as exemplified in the writings of the Earl of Shaftesbury (1671–1713) and the seventeenth-century Cambridge Platonists. These thinkers had followed Plato in distinguishing within human nature various components competing with each other for supremacy. In a well-ordered personality, the one that would prevail was the quality of rational insight into the universal good; the other elements of the soul would be kept in their proper places. A well-ordered commonwealth followed the same principles.[50] "God has given . . . all the faculties and principles of the human soul," Edwards wrote, "that they might be subservient to man's chief end, . . . that is, the business of religion."[51] Such an affirmation was typical of Christian Platonism. Among the God-given faculties were the affections, both benevolent and malevolent, prudential reason, and even a natural conscience, which "doth naturally, or of itself, . . . give an apprehension of right and wrong."[52] The Platonic tradition would remain an important element in the project of self-construction as carried on by New Englanders for another century and more.

More of a problem for Edwards than Platonism was how to define his relationship to the moral philosophy of his own time. Most of early-modern moral philosophy was the creation of theological Arminians, Christian thinkers seeking to refute Hobbes on the one hand and Calvin on the other by establishing a natural basis for human moral values. They believed human beings had a meaningful power to choose between right and wrong. In addition to Locke, writers answering to this description included Francis Hutcheson (1694–1746), Thomas Reid (1710–1796), Joseph Butler (1692–1752), most of the literary circle around *The Spectator,* and even the Cambridge Platonists whom Edwards so admired. Edwards respected the achievement of these moralists and undertook to relate it to another great system of thought, Reformed theology. Unlike Franklin, who thought religion mostly nonrational, though potentially useful, Edwards believed the doctrines of religion eminently rational: "there is the most sweet harmony between Christianity and reason," he declared.[53]

Jonathan Edwards set out to show that the moral philosophy of his age did not really dictate an Arminian theology; it could be comprehended within a Calvinist system as well. Furthermore, he believed that the Calvinist system was not simply viable but preferable on logical, scriptural, and empirical grounds. In fact, Edwards looked to Reformed theology to solve the problem of human nature posed by eighteenth-century faculty psychology. Edwards produced in the end a dual system of morality, one natural and one divine. What he called natural morality was essentially the conventional moral philosophy of the eighteenth century, based on man's own unaided faculties. As a consequence of original sin, however, these faculties were corrupted by pride, which alienated humanity from God and prevented the individual from following the dictates of reason. Since this fallen human nature was hopelessly self-centered and incapable of true virtue, Edwards called a divine system of ethics into existence to rescue it.[54]

Nowhere is the contrast between Edwards and Franklin more striking than in their attitude toward what Edwards called "the great Christian doctrine of original sin." Although he shared Edwards's low estimate of human nature, Franklin despised the doctrine of original sin, declaring it had been "invented . . . by priests (whether Popish or Presbyterian I know not) to fright and scare an unthinking populace."[55] For Edwards, original sin was the fundamental truth of the human condition, around which he constructed his ingenious moral philosophy.

The problem, for Edwards as for Franklin and so many others, began with the weakness of the rational faculty in the human will. In the conventional model, conscience was a faculty of both the understanding and the will. As far as the perceptions of the understanding went, there was little difficulty: people were capable of *knowing* the right by means of their natural conscience. The problem lay in the will, in the helplessness of the conscience to *motivate* right action. The natural conscience was a rational power, which perceived moral obligations as part of the proper fitnesses of things. But it did not control the will. In its fallen state, the human will was incapable of transcending self-interest to achieve the austere altruism Edwards insisted was the one true virtue. Only God's grace could supply this.[56]

Edwards's decision to define conscience as a rational power was important. It meant that he was defending the conventional view, going back to Plato, that moral judgments were real judgments and not (as Hutcheson and Hume claimed) emotional reactions. But it also

meant that conscience partook of the weakness of reason. Whether
reason could motivate to action at all was the subject of a long-standing
philosophical disagreement. The dominant school (sometimes called
intellectualism), looking back to Aristotle and Aquinas, held that
reason could motivate, even while deploring its weakness. A rival
school of thought (voluntarism), led by Augustine, held that reason
had no motivating power whatsoever.[57] Edwards associated himself
with the latter position, which helped him in his theological argument
against free will. (Our actions are prompted by our emotions; but we
do not voluntarily choose our emotions; therefore we do not have free
will.)[58]

It might seem that Edwards, in espousing voluntarism, was
excluding the rational conscience altogether from the operation of the
will and defining it as solely a faculty of the understanding. Such was
not the case. In matters of practical morality Edwards still expected
reason to regulate and legitimate the motives, though it could not
itself be a motive. "All things in the soul of man should be under the
government of reason, which is the highest faculty."[59] He accepted the
conventional terminological distinction that a passion was a bad affection, one that had usurped the governing role of reason. The Christian
life was a process of "ruling and suppressing the evil and unruly
passions" while "exerting and following good affections." The degree
of rational justification and order that natural emotions displayed provided Edwards with a basis for judging them. For example, anger was
legitimate or not depending on whether it was rationally appropriate.[60]

Edwards, then, agreed with Franklin that there was such a thing as
a natural morality, discoverable by human reason. "There are many in
this world, who are wholly destitute of saving grace," he wrote, "but
nevertheless have something of that which is called moral virtue."[61] In
accordance with standard eighteenth-century moral philosophy, the
natural conscience could invoke the aid of other faculties in the performance of its task; thus, Edwards explained, reason can ally with love
"to keep men's irascible passions down in subjection, so that reason and
love may have the regulation of them." Among the principles in human
nature that Edwards recognized as potentially helpful to the natural
conscience were prudential self-interest, benevolent affections, and the
force of good habits.[62]

Edwards would have found nothing actually wrong with most of
Franklin's homely devices for self-improvement, based as they were on

nature and the general Providence of God that made provision for human welfare in this world. No more would he have objected to the Founders' constitutional provisions for checks and balances, which imaginatively used human wickedness to combat wickedness. ("Ambition must be made to counteract ambition," as Madison explained it, invoking the principle of countervailing passions.)[63] Such devices took human nature as they found it, and did the best that could be done with it. They tamed the effects of evil without actually eradicating it. But, of course, all that could be achieved in such a fashion was better behavior; the basic self-preoccupation that corrupted the human heart remained untouched. True virtue, Edwards insisted, was a matter of inward disposition, not outward behavior.

Both Edwards and Franklin carried on inward dialogues in the course of trying to master their own subordinate faculties. Like Franklin, Edwards addressed good resolutions to himself. "Resolved to do whatever I think to be my duty, and most for the good and advantage of mankind in general." "Resolved, to be continually endeavoring to find out some new contrivance and invention to promote the forementioned things." "Remember to Read Over These Resolutions Once a Week."[64] Some of Edwards's private resolutions are as candidly prudential as anything Franklin ever expressed. The cover-leaf memoranda Edwards wrote for his projected monumental work on natural philosophy, for example, include: "The world will expect more modesty because of my circumstances—in America, young, etc. Let there then be a superabundance of modesty [in the work], and though perhaps 'twill otherwise be needless, it will wonderfully make way for its reception in the world."[65] Not only self-exhortation but also self-evaluation characterized the inward dialogues of Edwards and Franklin. The two were working within a cultural inheritance of Puritan introspection that had produced innumerable diaries, conversion narratives, and similar documents. The traditional purpose of such efforts was to assess the quality of one's motives, in order to ascertain whether they were grace-given or self-seeking. Both Edwards and Franklin show finely honed skills at detecting the dangers of self-deception, particularly "how exceedingly affection or appetite blinds the mind and brings it into entire subjection."[66]

Franklin, as we have seen, expected that his practice of self-discipline would eventually lead to the formation of good habits that would render virtue automatic and unproblematic. He realized that pride could never really be overcome, but treated this as a minor exception to the rule.[67] Edwards worked just as hard at self-discipline and industriousness. ("By a sparingness in diet," he wrote in his diary while a student at Yale, "I shall doubtless be able to think more clearly, and shall gain time.")[68] But he harbored no expectation that self-discipline would ever come easily; it would always be a struggle requiring conscious effort. The residue of pride was no small matter for Edwards. Besides, any good behavior that came reflexively, without manifesting an intention, might be useful but could not be truly virtuous in his eyes.

At most, Edwards's self-imposed rules of discipline might manifest a grace already received or in some vague way prepare one to receive it. Whatever practical payoff they had in this life must be set against the unremitting toil they cost him. Edwards's life, like his writings, was organized methodically, even painfully. The evidence that has come down to us provides little indication that Edwards enjoyed relaxation as Franklin obviously did.[69] Expecting so little from his regimen, why did Edwards subject himself to it? One is driven to the conclusion that he found austerity and hard work satisfying in their own right. If so, Jonathan Edwards was a more thoroughgoing exemplar of the work ethic than Benjamin Franklin.

There is a striking contrast between Franklin and Edwards in their attitude toward the faculty of prudence, or self-interest. In theory, Edwards admitted that self-interest, if properly enlightened, could be a legitimate motive.[70] In practice, however, he very seldom urged prudential considerations upon his audiences except with regard to the hereafter. Imprecatory sermons like the famous "Sinners in the Hands of an Angry God" were addressed to the prudential self-interest of sinners to awaken them to a proper sense of their danger. Perhaps this would be of some help in preparing them for grace. However, Edwards pointed out elsewhere that fear of hell was only a "natural" and loveless motive, not to be equated with true virtue.[71]

According to Edwards, the self-preoccupation of human nature was the essence of its sinful alienation from God; "selfishness is a principle natural to us, and indeed all the corruption of nature does radically consist in it."[72] To exploit this ultimate vice, even for limited ends, must have been too distasteful for the evangelical philosopher. Instead, over and over again, he inveighed against it. "A Christian spirit is contrary to a selfish spirit." "Men are not to act as their own or for themselves singly, for they are not their own." "If you are selfish, and make yourself and your own private interest your idol, God will leave you to yourself, and let you promote your own interest as well as you can."[73]

Social ethics was really too important to be left to the second-best devices of natural morality; Edwards insisted upon applying the standards of divine morality in his social thought. He demanded the transcendence of self-interest and the attainment of altruism, both of which only come through divine grace. Only a religious awakening, therefore, could redeem secular society. Once a person had been converted, he would be "greatly concerned for the good of the public community to which he belongs, and particularly of the town where he dwells."[74] The specification of the town is significant; practically all of Edwards's own interest in what we would call politics was expressed at the town level.

Rejection of individualism was a prominent feature of Edwards's social thought and social ethics. In one of his rare references to an American identity, Edwards criticized the individualistic culture he and his neighbors shared: "We in this land are trained up from generation to generation in a too niggardly, selfish spirit and practice." When he persuaded his parishioners to subscribe to a town covenant in 1742, he made its central theme the renunciation of "private interest" (including its corollary, party spirit).[75] In his sermons on economic life, usually based on Old Testament texts that emphasized communal responsibility, Edwards repeatedly denounced individualism, market values, and laissez-faire.[76] Edwards stood closer to the classical republican tradition than to the liberal one, but his views on political and social morality owed more to biblical sources than to any secular philosophy. His teachings exemplified ideals of Christian communalism often expressed in the church-centered villages of colonial New England.[77]

For Jonathan Edwards, society was ideally an organic whole, in which persons treated each other as fellow members of the body of Christ. This is clearly set forth in his sermon cycle on I Corinthians 13, entitled "Charity and Its Fruits," now available in the Yale edition of Edwards's works. The proper model for society he presented was not a contractual arrangement but the human family, with the magistrates acting "as the fathers of the commonwealth." In a good society, Christians "will not desire that all should be upon a level; for they know it is best that some should be above others and should be honored and submitted to as such."[78] (When Tryon Edwards published the work in the nineteenth century, he inserted some extra sentences at this point to try to soften and explain away his ancestor's endorsement of social inequality.)[79]

Edwards clearly believed that social morality was important. As a manifestation of grace, social morality was more important than acts of worship: "moral duties, such as acts of righteousness, truth, meekness, forgiveness, and love toward our neighbors . . . are of much greater importance in the sight of God than all the externals of his worship."[80] Edwards practiced what he preached and stood up for his social vision regardless of its unpopularity with a majority of his congregation. However, the social morality that interested him was properly only a by-product of true virtue, the faith of the heart. This relationship is clearly evident in the biography Edwards prepared of a model Christian saint, David Brainerd.

Although the account is nominally Brainerd's own journal, we know from the evidence presented by Norman Pettit that Edwards extensively edited and rewrote it, making it conform with his own theories concerning the religious affections.[81] The didactic life story that Edwards presented could hardly contrast more sharply with that of Franklin's *Autobiography*. Where Franklin chose himself as the subject, Edwards selected another. Where Franklin's subject lived to achieve wealth and fame at a ripe old age, Edwards's subject endured unremitting physical and psychological affliction, worked hard for very modest results, and died young. Yet Edwards held David Brainerd up as an example to young Christians of what life was really all about.

Like Franklin and Edwards, Brainerd was constantly in dialogue with himself. This dialogue concerns his relationship with God, the purity of his own motives, and his struggle to attain mastery over his baser faculties. His emotional highs and lows are vividly recorded. For all Brainerd's obsessive concern with overcoming pride, the dialogue seems in its own way totally self-absorbed. A missionary to the Indians, Brainerd only rarely notices the Indians as individual personalities. Most of the time they are means to his ends, his service to them an act of determined self-abnegation.[82] Franklin had thought personal religious practice could be useful as a spur to a life of public service, but Brainerd leads his life of service as a means to his personal religious practice. Franklin imposed personal discipline on himself as a means to temporal success; Brainerd uses self-discipline as a means to evangelical humiliation. In the end, the meagre results Brainerd achieved in his mission were irrelevant to him and his editor; Edwards was interested in Brainerd's state of mind, not in what Franklin would call his merit.

In practice, Edwards showed scarcely any concern with working for a just society through the devices of natural morality that Franklin and the other framers of the Constitution employed. While there was nothing wrong with these devices in principle, neither did they seem very important. They did nothing to liberate humanity from its prison of self-centeredness. Edwards wanted to change hearts, to be an instrument of divine grace for individuals. When enough individuals were saved, the community would be saved by the manifestation of their grace. In the meantime, a person would be foolish to attach much importance to what Edwards called "this world of pride and malice and contention and perpetual jarring and strife, . . . where all are for themselves and self-interest governs." The world Edwards described was the same one Franklin knew, but their responses to it were different. "What man acting wisely and considerately would concern himself much about laying up a store in such a world as this?" demanded Edwards.[83] Franklin could have cheerfully responded, "I would."

For Edwards, society was too individualistic because the people who composed it were too selfish; the problem of society was rooted in the problem of human nature, most specifically, in the defective human will. "The ruin which the Fall brought upon the soul of man consists very much in that he lost his nobler and more extensive principles, and fell wholly under the government of self-love." To supply the motivating power toward virtue that fallen human nature lacked, Franklin and the Arminian moral philosophers invoked prudence, instinctive emotions, and unthinking habits. But Edwards pointed out that none of these was *truly* virtuous: they might shape outward behavior but they did not alter one's egocentric state of mind. Preoccupation with self was a kind of prison, from which only Christ offered hope of deliverance. "God hath in mercy to miserable man contrived in the work of redemption . . . to bring the soul of man out of its confinement and again to infuse those noble and divine principles by which it was governed at first [before the Fall.]"[84]

"There is a distinction to be made between some things which are truly virtuous, and others which only seem to be virtuous," wrote Edwards in what is probably his most famous philosophical distinction. "True virtue," as distinguished from the various halfway measures and imitations that Franklin and the Arminians discussed, Edwards defined as "benevolence to Being in general."[85] This was not part of fallen humanity's natural make-up; it could only be bestowed through God's saving grace. In His "ordinary method," to be sure, God would "give grace to those that are much concerned about it," those who had worked to attain "a preparatory conviction of sin." Ordinarily, "God makes use of . . . a good understanding, a rational brain, moral prudence, etc."[86] But of course there were many exceptions and "surprising" conversions. There was no secret sure method, no gradual progression up the ladder of love (as Plato had supposed). Grace was a matter of all or nothing, a blessing from God, which one could neither earn nor resist. When it came, it shed "a divine and supernatural light" upon experience.[87] Of course even a sanctified person would not be sinless. But he or she would have been definitively liberated from the prison of self and weaned away from this world of selfishness. "By living a life of love, you will be in the way to heaven. As heaven is a world of love, so the way to heaven is the way of love."[88]

True virtue, "benevolence to Being in general," was an affection, that is, an emotion. Franklin had considered religious belief non-rational and morality rational. For Edwards, it was just the opposite: Christianity was rationally justifiable, but true virtue was an emotional quality. Being an emotion, the God-given power of true virtue conferred no additional knowledge about right and wrong; the natural conscience, if well informed, will "appprove and condemn the same things that are approved and condemned by a spiritual sense."[89] The difference was in the beholder, not in the principles beheld. Being an emotion, true virtue was involuntary: one does not love or hate as a result of a deliberate decision. Most importantly, true virtue, being an affection or emotion, had what the merely speculative, natural conscience lacked: the power to motivate. True virtue "not only removes the hinderances of reason, but positively helps reason,"[90] empowering one to act rationally, that is, rightly. True virtue overcame the limitations of self and opened the door to the world of love. Divine grace solved the problem of human nature.

As Norman Fiering has brilliantly demonstrated, Edwards's theory of natural morality was rationalistic, but his theory of divine morality or "true virtue" was a form of ethical sentimentalism.[91] It was also a form of ethical aestheticism. Like a number of other moral philosophers of his time, Edwards sometimes used the term "moral sense" as a synonym for "conscience." For him, the moral sense meant the natural conscience. True virtue, on the other hand, was not a moral sense but a quality of moral *taste*. Just as some people had an aesthetic sensibility that enabled them to react immediately to beauty, he explained in his famous treatise on the religious affections, "so there is likewise such a thing as a divine taste, given and maintained by the Spirit of God, in the hearts of the saints, whereby they are in like manner led and guided in discerning and distinguishing the true spiritual and holy beauty of actions."[92] As our responses to natural beauty are immediate, disinterested, and involuntary, so are the responses of the truly virtuous person to moral beauty. "The soul [of the saint] distinguishes as a musical ear."[93] What interested Franklin about morality was its usefulness, but what interested Edwards about morality was its beauty. In the last analysis, for Edwards, beauty and morality were the same thing.[94]

Like Franklin, Edwards was much interested in natural science; he projected, though he never wrote, a comprehensive work on natural philosophy, as the physical sciences were then called. The differences between Franklin and Edwards, however, are as apparent in their approach to science as in their moral philosophies. Where Franklin was primarily an experimentalist, Edwards was primarily a theoretician. Franklin was interested in applied science; Edwards, in pure science. Edwards's interest in science stemmed from his love of harmony, symmetry, and beauty. "Always a metaphysician and an artist," even in his scientific writings, "he wanted to fit all loose parts into a perfect whole," writes Paul Conkin. Scientist as well as logical determinist, Edwards wanted "to live in a universe in which nothing was left to chance."[95] Eventually, Edwards's scientific activities were crowded out of his life by his theological and evangelical efforts. From his point of view, the latter were more relevant to the needs of the human condition.

Edwards was always clear about his priorities. The work of Redemption was more important than either the study of the material universe or the promotion of social reform.

> The conversion of one soul, considered together with the source, foundation, and purchase of it, and also the benefit and eternal issue of it, is a more glorious work of God than the creation of the whole material universe. . . . More happiness and a greater benefit to man, is the fruit of

each single drop of such a shower [of grace], than all the temporal good
of the most happy revolution in a land or nation amounts to, or all that
a people could gain by the conquest of the world.[96]

Edwards could not more eloquently have summed up his differences
with Benjamin Franklin.

While Franklin and Edwards both addressed the problem of human
nature as posed by eighteenth-century moral philosophy, in the end
each of them transcended the conventional model of the faculties. That
model was based on the assumption that rationality ought to govern
human nature; its failure to do so was deplorable. Far from simply
bemoaning the failure of rationality, however, Franklin and Edwards
both found substitutes for it in the course of their quests for virtue.
Franklin substituted habit; Edwards, a divinely disinterested benevolence. One came through practice and the other through grace. Each
was, in its way, an answer to the problem of humanity's perverse
irrationality.

For Franklin, the process of self-construction was secular, deliberate,
and highly individualistic. For Edwards, self-construction was at best
a preparation for a divine grace that would be necessary to fulfill the
promise of rebirth; it was a preparation undertaken within the tutelage
and discipline of a local church community. Franklin encouraged
people to feel pride in their accomplishments, however partial; Edwards
deplored human pride. Surprisingly, however, after their deaths the
intellectual history of self-construction in America developed in the
direction of synthesizing their approaches rather than leaving them as
mutually exclusive alternatives.

?❧ EPILOGUE AND SYNTHESIS

Edwards's message urged people to let God take over their hearts, and
all else would follow. Franklin's message was that God helps those who
help themselves. There have always been many Christians in America
who cannot help feeling that both are somehow true. In the light of the
differences between Jonathan Edwards and Benjamin Franklin, it may
seem remarkable that there should be an American tradition drawing
upon both of their approaches to the problem of human nature. But
such there is, and it goes all the way back to their contemporary,

George Whitefield, the Christian evangelist from England who came to know and admire them both. Edwards and Whitefield had in common the desire to save souls; Franklin and Whitefield had in common a concern with social morality and organized social reform. Franklin welcomed Whitefield's energy, rhetorical power, and organizational skills in humanitarian causes.[97] The next several generations of evangelicals developed along the lines Whitefield pioneered and Franklin approved. In the nineteenth century, American evangelical Protestants created an impressive synthesis of the Edwardsian and Franklinian approaches to religion that had momentous historical consequences.

The Evangelical movement of the nineteenth century, international and ecumenical in scope, active in both political and private sectors, innovative in its use of the media of communication, became a major culture-shaping force for its age. Like latter-day Franklins, the evangelical Christians of the century after Franklin's death in 1790 were utilitarian, humanitarian, well organized, and not afraid to make big plans. But in the spirit of Edwards, they centered their personal lives upon an experienced relationship with Christ. As compared with *both* Franklin and Edwards, the evangelicals of the nineteenth century strike us as optimistic. They combined Edwards's faith in God's grace with a more positive estimate of human nature than that of either of the eighteenth-century thinkers we have been examining. When Jonathan Edwards's descendent Tryon Edwards edited "Charity and Its Fruits" in 1851, he found the conclusion of the seventh sermon, against selfishness, in need of revising. Edwards had ended on a note of pessimism regarding the likelihood of overcoming selfishness; his nineteenth-century successor added a more positive peroration, ending: "Let us strive to overcome it that we may grow in the grace of an unselfish spirit, and thus glorify God and do good to man."[98]

Edwards had thought Franklin's devices to improve natural morality valid but not very important. Franklin, however, felt the same way about Edwards's solution to the problem of human nature. "So Dr. Edwards assures us that a few people experience (now and then) a beatific vision of the divine," one can imagine Franklin complaining; "so what? The world needs solutions appropriate for everybody, not just for a few saints." The evangelicals of the nineteenth century shared Franklin's attitude on this matter. They preached *plenteous* grace, enough grace for all. And instead of relying on occasional "showers" of

grace in periodic revivals, the nineteenth-century evangelicals so organized and institutionalized their revival as to make it a continuous
downpour. By the same token, they organized the charitable fruits of
grace on a scale Cotton Mather could never have imagined.

The nineteenth-century evangelicals still conceptualized human
nature in terms of a faculty psychology, for they continued to use and
adapt the intellectual constructs of eighteenth-century moral philosophy. By their time, these had been codified by the Scots Thomas Reid
and Dugald Stewart and the Scottish-American John Witherspoon.
The form of Scottish moral philosophy that the American evangelicals
mainly used was actually closer to Franklin's than to Edwards's model,
for the sentimentalist side of Edwards's ethical theory did not win
broad acceptance, even within the Reformed community.

Within the framework of faculty psychology, Edwards's evangelical
descendents even found an ingenious way of accepting the legitimacy
of prudential self-love. The self-love of the regenerate was legitimate,
Edwardsean theologians decided, because a person who was full of
benevolence to Being in general would inevitably direct at least a little
of this benevolence toward his or her own being. And the self-love of
the unregenerate, while morally culpable, was still socially useful. Just
as God had turned the wickedness of Pharaoh to the good of the Exodus
or the wickedness of Judas to the good of Redemption, His Providence
could make good come out of evil on an everyday basis. As Adam
Smith himself pointed out, the self-interested labors of the baker provided society with its bread. The theology of Edwards thus made its
peace with the utilitarian psychology of Benjamin Franklin.[99]

Some of the credit for adapting Edwards's legacy to a new age
belongs to his disciple Samuel Hopkins (1721–1803). Hopkins taught
that in the millennial time to come there would be a larger population
and more virtue, so that God would in the end save many more people
than were damned. He reconciled divine sovereignty with revival
preaching and individual preparation by teaching that these were the
"occasions" of grace, if not the "causes" of it. He completed the divorce
of salvation from the fear of hell by teaching that after conversion a
person should be so caught up by benevolence to Being as to be willing
to be damned, if that was for the good of the whole. And through his
courageous opposition to the New England slave trade, Hopkins pioneered the humanitarianism that would become such an admirable
fruit of nineteenth-century evangelical piety.[100]

As mediated by Hopkins, Edwards became a heroic precursor and legitimator to the nineteenth-century evangelical humanitarian tradition. Joseph Tracy's magnificent centennial history of the revival of the 1740s (still indispensable for its lucid expositions of the context of events) typifies the respect that the Second Great Awakening felt toward the First.[101] Many a laborer in the vineyards of the Second Awakening drew inspiration and reassurance from *The Life of David Brainerd.* (Franklin's *Autobiography* was popular too in Victorian America, though not assembled and published in its present form until 1868.) The mantle of Edwards became a prize for which rival evangelical schools of thought grappled through prolonged theological debates. Meanwhile, religious liberals like Oliver Wendell Holmes the elder struggled to rid American culture of Edwards's towering presence.[102]

What happened in the nineteenth century was that evangelical Christians came to accept the importance of many of Franklin's concerns for temporal human welfare and incorporated them into their own version of the Edwardsian model of faith. Christian Sunday schools and Temperance organizations inculcated the habits of industriousness and sobriety that Franklin wanted encouraged. Edwards's concerns with church discipline and the social morality of the town were grandly generalized by his nineteenth-century admirers into a commitment to making the United States as a whole a Christian nation. His postmillennial speculations were likewise grandly elaborated by Lyman Beecher (1775–1863) and others as justification for social reform. This process reached a climax in the work of Charles Grandisson Finney (1792–1875), the central figure of the antebellum revival. Finney has been called a man with a "divided conscience": a utilitarian like Franklin, yet still committed to benevolent and religious motives like Edwards.[103]

Thus evangelical piety energized humanitarianism as deism never could—just as Franklin had expected. Franklin, who encouraged Whitefield's social enterprises, would have approved of the Evangelical United Front, perhaps viewing it as a Christian version of his United Party of Virtue. Since he looked upon all religions as means to temporal ends, we may surmise that Franklin would have thought the emancipation of the slaves alone sufficient justification for the religious faith of the Victorian era. Edwards, on the other hand, might well have worried about the strict doctrinal purity of many of those who so proudly claimed him. Philosophies that logic declares different, history may still reconcile.

*The American Founders and the
Scottish Enlightenment*

Benjamin Franklin and Jonathan Edwards engaged in a dialogue
about human nature that included participants throughout the
Western world. In the eighteenth century, however, no corner of
Western civilization was more deeply engaged with problems concerning human nature, the development of the self, and the relationship between the self and society, than Scotland. From Scotland came
many of the ideas that American thinkers of the eighteenth century
and after applied to the issues confronting them. For this reason it
seems desirable to look specifically at the Scottish Enlightenment and
its relationship to American thought during the generation after the
death of Edwards. Both the Constitution of the United States and the
arguments made on its behalf were deeply informed by contemporary
ideas about the self and society, many of which came from Scotland.

Evidence for the enormous contribution that Scottish thought made
to early America has accumulated slowly over a period of many years.
However, no attempt to base a general interpretation of early American
political thought on this circumstance was made until 1978, when
Garry Wills published his study of the Declaration of Independence,
Inventing America. Wills's work aroused a storm of controversy and
criticism, and by now it appears certain that his discussion of the
philosophical issues underlying the Declaration was garbled. Nevertheless, his book proved to be a landmark in the sense that it focused

attention on the relevance of the Scottish Enlightenment to the American revolutionary generation. Sometimes a forceful statement, even if wrong, can have a constructive effect, and so it seems to have been with Wills's account.[1] What I propose to do in this chapter and the next is offer another way of seeing the relevance of the Scottish Enlightenment to the American founders.

Behind the flashy performance of Wills lay a long historiography, going back to I. Woodbridge Riley's account of *American Philosophy: The Early Schools,* published in 1907. By 1946 Herbert W. Schneider could conclude that the Scottish Enlightenment was "probably the most potent single tradition in the American Enlightenment." The surveys of the Enlightenment in America by Donald Harvey Meyer and Henry F. May in the 1970s confirmed it.[2] These intellectual connections are not surprising in view of the many commercial, social, cultural, and institutional ties between Scotland and America in the eighteenth century, ties that have also been thoroughly documented by historians.[3]

Of course, all Americans of the eighteenth century did not respond the same way to Scottish ideas, nor were all these ideas alike. We shall be examining a group of Americans—the framers of the Constitution along with one of its prominent supporters, Thomas Jefferson—in light of the use they made of Scottish ideas. One does not need demonstrate all over again the links connecting the American Founders with Scotland: the people they knew, the books they owned and recommended, their educational lineages, the organizations they belonged to, their travels and correspondences. This information has already been compiled, the connections have been made.[4] Given, then, that we are aware of the American Founders' affinity with—and debt to—the Scottish Enlightenment, what difference does this make? Does it help us understand the Founders and the Constitution they created? How does it help us appreciate the importance the Founders attached to the proper development of the self?

Both the Scottish Enlightenment and the Constitution of the United States were the creation of particular social groups, located in particular historical contexts, and implementing particular agendas. The founders of the American republic were a flexible, innovative, and above all, practical lot. If they found the Scottish Enlightenment supremely relevant and helpful, this should reveal something of their ways of thinking and the purposes of their proposed Constitution. (Of course,

I do not claim that the thinking of the Founders or the Constitution they created were entirely shaped by Scottish influences. To do so would contradict my other premise, that the Founders were supremely practical.) In the last analysis, the framers of the American Constitution found the thinkers of the Scottish Enlightenment suited their purposes because the social situation and goals of the two groups were remarkably similar. Both were concerned with national identity; less obviously but equally importantly for our purposes, both were concerned with providing conditions facilitating the proper development of the self.

?⊷ THE SCOTTISH ENLIGHTENMENT

The European phenomenon we call the Enlightenment took on somewhat different forms in different contexts. In Scotland, the Enlightenment was a well-organized, elite-led movement of moderate reform.[5] Its principal adversaries were Jacobitism on the right and radical Protestantism on the left. The social base of the Enlightenment in Scotland was clearly defined; it consisted of an alliance between the modernizing aristocracy of the lowlands and the middle class of the cities. The number one item on the agenda of these groups was the economic development of their backward country on the fringe of Europe. They supported Scotland's Union with England in 1707 because it promised economic advantages, and they refused to join the reactionary Jacobite uprisings of 1715 and 1745. Scientific agriculture and the consolidation of land holdings into commercially viable units were favorite projects with them; in the jargon of the age, these were called improvements, a term that then came to be applied to Scottish reform in general. Significantly, the word "improvement" also acquired an important meaning in relation to the development of the self, to which we shall return.

 Before going any farther, let us clarify and personalize the Scottish Enlightenment by calling the roll of the most important of its thinkers. Francis Hutcheson (1694–1746) was the acknowledged Father of the Scottish Enlightenment. Those who built upon his work included Lord Kames (1696–1782), Thomas Reid (1710–1796), Hugh Blair (1718–1800), William Robertson, (1721–1793), Adam Ferguson (1723–1816), John Millar (1735–1801), and Dugald Stewart (1753–1828).

The last named was significant as the most important transmitter of the Scottish Enlightenment to the nineteenth century.[6] In a class by themselves are the giants of the Scottish Enlightenment: David Hume (1711–1776) and Adam Smith (1723–1790). To examine the origins of the leading writers of the Scottish Enlightenment is to confirm their clear identification with the modernizing elements in Scottsh society: all save Kames and Hume were middle-class (these two were related to each other and came from an aristocratic family); all save Ferguson were lowlanders (and his thought showed the influence of his unique highland origins).

Scotland in the eighteenth century was a land of dramatic contrasts, and these contrasts dictated a high degree of organization and self-consciousness on the part of the proponents of its Enlightenment. The most important contrast was that between the lowlands, where the Enlightenment took root, and the primitive highlands, where a pre-medieval tribalism still prevailed. The backwardness of the highland economy is almost impossible to exaggerate: in parts of Scotland, the *wheel* was unknown until the eighteenth century. ("When a cart appeared in East Kilbride, 12 miles from Glasgow, in 1723, the crowds collected round so wonderful a machine: it might have been a satellite from the moon.")[7]

Another sharp contrast was that between the two rival parties in the Church of Scotland. Scotland had a powerful established church of its own, and it was in ecclesiastical politics that the Scottish Enlightenment took on its chief institutional form. The Popular Party, drawing support from what must have been a majority of the population, strongly affirmed evangelical Calvinism and an undeviating loyalty to the theology of the Westminster Confession of 1647. The Moderate Party, supported by the alliance between improvement-seeking aristocrats and the urban middle class, synthesized Christianity with the Enlightenment on terms similar to those of English Latitudinarism. The two parties fought constantly over clerical appointments. The law sanctioned the right of landholders to "patronage," that is, to choose the minister for the local church. Naturally, the Popular Party frequently opposed the patron's choice, and from time to time groups of disaffected evangelicals took the drastic step of seceding from the national church. The Moderate Party, which defended the patronage system, was the stronghold of the Enlightenment.[8] Being liberal Christians, the Moderates believed as Locke did in religious toleration.

When David Hume's skeptical philosophy was challenged by angry
evangelicals, it was his friends in the Moderate Party who protected his
freedom of expression (though they were never able to get him the
university professorship he justifiably craved).[9]

The intellectual agenda of the thinkers of the Scottish Enlightenment was set by the practical issues of their time and place. Despite
parallels with the moderate Enlightenment of the English Latitudinarians, there were important differences too, giving the Scottish
Enlightenment its unique quality. Scottish Calvinism had a stronger
intellectual tradition than did Anglicanism, and the universities of
Scotland were more numerous and took their tasks more seriously than
eighteenth-century Oxford and Cambridge did. Also, Scottish intellectuals were acutely conscious of their provincialism and both defen-
sive about it and anxious to overcome it; this marginal status seems to
have spurred them to achievement, as it has so many other people. One
of the features of the Scottish Enlightenment is that its proponents did
not define themselves primarily as Scotsmen: they thought of themselves as cosmopolites and men of the Enlightenment. Most important
of all, the glaring contrasts they encountered between sophisticated
prosperity and primitive backwardness provoked Scottish intellectuals
into serious reflection on the nature of social and economic progress.
Economic development simply was not an issue for eighteenth-century
English thinkers in the same way. The Scottish Enlightenment, then,
consisted of a self-conscious band of programmatic intellectuals,
indebted to a provincial Calvinist heritage they were trying to escape,
and seeking to enlist private wealth on the side of their country's
public good. Out of the tensions of this cultural matrix, a small and
comparatively remote country produced an astonishingly dispropor-
tionate share of the eighteenth century's intellectual achievements.[10]

From the Scottish Enlightenment's dedication to analyzing and promoting economic development came the origins of modern social science—psychology, sociology, political science, and economics. These
social sciences were gestated in the womb of moral philosophy, a
wide-ranging early-modern academic discipline that included not only
what we call moral philosophy, meaning ethical theory, but the whole
study of human nature, both descriptive and prescriptive. The Scottish
thinkers of the Enlightenment were all of them moral philosophers, so
their specialized analytic innovations were housed in a framework that
was generalized and normative. Notwithstanding this moral frame-

work, the Scottish thinkers strove to be flexible and empirical rather than deductive in their approach to problem-solving.[11] They constituted themselves, in twentieth-century terms, a brain trust for the modernization of Scotland.

To make their case for economic development, the thinkers of the Scottish Enlightenment had to confront a venerable tradition of social thought called civic humanism, originating in the revival of classical learning in the Renaissance. Out of this tradition came the political ideals we have been calling classical republicanism. In this paradigm, a healthy commonwealth was based on the "virtue" of the political community, reflecting an unselfish public spirit, and "mixed" institutions of government, balancing the orders of society (monarch, nobility, commons). Commercial values were thought to pose a danger to free institutions by encouraging self-interest and corrupting public virtue. Large, wealthy empires were doubly vulnerable: their commerce would undermine their liberty, and because of their size they could only be governed by absolute monarchies.[12] Scottish Calvinist particularists like Andrew Fletcher invoked this civic humanist tradition in opposing the legislative Union with England in 1707. Naturally, the Scottish programmatic Enlightenment had to come to terms with such a well-established pattern of thought. It is possible to conceptualize much of the Scottish Enlightenment as an extended dialogue and debate with civic humanism.[13]

As defenders of the Union with England, the writers of the Scottish Enlightenment were committed to two tasks, both of which brought them into potential conflict with civic humanism. First, they had to defend economic development as natural and beneficial; second, they had to minimize the significance of Scotland's loss of self-government. The defense of economic development led the Scottish thinkers into analyzing the evolution of society through stages. Typically, they identified four such stages: hunting (or "savage"), pastoral, agricultural, and commercial. Each represented an enrichment of the human condition, a growing technological power, and a refinement of manners.[14]

The Scottish writers coped with their country's loss of political autonomy by the ingenious device of arguing that politics was not really all that important. The evolution from one stage of social development to the next was governed by fixed laws of human behavior over which individuals, including statesmen, had little control. According to these thinkers, many of the most important changes in society came about imperceptibly or inadvertently; social actions often had unintended consequences. David Hume pointed to the growth of English liberty as a historical example. The religious fanaticism of the Puritans, he observed, by opposing the power of the crown, had inadvertently strengthened English freedoms. (The seemingly "ridiculous" principles of the Puritans kindled "the precious spark of liberty.")[15] Adam Smith carried this logic to its fullest in the *Wealth of Nations* in 1776: in the economic realm, political manipulation was downright harmful. The workings of the marketplace had been designed by a benevolent Providence, just like those of eighteenth-century celestial mechanics. The "invisible hand" would direct all for the best if only men would leave it to do its work.[16]

The disposition of the Scottish thinkers to minimize the importance of law as compared with other social forces had lasting consequences. It helps explain the determination of their followers, across the eighteenth and nineteenth centuries, to rely whenever possible on custom, moral exhortation, voluntary societies, and education as instruments of virtue in place of legal sanctions. One of the most famous of these followers was Edmund Burke, whose statement on the importance of manners became a favorite on both sides of the Atlantic. "Manners are of more importance than laws. Upon them, in a great measure, the laws depend. The law touches us but here and there, and now and then. Manners are what vex or soothe us, by a constant, steady, uniform, insensible operation like that of the air we breathe in. They give their whole form and colour to our lives. According to their quality, they aid morals, they supply them, or they totally destroy them."[17] Burke was using the word "manners" in a broad sense here, but Anglo-American opinion leaders did not adopt a merely passive attitude toward them. The cultivation of good manners as essential to free society would be a major cultural development, a widespread popular aspiration, and a principal goal of reformers throughout the period covered by this book.

The Scottish philosophers themselves were both practitioners and promoters of polite culture, especially of polite discourse among gentlemen, as creating the preconditions for political civility and therefore for political freedom.[18] The version of politeness they embraced was that of *The Spectator* of Addison and Steele, not that of the French court at Versailles. Theirs was an explicitly upper-middle-class politeness, created for a world of coffeehouses, clubs, and debating societies—not of nobles or courtiers. To a remarkable extent, it was a culture that recognized women as members and included them in the audience for which polite literature was written. This version of politeness endorsed "a proper blend of seriousness and ease, Christianity and worldliness." Whig rather than Tory, it accepted the new world of commercial relationships. In contrast to the fawning dissimulation of the courtier, it valued sincerity and regulated "the free relations between equals." It was "a politeness for the *polis*."[19] Good manners and good taste were valued as moral qualities, while mere fashion was deplored as snobbish and frivolous. The essence of polite culture was the balanced cultivation of the self, especially of the faculties of dispassionate reason, virtue, and sensitivity. The cultivated gentleman or lady, the responsible citizen, the objective observer of society: this was the ideal self. Such a person had internalized the stable, objective values of Scottish moral philosophy.[20]

In the upper-middle-class polite culture typified by *The Spectator,* Scottish moral philosophers found a program of individual improvement analogous to their program of national improvement in commerce and manners. These two programs, the improvement of the nation and that of the individual, were mutually reinforcing. A nation that had progressed to a higher stage of civilization offered greater opportunities for individual self-realization. "In the political union, and in the gradual improvement of which it is susceptible," Dugald Stewart explained, "nature has made provision for the gradual improvement of our intellectual and moral powers."[21] Through such media as the *Edinburgh Review* and the writings of Stewart's followers among American moral philosophers, his faith in balance and in progress both individual and political would be perpetuated on both sides of the Atlantic for much of the nineteenth century.[22]

One of the reasons why Reid, Stewart, and other Scottish Moderates rejected David Hume's radical skepticism in favor of an epistemology of common sense is that Hume dissolved human consciousness into a mere chain of sensory experiences. Reid and his circle were determined to retain the integrity of the individual *self,* as they believed the self could be improved and its powers cultivated. Their agenda of education and politeness would be threatened if the very existence of the self were called into question.[23]

The Scottish philosophers did not constitute a unified front on all political questions, though in general they were strong friends to civil liberties and sympathetic to the views of the American colonists.[24]

Ultimately, however, they were perhaps less interested in the political order than in the socioeconomic order. This is revealed in their ambiguous relationship to the ideas of John Locke. The founder of their school, Francis Hutcheson, continued to accept Locke's notion of a series of contracts creating society and government, but devoted most of his attention to noncontractual, nonrational social bonds (the "social affections"). Society itself was stronger and more durable than government, Hutcheson implied.[25] In 1757 the Scotsman John Dalrymple undertook to investigate Locke's theory that government originated in a desire to protect property. Dalrymple concluded that the idea of property was a social construct, which had evolved along with the changing material nature of the things that became property, through the different stages of society.[26] Thereafter, spokesmen of the Scottish Enlightenment tended to emphasize the gradual evolution of human institutions rather than their origin in a hypothetical contract, though they never surrendered Locke's defense of the integrity of private property. In Hume, though not in other Scottish thinkers, this tendency led to a thoroughgoing positivism and abandonment of the whole notion of natural rights.[27] The Scots always honored Locke and considered themselves to be working within his tradition; as time went by, however, they modified his doctrines considerably in all the fields of moral philosophy as then defined, including epistemology and ethics as well as social theory.

It would oversimplify intellectual history to describe the Scottish Enlightenment as a straightforward repudiation of civic humanism. Some of the time, the terms of Scottish discourse were dictated by civic humanist premises. The new Enlightenment and the old civic humanism had much in common, after all. Both were fundamentally concerned to protect civil liberty against tyrannical government. Both could make use of the examples of the ancients.[28] Montesquieu, probably the most widely read of all Enlightenment *philosophes* and one to whom the Scots were greatly indebted, showed many continuities with the civic humanist tradition. Just as Scottish thinkers acknowledged Locke while moving beyond him, so too did they let elements of the old civic humanism crop up in their thinking. (For example, Hume worried about the effects of the new national debt—a typically civic humanist attitude.) Most importantly, the thinkers of the Scottish Enlightenment continued to endorse the features of mixed and balanced government embodied in the British constitution. It is necessary to keep these complications in mind without losing sight of the fundamental contrast between the modern empiricism of the Scottish Enlightenment and the ancient natural law that underlay Renaissance civic humanism and classical republicanism.[29]

Although the broad outlines of the Scottish Enlightenment are clear—support for the economic "improvers," the religious Moderates, and the Union with England—within this basic orientation there was a rich variety of philosophical positions. There was no strict party line in Scottish moral philosophy: that was part of its greatness. The issues the Scots debated in the course of addressing their agenda were intellectually momentous. Among them were social organicism v. contractualism, government intervention v. laissez faire, free will v. determinism, Christianity v. skepticism, ethical sentimentalism v. ethical rationalism. The Scots spread a rich intellectual table where the Americans would pick and choose and feast.[30]

❧ THE FRAMERS OF THE AMERICAN CONSTITUTION

In America, the Scottish Enlightenment came to a kind of fulfillment denied it at home. Scottish intellectuals felt keenly their isolation from the major seat of power in London. They had to content themselves with their magazines and literary clubs, the promotion of polite culture, ecclesiastical and academic patronage, and their role as a brain trust. In the America of the revolutionary generation, by contrast, the leading intellectuals *were* the statesmen. In America, the social thinkers were empowered to implement their ideas and free to choose which ideas to implement. When they chose to promote polite culture, it was a complement to, not a substitute for, their power to shape institutions. It was a combination of intellectual and political power rare, if not unique, in the annals of history.[31]

To see why the framers of the American Constitution found the Scottish Enlightenment so relevant helps us characterize the framers and clarify their agenda. Like the Scots they admired, the framers were advocating an enlargement of the political arena through a union—in their case, transforming a confederation into a true union of the states. The benefits they looked to achieve through unification were to a large extent economic. Like those Scots again, the Americans were socially conservative but economically progressive—progressive in the sense of wanting commercial development, not in the sense of wanting a redistribution of wealth. Like the Scots, finally, the American framers were concerned with the cultivation of the self.

To take a comparative look at the societies of Scotland and America in the eighteenth century is to be struck by many parallels. The hinterlands of the American frontier were analogous in important ways to the Scottish highlands. Transportation and communication were difficult, and the region's economic potential was undeveloped. Though the weight of the past (in the form of deferential custom) was less crushing on the American frontier folk, in other ways their situation was even worse than that of the highlanders: distances were longer, their geographic isolation greater, and the intermittent frontier warfare with Indians, Spanish, French, and British even more dangerous than the feuds among highland clans. Bernard Bailyn has recently described eighteenth-century America as a "marchland" of Western civilization, and has graphically reminded us of the social barbarism of the frontier in particular.[32] It was a land of violence, primitive and regressive. If the Scottish highlands had their archaic system of clans, the Americans had chattel slavery, outlawed for its inhumanity in the mother country. The Scottish Enlightenment derived its stimulus from the contrast between the primitive and modern. The founders of the American republic confronted problems of modernization fully analogous. They too faced a juxtaposition (in Bailyn's words) of "primitivism and civilization."[33]

Not only did the task before them resemble the agenda of the Scottish Enlightenment; the framers of the American Constitution themselves occupied a situation not unlike that of the Scottish *literati.* They represented the more civilized parts of America—the cities and accessible river valleys—as well as the more prosperous, cosmopolitan social classes—the landowners, merchants, and professionals. These were the people, in America as in Scotland, with a stake in a sound currency, public credit, and a unified customs-free trade zone. These were the social groups that had made the Scottish Enlightenment, and they would be the principal political supporters of the proposed Constitution of the United States. Scientific agriculture did not become a political issue in the United States until later; when it did, it was supported by the same social groups.[34]

The religious context in which the framers found themselves also bore marked similarities to that of Scotland. In America too the liberalization of Calvinist theology and the conflict between evangelical and rational religion were major issues. In the absence of an ecclesiastical patronage system expressing the power of a ruling class, evangelicalism was stronger and rational religion correspondingly weaker in America. But the same theological authorities were invoked, and a Scottish clergymen like John Witherspoon (1723–1794) could achieve a career of distinction on each side of the Atlantic. In America, as in Scotland and England, the Enlightenment defined itself in large measure as a rejection of religious "enthusiasm." The framers at Philadelphia represented a variety of religious affiliations, but there was no one who could even remotely be characterized as an enthusiast.[35]

An interesting if little-noticed parallel between the cultural agenda of the Scottish Enlightenment and that of the American Federalists was their common support for politeness. In contrast to the dour neopuritanism espoused by the First Continental Congress (which banned horseracing and the theater along with gaudy dress in 1774),[36] the framers of the Constitution embraced an Addisonian public ethic. James Madison, for example, was an avid reader of *The Spectator,* the leading proponent of eighteenth-century polite culture. But the parallel is most clearly delineated in the writings of the Scottish-born American Constitution-framer James Wilson (1742–1798). Wilson's first publication was a set of essays entitled "The Visitant" (cf. *The Spectator*), defining politeness as "the natural and graceful expression of the social virtues." Wilson's co-author of "The Visitant" essays was William White of Philadelphia, future founding bishop of the Episcopal Church in the United States. Influenced by Scottish common-sense philosophy, Wilson and White considered politeness a moral quality, based on "perception by the moral sense."[37]

In later years, after accepting the first professorship of law in the College of Philadelphia, James Wilson devoted considerable attention in his lectures to the subject of politeness and its relationship to republican citizenship. There, in the words of Stephen Conrad, the scholar who has done the most to elucidate this subject, Wilson developed "an argument implying that politeness is an essential element of the social foundation of republican citizenship." According to Conrad, Wilson was aware of the potential contradictions between liberalism and classical republicanism as theoretical foundations of the American polity. Wilson employed Scottish common-sense philosophy to analyze this problem, and prescribed polite culture as the remedy. "If the moral sense was amenable to refinement through the routines of polite culture, then even the most vexed contradictions in the theory of republican citizenship could be 'reconciled.' " Polite culture would train citizens in civilized discourse, preparing them for both the private and public spheres of activity.[38] Certainly this framer of the Constitution believed, with Edmund Burke and Scots like Thomas Reid, that manners were at least as important as laws in providing the foundation for free government.

In any consideration of the parallels between eighteenth-century Scotland and America, one must reckon with the issue of cosmopolitanism versus provincialism. Both Americans and Scots lived on the periphery of the English-speaking world and needed to come to terms with their identity in relation to their metropolis. Part of their common dedication to politeness stemmed from their determination to overcome the cultural inferiority of their provincial status.[39]

The opposition that the supporters of the Constitution faced raised many of the same issues that the friends of the Enlightenment had had to confront in Scotland. The Antifederalists made use of principles from Montesquieu and the civic humanists to justify political particularism and oppose strengthening the union. They questioned whether the commercial advantages the union was designed to promote would outweigh the loss of participatory self-government.[40] In their defense of local majorities against the power of distant elites, the Antifederalists sometimes sound like the evangelical Popular Party in the Church of Scotland. And, of course, many Antifederalists were Calvinist sectarians, following the New Light of spiritual inspiration, suspicious of rationalism and secularism. (The terms Old Light and New Light were used in Scotland too, and may have originated there.)[41]

The framers and supporters of the proposed American Constitution defended their work with what they believed were scientific principles. If justified on a traditional historical basis, the new government would seem mutable, exposed to the cycles of corruption and decline. Eighteenth-century science, on the other hand, dealt with timeless principles. As one Federalist put it, under the Constitution the American states "shall resemble the Solar System, where every obedient planet moves on its proper path."[42] Of course the Founders made use of the wisdom of the past, including medieval legal and constitutional practice, because experience was part of what Enlightenment science valued. But as Richard D. Brown has written, "the Constitution itself, as the deliberate, self-conscious offspring of the most erudite political science of its day, was essentially modern. . . . Its origins were not lost in the mists of time, nor was it the work of legendary sages or divinities. . . . It was a government made in a test-tube."[43] What more logical place for the supporters of the proposed government to turn for ideas than the Scottish Enlightenment, which had been concerned with so many of the same issues? The fact that the Scottish thinkers themselves had respected the past and synthesized their social science with the defense of balanced government made them all the more relevant.

One of the most pervasive influences of the social thought of the Scottish Enlightenment on the Americans is a very broad one, not attributable to any individual thinker. This is the Scots' concern with *unintended outcomes.* The Founders and their supporters thought of themselves as a wise and virtuous elite, creating a Constitution that would have to be administered by lesser mortals. "Enlightened statesmen will not always be at the helm," warned *The Federalist Papers.*[44] In Herman Wouk's novel, *The Caine Mutiny,* the United States Navy is described as "a system designed by geniuses to be run by idiots." The framers of the American Constitution wanted to construct just such a system, so that the unintended outcome of short-sightedness and selfishness would be the public good.

The Scots offered hope that this would be possible. Hume was particularly helpful; he taught that men could be governed through their passions and ambitions.[45] This was, of course, the opposite of the civic humanist reliance on public virtue to make government work, but it seemed more relevant to the Founders. They were fed up with the weakness of the Articles of Confederation and their reliance on uncoerced popular virtue.[46] If anything, America suffered from an excess of public spirit: too much hasty legislation by ill-informed citizens. The Scots were helpful here too: they had decided (for altogether different reasons) that widespread participation in government was not the key to the health of the body politic.

The Constitution, with its system of checks and balances, was based on the principle that even without enlightened statecraft, the vices could, through wise contrivance, be made to do the work of virtues. But the document's elaborate system for the indirect selection of presidents, senators, and federal judges was also based on the principle that what little virtue society possessed could be filtered out and concentrated in a few wise representatives, who would do a better job of governing than the people could do for themselves. Both principles had an intellectual basis in the Scottish Enlightenment: one in Hume, the other in Reid and his followers. In theory the two are not perfectly compatible, since the former is based on the premise that no one can be trusted, while the latter is based on the premise that there are a few who can be trusted more than most. But between the two systems, republican government could survive even if public virtue was scarce, or so *The Federalist* argued. Later generations of Americans, as we shall see, were by no means as confident as the Founders that vices could be made to do the work of virtues, or that wise institutions of government could sufficiently make up for a scarcity of public virtue.

Like the theorists of the Scottish Enlightenment, and like the authors of *Cato's Letters,* the practical statesmen of the American Enlightenment synthesized what they found enduring in the old classical republicanism with the new science of government. The Federalists created a Union to promote economic development while checking democratic majorities through balances reminiscent of "mixed government." The Constitution made the imaginative leap of balancing, not the estates of the realm, but the component parts of government itself, each chosen in a different way by a different constituency. It was a contrivance to preserve what the framers felt were the procedural benefits of mixed government in a country without traditional social orders. It was a triumph of eighteenth-century political engineering.[47]

For their part, the Antifederalists too synthesized civic humanism with the Enlightenment. While most of their criticisms of the proposed Constitution dealt with its creation of a distant, unresponsive elite that violated the traditional connection between republicanism and localism, the major concession they extracted from the Federalists in the end was an implementation of Lockean principles: the American Bill of Rights. The Antifederalists conceived the governments of the states in terms of empowering popular virtue, but when it came to the central government, they insisted on a Lockean construction of strictly delegated powers.[48]

Tracing the parallels between the Scottish and American Enlightenments has helped us characterize the Founders and clarify their goals. They were enlightened statesmen (in both the capitalized and lower-case senses of the word "enlightened"), but not spokesmen of a democratic populace. Instead, they spoke for a republican elite of cultivated gentlemen. The Addisonian polite culture they endorsed was compatible with, and indeed helped to reconcile in their minds, both classical republicanism and political liberalism. Like the great Scottish philosophers, the American framers sought to unify and rationalize their country's economy. Practical politicians, they were also well informed and respectful of learning. They applied the most relevant and sophisticated social theory available to the Constitution they created. The Scottish Enlightenment provided them with much of this theory. As later chapters will demonstrate, however, polite culture and Scottish moral philosophy—like the American Constitution—were destined for a much broader and more democratic application in the nineteenth century.

Ꮽ THE PSYCHOLOGY OF THE FACULTIES

Of all the borrowings that Americans made from the Scottish Enlightenment, the one that concerns us the most in this book is their use of faculty psychology. Faculty psychology was relevant to the founders of the American republic for two broad reasons. In the first place, they envisioned the nation they were creating as one where the citizens would be free to develop their faculties, to engage in self-improvement or the "pursuit of happiness." Secondly, they conceptualized the constitutional order they were creating, the institutions themselves, in terms analogous to the faculties of human nature. Before we follow this analogy, it is necessary to explain faculty psychology itself.

Faculty psychology was not peculiar to the Scottish Enlightenment. We have already seen how it was employed by the English authors of *Cato's Letters* in the 1720s. But the version most influential in the United States was the codification formulated by the Scottish philosophers Thomas Reid, Lord Kames, and Dugald Stewart. Faculty psychology was one of the subjects about which Scottish philosophers disagreed with each other. David Hume was an avowed critic of faculty psychology, and we know that *The Federalist Papers* used several of his arguments. But when it came to the fundamentals of human nature, Publius (the pseudonym used by Alexander Hamilton, James Madison, and John Jay in writing *The Federalist*) stood by the more conventional outlook typified by Cato and Reid.[49] Hume was by no means universally popular in America; his *History of England* was considered outrageously Tory and his *Dialogues on Natural Religion* scandalous. Indeed, when Madison made use of Hume's arguments about the advantages of a large commonwealth, he did so without attribution—probably because to have avowed indebtedness to Hume would have been a tactical mistake.[50] By contrast, Reid and his school were safe authorities for generations of Americans to cite.

The word "faculty," like the word "facility," is derived from the

Latin for "power." "What is a power but the ability or faculty of doing a thing?" asks Publius, rhetorically.[51] Faculty psychology in ancient, medieval, or modern times is the study of the human powers. From Pythagoras, Plato, Aristotle, and the Stoics onward, human nature has been sorted out into different powers, some shared with plants, some with animals, and some—the rational and moral powers—with God. The medieval scholastics elaborated the system and the Protestant reformers retained it. John Locke and other philosophers of the Enlightenment modified the tradition but carried it forward. As we saw in our examination of Edwards and Franklin, the form of faculty psychology that the Americans inherited was still hierarchical. It treated human nature as including all the components of "the great chain of being," from mere existence to animation, sensation, and rationality. Mankind lived in a middle state, part of nature yet above it—both body and spirit, animal and divine, neither all good nor all evil.[52]

All systems of faculty psychology are essentially teleological, since the faculties are defined in terms of their purpose. As the Scottish moral philosopher Francis Hutcheson explained, divine Providence so designed the human faculties that "they form a machine, most accurately subservient to the necessities, convenience, and happiness of a rational system."[53] When a person allowed certain faculties to get out of control, he was perverting the divinely intended harmony of the system. Earlier generations had synthesized faculty psychology with Christianity, identifying the perverse misuse of God-given faculties with sin. Human passions (or affections, as they were also termed) were legitimate faculties in their place, but there was a standing danger that they might be indulged or followed to excess. Archbishop Cranmer had expressed it in his Litany: "From all inordinate and sinful affections, . . . Good Lord, deliver us." The conventional theological formulation held that the proper supremacy of reason among the faculties had been jeopardized by the corruption of human nature in the Fall. As Milton wrote in *Paradise Lost,*

> Reason in man obscured, or not obeyed,
> Immediately inordinate desires
> And upstart passions catch the government
> From reason, and to servitude reduce
> Man till then free . . .[54]

In his studies at Princeton, Madison had been exposed to the same Calvinist tradition as Milton, in which both freedom and virtue were equated with the supremacy of rationality. To be enslaved by one's own passions was accounted one of the cruelest forms of slavery.[55]

Eighteenth-century science was taxonomic in its preoccupations, and the faculty psychologists of the time struggled toward greater precision and debated definitions. Human mental powers were arranged in a kind of natural history of the mind by a series of Enlightenment moral philosophers beginning with the Earl of Shaftesbury. In the elaborate system developed by Thomas Reid, the human faculties were classified as "mechanical," "animal" (called "sensitive" by Aristotelians), and "rational." The mechanical powers were involuntary reflexes. The animal or sensitive powers were physical appetites (hunger and sex), instinctive desires (like gregariousness), and—most important for American writers on politics—the "passions" or "affections," which we would call the emotions. The rational powers were two: conscience (called the "moral sense" by many writers) and prudence, or self-interest.[56]

An excellent example of how the American revolutionaries employed faculty psychology is John Witherspoon's jeremiad, "The Dominion of Providence over the Passions of Men," preached on May 17, 1776, in reponse to a day of fasting and humiliation proclaimed by the Continental Congress. Witherspoon dedicated his sermon to the President of the Congress, John Hancock. He took as his text Psalm 76:10: "Surely the wrath of man shall praise thee." Even the corruptness of human nature, even the disorderly passions of man, are in the service of God's providential purposes; out of the horrors of "civil war" God will vindicate the right, he reassures his congregation. Witherspoon places his Whig politics in the context of faculty psychology. He does not accuse the King and Parliament of any *unusual* degree of passionate evil; it is necessary to "refuse submission to their unjust claims" simply "because they are men, and therefore liable to all the selfish bias inseparable from human nature." We Whigs should try to keep our own passions in order, he exhorts, and not wage war in a "turbulent" spirit but in one of discipline, "industry," and "frugality," demonstrating "a dignity in virtue."[57]

The version of faculty psychology formulated by the school of Reid and Witherspoon, and adapted by the American Founders to their own purposes, had two distinctive characteristics. The first of these was the degree of rationality accorded to self-interest. This accorded with Benjamin Franklin's usage but contrasted sharply with the faculty psychology of the medieval scholastics and Protestant reformers, who had treated motives of self-regard (or self-love) as passions. The second distinguishing mark of this school was that the moral sense was considered a rational faculty, in contrast with the opinion of such thinkers as Francis Hutcheson, David Hume, and Adam Smith, who held that the moral sense was an affection, that is, an emotion.

Of central importance to eighteenth-century American writers on politics were motives of self-interest. In their day, interest was not yet simply equated with economic interest but meant self-regarding motivation broadly understood. Publius recognized that "it is a general principle of human nature that a man will be interested in whatever he possesses," especially his material possessions. Albert O. Hirschman has shown how, in the course of the eighteenth century, certain self-regarding motives such as avarice and ambition, which had previously been classified as "passions," came to be grouped into a new category called "interests" and ranked as rational rather than sensitive powers, even though they still retained some of the characteristics associated with passions.[58] An emphasis on rational self-interest, or prudential calculation, was particularly important in the construction of liberal, or contractual, political theories. Jefferson's *Declaration of Independence* invokes this faculty: "prudence, indeed, will dictate that governments long established should not be changed for light and transient causes."

The Federalist Papers make extensive use of faculty psychology in the course of a sustained analogy between the construction of a polity and the construction of an individual self. The "balanced government" Publius was advocating rested on the correspondences that he thought he saw between political institutions and social classes on the one hand, and the faculties of human nature on the other. But before opening that discussion, we shall look at the meaning of faculty psychology for another leading exponent of the American Enlightenment: Thomas Jefferson.

✇ THE FACULTY PSYCHOLOGY OF THOMAS JEFFERSON

Thomas Jefferson frequently employed the model of faculty psychology current in his day, including the principle that the passions needed to be kept subordinated to reason. An accomplished classical scholar, Jefferson declared that he revered the ancient philosophers primarily for the counsel they provided on governing the passions—"which, unrestrained, would disturb our tranquillity of mind." In his proposed revision of the Virginia criminal law (1779), he attributed crime to "wicked and dissolute men resigning themselves to the dominion of inordinate passions."[59] And although he thought British interests, rightly understood, lay in good relations with America, Jefferson regretfully noted that "interest is not the strongest passion in the human breast."[60]

Nevertheless, Jefferson valued the passions/affections in their place and believed they served indispensable functions; like others who applied the psychology of the faculties, Jefferson believed in their harmonious integration, or balance.[61] "The perfection of the moral character is, not in a Stoical apathy, so hypocritically vaunted, and so untruly too, because impossible, but in a just equilibrium of all the passions."[62] Understanding Jefferson's use of faculty pychology helps us understand several aspects of his thought, including three that have been of particular interest to historians in recent years: his Lockean liberalism, his classical republicanism, and his racism.[63]

Like the authors of *Cato's Letters,* whose Radical Whig political orientation he shared, Jefferson was more concerned to restrain the passions of the rulers than those of the ruled.[64] "Sometimes it is said that man cannot be trusted with the government of himself. Can he, then, be trusted with the government of others?" he asked rhetorically.[65] The Congressional declaration of "the Causes and Necessity of taking up Arms" (1775), which Jefferson co-authored, condemned Parliament's "inordinate passion" for power. In the Kentucky Resolutions of 1798, he appealed to state sovereignty to provide protection against "the passions" of a Congressional majority.[66]

Jefferson shared with most of his educated American contemporaries an enormous intellectual debt to the Scottish Enlightenment. So widespread was this influence at the time that it would have been surprising if he had escaped it.[67] But just as all members of the Scottish Enlightenment did not think alike, neither did all representatives of the American Enlightenment. Jefferson's attitude toward human nature is different from those of Franklin, Edwards, and most of the men who framed the Constitution, including even his longtime friend James Madison.[68] Although Jefferson supported the new Constitution and endorsed its principles of limited and balanced powers, he did this not so much because he shared the others' anxieties about human nature and the passions of the multitude as out of an optimistic faith that human nature was basically good.

"I am among those who think well of the human character generally," Jefferson acknowledged. How different is this affirmation from anything that Jonathan Edwards or even Benjamin Franklin would have said! Whereas they saw human nature as constituting a *problem* demanding solution, Jefferson did not view it that way. What he meant by his high estimate of human nature was that man was not naturally antisocial: "I consider man as formed for society, and endowed by nature with those dispositions which fit him for society." Individuals whose faculties—rational and emotional—were harmoniously integrated would naturally create a harmonious and integrated society.[69]

As we have seen, Jefferson shared the prevailing assumption of the faculty psychology paradigm that the passions were stronger than the reason. On balance, however, he accounted the presumed power of emotion to the credit rather than to the debit of humanity. The individual's emotional makeup could work for good, especially if the personality were properly cultivated. What moral philosophers called the "social affections" or "benevolent affections," the instinctive ties of family, friendship, honor, and empathy, seemed to him bonds of tremendous importance and promise. They justified calling man "a social animal." They gave him confidence that the ruthless selfishness portrayed by Hobbes could be overcome. Collectively, they overcame the rationale for tyranny.[70]

Assuming the role of a national spokesman and attributing his confidence to all Americans, Jefferson wrote: "We consider society as one of the natural wants with which man has been created; that he has been endowed with faculties and qualities to effect its satisfaction, [and that] by the exercise of these faculties, he has procured a state of society." His justification for republican government and his commitment to citizen involvement at the local level flowed naturally from this confidence in the normal harmony between the competent individual and the interests of the community. And since individuals did not need to be coerced into social behavior, they could be safely left to their own self-direction. Thus Jefferson's moral philosophy entailed his liberalism as well as his classical republicanism. Jefferson's laissez-faire politics was the analog to Adam Smith's economics, and like it was based on a positive estimate of human moral sentiments.[71]

Jefferson's thoughts on moral philosophy were expressed over his lifetime in disconnected fragments that must be pieced together by those who would construct his overall opinion. Although Garry Wills has argued that Jefferson followed the Scottish philosopher Francis Hutcheson in basing moral values on an emotional moral sense, Morton White has provided a more accurate characterization of Jefferson's understanding of moral theory in *The Philosophy of the American Revolution*.[72] There White argues persuasively that Jefferson in fact considered moral judgments properly rational—as did John Locke, Thomas Reid, Richard Price, a majority of the Scottish philosophers, and most of the other subjects of this book. Of all the Scottish philosophers, Kames probably exerted the strongest influence upon Jefferson, though Dugald Stewart became his close friend when both were in Paris, and their ideas have much in common, particularly their faith in the progressive improvement of the moral sense.[73] Such use as Jefferson made of Scottish ideas was by no means incompatible with his Lockean orientation, since the Scots themselves were working in Locke's tradition.[74]

For Jefferson, moral judgments should be rational, and our moral feelings should be properly subject to the guidance of reason, which could calculate the greatest good of the greatest number. Like Franklin, Jefferson believed that social utility was the real ground of virtue. "Happiness [is] the aim of life. Virtue the foundation of happiness. Utility the test of virtue," he wrote in a set of didactic maxims worthy of Franklin.[75] But most of the time calculation of utility was not necessary. Most of the time, for most of the people, moral feelings were reliable enough. Such was the benevolence of the divine Creator in giving humanity these feelings, making man a sociable animal. This was why (in a famous example Jefferson gave) the untutored impulses of the ploughman might sometimes be a better guide to moral action than the labored reasonings of a professor who had been led astray by some false philosophy.[76] His example does not mean, however, that we should abandon rationality for emotion or that no true knowledge of moral principles can be discovered. Jefferson believed that reason should judge of all questions, including moral, metaphysical, and religious ones. The moral feelings were the uneducated person's safeguard. The educated person realized that the true value of these feelings lay in their social utility.[77]

One can see why Wills made his mistake of thinking Jefferson espoused an emotivist theory of ethics. It was to the instinctive moral feelings that Jefferson gave the term "moral sense" (or "moral faculties"). This produced a terminological confusion, since Reid, for example, used the term "moral sense" to mean the reason in the exercise of its moral function. But Jefferson's "moral sense" was Witherspoon, Kames, and Stewart's "benevolent affections" or "social affections."[78] Wills failed to notice that Jefferson did not accord these moral feelings the highest authority, but subordinated them to that of the understanding (that is, reason) for guidance and improvement.[79]

Wills was concerned to elucidate the Declaration of Independence, and most of (the surviving evidence for) what Jefferson had to say about moral philosophy was written well after 1776, though it nevertheless hangs together in a broad consistency across the years. But even the Declaration itself contains a powerful clue to Jefferson's school of ethical theory. It proclaims the truth that "all men are created equal" to be "self-evident." The drafting committee of Jefferson, Franklin, and John Adams chose the term "self-evident" with some care, preferring it to the earlier expression, "sacred and undeniable." "Self-evidence" is a powerful term in moral philosophy, used by defenders of rationalist ethics to characterize the fundamental premises of morality, claiming that they rest on the same logical basis as the axioms of mathematics. Wills recognized the importance of the term "self-evident," but not the fact that it pointed away from an emotivist understanding of ethics and toward a rationalist one.[80]

The importance attached in the Declaration to the faculty of prudential self-interest helps reconcile its faculty psychology with Lockean political principles. Intermediate between conscience and the passions, we have seen, was the faculty of self-interest, exercising prudence. Prudence was a form of rationality, and one that played an essential part in the contractual philosophy of government. The Declaration of Independence acknowledged that "Prudence, indeed, will dictate that Governments long established should not be changed for light and transcient causes," and affirmed that Americans had given due weight to prudential considerations by not rushing into their revolution.

Jefferson's understanding of faculty psychology is illuminated by his celebrated dialogue between *Head* and *Heart*. While in Paris during 1786, the widower Jefferson was smitten by an attractive married woman named Maria Cosway, to whom he sent the dialogue. The most appealing lines are given to *Heart,* represented as pleading for a continuation of their relationship.

Heart: Morals were too essential to the happiness of man to be risked on the incertain combinations of the head. [Nature] has laid their foundation therefore in sentiment, not in science. That she gave to all as necessary to all: this to a few only, as sufficing with a few. I know indeed that you [*Head*] pretend authority to a sovereign controul [sic] of our conduct in all its parts: and a respect for your grave saws and maxims, a desire to do what is right, has sometimes induced me to conform to your counsels.

Heart goes on to claim that she is sometimes a better guide to action than *Head.* But of course, the fact that Jefferson attributed daring sentiments to *Heart* in a romantic dialogue does not mean he actually endorsed them, only that he was titillating himself and his correspondent with them. Eventually, Jefferson followed the prudential dictates of *Head* and allowed his relationship with Mrs. Cosway to wind down.[81]

Not considering human nature to constitute a problem, Jefferson instead regarded it as a potential to be realized. All aspects of human nature—mental, moral, emotional, and physical—were responsive to proper cultivation. Instead of suppressing certain aspects of human nature, Jefferson was concerned with the proper nurture and development of all. The many didactic letters of advice he wrote to his daughters, grandchildren, and other young friends and relatives testify to this. Indeed, Jefferson's letters can be also seen as important vehicles for his own self-construction, as well as vehicles for the construction of the young personalities under his moral tutelage.[82]

Like Franklin, Jefferson was an exponent of self-discipline. He instructed his correspondents that it was important to exercise virtue early and often so as to strengthen it with the force of habit: "lose no occasion of exercising your dispositions to be grateful, to be generous, to be charitable, to be humane. . . . Consider every act of this kind as an exercise which will strengthen your moral faculties."[83] Jefferson also believed it important for young people to keep before them models of virtue, drawn from history, literature, and personal acquaintance. Conscious self-improvement was the key to the fulfillment and therefore the happiness of the individual.[84] It is not too much to say that the meaning its author attached to "the pursuit of happiness" mentioned in the Declaration of Independence was the realization of one's full potential.[85]

Jefferson's commitment to the development of human potential led him to his strong support for public education. This aspect of the cultivation of the faculties was a collective rather than an individual responsibility. For him, education was not only intellectual, and certainly not narrowly vocational, but concerned with the well-rounded culture of the self. He conceived this, of course, in terms of the prevailing faculty psychology and the development of the human powers—intellectual, moral, and emotional—in their proper harmony. Self-development had political implications. Only an educated, self-disciplined people could make liberal and republican institutions work, for only they would have the necessary sense of their "duties" as well as their "rights." The United States was a laboratory for demonstrating "what is the degree of freedom and self-government in which a society may venture to leave its individual members."[86]

The report Jefferson wrote for the Commisioners for the University of Virginia in 1818 described his educational philosophy. "Education generates habits of application, of order, and the love of virtue, and controls, by force of habit, any innate obliquities in our moral organization." The culture of the moral feelings was particularly important to the progress of the whole human race over time. "We should be far, too, from the discouraging persuasion that man is fixed, by the law of his nature, at a given point; that his improvement is a chimera, and the hope delusive of rendering ourselves wiser, happier or better than our forefathers were. As well might it be urged that the wild and uncultivated tree, hitherto yielding sour and bitter fruit only, can never be made to yield better." The analogy from agriculture came naturally to the Virginia planter.[87]

Besides the achievement of individual self-realization, the other general goal of Jefferson's plans for public education was the recruitment of those persons "whom nature hath endowed with genius and virtue" and their training for public service. To make sure the commonwealth really got the best possible leaders, this process should be purely meritocratic, "without regard to wealth, birth or other accidental condition."[88] The persons who would be thus selected constituted what Jefferson called "the natural aristocracy," the "aristoi" of "virtue and talents." This group he differentiated, in a now-famous letter to John Adams, from the "artificial aristocracy founded on wealth and birth, without either virtue or talents." He went on to ground his political science in this model of human nature: "May we not even say that that form of government is best which provides the most effectually for a

pure selection of these natural aristoi into the offices of government?"
This had in fact been the goal of the framers of the Constitution as set
forth in *The Federalist,* and Jefferson was satisfied that they had achieved
it well.[89]

The natural aristocracy represented Jefferson's desire to democratize
his ideal of the development of human potential. But although he
imagined a natural aristocracy without regard to "accidental," irrelevant criteria, in practice his vision was restricted by race and sex, if not
by class. Only white men possessed the full range of human potential
in his eyes, for only they possessed the faculties appropriate for public
leadership. The human nature in which Jefferson felt confidence was
that of white men. Although contemporaries of his like Mary Wollstonecraft and Abigail Adams were raising feminist issues, Jefferson
showed no interest in questioning patriarchal traditions. When asked
about "female education," he confessed to not having devoted any
thought to the subject except as it related to his own daughters, whom
he educated for the role of republican motherhood. He did, however,
agree with the Scottish moral philosophers that the status of women
was an index of the advance of civilization.[90]

Jefferson's racism has been the subject of so much comment by
historians in recent years that it will not be necessary to cover the
ground in detail again here.[91] In his *Notes on the State of Virginia* he
declared blacks "much inferior" in reasoning power to whites, though
not in their emotional faculties (and therefore not in their emotional
moral sense). "Their existence appears to participate more of sensation
than reflection." In the terminology of faculty psychology, he found
their "animal faculties" more developed than their distinctively human
ones—even crediting tales that Africans mated with orangutans.[92] To
be sure, there is a contrast between the substance of Jefferson's opinions
on race, which we find abhorrent, and the tentativeness with which he
expressed them. Jefferson qualified his assertions about the racial inferiority of Negroes by saying that further evidence might show their
apparent limitations were not innate but due to environmental disadvantages; if such evidence materialized, he insisted, he would be only
too happy to revise his opinion of their inferiority. In practice, however, he tended to discount evidence of black achievement.[93] Perhaps,
therefore, we can call him a prejudiced man who respected the ideal of
an open mind, at once a bigot and a *philosophe.*

When it came to the Native Americans, Jefferson adopted a different stance. He considered them representative of an earlier, "savage," stage of human history (such as the Scottish philosophers had identified), but not racially inferior to whites. He hoped, indeed, for their assimilation, first economically and then through intermarriage into the general body of the United States population, in sharp contrast to his insistence that African-Americans, if and when they were emancipated, must be deported. Whether assimilated or not, however, the most important thing about the Indian tribes from Jefferson's standpoint was that they must be expropriated and their lands turned over to white cultivators.[94]

Despite his belief in the inferiority of the Negro race, Jefferson was no apologist for slavery. In principle, he admitted that black people possessed the same natural rights as others: "whatever be their degree of talent it is no measure of their rights. Because Sir Isaac Newton was superior to others in understanding, he was not therefore lord of the person or property of others."[95] Jefferson believed slavery corrupted the faculties of both master and slave. He was particularly concerned about its negative effects on whites, which he characterized in terms of faculty psychology and the construction of the personality:

> The whole commerce between master and slave is a perpetual exercise of the most boisterous passions, the most unremitting despotism on the one part, and degrading submissions on the other. Our children see this, and learn to imitate it; for man is an imitative animal. . . . If a parent could find no motive either in his philanthropy or his self-love, for restraining the intemperance of passion towards his slave, it should always be a sufficient one that his child is present. But generally it is not sufficient. The parent storms, the child looks on, catches the lineaments of wrath, puts on the same airs in the circle of smaller slaves, gives a loose to his worst of passions, and thus nursed, educated, and daily exercised in tyranny, cannot but be stamped by it with odious peculiarities. The man must be a prodigy who can retain his manners and morals undepraved by such circumstances.

Accordingly, Jefferson looked forward to the end of slavery as "a complete emancipation of human nature," white as well as black.[96] He hoped for the deportation of the freed people and their colonization elsewhere to avoid further race conflict.

The concern Jefferson expressed for the effect of slavery was typical of his interest in social "manners and morals." Like the Scottish moral philosophers, he was deeply concerned with the close association between manners and morals and their effect on national character. "It is the manners and spirit of a people which preserve a republic in vigour." Confident as he was in the probity of innate (white male) human nature, he still worried that degenerate manners could corrupt it. The Euro-Americans could not be so trusted to exercise their "common sense" in self-government, he remarked, had they not "separated from their parent stock and kept [themselves] from contamination" by its "ignorance, superstition, poverty, and oppression." As ambassador to the royal court in Paris, he observed the manners of the French aristocracy with disgust, commenting that their fashionable pursuits were such as "nourish and invigorate all our bad passions."[97]

Popular government could not rest simply on the faculties of universal human nature alone; acquired as well as innate qualities went into shaping a national character suitable for free institutions. Jefferson rejoiced that, in the United States, the widespread ownership of family farms and the broad distribution of property among white men that this entailed provided a basis for republican civic virtue superior to the class society of Europe. "Every one, by his property, or by his satisfactory situation, is interested in the support of law and order. And such men may safely and advantageously reserve to themselves a wholesome controul {sic} over their public affairs, and a degree of freedom, which in the hands of the Canaille of the cities of Europe, would be instantly perverted to the demolition and destruction of every thing public and private."[98] Political freedom was appropriate only for those who were ready for it. Americans had shown themselves ready; continental Europeans had not. Much depended on the national character, in other words, on the state of "manners and morals." By them, the collective moral sense could be improved just as the moral sense of the individual child was improved through education.[99]

A relevant aspect of national manners was the state of polite conduct. In contrast to the degenerate manners of the French upper and lower classes, a virtuous and gentlemanly politeness won Jefferson's admiration. Like so many other members of the American gentry, he endorsed *The Spectator* and *The Tatler*.[100] Proud of his own manners and taste, he hoped to spread them among his fellow countrymen. "With respect to what are termed polite manners," he observed, "I would wish [my] countrymen to adopt just so much of European politeness, as to be ready [to] make all the little sacrifices of self which really render

European manners amiable, and relieve society from the disagreeable scenes to which rudeness often exposes it." Accordingly, he urged his grandson to acquire good manners, for "politeness is artificial good humor[;] it covers the natural want of it, and ends by rendering habitual a substitute nearly equivalent to the real virtue." He commended the precepts and example of Dr. Franklin on politeness as a way of getting on in the world by cultivating the good will of others.[101]

Politeness was important to the community as well as to the individual. It provided a framework of civil public discourse in republican society. The "new social virtue was less Spartan and more Addisonian, less the harsh self-sacrifice of antiquity and more the willingness to get along with others for the sake of peace and prosperity." As Jefferson put it, "When I hear another express an opinion which is not mine, I say to myself, he has a right to his opinion, as I to mine; why should I question it? . . . If he wants information he will ask [for] it, and then I will give it in measured terms; but if he still believes his own story, and shows a desire to dispute the fact with me, I hear him and say nothing."[102] Politeness represented the kind of habitual self-control and consideration for others that made liberal and republican government possible. As a model of the political virtues of politeness, Jefferson held up his friend and collaborator James Madison:

> He acquired a habit of self-possession which placed at ready command the rich resources of his luminous and discriminating mind. . . . Never wandering from his subject into vain declamation, but pursuing it closely in language pure, classical and copious, soothing always the feelings of his adversaries by civilities and softness of expression, . . . he sustained the new constitution in all its parts, bearing off the palm against the logic of George Mason, and the fervid declamation of Mr. Henry. With these consummate powers were united a pure and spotless virtue, which no calumny has ever attempted to sully.[103]

The politeness Madison exemplified was not only a pattern of self-discipline and social behavior, it was a cultivated style of rhetoric and leadership. When we look at *The Federalist,* we shall be observing, among other things, the polite style of rhetoric and persuasion.

Jefferson's moral philosophy may be summarized as a belief in objective standards of goodness and right, which were rationally comprehensible and based like Franklin's on social utility. He also accepted the model of faculty psychology prevailing in his day, according to which the emotions were stronger motivations than reason. Among the emotions, however, Jefferson believed the benevolent ones to be stronger, on the whole, than the malevolent. It was this confidence in the strength of the social affections that gave Jefferson his confidence in human nature as a whole and in the possibility of free government, liberal and republican.

Jefferson's confidence in human nature had profoundly ambiguous consequences. On the negative side, it encouraged him in an attitude of procrastination: the future was bound to be better, because human nature worked for good, and human beings were sure to emancipate themselves progressively from the constraints and corruptions of the past. Thus it would be safest to leave difficult social problems like slavery to the next generation.[104] The time never came when Jefferson was willing to confront in practice the problem of slavery. For when the issue was actually raised in the Missouri Controversy of 1820, the old man perceived it not in terms of a long-deferred promise but only as a threat to the Union and to his political party. Observing the antislavery movement of the next generation at first hand, he condemned, in the strong terms of faculty psychology, its "unwise and unworthy passions."[105]

In a more positive way, Jefferson's confidence in the human faculties encouraged him to have faith in freedom of inquiry and expression as the ultimate guarantors of human welfare and progress. If tyranny and priestcraft (which was a form of tyranny) were prevented, the wholesomeness of human nature would have its chance. "To preserve the freedom of the human mind then & freedom of the press, every spirit should be ready to devote itself to martyrdom; for as long as we may think as we will, & speak as we think, the condition of man will proceed in improvement."[106] Improvement was a subject on which the Scottish philosophers had had much to say, and for Jefferson, America was a nation dedicated to the opportunity for self-improvement, both individual and collective.

CHAPTER 3

The Political Psychology of The Federalist

No document relating to the Constitution of the United States has received more attention than *The Federalist Papers*. The papers were written in 1787–88 for the purpose of persuading the people of the state of New York to elect a convention that would ratify the proposed Constitution of the United States. In this immediate objective they failed, though in the end New York did ratify and the Constitution went into operation. Thereafter *The Federalist* was transformed from a failure into a success, becoming a canonical text of American constitutionalism, next in importance only to the Constitution itself and the Declaration of Independence. Ever since Jefferson prescribed it as a text at the newly founded University of Virginia, the work has been treated as an authoritative statement of how American political institutions work or should work.[1]

Probably every reader of *The Federalist* has noticed that its arguments are based on ideas about universal human nature. These ideas form a coherent model, which is what will concern us in this chapter. One can identify the sources of this model and show how the authors of the papers used it in defining their audience and constructing their case. The authors of *The Federalist*—Alexander Hamilton, James Madison, and John Jay—were practical men, writing under intense pressures, with a strong sense of the campaign strategy they were pursuing. They submerged their individual differences in the collective *persona* of Publius, who for our purposes may be treated as a single author.[2]

Over the past generation, scholarship has demonstrated the importance of the intellectual conventions of an age in defining an author's intentions. This chapter addresses what J. G. A. Pocock terms "the politics of language"—that is, the study of how the vocabulary and assumptions of an intellectual paradigm can be put to political use.[3] The conventional paradigm that did the most to shape the argument of *The Federalist* was eighteenth-century faculty psychology. By examining the authors' use of the language of faculty psychology we can discover what they meant by such crucial terms as "interest," "balance," "reason," "passion," and "virtue" in *The Federalist*. Only then can we appreciate how they were adapting conventional conceptions to the needs of a new nation and a new political order, and the powerful analogy they made between the construction of a polity and the construction of a self.[4]

By his use of faculty psychology Publius placed his arguments in the context of Enlightenment behavioral science. Throughout, *The Federalist* appeals to immutable scientific laws of human behavior, illustrated by historical examples and confirmed by the Americans' own experiment in free government.[5] But the strategy also connected Publius with an even larger context. This was the classical, medieval, and modern tradition identifying liberty with order.[6] Faculty psychology had always taught that the liberty of the individual's will required preventing any faculty from disturbing the harmony of the mind (especially any passion from usurping the authority of reason). Publius made use of the paradigm to present his case for guarding political liberty with social and psychological order. The relationship between political liberty on the one hand and social and psychological order on the other would remain a leading concern of American thinkers for the next century.

We may infer that Publius advocated adoption of the Constitution in the terms he did not only because he believed in a certain model of human nature but also because he expected that model would promote an effective presentation. The particular version of faculty psychology that Publius employed influenced not only his substantive arguments (his political science) but also his techniques of persuasion (his rhetoric). Indeed, the political science and the rhetoric of *The Federalist* are intimately related to each other through their common dependence on this psychological vocabulary. Madison and Hamilton did not need to confer about whether to accept the conventions of faculty psychology; these were presuppositions of their argument. But it is a mark of their successful collaboration that they both resorted to faculty psychology with such eloquence and power in the construction of their case.[7]

In the eighteenth century, the influence of psychology on political theory and rhetoric was facilitated because all three subjects were often treated at the time in connection with the enormous intellectual structure defined as moral philosophy. Rhetoric had a history of its own going back to the medieval *trivium,* but in the eighteenth century a new rhetoric appeared, associated with moral philosophy, particularly in Scotland. Adam Smith lectured on rhetoric while holding the chair of moral philosophy at Glasgow; Hugh Blair, the age's most widely read writer on rhetoric, was strongly influenced by Scottish moral philosophy. Other writers bridging the two disciplines included George Campbell and Lord Kames.[8] This philosophical connection gave to eighteenth-century psychology and political economy their strongly normative coloration. The interlocking relationships among various disciplines within moral philosophy made it all the easier for the founding generation of American leaders to apply faculty psychology to both ideas about good government and techniques for persuading men to adopt it.

Most interpreters of Publius have presented only a partial picture of his model of human nature. Some have considered him a pessimist in the tradition of Thomas Hobbes and John Calvin, emphasizing the need to impose control on the evil passions of man.[9] More often, Publius has been treated as a proto-liberal, concerned with men pursuing their own interests, sometimes rationally calculated, in a system more amoral than immoral.[10] Most recently, some scholars have treated Publius as a classical republican who believed in the possibility of virtue in human affairs.[11] Actually, all these interpretations can be synthesized within the paradigm of the faculty psychology Publius employed, which found places in human nature for passion, interest, and virtue.

The faculty psychology Publius employed was representative of a large and distinguished school of thought which included the Scottish moral philosopher John Witherspoon, who emigrated to America to become president of Princeton, a signer of the Declaration of Independence, and the teacher of James Madison.[12] Not that the influence of this form of faculty psychology has to be traced through personal connections: it was common intellectual property in the eighteenth century, and both Madison and Hamilton (who had been educated at Anglican King's College) employed it in *The Federalist.* At the time Madison and Hamilton were writing *The Federalist,* the last volume of the definitive redaction of Thomas Reid's lectures on moral philosophy, with their codification of faculty psychology, was just being published. It is not clear whether either of them had access to it, but the psychology they drew on was a pattern of thought with which they and their readers were thoroughly familiar, not a paraphrase or transcription of any single book.[13] Indeed, the principles of psychology used in *The Federalist Papers* were essentially the same as those that had been used half a century earlier by the authors of *Cato's Letters;* the similarity is the more remarkable in view of the fact that Cato was arguing for limitations on government and Publius for the strengthening of government.

As we have seen, faculty psychology was capable of more than one interpretation in the eighteenth century. If the harmonious relationship among the faculties was emphasized, it could inspire confidence in human nature. If the potential for conflict among the faculties was emphasized, it could inspire more caution. While Thomas Jefferson's trust in human nature—and specifically in the social affections—led him to embrace a combination of direct citizen participation and little government, Publius's more pessimistic assessment of the faculties led him to espouse a revised form of the ancient theory of mixed government.

?◕ THE HIERARCHY OF MOTIVES

The faculty psychology employed by Publius posited the same sequence of rightful precedence among conscious motives that Franklin and Edwards had recognized: first reason, then prudence (or self-interest), then passion.[14] Majority opinion among the thinkers of the Enlightenment, however, held that this sequence did not come naturally to mankind. John Locke's classic statement of religious liberalism, *The Reasonableness of Christianity,* deplored the weakness of human reason in controlling the passions. John Adams agreed: "Human reason and human conscience," he recorded sadly, "are not a match for human

passions, human imaginations, and human enthusiasm." Alexander
Pope, who summed up so much of the conventional wisdom of the age,
declared, "The ruling passion conquers reason still."[15] Upon this model
of human nature's contrariness Publius based his political philosophy.
"Why has government been instituted at all?" asked Hamilton's Publius. "Because the passions of men will not conform to the dictates of
reason and justice without constraint." Madison's Publius agreed:
"What is government itself but the greatest of all reflections on human
nature? If men were angels, no government would be necessary."[16]

The juxtaposition of "reason and justice" was typical of Publius;
sometimes he spoke similarly of wisdom and virtue.[17] The rational
faculty, for Publius as for Thomas Reid, was the capacity to apprehend
objective truth, both descriptive and normative (or, as they would have
said, "speculative" and "practical"). Yet reason-cum-conscience was
but a feeble monarch over the other faculties. If it had might, as it has
right, it would rule the world, the well-known eighteenth-century
moralist Joseph Butler had affirmed. Publius put it this way: "There
are men who could neither be distressed nor won into a sacrifice of their
duty; but this stern virtue is the growth of few soils."[18]

To strengthen the power of conscience, one possible resource was the
faculty of prudential self-interest, as Franklin had demonstrated so
effectively. Eighteenth-century faculty psychology was a discipline in
flux, Publius knew. Whereas medieval and Reformation thinkers had
stressed the passionate side of self-interest, Enlightenment thinkers
had come to see the faculty as potentially rational.[19] Publius took
remarkable advantage of this transitional moment in the history of
ideas. He treated self-interest as an intermediate motive, sometimes
partial, short-term, and passionate (in the derogatory sense of "selfish
passions"), but capable of being collective, long-range, and rational.
Short-term self-interest he identified with the Articles of Confederation and with his adversaries; long-term self-interest he allied with
reason, virtue, and the Constitution.[20]

Within the category of self-interest, "immediate interests," as Publius called them, "have a more active and imperious control over human
conduct than general or remote considerations." Consequently, the
interests that most resembled passions were stronger than those par-
taking of the nature of prudential reason. These rules of individual
motivation were also applicable to political entities. "The mild voice of
reason, pleading the cause of an enlarged and permanent interest, is but

too often drowned before public bodies as well as individuals, by the clamors of an impatient avidity for immediate and immoderate gain."[21] Distinctions could also be made among the social affections (or passions) in terms of their power. People show less emotional attachment to groups as these get progressively larger: "a man is more attached to his family than to his neighborhood, to his neighborhood than to the community," and so on. More tragically, "to judge from the history of mankind, we shall be compelled to conclude that the fiery and destructive passions of war reign in the human breast with much more powerful sway than the mild and beneficent sentiments of peace."[22]

This psychology gave Publius his basis for discrediting the Articles of Confederation, the institutional framework that preceded the Constitution and conferred no coercive power upon the federal government. The Articles relied too much on "the weaker springs of the human character." "It was presumed that a sense of their true interests, and a regard to the dictates of good faith, would be found sufficient pledges for the punctual performance of the duty of the members to the federal head. The experiment has, however, demonstrated that this expectation was ill-founded and illusory."[23] As usual, history confirmed the precepts of moral philosophy.

Yet the same psychology that taught the statesman that political institutions must take account of the perversity of human nature posed a serious problem for the political advocate. How could one persuade the public to adopt the institutions it so sorely needed? Some eighteenth-century rhetorical theorists, such as the highly regarded Scot Hugh Blair, openly advised the judicious invocation of the passions in persuasive expression.[24] Yet Publius does not invoke them; indeed, he deplores them. "It is the reason of the public alone that ought to control and regulate the government," writes Madison-Publius. "The passions ought to be controlled and regulated by the government."[25] His own rhetoric is coolly and carefully rationalistic, as in the famous Number 10, where he argues on the basis of a sequence of dual alternatives to create an impression of impeccable deductive logic. Sometimes Publius reasons from "axioms," as in Number 23; elsewhere he prefers an inductive approach citing the "lessons of history," as in Number 20. Throughout, the reader Publius addresses is "an impartial and judicious examiner," one who is "dispassionate and discerning."[26]

Norman Fiering has described the eighteenth century as the time of an intellectual revolution in which reason was displaced from supremacy by "the lowly and dangerous passions."[27] There is indeed much evidence for such an emerging rebellion against the conventional wisdom. Shaftesbury, Hutcheson, and their sentimentalist school of moral philosophy challenged the rational nature of the moral sense; rhetoricians like Blair legitimated the passions; religious pietists and evangelicals demanded an awakening of holy affections; the subversive psychology of Hume, like that of Hobbes earlier, attributed all human motivation to passion, denying even the possibility of rational control. Jonathan Edwards's doctrine of "true virtue" may be considered part of this widespread reassessment of the affections or passions. Thomas Jefferson clearly participated in such an upward revaluation of the "heart" as compared with the "head." But any such revised attitude toward the passions was alien to Publius; if it was a revolution, he was a counterrevolutionary. To him, the passions were dangerous. Like the Old Lights who opposed the Great Awakening, Publius distrusted "enthusiasm."[28] *The Federalist* may be considered one of the masterpieces of what Henry F. May has called the Moderate Enlightenment. One of the defining characteristics of this version of the Enlightenment was its steadfast commitment to strengthening the power of reason over passion. Publius judged policy questions by whether they conduced to the supremacy of reason, rejecting a proposal to call frequent constitutional conventions because "the passions, therefore, not the reason, of the public would sit in judgment." He deplored the formation of political parties because they appealed to passion rather than reason.[29]

If Publius was rather old-fashioned in his distrust of passion, he was quite up to date in his techniques for controlling it. While Christian philosophers of earlier times had typically striven to repress undesirable feelings, the Enlightenment hit upon the technique of balancing them off against each other, "like the antagonist[ic] muscles of the body," in Hutcheson's simile. Even antisocial motives could have their uses in a system making proper use of the principle of countervailing passions.[30] Madison-Publius heartily endorsed "this policy of supplying, by opposite and rival interests, the defect of better motives." He summed up the advantages of the separation of political powers in terms of opposing psychological passions: "Ambition must be made to counteract ambition." Hamilton-Publius applied the same psychology when urging the wisdom of making the president eligible for re-election: the temptation to abuse power would be counterbalanced by the desire to stay in office, so that "his avarice might be a guard upon his avarice."[31] In *The Federalist,* the Constitution is presented as a marvel of political engineering, based on a sound psychology, that will use human nature to control human nature, among both governors and governed, without requiring recourse to tyrannical coercion.[32]

Publius's rhetoric, like his political science, sought to turn selfishness to advantage. He enlisted prudential motives on the side of reason and virtue, to add "the incitements of self-preservation to the too feeble impulses of duty and sympathy." It was a mode of argument that the aged Franklin no doubt approved. The argument was designed to show that "the safety of the whole is the interest of the whole." The crisis of the Revolutionary War had temporarily "repressed the passions most unfriendly to order and concord"; what was needed now was a new sense of crisis, which would once again ally an enlightened prudence with reason and virtue to overcome passion and petty self-seeking.[33]

The rhetorical posture of Publius remains remarkably consistent throughout *The Federalist.* Number 1 begins by asking "whether societies of men are really capable or not of establishing good government from reflection and choice," or must forever be bound by "accident and force." "Happy will it be if our choice should be directed by a judicious estimate of our true interests"—but this is unlikely. The proposed plan affects too many "particular interests" not to arouse "views, passions, and prejudices little favorable to the discovery of truth." What Publius fears is that "a torrent of angry and malignant passions will be let loose," frustrating all attempts at rational discourse.[34] He himself will engage in rational argument, without impugning the motives of individuals. (The motivation of the human race, however, is quite another matter.) Publius makes his own style of rhetoric a pattern for how he hopes the debate as whole can be carried on—confident that in elevating it to the general welfare, he will force his adversaries to meet him on his own ground, instead of descending to a level where pettiness and passion rule. However he may feel provoked, Publius will take his stance with Prospero in *The Tempest:* "Though with their high wrongs I am struck to the quick,/Yet with my nobler reason 'gainst my fury/Do I take part."[35]

While recognizing that it is not easy to know the good, Publius has no doubt that the good does objectively exist.[36] And for all his disparagement of the strength of rational and virtuous motives, he still assumes they too exist and have a fighting chance to prevail. "As there is a degree of depravity in mankind which requires a certain degree of circumspection and distrust, so there are other qualities in human nature which justify a certain portion of esteem and confidence. Republican government presupposes the existence of these qualities in a higher degree than any other form."[37] Unlike Franklin and Jefferson, Publius never goes so far as to embrace utilitarianism; he never actually defines the moral good in terms of collective benefits. But he does argue that a collective prudence can assist and foster virtue. The Constitution, Publius is confident, will provide a setting designed to promote the worthy qualities over the unworthy ones—and, as we shall see, the worthy people over the unworthy ones as well.

✌ FACULTY PSYCHOLOGY AND THE POLITICAL ORDER

The analogy between the human mind and the political commonwealth, "in which there are various powers, some that ought to govern and others that ought to be subordinate," is one of the oldest staples of philosophical discourse.[38] It remained as popular with the eighteenth-century moderns as it had been with the ancients; indeed, the grouping of both psychology and civil polity (political theory) under the umbrella of moral philosophy encouraged it. Publius was convinced that groups had dynamics analogous to those of individuals, with the same tragically inverse relation between the legitimacy of motives and their power. "In all very numerous assemblies, of whatever characters composed, passion never fails to wrest the scepter from reason," and the more numerous the assembly, "the greater is known to be the ascendancy of passion over reason." Once dominated by passion, an assembly became a "mob."[39]

Publius wanted a system of government that would provide scope for the exercise of the faculties, which he called "liberty," and offer security to retain their fruits, which he called "justice."[40] The faculties of different people were not equally developed; some individuals were more wise and virtuous than others, just as some were more adept at making money. A well-designed system of government should allow men the exercise of their political faculties and favor those whose "fit characters" were most politically desirable. "The aim of every political constitution is or ought to be," Publius wrote, "to obtain for rulers, men who possess [the] most wisdom to discern, and [the] most virtue to pursue, the common good of the society"—though he was cautious enough to add, "and in the next place to take the most effectual precautions for keeping them virtuous."[41]

Publius did not envision a free-for-all like that of the later social Darwinians; he wanted a teleological—that is, purposeful—system designed to favor wisdom and virtue. Of course there would always be struggles, just as there are within the breast of even the upright citizen, but a good constitution would moderate them and influence their outcome.[42] Modern readers have varying reactions to Publius's allegiance to the leadership of a wise and virtuous elite; an element of class hypocrisy has been detected in it, even by a historian who stresses that the Constitution and the theory of popular sovereignty invented to justify it were later put to democratic use.[43]

The best example Publius could offer his readers of a wise and virtuous elite was the Constitutional Convention itself. "Without having been awed by power, or influenced by any passions except love for their country, they presented and recommended to the people the plan produced by their joint and very unanimous counsels." This is a highly idealized picture of the Convention, crafted for rhetorical purposes to illustrate a perfect rationality. ("Love of country" as a good passion will be considered below.) The delegates rose above party and faction to achieve "unanimity," Publius claimed.[44] That the delegates were actually far from unanimous in endorsing the outcome of their deliberations was irrelevant. The Fathers of the Convention occupied a place in Publius's scheme analogous to the semimythic lawgivers of antiquity—Solon, Lycurgus, and Romulus. They required some veneration even before their work was implemented. "Let our gratitude mingle an ejaculation to heaven for the propitious concord which has distinguished the consultations for our political happiness," Publius wrote, in a rare expression of religious devotion.[45] As a benevolent Providence had designed the faculties of (unfallen) man for the welfare of the individual, the wise lawgiver contrived a complex machinery in harmony with (fallen) human nature for the welfare of the community.

Throughout *The Federalist* there runs an implicit analogy between the human mind and the body politic. Just as the mind has faculties of reason (knowing wisdom and virtue), prudence (knowing self-interest), and the passions, so does society contain a small natural aristocracy of wisdom and virtue, a larger group of prudent men capable of understanding their enlightened self-interest, and the turbulent masses, who are typically motivated by passion and immediate advantage. Publius recognized a certain correlation between the development of the faculties and social class. A man whose station in life "leads to extensive inquiry and information" would be able to rise above "the momentary humors or dispositions which may happen to prevail in particular parts of the society" and make a good political leader. Artisans, on the other hand, "are sensible that their habits in life have not been such as to give them those acquired endowments, without which in a deliberative assembly the greatest natural abilities are for the most part useless," and would tend to elect better-educated merchants and professional men as their political representatives.[46]

The elitism in this model will come as no surprise to the historian in the light of what we have learned about patterns of deference in eighteenth-century American political culture. Although Publius was probably not writing for an audience of artisans, he claimed that artisans would agree with him and credited them with sense. He noted that "there are strong minds in every walk of life that will rise superior to the disadvantages of situation," but felt that "occasional instances of this sort" did not invalidate the general rule. It is worth noting that the distinctions Publius drew between the faculties of men in different classes were based upon acquired characteristics, not innate ones; they were an invitation to self-improvement. His elitism was meritocratic, and left the door open for the democratization of his gentlemanly ideals in the generations to come.[47]

In the meantime, however, there could be no doubt that what he envisioned was a gentry politics. "The idea of an actual representation of all classes of the people by persons of each class is altogether visionary," Publius insisted. Most political representatives in the new government would and should be large landholders, merchants, or professional men. If a single social group could be identified as impartial, it was the professionals, who were not tied to any particular property interest as the landowners and merchants were. The shortsighted masses were not likely to look after the general interests of society as well as these elite groups.[48] To be sure, "the people commonly intend the PUBLIC GOOD," Hamilton-Publius granted. "But their good sense would despise the adulator, who should pretend that they always reason right about the means of promoting it." Madison-

Publius, enumerating examples of "wicked" legislation in Number 10, cited only instances that, in their eighteenth-century context, favored the have-nots against the haves: paper money, an abolition of debt, an equal division of property.[49] It was all to the good that only a few farsighted "speculative" men would pay attention to the affairs of the new national government, while the "feelings" of the average citizens were occupied with the mundane affairs of their particular states. Federal tax policy was a subject Publius considered particularly well entrusted to a small group of "inquisitive and enlightened statesmen" that did not attempt to mirror the diverse composition of society.[50]

Publius defined his audience as consisting of "the candid and judicious part of the community."[51] Yet he was not engaged in an academic inquiry; he was an advocate, a campaigner. He had to combine rationality with motivation in order to persuade effectively. He found the key to his rhetorical problem in eighteenth-century faculty psychology, in the concept of enlightened self-interest. Publius, for all his pessimism about the weakness of unaided reason, was convinced that a well-designed constitution could make rational and moral use of self-interested motives. Before such a constitution could be implemented, however, the public would have to be persuaded that it was not only just but also in their own true interest.

Publius credits his audience with being members of the wise and virtuous elite. But he does not appeal only to disinterested motives. He is eager to demonstrate how the proposed Constitution can be of tangible benefit to various economic interests (especially in Numbers 4, 11, 12, and 13) as well as to "the prosperity of commerce" in general and, in the largest sense, to all who have an interest in "the effects of good government."[52] There are, then, two audiences implied for his presentation: the direct audience of dispassionate inquirers and the larger, indirect audience capable of enlightened self-interest. Even if most members of the direct audience already supported the Constitution, *The Federalist* serves a campaign function. The indirect audience will be enlisted in the cause (presumably by the readers) in order to help control the passionate multitude. Although Publius does not make it explicit, an analogy is implied here with the cooperation he foresees in Congress between the disinterested professional men and the representatives of the great landed and mercantile interests. This interpretation, derived from internal analysis of *The Federalist,* is supported by what we know from other sources about the conduct of eighteenth-century electioneering. Robert H. Wiebe describes it thus: "The gentry addressed their speeches and pamphlets, rich with learned allusions and first principles, to one another, not to the people, who would have to receive their instruction from others closer to them in the hierarchy. The art of persuasion centered around the conversion of a secondary tier of gentlemen."[53]

Against the rationalistic and elitist appeal of *The Federalist,* the Antifederalists seem to have employed a rhetorical strategy of their own. They concurred in the faculty psychology's estimate of the weakness of human nature, perhaps even more consistently than Publius did: they refused to believe in the ability of even an elite few to follow the guidance of wisdom and virtue. If there was any hope of overcoming evil, it lay in the common sense and feeling of the common man, which they addressed.[54] Publius complained that the Antifederalists' rhetoric suggested "an intention to mislead the people by alarming their passions, rather than to convince them by arguments addressed to their understandings." To their distrust of any officeholders Publius replied that "the supposition of universal venality in human nature is little less an error in political reasoning than the supposition of universal rectitude." If supporters of the Constitution were willing to trust the rulers, its opponents (according to Publius) placed too much faith in the masses who were ruled—"but a nation of philosophers is as little to be expected as the philosophical race of kings wished for by Plato."[55]

❧ FACULTY PSYCHOLOGY AND MIXED GOVERNMENT

The Constitution, most recent scholarship agrees, broke with the venerable tradition of mixed government that balanced monarchy, aristocracy, and democracy by rejecting the European practice of representing different orders of society in the legislative body. Publius indeed boasted that Americans had discovered the secret of "unmixed" republican government.[56]

Yet Madison, Hamilton, and the other framers of the Constitution also respected many of the values of mixed government as these had been passed down from ancient, medieval, and early modern political writers—such values as stability, balance, and the supremacy of common over partial interests.[57] Could these be salvaged in the new polity? Publius's creative response to this problem was to argue that the proposed Constitution conferred the procedural benefits of mixed government without its social inequities. The elements it mixed were no longer monarchy, aristocracy, and democracy, but executive, legislative, and judicial. Checks and balances among these branches were "powerful means by which the excellencies of republican government may be retained and its imperfections lessened or avoided."[58] Publius provided a kind of mixed government with a psychological rather than a social justification. Through faculty psychology, he described what he saw as the advantages of mixed government that the Constitution would preserve, even for a country without a European social structure.

For Publius, the art of governing was a decision-making process analogous to that undertaken by an individual; the institutions of government were analogous to the individual's faculties of mind. In both cases, reaching a right decision required a careful act of balancing. Precipitate, ill-advised action was to be avoided; long-term prudence and morally right actions were desired. An individual did well to act from more than one motive, since reason was weak and the passions were unreliable. In politics, then, a measure of institutional complexity was advantageous, since "the oftener a measure is brought under examination, the greater the diversity in the situations of those who are to examine it, the less must be the danger of those errors which flow from want of due deliberation, or of those missteps which proceed from the contagion of some common passion or interest." The intention was not so much to frustrate particular social groups as to provide the right mix of motives. A well-structured government would resemble the balanced mind of a wise person, while a poorly constructed government, like a weak mind, was prone to fall under the tyranny of some capricious passion.[59] Publius's line of argument was not unprecedented: the seventeenth-century English classical republican theorist James Harrington had argued that government should be designed to maintain the supremacy of reason over passion, and had blamed passion for the degeneration of monarchy into tyranny, aristocracy into oligarchy, or democracy into anarchy.[60]

In Publius's presentation there is a marked, if implicit, tendency for the different branches of government to mirror particular faculties of mind. As we have seen, Publius's rhetoric sorted his potential audience into three horizontally defined, hierarchically ordered groups—rational men, self-interested men, and passionate men—and addressed only the

first two. But these groupings would not do for the structure of government, since all the functions of government should be rational.
Therefore Publius invoked a different set of faculties in explaining the
structure of government, a grouping equally legitimated by psychological tradition but vertical rather than horizontal in conception. The
psychological faculties to which the branches of government correspond were all aspects of reason: understanding, will, and conscience.
These conventional terms of faculty psychology provide keys to Publius's exposition of the powers of the legislative, executive, and judicial
branches of government, respectively. In an individual, the understanding received and processed information, the will took action, and
the conscience or moral sense judged right from wrong. In the system
of faculty psychology Publius was following, all were supposed to
operate rationally and resist the "impulse of passion."[61]

The judiciary, in Publius's scheme, was the conscience of the body
politic, interpreting its common moral standards. Not only did Publius invest this branch with the power of judicial review of legislation;
he even asserted that judges had a power to correct the operation of
"unjust and partial laws," whether or not these were unconstitutional.
For one who doubted the virtue of mankind in general, Publius reposed
astonishing confidence in that of judges—but this was because of the
faculty they exercised, which was at once the most reliable and the
weakest. "The judiciary, from the nature of its functions, will always be
the least dangerous" branch of government, he explained, because it
has "neither force nor will, but merely judgment."[62] The executive
branch partook of the qualities of the "will," which explains why
"energy" and "unity" were so essential to it, even in a republican
system. As the will ought to implement fixed principles and the con-
clusions of the understanding in Reid's psychology, so the executive
ought to enforce only the laws enacted by the legislature. In identifying the executive with the will, Publius was not making the presidency supreme but emphasizing its rationality and subordination to
the law.[63]

The understanding was the faculty through which the individual
acquired knowledge of the world, and Publius conceived of the legislative branch as the one through which the government acquired "a
due knowledge of the interests of its constituents." Interests, as we
know, could be either rational or passionate. The faculty of the understanding included both rational and sensitive aspects; among the latter
were dangerous motives of passion. The legislature likewise had both

rational and emotional aspects; indeed, it possessed a weakness for "all the passions which actuate a multitude."[64]

In traditional faculty psychology the will "had the special task, among others, of controlling the passions lodged in the sensitive appetite."[65] Fortunately, the President, embodiment of the faculty of the will, had a veto over congressional legislation that could prevent "unqualified complaisance to every sudden breeze of passion, or to every transient impulse." Within the legislature itself, Publius looked to the Senate to impart more of the rational quality he feared might be deficient in the House of Representatives. Due to their longer terms, larger constituencies, and indirect method of election, senators would be "more out of the reach of those occasional ill humors or temporary prejudices" to which democratic assemblies were prone.[66]

Discussions of the ratification of the Constitution usually point out that its proponents wanted a stronger, more energetic government. Yet analyses of *The Federalist* often emphasize the limitations on governmental power it endorses. An understanding of Publius's faculty psychology helps resolve this seeming paradox. The branches of government he wanted to strengthen were ones he associated with the most rationality: the judiciary, the executive, and the Senate; the elements he wanted to limit he associated with narrow self-interest and the passions: the state governments and all popular assemblies, including the House of Representatives. While the national government would express the general welfare, Publius identified the states with partial views; and when the states became subject to "violences" and "passions," he expected that the federal government "will be more temperate and cool."[67]

More important even than one-to-one correspondences between governmental institutions and psychological faculties is Publius's pervasive argument that just as a healthy human mind balances short-, intermediate-, and long-term goals, so should a healthy polity. As the individual's powers respond to each of these objectives, so should those of a commonwealth. This carryover of attitudes derived from faculty psychology into the realm of politics helps explain Publius's misgivings about majority rule. Hamilton-Publius and Madison-Publius agreed that only the "deliberate sense of the community," not every transitory numerical majority, was entitled to prevail. *The Federalist* quoted Jefferson with approval: "An elective despotism was not the government we fought for."[68]

As Publius presented the matter, it was not so much the people themselves who were being limited as their passions, nor any aristocracy that was being empowered, but the qualities of virtue and wisdom. From our point of view, of course, the result was a compromise of majority rule. "The people," Publius warned, "stimulated by some irregular passion, or some illicit advantage, or misled by the artful misrepresentations of interested men, may call for measures which they themselves will afterwards be the most ready to lament and condemn." Enforced delay was the appropriate remedy, "until reason, justice, and truth can regain their authority over the public mind."[69] Publius wanted calm and thorough deliberation; if this should occasionally prevent a good law from passing—a possibility he admitted—so be it. "Every institution calculated to restrain the excess of law-making, and to keep things in the same state, in which they may happen to be at any given period, [is] much more likely to do good than harm."[70]

ᚈ❧ FACULTIES AND FACTIONS

Publius's analogy between psychology and political science extends to his treatment of factions, which has been the most interesting aspect of *The Federalist* to twentieth-century commentators. *Cato's Letters* had described a "faction" as "the gratifying of private passion by public means."[71] Madison's Publius defines "faction" similarly, as the collective expression of "some common impulse of passion, or of interest, adverse to the rights of other citizens, or to the permanent and aggregate interests of the community." Hamilton's Publius uses the word in the same sense. "The latent causes of faction are thus sown in the nature of man."[72] "Faction" was not a value-free concept for Publius; it was by definition an evil. The idea of inevitable evil in human nature did not surprise men who were well acquainted with the Christian doctrine of original sin and its secularized versions in eighteenth-century faculty psychology.

Although Publius mentions only "passion" and "interest" in his initial definition of faction, his discussion also refers to "opinion" as a source of faction. It would appear that even the faculty of reason, being "fallible" and prone to corruption by "self-love," can give rise to factions of an ideological nature.[73] More often, however, factions stem from passions—writ large and inflamed by ambitious demagogues. In this collective form, passions become more dangerous than ever: "a

spirit of faction" can lead men "into improprieties and excesses for
which they would blush in a private capacity," pointed out Hamilton's
Publius.[74] "But the most common and durable source of factions,"
continues Madison's Publius in Number 10, derives from motives of
self-interest, specifically, "the various and unequal distribution of property"—an inequality that has already been traced to "the diversity in
the faculties of men."[75]

Most of the modern analyses of what Publius says about faction have
focused on property interests rather than on psychological faculties.
Recently, however, scholars have begun to devote attention to the
important connection between faction and passion.[76] Indeed, one could
say that Publius considers faction the collective form of passion. All
factions, even those that do not originally derive from passion, have the
effect of unduly strengthening passion over reason. Partisanship comes
to substitute for independent judgment. Publius has a horror of "the
arts of men who flatter [the people's] prejudices to betray their interests."[77] The demagogue is a sinister figure in *The Federalist.* He lurks
ready to exploit the passions and create a faction. He is the natural
enemy of the statesman, who has virtue and the common interest at
heart. The Constitution, Publius argues, will provide a context within
which the statesman can defeat the demagogue. Fittingly, he both
begins and ends his series of letters with warnings against demagogues.[78]

Most factions arise from the class of motives called interests, intermediate between passion and reason. There is a legitimate scope for the
rational pursuit of one's interest, but only in a broad context.
Eighteenth-century moral philosophy invariably drew a distinction
between benevolent and malevolent passions; implicit in *The Federalist*
is an analogous distinction between benevolent and malevolent interests. The Constitution will be in the true common interest. By definition, the interests that produce faction are adverse to the common
interest, therefore they are narrow and evil. Publius also condemns
motives of short-term interest that are closely akin to passion.[79] Narrow
or short-sighted interests are unworthy; a good government will "break
and control" their violence, not be the vehicle for their expression and
rule. Such interests pose a particular problem in the legislative branch.
One of the reasons why that branch is so prone to the evils of factionalism, Publius argues, is that legislators are constantly cast in the dual
role of advocates and judges in the causes before them. Their self-

interest corrupts what should ideally be a disinterested pursuit of the common good.[80]

Publius maintains that the Constitution will be able to limit "the violence of faction" in three different ways. The first is suppression by military force. This is discussed by Hamilton's Publius in Number 9 and Madison's Publius in Number 43; it shows how seriously they took the threat that factions posed to legitimate government. However, there were two alternatives to force in dealing with factions. Both alternatives derived from models developed in faculty psychology; they are described primarily in Madison's Number 10. One of these methods was to enlighten the quality of the self-interest involved, in this case by refining it through the medium of representatives who would take broader views than their constituents and hence be less susceptible to demagogy and factionalism. Representatives of "enlightened views and virtuous sentiments" would be "superior to local prejudices and to schemes of injustice." The other method was to pit factions against each other so that they cancel each other out, just like countervailing passions. Both methods work better in a large republic than a small one, Madison points out, since the larger constituency provides a more effective filter for the talents of representatives and also a larger number of "parties and interests," reducing the chance that any one of them will be able to oppress the rest.[81] "In the extent and proper structure of the Union, therefore, we behold a republican remedy for the diseases most incident to republican government," concludes Number 10. The Constitution will be beneficial not only because of its carefully designed structure of checks and balances, but also because it creates a large, and therefore stable, republic. (Later, when Jefferson was defending the Louisiana Purchase, he did so in the same terms, identifying "passion" with Madison and Hume's theory of faction: "The larger our association, the less will it be shaken by local passions.")[82]

Madison's Publius placed less faith in enlightened representatives to mitigate the evils of faction than in the countervailing effect of other factions. Hamilton's Publius, though he had much less to say about the principle of countervailing factions, also endorsed it.[83] This does not mean that Publius considered factions good, but only that he accepted their inevitability and sought to mitigate their effects. The "policy of supplying, by opposite and rival interests, the defect of better motives, might be traced through the whole system of human affairs, private as well as public," he pointed out, placing his political science in the context of his psychology. Just as passions like ambition could be made to counteract the ambition of others, so could factions neutralize each other's evil—especially if there are enough of them that "you make it less probable that a majority of the whole will have a common motive to invade the rights of other citizens." "In the extended republic of the United States, and among the great variety of interests, parties, and sects which it embraces, a coalition of a majority of the whole society could seldom take place on any other principles than those of justice and the general good."[84] Justice and the general good were the goals. What looks to twentieth-century eyes like broker-state pluralism was, to Publius's contemporaries, subsumed within a familiar scheme of eighteenth-century moral philosophy, the principle of countervailing passions.[85]

Of course, factions could be majorities as well as minorities. Indeed, the factions Publius was chiefly worried about were the ones that commanded a majority; minority factions were easily limited. But "when a majority is included in a faction, the form of popular government . . . enables it to sacrifice to its ruling passion or interest both the public good and the rights of other citizens."[86] Thus Publius's desire to limit faction was related to his desire to limit majority rule, as well as to his desire to control passion and affirm the supremacy of reason and virtue.

◌⊷ POLITICAL REPRESENTATION AND VIRTUE

If political science builds on the model of faculty psychology, it follows that political representation should identify an elite of wisdom and virtue. The governors of a polity should be analogous to the higher faculties of an individual. A "republic," which Publius defined as a representative democracy, was preferable to a direct democracy because of the superior quality of the representatives as compared with the people as a whole. A system of representation could "refine and enlarge the public views by passing them through the medium of a chosen body of citizens whose wisdom may best discern the true interest of their country and whose patriotism and love of justice will be least likely to sacrifice it to temporary or partial considerations."[87]

As means of achieving the proper ends of representation, Publius considered large constituencies superior to small ones. They provide a

larger pool of talent from which to recruit "fit characters," and those
who represent large constituencies "will be less apt to be tainted by the
spirit of faction," since they would have more varied interests to serve.
Publius accordingly argued that the national government would successfully recruit "the best men in the country" for its elective offices.[88]
It has been observed that Publius was adapting what had been considered the traditional advantages of "virtual" representation (the
wisdom of the representative) to a political situation where only
"actual" representation was practiced.[89] This may be compared with
his adaptation of the advantages of mixed government to a situation
where no legally recognized estates of the realm existed.

Representation, according to Publius, was a refining process in which
higher faculties (that is, motives and abilities) were sorted out, concentrated, and strengthened. Indirect elections performed this function
better than direct ones. This is why he reposed special confidence in
senators and presidents, who would be elected indirectly.[90] Repeatedly,
we have seen how Publius put his faith in complexity as a means of
inhibiting passion, both in individuals and in groups. Government is
divided into state and federal authorities along one axis, and into
legislative, executive, and judicial branches along another. Society itself
is beneficially complex, being composed of many interests, as is human
nature with its varied faculties. By the same token, complex elections
are safer and more effective than simple ones. Publius also believed
long terms better than short ones, since experience is so valuable,
and—within limits—fewer representatives better than many, since
smaller bodies are more selective and partake less of the "infirmities
incident to collective meetings of the people." The danger in large
assemblies is that "ignorance will be the dupe of cunning and passion
the slave of sophistry."[91]

Clearly, Publius believed that the Constitution was designed to
provide scope for the individual to develop his own faculties and to
enjoy the fruits of their development.[92] But can one make an even
stronger claim? Did Madison and Hamilton believe it was the responsibility of government actively to promote virtue in general, or that the
Constitution would make Americans a more virtuous people than they
already were? It seems likely that they did, though scholars have had
to draw on evidence outside *The Federalist* to make the case.[93] The most
persuasive such argument is that of Colleen Shehan, based on Madison's unpublished "Notes on Government." She finds that "Madison's
deepest concern is with the moral and intellectual character of repub-

lican citizens and thus with the decisive influences on their character."
Madison was particularly eager for public education and the wholesome effects of participation in free government to counteract the
deleterious influences of slavery on the characters of white men.[94] He
thus shared his friend Jefferson's concerns over the construction of the
responsible citizen's self.

Even if we restrict ourselves to *The Federalist* alone, it is clear that
Publius tried to enlighten self-interest and enlist it on the side of
reason rather than on the side of passion. It is also clear that he wished
to reward the qualities of *public* virtue and wisdom with political
power. However, *The Federalist* has little to say about the highest
faculties of *private* morality and speculative reason because the specific
purpose of the papers did not require discussing them. No one then felt
that ratification of the Constitution touched upon the educational or
religious institutions of the country, for example. Publius's letters are
single-minded in their focus on the campaign for ratification. They are
masterpieces of special pleading. Accordingly, it is a mistake to try to
extract from them a complete political theory or a comprehensive
statement of the relation between government and personal virtue such
as one finds in Aristotle.

Despite the knowledge and admiration of the ancients that Publius
and his generation possessed, the classical conception of civic virtue
was alien to *The Federalist.* The ancient philosophers, particularly Aristotle, held that human nature could only be properly fulfilled through
political participation; the truly good man had to be politically
active.[95] Publius acknowledged no such imperative. In Number 10 he
praised representation, which the ancient world never developed, as
superior to participatory self-government. Life under the Articles of
Confederation had left him disillusioned with widespread political
participation and American public virtue; that is why he felt American
political institutions needed to be restructured to strengthen the hand
of virtue. The experience of public service would no doubt benefit the
representatives themselves by broadening their views, so one could
argue that Aristotelian virtue was still relevant to them. And, after all,
Aristotle never expected his standards of civic virtue to apply to any
but a small elite. But it would not have served Publius's purposes to
pursue this subject explicitly, and he did not. He was more interested
in proving the utility of the representatives to the government than the
utility of the government to the representatives.[96]

The neoclassical school of Machiavelli, Harrington, and Montesquieu developed its own elaborate tradition of civic virtue as a pre-condition for free government. The Antifederalists drew heavily upon these writers, especially Montesquieu, to argue that republican virtue would be corrupted in a large and centralized polity, although they also invoked Lockean liberalism, for example, in their demands for a Bill of Rights.[97] Publius's use of the neoclassical tradition was even more selective than that of the Antifederalists. The neoclassical idea of balanced government as a safeguard against faction and demagogy was still relevant to him, but the conception of the sentiment of patriotism played only a very small role in *The Federalist*. "Virtue," as Publius used the word, was not simply equivalent to love of country, as it was for Montesquieu; it was a moral quality that included a sense of honor and justice. Still less did it resemble Machiavelli's *virtù,* the dynamic force of character that can reshape a polity. Publius's "virtue" was a quality of rational insight, not a sentiment or feeling.[98] When Publius had occasion to mention patriotism or love of country, he clearly labeled it a "passion," and he treated it as something quite different from virtue. He assumed that such sentiments of loyalty would attach themselves more firmly to the states than to the new national government.[99] To the extent that national institutional traditions could be cultivated, adding the sentiments of habit to other motives for obedience to government, that would of course be all to the good.[100]

Both the classical and the neoclassical schools had based republican institutions on civic virtue. Publius retained a connection between republicanism and virtue, but he considered civic virtue a rarity and used the paradigm of faculty psychology to prove it. He went on to justify the Constitution as a system that could augment the power of public virtue, drawing on principles developed by moral philosophers for enhancing the power of virtue in the individual. As Publius understood human nature, self-interest was a stronger motive than altruism. Accordingly, liberalism, which grounded the authority of the state on a compact among rational individuals, provided a stronger basis for effective government than classical or neoclassical republicanism. In Publius's model, the enlightened prudence of liberalism would work where the civic virtue of classical republicanism would be too weak.[101]

?☞ CONCLUSION: FACULTY PSYCHOLOGY
AS RHETORICAL STRATEGY

At the end, Publius recurs to his rhetorical strategy and points with modest pride to his success. "I have addressed myself purely to your judgments and have studiously avoided those asperities which are too apt to disgrace political disputants." He has proved at least some parts of his case with the conclusiveness "of mathematical demonstration."[102] The tone has been in keeping with Publius's objectives. He writes on behalf of a small group of lawgivers to a minority audience, through whom he hopes to reach a decisive segment of the political community. He writes to demonstrate that the Constitution will appeal to the enlightened self-interest of practical men. He writes of society through psychological metaphors, showing that the Constitution will control the disorders and instabilities he terms "passion."

The argument itself is at one with the rhetoric in which it is couched. An elite of wise and virtuous lawgivers have constructed a system to pool and maximize society's small store of reason and morality. The system depends on mingling these scarce resources with baser but more plentiful ones to achieve a serviceable alloy of mixed motives. Not even the most complex, carefully devised electoral system can guarantee the best rulers, so "enlightened statesmen will not always be at the helm." But if a virtuous person is unavailable, a selfish one may do, provided his self-interest coincides with social utility. Hence the emphasis on broadening and enlightening self-interest. Even some of the passions can be put to work: "the love of fame," for example, "the ruling passion of the noblest minds," can motivate a statesman to deeds of public service.[103] Like Jonathan Edwards, Publius considered disinterested true virtue a rare and precious metal; unlike Edwards, he would accept the counterfeit tender of self-interest if it could purchase social advantage.

Publius was actually more typical of eighteenth-century writers on moral philosophy than was Edwards. Publius was writing in a tradition stemming from Bernard Mandeville's once startling dictum: "Private vices by the dextrous management of a skillful politician may be turned into public benefits." A far greater moral philosopher, Adam Smith, had applied this principle to the economic realm. A well-designed economic system, Smith taught, would take advantage of the psychological fact that individuals pursue wealth for themselves under the (mistaken) impression that it will bring them happiness. It was a Providence of God that men's very selfishness and foolishness could serve society. Like Publius, Smith never confused socially useful behavior with genuine virtue.[104] We have already seen how an older contemporary of Publius, Benjamin Franklin, also sought to enlist selfishness in the public cause by teaching that honesty was the best policy.

The language of faculty psychology provided Publius with a familiar vocabulary in which to conceptualize an unfamiliar Constitution. It was a vocabulary his audience understood and respected. Through it, he could invoke conventional wisdom on behalf of the drastic innovation he was advocating. By analogy to the faculties of the human mind, Publius showed how the balance of powers in the Constitution, like that in a wise individual, would lead to balanced decisions. The new government would set reason and justice over passion and partisanship, he argued. A letter from Madison to Washington in 1787 shows how he was already starting to think in these terms before composing his share of *The Federalist:* "The great desideratum which has not yet been found for Republican Governments seems to be some disinterested and dispassionate umpire in disputes between passions and interests." In faculty psychology, the conscience was the umpire over the passions and interests. As Madison used the term in *The Federalist,* the national government would be umpire over the states' "violent factions"—not in the sense of a passive arbitrator but in the sense of a dispassionate authority constituted with the power to back up its decisions.[105]

Given the task of advocating the Constitution in the America of 1787–88, the way Publius made use of faculty psychology was brilliant. It put him in the mainstream of eighteenth-century educated opinion and spoke directly to the cultural values of the gentry class who were his primary audience, while avoiding any tactically unwise hint of a direct challenge to more democratic values. The model of faculty psychology that Publius used, emphasizing the supremacy of reason rather than revelation or tradition or even the will of the majority, enabled Madison and Hamilton to pick and choose widely from the theories and experiences of the past to suit the circumstances of the present. Elements of classical republican theory, such as a concern with balance and virtue, survived in new guises, synthesized with insights from Scottish moral philosophy. Within the overarching frame of reference provided by faculty psychology, Publius found it possible to invoke a variety of political authorities on particular issues, even including one of the leading critics of faculty psychology, David Hume.

Working within the intellectual and social conventions of his age, Publius adapted the language of faculty psychology to an original and distinctive message. Despite its pessimism about human nature, his message is ultimately optimistic. Chaos and coercion are not the only alternatives: both individual and society can be improved by conscious effort and made more rational. If aided by wisely contrived institutions, reason can reassert its rightful supremacy. Part of the beauty of the system was that it did not require passion and partisanship to be repressed altogether, but took advantage of them to overcome them. The model of countervailing passions, so carefully constructed by eighteenth-century moral philosophers, offered Publius a means to reconcile political conflict with order. *E pluribus unum* was the paradoxical motto of the Union: "out of many, one." Publius had argued just such a set of paradoxes: out of passion, reason; out of complex procedures, a just result; out of selfishness, the common good.

Its use of faculty psychology, originally designed for the circumstances of 1787–88, also helps account for the lasting popularity of *The Federalist* and its status as a canonical text. Membership in Publius's audience is not restricted by time and place; anyone who wants to can participate. Conceptualizing his readers in terms of their faculties, Publius addresses the better nature within each complex person. He wins us over by insisting that he will not *(sic!)* flatter us, that he trusts our judgment because we too understand the weakness of human nature. Whatever selfishness may characterize most people, "no partial motive, no particular interest, no pride of opinion, no temporary passion or prejudice" must influence us. Each of us can act "according to the best of his conscience and understanding." "What more could be desired by an enlightened and reasonable people?"[106]

⁂ PART II

Constructing Character in Antebellum America

CHAPTER 4

The Emerging Ideal of Self-Improvement

"It is the age of the first person singular," Ralph Waldo Emerson wrote in his journal at the beginning of February, 1827.[1] Like so many of his aphorisms, this observation offers several levels of meaning. Antebellum white Americans not only asserted themselves in a variety of ways, they were increasingly able to define themselves through voluntary choice. Contemporaries were quite aware of this novel power and felt that it presented both opportunities and dangers. The origins of the goal of personal self-definition may be sought in evangelical Christian "new birth" and in the cultivated self of eighteenth-century politeness, but the ideal spread widely and took on new forms in the United States during the nineteenth century. A combination of weak institutional constraints and the market revolution, which multiplied occupational and consumer options, provided favorable conditions for such widespread personal autonomy. This chapter will outline broadly some of the forms that self-definition took. It was an age of self-reliance, but also of self-control and self-improvement. (On the other hand, it was not an era that celebrated self-indulgence; "the age of the first person singular" meant something quite different from the "me generation" of the 1980s.) Surprisingly, the Enlightenment model of the balanced character, in which reason reigned supreme over the passions, remained relevant and widely accepted, even in an era of democratic Romanticism.

❧ THE QUEST FOR IDENTITY

"Now that the republic—the *res publica*—has been settled, it is time to look after the *res privata*—the private state," declared Henry David Thoreau in 1854.[2] Many of his neighbors agreed, on this much at least, with the great iconoclast and undertook their own brave experiments with shaping a new personal life for themselves. In this respect, the individualism of Walden Pond may serve as a symbol for a mass movement: of innumerable quests for new identities and new births; to reexamine past lives; to reshape human nature. The Declaration of Independence proclaimed that all men had an unalienable right to the pursuit of happiness. In practice, Americans defined this pursuit not only in economic and political terms but also in moral and spiritual ones, and in terms of manners and lifestyle. The decades following the American Revolution and establishment of the Constitution witnessed an extraordinarily rich and varied experimentation by the people of the new nation with new, voluntarily chosen identities.[3]

In eighteenth-century North America many, probably most, people still thought of themselves less as autonomous individuals than as members of small communities—families, towns, gathered churches. The individual self did not yet enjoy the unambiguous moral legitimacy that it has today.[4] Jonathan Edwards, deploring self-interest and exalting the corporate interest of the village community, spoke for the traditional and predominant view; Benjamin Franklin, in advocating a more positive view of self, was conscious of having to fight against the cultural hegemony of Reformed Protestantism and the doctrine of original sin. Acceptance of personal autonomy, the deliberate construction of personal identity, and the pursuit of a balanced character were still normally characteristic only of elite males. Franklin had labored to extend the opportunity for self-definition to include urban artisan-tradesmen. In the years to come, the range of his work was dramatically extended. The first half-century of independence witnessed a still broader expansion of personal autonomy. More opportunities arose for individuals to exercise choices, and among them was the power to choose and shape a personal identity. But the devotion to moral order did not vanish with the increase in individual power to choose. For one thing, many people continued to embrace various kinds of communities, especially in the newly founded religions; a communal identity

could be just as voluntary as an individual one. Even more characteristic of the nineteenth century, however, was the substitution of *personal* discipline for *community* discipline.

The quotation from Thoreau proclaims a shift of priorities: away
from the public and toward the private, away from politics and toward
the cultural and personal. For many Americans, of course, the *res publica*
and the *res privata* were not incompatible, and the quest for identity
was conducted through the fervently partisan politics of the antebellum era as well as in extrapolitical ways. For those Americans
excluded from participation in electoral politics, the opportunity to
engage in other forms of self-definition was particularly important, and
for women—the largest of the excluded groups—it was a time of
expanding opportunities to define themselves. There was a growing
interest in the shaping of individual and collective identities, not
through the kind of institutional engineering that had concerned the
framers of the Constitution, but through such cultural means as manners, literature, religion, education, and voluntary benevolence.

The heightened sense of the importance of the individual that
emerged in the nineteenth century did not (as one might imagine)
produce a diminished sense of community. Instead, a heightened sense
of national community actually accompanied the rise of individualism.
Where the Founders had emphasized the division of society into many
conflicting groups, social thinkers of the antebellum era tended instead
to hope for consensus, and to try to build it through an awakened
personal sensibility. Where the debates over the Constitution had occupied the former generation of thinkers, the controversial revival and
reform undertakings of the Second Great Awakening focused the attention of the latter. Above all, American social thought in the nineteenth
century showed a tendency to expand the number of people who were
entitled to an autonomous sense of self, and the climate of opinion
encouraged them to construct an identity of their own.

The heroic ideal of the self-constructed individual became widespread throughout Western civilization in the nineteenth century, and
was typical of the Romantic movement. At the same time, the institutions and conditions of life in the United States permitted the ideal
to be more widely relevant and celebrated in the young republic than
in any other country. That white Americans of the antebellum period
enjoyed more liberty than people ever had before is a historical commonplace, and a number of powerful explanations have been offered to

account for it: the absence of feudalism, the material abundance of the continent in relation to its population, the experience of life on the frontier of white settlement, and the relatively free military security enjoyed by a country with no powerful foreign enemies nearby.[5] In recent years, historians have reminded us that a majority of the population, including African-Americans, women, and others were denied the full benefits of antebellum freedom. Yet if we widen the traditional universe of historical inquiry to include nonpolitical activities, we find that working-class people, women, minority groups, even slaves were able to participate to a degree in certain kinds of voluntary self-definition, through (for example) religion, manners, and self-discipline.[6] And, if we look at antebellum social criticism, we find that denials of opportunity for self-development were increasingly protested as deviations from the norm.

Freer than people had ever been to decide things for themselves, antebellum white Americans used their freedom to reshape their physical surroundings, their society, and themselves. The first we call technological progress, the second, social reform. The third, their experimentation with new identitities and social roles, is perhaps no less important. One relatively straightforward way of claiming an identity was to affiliate with a voluntary association. Americans had a reputation as a nation of volunteers. As Alexis de Tocqueville and numerous subsequent commentators have observed, Americans of the time redefined themselves through membership in innumerable organizations and denominations, as Masons or Anti-Masons, as militiamen or Associationists or Shakers. They joined labor unions, women's auxiliaries, and volunteer fire brigades.[7]

The quest for personal identity was not confined to joining organizations, however: it often took the form of a serious effort to reshape one's personal life and character. Evangelical Protestantism, the most pervasive religious tradition in America, encouraged converts to conceive of their spiritual life in terms of "re-birth" as a new person. Victorian ideas of morality and socially acceptable behavior set standards to which people struggled to conform. Americans were undertaking to live Christian lives, temperate lives, disciplined lives, and polite lives—sometimes all at the same time. Members of restorationist religious movements attempted to live ancient lives.[8]

The expansion of the market economy in the nineteenth century increased the opportunity for ordinary white Americans of both sexes to engage in various other forms of self-definition. Entrepreneurs formed business partnerships and joint-stock companies; employees formed associations of working men and women. The commercial nexus that Franklin had exploited in his process of didactic self-construction became ever more widespread. Even in the countryside, the expansion of the market affected peoples' range of choices. As recent scholarship has shown, commercial activities presented rural people with additional resources for their family survival strategies.[9] Women in particular derived greater autonomy from earning money outside the home (as they would in twentieth-century developing countries). Surely one explanation for the continued relevance of the Scottish Enlightenment to the intellectual needs of nineteenth-century Americans lies in the continued relevance of questions arising from the adaptation to commercial values. The tensions between cosmopolitanism and provincialism, rationalism and enthusiasm, politeness and rudeness, which had so preoccupied the eighteenth-century gentry in both Scotland and America, remained a feature of American life and became relevant to more and more people during the long-drawn-out market revolution.[10]

Nineteenth-century Atlantic civilization celebrated the ideal of careers open to talent—but this ideal, to be meaningful, required an appropriate variety of careers from which to choose. Urbanization and the growth of commerce multiplied occupations, especially those making use of formal education, far beyond what subsistence husbandry could provide. Meanwhile consumer goods were also multiplying, and opportunities arose for self-definition in terms of taste. While the market was providing new economic resources, it provided new cultural resources as well: cheaper newspapers, magazines, and books, a better postal system, and beginning with the invention of the telegraph, virtually instantaneous communication over long distances.[11] Urban life in the nineteenth century provided greater variety in available recreations, and these too, both the new mass culture and the new high culture, offered opportunities for self-definition to consumers.[12] In sum, the expansion of the market economy widened the scope for personal autonomy on a scale previously unparalleled: choice of goods and services to consume, choice of occupations to follow, choice of life styles and identities.

Nor was the emergence of the market economy without relevance to religious life, at least by way of analogy. Just as antebellum Americans experienced free enterprise in commerce, they also experienced it in religion. Each religion, like each product for sale, was one among many available; each religion, like each product, had to be marketed to potential customers if it were to survive competition. If the result was sometimes crass and corrupt, marketplace logic was not an entirely negative influence on American religion. It kept the churches adaptable, dynamic, and growing.[13]

The pursuit of self-defined identity in antebellum America almost always had two sides: voluntary choice and self-discipline. Most of the new religious faiths and secular lifestyles required voluntary commitment but also imposed novel restraints. These might involve anything from the temperate use of alcohol (or total abstinence from it), to unpaid labor in a utopian community, to the proper use of a fork. Historically, the members of Reformed and sectarian churches had assumed collective responsibility for each other's behavior, a "watch and ward" over church discipline. The new American religions had their own versions of church discipline; among the strictest was that of the Latter-day Saints, founded by the prophet Joseph Smith in 1830.[14]

Sometimes Americans went beyond self-reformation and the discipline of those in their own group to a concern with the reformation and discipline of others throughout society: to redeem the insane through asylums or convicts through penitentiaries, for example. From this outreach derives the antebellum reformers' reputation as promoters of social control. It is useful, however, to recognize that concern with social control was one aspect of a concern with discipline and character-formation that typically began with the self and was then extended to others. To be sure, the reformers' efforts to redeem others dovetailed with the needs of industrial and commercial employers for a disciplined work force. But from the point of view of the ordinary people involved in reform organizations—the foot-soldiers of reform—their participation "might reflect less the wish to control others than an impulse toward self-definition," that is, a wish to avow publicly their own values and aspirations.[15]

One of the most insightful of recent studies to address the issue of discipline is Martin Wiener's discussion of punishment in Victorian Britain. Wiener shows how reformers were not simply concerned with disciplining the criminals themselves, but with discouraging reckless motives and cruel passions in the public at large. Victorian opinion leaders—secular as well as religious—feared that the culture of the market was encouraging impulsive, willful passions, partly by stimulating consumer desires for easy gratification and partly by permitting women and young people the independence that went with earning their own money. In response, a wide variety of measures were taken to promote self-discipline. Among other things, new legal rules were developed applying stricter standards of reasonableness, prudence, and intent. Public executions and other public punishments were abolished because, whatever their efficacy as deterrents, they aroused the wrong passions in the audience. The whole objective of reform was the construction of disciplined individual selves.[16]

The political history of antebellum America, with its struggles over issues like temperance, sabbatarianism, nativism, and the restriction of slavery, can only be understood in terms of this dynamic context of social and individual reformation. Although much of the preoccupation with reformation of character was nonpolitical, some of it spilled over, so to speak, into the political arena. The political parties themselves can be seen as one manifestation of the search for identity: ethnocultural political historians have shown that affiliation with a political party (of which there were many) might be as much an assertion of personal identity as a judgment upon the questions of the day.[17] Beyond the political mainstream, traditional lifestyles were undergoing still more drastic revaluations: new gender roles were debated; experiments in complex marriage, celibacy, and polygamy were conducted. Political participation for women was demanded at Seneca Falls in 1848. Secondary education for women was expanded and the first colleges open to women founded.[18]

The commitment to discipline was by no means confined to employers and social reformers. One widespread form of self-imposed discipline in nineteenth-century America was politeness. As historians of eighteenth-century England have shown, polite culture was one of the large consequences of the commercial revolution and the concomitant rise of the middle class.[19] This new code of behavior represented a giant undertaking of voluntary self-reconstruction and became an aspect of the identity of respectable people everywhere in the Western world. Polite culture may be conceived as the form of self-imposed discipline that accompanied the new freedoms offered by the market revolution. With a rising material standard of living and wider availability of consumer choices, acceptance of polite standards of behavior reflected a quest for an improved *quality* of life, what Richard Bushman has termed "the refinement of America."[20] Just as obedience to the discipline of a church defined its membership, good manners defined a person as a member of the middle class—"polite society," as it was called.[21]

Unlike the hierarchical behavioral codes of traditional European society, the new polite culture was inclusive rather than exclusive, open to all who would adopt it. The impulse to self-discipline probably came as much from "below" (that is, from people aspiring to middle-class status) as it did from "above" (that is, from elite members hoping to impose order). It was part of the program of self-improvement whose patron saint was Benjamin Franklin, a program that included education and economic security. Etiquette books promoting politeness formed part of a massive effort to remake the face of America.[22]

The etiquette books taught a prudential basis for social ethics that Franklin would have endorsed: the reason for treating others politely was to demonstrate that one deserved to be treated with reciprocal politeness. But they also insisted that polite culture demanded sincere consideration for others. The project of self-improvement was supposed to produce true gentlemen and ladies, not hypocrites masquerading as respectable. Nevertheless, the authors of the manuals worried (with good reason) that they might be providing instruction in behavior not only for well-meaning young people, but also for "confidence men" and "painted women."[23] In the end, the promoters of sincere politeness always found the going tough; there were many temptations to unbridled self-aggrandizement in the United States. Foreign observers during the antebellum period generally complained about the low state of American manners.[24]

✷ EVANGELICAL RELIGION

Most antebellum American religion was, in one way or another, evangelical. The distinguishing feature of evangelicalism among the varieties of Christianity is its insistence upon a new birth, that is, a conscious commitment to Christ, undertaken voluntarily at an identifiable moment and generally conceived (depending on the theology of the particular evangelical group) as a response to divine grace. How the offer of grace and the human response to it should be described became a central issue for rival schools of American evangelical theology during the antebellum period. Theologians—both learned and unlearned—

reconsidered the Reformation formulations of doctrine and, for the most part, strengthened assertions of the freedom of human will at the expense of the irresistibility of divine grace. Protestant theological discussion of the freedom of the will constituted one of the most sophisticated dialogues in antebellum America.[25]

The essence of evangelical commitment to Christ is that it is undertaken voluntarily, consciously, and responsibly, by the individual for himself or herself. (That, after all, is why evangelicals, in any century, are not content to let a person's Christianity rest on baptism in infancy.) Evangelical Christians were (and are) people who have consciously decided to take charge of their own lives and identities. The Christian discipline they embrace is at one and the same time liberating and restrictive.

In the evangelical tradition, conversion, that is, commitment to Christ, initiates a long process on the part of the convert to lead a better life, to remake himself or herself. It is a process that typically demands sustained self-discipline. In nineteenth-century America, this subsequent process, like that of conversion itself, had elaborate and various theological descriptions. Converts could be assisted by devotional programs such as John Wesley's famous "method," from which his followers got their name. The goal, which might be termed sanctification or holiness or perfection, was, needless to say, elusive, but its pursuit involved believers in self-examination, repentance, and efforts at improvement. The discipline and supportiveness of their fellow church members were intended to encourage these efforts. Despite the importance of this subject, there has been only a little scholarly work on it, mostly on the colonial rather than the antebellum period. Conversion itself and the preparation for it have been better studied than the subsequent struggle for self-discipline and personal improvement.[26]

The present state of historiography leaves unresolved two different perceptions of evangelical Christianity in early America. The scholarship on the eighteenth century treats evangelical Christianity as a democratic and liberating force, whereas much of the literature on the evangelical movement of the nineteenth century emphasizes its implications for social control. Did some dramatic transformation of the revival impulse come about at the turn of the century? It seems improbable; more likely, historians have concentrated on what might be called the "soft" side of evangelicalism in the eighteenth century and the "hard" side in the nineteenth, but both were consistently present. Evangelical Protestantism did not mysteriously mutate from a democratic and liberating impulse into an elitist and repressive one when it moved from the eighteenth to the nineteenth century. Austerity and self-discipline were present even in eighteenth-century evangelicalism; individual autonomy was asserted even in nineteenth-century evangelicalism.

At bottom, the difficulty in understanding the dual nature of American evangelicalism, voluntary yet restrictive, may reside in the limitations of our concept of social control.[27] The problem is that the idea of social control, implying *one* person or group imposing constraints on *another,* does not take account of the embrace of *self*-discipline, so typical of evangelicals. Even what looks to us like social control was generally undertaken by nineteenth-century evangelical reformers in the name of *self*-discipline. Their reforms typically attempted to redeem people who were not functioning as free moral agents: slaves, criminals, the insane, alcoholics, children, even—in the case of the most logically rigorous of reformers, the feminists—women. The goal of the reformers was to substitute for external constraint the inner discipline of responsible morality. Liberation and control were thus two sides of the same redemptive process.[28] For this reason, the more comprehensive category of "discipline" seems more useful as a tool of analysis than that of "social control," and enables us better to understand the evangelical movement and the continuities between its colonial and antebellum phases. It also calls attention to the important psychological issues of personal identity that have been raised by historians of evangelical reform.[29]

The individualism of evangelical religion is modified during a religious revival, which has come to mean an evangelical undertaking to secure mass, rather than individual, conversion experiences. Conversions during a revival are typically public rather than private, and induced by preaching rather than meditation or other private devotions. The promotion of organized revivals became a central feature of antebellum American society, and it has stimulated a large body of historical writing.[30] Revivalism, by promoting collective conversion, also leads to a concern with collective discipline—that is, social reform.

Scholarship on antebellum revivalism has reached a high point of sophistication in two recent case studies. Randolph A. Roth has examined the Connecticut River Valley in Vermont. He finds revivals were a way of promoting Christianity within a liberal society; they put religion on a voluntary rather than traditional or coercive basis. Roth portrays his subjects as people trying "to reconcile their commitment to competition, toleration, and popular sovereignty with their desire to defend an orderly and pious life." Like others before him, Roth interprets the antebellum revivals as having been conditioned by economic circumstances; he believes revivals flourished best in manufacturing towns because there they represented a conjunction of the values and interests of the owners and the workers.[31]

David G. Hackett examines a more urban environment: Albany, New York. He relates revivalism there to ethnic, economic, and ideological changes across several generations. He points out the similarity in values between the evangelicals and the Workingmen's political party, both affirming self-discipline and temperance. Hackett identifies evangelicalism with a personality type arising out of the breakdown of early-modern European (in this case, Dutch) organic community and the emergence of individualism and the power of choice.[32] Taken together, the books of Roth and Hacket provide a picture of evangelical religion as a broad popular movement, evincing a search for order in both private and public life and an acceptance of voluntarism with self-discipline.

Nineteenth-century evangelicalism synthesized the impulse to reorganize society along humanitarian lines that we identified in Franklin with the longing for a personal relationship to Christ that was so strongly manifested in Edwards. The synthesis developed through a dedication to the redemption of the private person. This redemption, coming from God, eventuated in the moral reordering of the individual's faculties in a way both disciplined and empowering. Those who had been saved by God felt commissioned by Him to save the world.

There were losses as well as gains in the emergence of the nineteenth-century evangelical personality. The new seriousness left little room for the genial tolerance and generous pluralism of Franklin or Jefferson, and Edwards's mystical love of beauty was often neglected in the stark literalism of his Christian successors. But the evangelical movement played a major part in democratizing the ideal of personal self-construction.

❧ POLITE CULTURE AND FEMALE IDENTITY

The rise of evangelical Christianity in the Atlantic world coincided broadly in time with the rise of polite culture. To the extent that both expressed a search for social order and personal identity, the two were sometimes rivals and sometimes allies. It is important, therefore, to understand the changing relationships of these two cultural programs with each other. In Britain, middle-class polite culture had originated in the early eighteenth century, propagated by such publications as *The Spectator* and *The Tatler*. Like the political philosophy of John Locke, it was associated with the Whig regime that came to power after the Revolution of 1688 and with Latitudinarian Anglicanism. It endorsed commercial activity and the aspiration of the middle classes to a better life, while criticizing the fashionable luxury of the rich. The ideology of politeness applied to literary taste and religious sentiment as well as interpersonal relations; it emphasized the need for control of the irrational passions and deplored religious appeal to such passions, calling it "enthusiasm."[33]

To many eighteenth-century British and American evangelicals, the conjunction of politeness and religious Latitudinarianism was unappealing. These evangelicals embraced a more austere life-style and rejected polite society, treating it as a negative reference group. They were dedicated to recovering the piety of the primitive church, not to the modernizing civility of Latitudinarianism. In America, the Great Awakening revealed differences in the style of communication between Old and New Lights: Old Light preachers accepted polite standards of literary taste, based on the proper supremacy of reason over passion, but New Lights repudiated them in favor of extemporaneous preaching that employed more frankly emotional appeals. The countertradition of popular rhetoric was continued in antebellum times by some of the aggressive sectarian preachers and pamphleteers of the Second Great Awakening.[34]

Yet a remarkable feature of the Second Great Awakening was that a large number of evangelicals came to embrace polite culture as a welcome ally in the struggle to civilize America. Instead of regarding politeness and evangelicalism as rival codes, this group forged a remarkable synthesis of the two. There was actually a strong basis for such an alliance: polite culture can be considered as a kind of secular perfectionism, sharing many of the goals of religious perfectionism. Both polite and evangelical culture were concerned with disciplining wayward human nature, and in the tumultuous society of antebellum America, each might well welcome the aid of the other. Many evangelical leaders, after all, felt a strong commitment to reason and did not wish their message to be dependent upon appeals to the irrational passions. The desire to synthesize evangelical Christianity with polite culture became a typical characteristic of mainstream evangelicals in both the Northern and Southern United States, as indeed of many evangelicals in other countries. In the end, both evangelical and nonevangelical versions of polite culture came into existence, with the evangelical version the more restrictive of the two.[35]

To some extent this alliance with politeness was a natural consequence of the evangelicals moving away from an exclusively oral culture and into the world of print. The prevailing literary standards were polite, and when evangelicals enlisted printed media in their service it would have seemed unnatural not to conform to them. Polite culture taught respect for classical education, and so had Christianity ever since the founding of the medieval universities. Literacy and education accordingly became important vehicles for cooperation between evangelicalism and politeness. Other examples of the alliance of the evangelical movement and politeness would include efforts to control violence, sexuality, and alcohol, and to promote respect for women.[36]

During the Victorian period, polite culture became the more or less official ideology of home life and (accordingly) was increasingly viewed as the province of women. In earlier times, politeness had been associated with male "gallantry" toward women, but in the nineteenth century it was actually taken over by women and used to promote their own objectives, social and intellectual. From their power base as guardians of polite culture in the home, influential women extended their sphere to include literature and the arts, religion and moral reform.[37] A key figure in this development was the moral philosopher of domesticity, Catharine Beecher (1800–1878).

Catharine Beecher belonged to Victorian America's most prominent family of Christian preachers, authors, and activists: daughter of Lyman Beecher, sister of Harriet Beecher Stowe, Henry Ward Beecher, and other siblings only slightly less famous. As a writer and teacher of moral philosophy, Catharine Beecher held that women had a special responsibility to redeem American society. Coming from an evangelical background, she accepted the Edwardsean definition of virtue as selfless benevolence and made it the foundation of an astonishing assertion of the moral superiority of her gender. Since the social role of women mandated "submission of the self to the general good," Beecher argued, it paradoxically conferred "moral leadership" upon women.[38]

Beecher's moral ideal, expressed in both writing and teaching, was an amalgam of evangelical religion with polite culture. "The only difference between the politeness inculcated by Lord Chesterfield, and that of St. Paul," she explained in her book on moral philosophy, was that the courtier was only concerned with the *"exterior"* of benevolence; the apostle, with the *"interior."* Jesus, although supporting the common people against the Scribes and Pharisees, was never ill-mannered. She quoted Thomas Reid to the effect that *"good breeding"* was a natural sign of "benevolence" (that is, true virtue).[39] Through this synthesis of religion and politeness she hoped to create an ecumenical Christianity that could serve as a kind of informal established church or national ideology for the American republic.[40]

According to Catharine Beecher's adaptation of faculty psychology, women were forced by the logic of their social situation to acquire especially strong benevolent affections and capacity for self-denial. These qualities defined women's constructive social role, even while their lack of manly rationality debarred them, she conceded, from political decision-making. Women had a higher calling than the political; they were entrusted with not simply a maternal but a civilizing mission; they were the transmitters of moral values. Although the men were the voters, only the women could make American democracy work. Within the family, women could construct the character of the next generation of citizens. Furthermore, the role of women extended beyond the domestic circle to include moral and educational reform causes, if not electoral politics.[41]

Beecher's book, *The Duty of American Women to Their Country,* begins with a horrific account of atrocities committed during the French Reign of Terror, then claims that only American women can prevent like scenes from being enacted here. Women can discharge this duty by instilling the proper values into the younger generation. Motherhood is by no means the only avenue for women to exercise this moral guidance. Some of them can do it by becoming schoolteachers, others by donating time or money to reform causes; some by teaching Sunday school, others by lobbying for prayer and Bible-reading in the public schools.[42]

Catharine Beecher, though she has been remembered principally as the founder of the teaching of home economics in schools, had in fact presented American women with a strong and positive conception of female identity as an alternative to male identity. Where men were competitive and aggressive, women should be unselfish and nurturing. In this way they would establish a compensatory cultural influence in an otherwise dangerously anarchic society.[43] Benjamin Franklin had believed that a social order could be based entirely on competitive individualism. His nineteenth-century successors were no longer confident of this, and Beecher's doctrine of the social role of women provided an appropriate centripetal balance to the centrifugal tendencies in the social role of men. In the language of faculty psychology, women would provide a "countervailing power" to balance that of men in the social organism.

Catharine Beecher's emphasis on the cultivation of benevolence was typical of the moral philosophy of the Victorian age. In the eighteenth century, Franklin and Publius had sought to invoke the power of prudential self-interest on the side of conscience. In the nineteeth century, moralists like Beecher followed instead the example of Thomas Jefferson and turned their attention to the power of the social affections. While the dominant moral philosophy of the eighteenth century had viewed the power of the emotions as a problem, to be overcome by reason or (in the case of Edwards) by divine grace, Victorian thinkers were more likely to see the power of the *right* emotions, properly cultivated, as part of the solution. Given the strength of the emotions, the argument went, they should be enlisted in the cause, not stubbornly suppressed. The benevolent affections (or social affections) such as gratitude, pity, friendship, and love became more and more valued as potential allies of conscience within human nature.[44] The ideology of politeness taught that a cultivated emotional sensibility could be an invaluable aid to conscience. It was logical, therefore, that women, having been forced (as Beecher explained) by the logic of their social situation to develop their benevolent affections, should be propagators of the ideology of politeness. But it was also a turn toward a broader conception, a more fully human conception, of that self which should be nurtured and constructed: not only the rational, but also (with care) the emotional; not only the masculine, but also the feminine.

?◦ CHARACTER AND SELF-IMPROVEMENT

During the nineteenth century, people who enjoyed the benefits of the expanding economies of the Western world found a kind of liberty that went beyond the right to consent to government and even beyond freedom of expression. This was a much wider scope of *personal* freedom, the right to choose what kind of person one would be. The consequences of this freedom involved more than occupational and consumer choices (important though these were) and more than affiliating with organizations of like-minded people sharing a common label. Most interesting of all, many people consciously committed themselves to a process of self-reconstruction. We might call this personality development; nineteenth-century people were more likely to speak in terms of character development, an expression that implied self-mastery rather than self-gratification or the projection of an advantageous image to others.[45]

"The Victorian concentration on character," Stefan Collini has pointed out in his study of British political thought, "gave a new form to an old concern." This old concern was "the moral formation of citizens," which can be traced all the way back to the rigorous discipline of Sparta. "A more restrained and less specific commitment to fostering the moral qualities appropriate to a citizen in a free state was a constitutive element in the long tradition of civic republicanism which derived from Aristotle, was renewed by Machiavelli, and which featured significantly in European, and particularly in Anglo-American, political thinking down to at least the end of the eighteenth century."[46] Looked at in this light, Victorian character formation was the heir to civic humanism as well as to evangelical pietistic self-discipline. However, by comparison with both these earlier forms of character formation, the nineteenth-century form was more concerned with positive self-development and less exclusively preoccupied with self-repression. It thus had more in common with eighteenth-century politeness and its concern with the cultivation of the self.

The people of the nineteenth century conceptualized character development in terms of what they called self-improvement, by which they meant the development and discipline of the innate human powers, or faculties, in accordance with a desired model. The term "self-improvement" had an interesting evolution. The word "improvement" originally derived from agriculture; to improve land or something else meant to turn it to good account, to make profitable use of it. One could improve an occasion, that is, take advantage of it. The word was sometimes used in a spiritual or moral sense: a preacher would improve a biblical text, that is, unfold its edifying application. As early as 1766, we find this usage in Scotland: "[She] had from her youth improved herself by reading." Especially in America, the terms "improve" and "improvement" were often applied to persons as well as things, with a moral as well as a material meaning.[47]

The moral ideal of self-improvement was taught to children by the famous hymn writer, Isaac Watts, in his poem, well known in its day:

> How doth the little busy bee
>   Improve each shining hour,
> And gather honey all the day,
>   From every opening flower!
> How skillfully she builds her cell!
>   How neat she spreads the wax!
> And labours hard to store it well,
>   With the sweet food she makes.[48]

The weak rhyme at the end is all too typical of Watts, but his doggerel illustrates the use of the word "improve." To improve oneself was not only to make oneself better—mentally, morally, and physically—but also to use one's abilities to proper advantage. Watts's poem would be forgotten had it not been the subject of Lewis Carroll's wonderful parody in *Alice in Wonderland:*

> How doth the little crocodile
> Improve his shining tail,
> And pour the waters of the Nile
> On every golden scale!
> How cheerfully he seems to grin,
> How neatly spreads his claws,
> And welcomes little fishes in,
> With gently smiling jaws![49]

Isaac Watts, writing in early eighteenth-century England, was expressing the Christian doctrine of stewardship. He wanted children to learn habits of industry, because God would hold them accountable for the use they had made of their talents. He made this explicit in the conclusion to his didactic poem.

> In works of labour or of skill,
>   I would be busy too;
> For Satan finds some mischief still
>   For idle hands to do.
> In books, or work, or healthful play,
>   Let my first years be passed,
> That I may give for every day
>   Some good account at last.

By the nineteenth century, Watts's Protestant ethic had been secularized (although the religious version persisted too, of course). It had become the ethic of self-improvement, in which the diligent exercise of human powers was rewarded not only on the day of divine judgment but throughout this life. And the most immediate of the temporal rewards for the proper exercise of the faculties was their increasing power—that is, they were "improved" in both senses of the word.

The greatest of all expositions of the nineteenth-century ideal of self-improvement was written by a Scotsman: Samuel Smiles's *Self-Help,* published in 1859. Smiles sought to encourage the working-class youth of Victorian Britain to take pride in themselves and their accomplishments, to cultivate good habits and avoid self-destructive behavior, to realize their potential. His book is about achieving self-esteem through work and self-discipline; his exemplary characters are altruistic rather than self-interested. Wealth is by no means the only or even the principal reward held out for effort, and both the "use and abuse" of money are carefully delineated. Smiles's work was immediately popular in the United States and had gone through several American editions by 1866.[50]

The American writers in the self-improvement genre likewise concerned themselves more with character-building than with formulas for material success. The leading historian of the antebellum self-improvement manuals, John Cawelti, has concluded that these manuals were not so much guides to behavior as they were attempts to reaffirm traditional values in the face of rapid social change. Since the manuals were not about social *mobility,* Cawelti argues that they must have been about social *control,* admonishing the young to cultivate conventional virtues and rest content with their station in life. Cawelti writes out of a conviction that the writers who encouraged individuals to better themselves through education should instead have been working for the transformation of society through politics.[51] This is a false opposition; educational policy was an important aspect of political debate then as now. But one can also look at self-improvement somewhat differently, by taking the ideal on its own terms as involving both self-development and self-discipline, and examining it as a widely disseminated model for the construction of the self.

In antebellum America, countless ordinary people sought to improve themselves, as they put it. Although the project of self-improvement is often thought to have been middle-class, its appeal cut across class lines, as Joseph Kett has amply demonstrated.[52] It is unduly patronizing to assume that working-class people who professed the values of respectability cannot really have meant to do so, or must have been the victims of a false consciousness. Surely such values as independence, self-discipline, and self-improvement could be taken seriously by working men and women.[53] The project of character-building was not even peculiar to believers in the ideology of capitalism. In the nineteenth century, "Socialists, too, justified their preferred economic arrangements on the grounds that they would produce 'a higher type of character', and even members of the Fabian Society could be found arguing that 'the end of the State . . . is, in fact, the development of character'."[54]

Upward social mobility as such was not called self-improvement, although it could be a consequence of self-improvement. The goal of those who pursued self-improvement as here defined was the ultimate identity of choice, that is, the full realization and development of their human powers. The enterprise was one of character formation, both moral and intellectual. The model character as defined in antebellum America was largely independent of occupation; more or less the same character was thought ideal for any man, regardless of occupation. It was, however, gender-specific, and the differences between the ideals for men and women will be explored further in later chapters.

People undertook self-improvement principally through education, which they pursued not only in schools and universities but also in lectures, lyceums, seminaries, and conversation groups, as well as by themselves. The historian Richard D. Brown has recently provided a fascinating portrait of the pursuit of self-improvement in the antebellum urban setting by three young men of different backgrounds.

Brown is especially interested in the way they made use of sources of information available through the development of commerce and technology.[55] Just what percentage of the population actively pursued this ideal, it would take a wiser—or bolder—historian than I to affirm. But that the ideal was much advocated and celebrated is clear. One contemporary statement to that effect was made in a speech at a county school association meeting, reported in the *Common School Journal,* February, 1839:

> Why should that grim craftsman [the blacksmith] have a mental cultivation beyond the ability to keep account of his horse-shoes and plough-irons, and read his Bible and newspaper? [Answering his own rhetorical question, the speaker proceeds,] Why, is he not an immortal man, or only a . . . working machine? Is he not an *end* to himself? Are not his own worth, power, wisdom the greatest of all ends to him? If I send my son away from home to learn the trade of a builder, I do not want him to be a mere carpenter and nothing more. I want him to be a whole man, of enlarged mind and liberal sentiments.[56]

Self-improvement was not only an individual but also a collective priority. Educational activities played a central cultural role in antebellum America, a society still in the process of self-definition, as were the individuals within it. Educational institutions expanded at all levels, public and private, denominational and secular. New types of institutions for professional and vocational training were created. The public schools were considered the foundation of political democracy. And although women did not vote, still they needed to be trained for "republican motherhood," so secondary education for women was expanded and the first colleges open to women founded.[57] One of the differences between North and South that was most conspicuous to contemporaries was the greater development of public education in the North. When the North won the Civil War, one of the top priorities in the Reconstruction of Southern society was the creation of public schools there for both whites and blacks.[58]

This was also a period when many other institutions, in addition to those we think of as comprising the educational system, came to profess educational or didactic objectives. Some of these were concerned with voluntary self-improvement, such as library companies, literary societies, and mutual improvement associations; the grand American adult education program called the lyceum flourished.[59] Meanwhile, other institutions undertook to improve people who could not do it for themselves. Prisons, poorhouses, and insane asylums began to address the redemptive transformation of their inmates; our word "penitentiary" derives from this impulse. The churches increased their missionary activities at home and abroad, and Protestantism achieved greater success in its foreign missions than at any other time in its history. Intensely partisan newspapers pursued political converts as zealously as the churches pursued religious ones. Voluntary associations promoted causes and tried to win people over, to change their minds, to reeducate them. In short, education, broadly conceived, stood at the very heart of American experience, public and private, during the first century of independence.[60]

A broad definition of education was characteristic of antebellum Americans. Education was thought to involve the development and discipline of the character as a whole, not just the intellect. As a contemporary educational theorist put it, "Education is developing, in due order and proportion, whatever is good and desirable in human nature."[61] Horace Mann, America's leading educational publicist, was particularly explicit in his address to the graduating seniors of Antioch College in 1859: "There are two grand laws respecting mind-growth, more important than the laws of Kepler. The first is the law of symmetry. The faculties should be developed in proportion." Each of the faculties, that is, should be developed in accordance with its proper place in human nature: "they should be balanced, not tilted." To achieve such balance of character required a balanced educational program. "The next law is as important as the first. It is that all our faculties grow in power and in skill by use, and they dwarf in both by non-use."[62] The faculties must be improved, therefore, in both senses of the word. Like most such ceremonial orations, this one was grandly platitudinous; it expressed that which was generally believed.

Among the many identities available to antebellum Americans, one of the most widely acknowledged and celebrated was that of the sound, well-balanced character. To have such an identity was to have all one's faculties properly exercised, developed, and disciplined. We may identify the practice of self-improvement with democratic Romanticism. But the ideal of the well-balanced character—the goal of the self-improvement efforts—was much older, and derived ultimately from the natural law tradition going all the way back to Aristotle. In the form that antebellum Americans knew it, it dated from the Enlightenment and had changed surprisingly little since it had influenced Jefferson and Madison.

In the eighteenth century, this model of the sound, well-balanced character had related chiefly to men of the elite (as we have seen), though Franklin and Jefferson, among others, had sought to broaden its application. In nineteenth-century America the ideal was significantly democratized in practice. In antebellum America, a sound character was considered essential to responsible political behavior, to holding a decent occupation, and to becoming a respectable person in general. Since the electoral franchise generally became open to all white males, it was logical that they should all be thought capable of developing a moral character justifying its exercise. The best opportunities for self-improvement, like the electoral franchise, were available only to white males, although that restriction was powerfully challenged by a few courageous individuals. The spread of free public schools and the increased educational provision for women and girls indicate the widening demand for opportunities for self-improvement. So does the proliferation of newspapers, magazines, books, and lectures. And so does the multiplication of handbooks on polite culture, showing how widespread was the aspiration toward self-construction. What had once been the exclusive badge of the courtier, and was then made available in the eighteenth century to upper-middle-class ladies and gentlemen, was now freely offered, like Methodist grace, to all who would accept it.

?• MORAL PHILOSOPHY AND THE CULTURE OF THE FACULTIES

The construction of a well-balanced character contained elements of both evangelical self-discipline and the acquisition of sincere politeness, as these were understood in antebellum America. Allusions to the model character can be found in fragmentary form in countless sources, private as well as public: literary, social, educational, religious, and political. For a formal description of the character, however, one must turn to the Scottish-American moral philosophers of the time, and specifically to their faculty psychology.

In its eighteenth-century origins, as we have seen, the Scottish school of moral philosophy had provided an academic rationale for Arminian theology and polite culture. Scottish moral philosophy was the creation of thinkers associated with the so-called Moderate wing of the established (Presbyterian) Church of Scotland. The Moderates were the Scottish counterparts of the Latitudinarian Anglicans in England: Arminian in theology, polite in culture, Whig and Lockean in politics. In a surprising twist of intellectual history, however, this school of thought was taken over in America during the late eighteenth and early nineteenth centuries by evangelical Calvinist scholars of energy and vision who made it into their own. The leading figures in this transformation were John Witherspoon and Samuel Stanhope Smith of Princeton, who synthesized evangelical Christianity with the science, the political liberalism, and the polite standards of the Enlightenment.[63] As a result of this development, there was a broad area of agreement on moral philosophy and faculty psychology as taught at most colleges in the antebellum United States, whether Calvinist or Arminian.

The domestication of the Scottish tradition of moral philosophy in the United States, begun at Princeton, was sustained in the nineteenth century by a large number of academic moralists, usually teaching at Protestant denominational liberal arts colleges. Frequently they were also the college presidents. The tradition persisted at some institutions until the end of the nineteenth century; James McCosh of Princeton and Noah Porter of Yale may be considered the last important exemplars before it ran its course.[64] What was being transmitted was a comprehensive philosophical system that usually included an ethics (which can be technically termed deontological intuitionism), an epistemology based on common sense, a teleological natural religion, and a metaphysical dualism of mind and matter. The resolute confidence of the Scottish philosophical tradition that morality was grounded in universal common sense provided a firm basis upon which nineteenth-century people could pursue their cultivation of the qualities of character. The influence of Scottish moral philosophy was by no means restricted to elite denominations but extended to such popular "primitivist" movements as the Disciples of Christ.[65]

Most relevant to our purposes was the preoccupation of Scottish-American moral philosophy with what may be termed the natural history of the mind. Following the example of Scottish mentors like Francis Hutcheson, Thomas Reid, Dugald Stewart, and Thomas Brown, the American moral philosophers sorted out the various faculties of perception and motivation, classifying them, organizing them, and describing how each should be developed. Often, the moral philosophers called their faculty psychology "moral science" to distinguish it from "moral philosophy" proper, which dealt with theories about the nature of right and wrong. Although there were variations in the way American moral philosophers presented their taxonomy of the faculties, a broadly similar picture of the ideal human character emerged. However the individual powers were identified, the categories of moral, rational, and passionate faculties were generally retained as they had been conceptualized in the eighteenth century.[66]

The antebellum moral philosophers' model of human nature postulated a hierarchical sequence of the human faculties in which the moral sense was properly supreme, followed in an order of rightful precedence by rational self-interest and the affections or passions. All the faculties were legitimate in their proper place. As we have already noted, however, the strength of these motives varied inversely with their position. Conscience, or the moral sense, which *should* be the supreme governor of conduct, was in fact naturally the weakest of motives, while the passions were the strongest, with prudential self-interest somewhere in between. The ultimate goal of the process of 'self-improvement' was to correct this problem and strengthen the higher faculties within the character, rendering morality superior to self-interest and reason superior to passion. The antebellum American moral philosophers passed readily from describing and analyzing human nature to prescribing for its cultivation.[67] In fact, the educational theory of mental discipline, relating the entire educational process to the development and discipline of the faculties, dominated American formal education at all levels. The theory of mental discipline received its fullest exposition when it was invoked by the Yale Faculty to justify the classical curriculum of a liberal arts college in the famous Yale Report of 1828.[68]

?⊛ SELF-CULTURE

Theological developments within nineteenth-century Protestantism facilitated, and were in turn facilitated by, an increasing emphasis on the cultivation of the faculties. In many denominations, theologians were emphasizing human agency and effort, rather than divine grace, in the process of conversion, and this evangelical Arminianianism came to be the most typical form of American Protestantism. There were

even some Christians who went so far as to make the conscious cultivation of character an actual substitute for the conversion experience
itself. The pioneers of this viewpoint were the religious liberals of
seaboard New England. Strongly influenced by Latitudinarian theology
from Britain and receptive to the polite culture that went with it, these
descendents of the Puritans came to reject the orthodox Christian
doctrine of original sin. The human faculties, while sadly under-
developed, were not innately depraved, they maintained. Contrary to
the view of Edwards, neither divine atonement for human sinfulness
nor irresistible divine grace to overcome it was necessary in their
theological system. Instead, they believed that the cultivation of a
Christian character could be pursued without reference to a single
dramatic moment of divinely inspired decision.[69]

The Unitarians, as the religious liberals eventually came to be called,
never constituted more than a small movement within American Protestantism, but they played an important part in the propagation of
ideas of individual and collective improvement in nineteenth-century
America. (The evangelical majority paid them the backhanded compliment of devoting a massive effort to their refutation.) The Unitarians contributed an astonishingly large proportion of the country's
intellectuals, reformers, and literary figures, which probably explains
why their history has been pursued more by literary scholars than by
students of American religion.[70] For our purposes, what will be important is their role as promoters of education and self-cultivation.

A comprehensive and lucid exposition of the project of self-
improvement, perhaps the most famous of them all in its day, was
given by William Ellery Channing (1780–1842). Channing was a
prominent spokesman of the young Unitarian religious denomination,
which had recently separated from the Congregationalists; he was a
clergyman of literary taste and enlightened political views respected in
Europe as well as the United States.[71] Educated at Harvard, the intellectual center of New England liberal theology, Channing had retained
a close connection with that university as a Fellow of the Harvard
Corporation, and played a role in founding its Divinity School. He was
deeply interested in moral philosophy and planned, but never wrote, a
book on the subject.[72] As a religious liberal, Channing espoused the
same strand of thought that Scottish moral philosophy had originally
represented. Befitting one who no longer believed in original sin, he
taught that the human faculties stood more in need of development

than of control. Consequently, in his teachings, education was emphasized more than discipline. Channing called his version of self-
improvement by the name "self-culture." Unitarian self-culture and
evangelical self-discipline had much in common, and both could motivate Whig philanthropy and social reform.[73] Channing's disciples
played a particularly important part, however, in reforms designed to
educate or develop human potential.

"Self-Culture" was originally the title of a lecture commemorating
Benjamin Franklin that Channing delivered to young working men of
Boston in 1838; later it was enlarged and published as a tract. It
became one of his best-known works, widely read and reprinted
throughout the English-speaking world. He addressed the lecture/essay
to "the mass of the people," not because of their usefulness to society
as a whole, still less because they needed social control, but because of
"what they are in themselves." "The nature which is common to all
men" is one of immeasurable "grandeur," Channing declared. In this
fortunate country, the masses enjoyed "means of improvement, of self-
culture possessed nowhere else." "To incite them to the use of these"
was the speaker's object.[74]

The "true greatness of human life" is often hidden from view, Channing believed; it consists of inward struggles to develop what is good
and control what is evil in our own characters: "the conflicts of reason
with passion" or "the victories of moral and religious principle over
urgent and almost irresistible solicitations to self-indulgence." Yet
despite difficulties we should never lose sight of God's purpose for us;
we were made for "Perfection as the end of our being." Not only are we
able to "enter into and search ourselves" to decide how we would like
to improve: "We have a still nobler power, that of acting on, determining, and forming ourselves," he explained. "We have the power not
only of tracing our powers, but of guiding and impelling them; not
only of watching our passions, but of controlling them; not only of
seeing our faculties grow, but of applying to them means and influences to aid their growth." This power over ourselves "transcends in
importance all our power over outward nature."[75]

The words "culture" and "cultivated," like the word "improvement," derived from agriculture. The agricultural origins of the terms
were still very much in people's minds, and it was no accident that
among those who were most dedicated to self-cultivation were
gentlemen-farmers.[76] Channing was well aware of this connection. "To

cultivate anything, be it a plant, an animal, a mind, is to make [it] grow," he noted. "Accordingly, in a wise self-culture, all the principles of our nature grow at once by joint, harmonious action." For the sake of analysis, however, it was necessary to address the culture of the faculties one by one, and Channing took them up in their order of importance.

He led off with the "moral sense." Channing conceived of it as a rational power, following in the path of Thomas Reid and the English Unitarian moral philosopher Richard Price.[77] "It is the supreme power within us, to be cultivated above all others," he admonished. "The passions indeed may be stronger than the conscience, may lift up a louder voice; but their clamour differs wholly from the tone of command in which the conscience speaks. They are not clothed with its authority." "In the next place, self-culture is Religious." The "religious principle" was a part of the human personality that needed fulfillment. Thirdly, "Self-culture is Intellectual."[78] Channing regretted that education was so generally regarded as entirely intellectual, instead of seeing that the intellect should properly be subordinated to the moral and religious principles of human nature.

Channing took comparatively little interest in the education of a rational self-interest, not even for the sake of broadening and enlightening it. Like Edwards but unlike Franklin, Channing insisted that "Disinterestedness" was a *sine qua non,* "the very soul of virtue."[79] Balancing one self-interest against another in the hope of achieving a just equilibrium of forces did not capture his enthusiasm either, despite the example of the framers of the Constitution. Elsewhere, this proto-Victorian moralist expressed his "distrust" for the expedient of pitting "men's passions and interests against each other," in an attempt "to use one man's selfishness as a check against his neighbor's." In Channing's opinion, "the vices can by no management or skilful poising be made to do the work of virtue."[80] So much for the political contrivances recommended by Publius and Hume! Enlightened prudence was not an ally the moral sense could really depend on.

Next in Channing's sequence of faculties to cultivate came the "social affections," those benevolent emotions of family love, friendship, and patriotism that contribute so much to warm and dignify human life. Like religion, they were important for the motivation they could supply for moral action. Channing was a typical American Victorian in sharing Catharine Beecher's high estimation of their value. And then, in fifth place, "self-culture is Practical." Even so far down on his list of priorities, Channing was unwilling to say that this aspect of self-culture was concerned only with vocational training; in a larger sense, practical culture was designed "to make us efficient in whatever we undertake, to train us to firmness of purpose and to fruitfulness of resource in common life, and especially in emergencies, in times of difficulty, danger, and trial."[81]

Two more objects of self-culture still remained. "The sense or perception of Beauty" was a faculty that Channing felt was sadly neglected in America—though even he, its professed apologist, defended it chiefly as leading the soul to religion and the mind to morality. Finally, "there is another power, which each man should cultivate according to his ability, but which is very much neglected in the mass of the people, and that is the power of Utterance." To express oneself effectively was a key to all forms of social power and confidence. "A man who cannot open his lips without breaking a rule of grammar, without showing in his dialect or brogue or uncouth tones his want of cultivation, or without darkening his meaning by a confused, unskilful mode of communication, cannot take the place to which perhaps his native good sense entitles him."[82]

For the rest of his lecture/tract, Channing defended the ideal of self-culture as relevant to the common man, not merely to an elite. He cast the entire discussion in masculine gender, though some who heard him applied his teachings to women, as we shall see. He alluded to the slaves of the South but once (he was, after all, addressing an audience of northern workingmen), as examples of people who had been deprived of their instrinsic value as human beings worthy of culture and treated as if they were mere engines of work.[83]

There was practical advice on how to find or make time for self-culture in a working man's week. One suggestion was to take advantages of opportunities in work itself to improve one's skills. Channing actually showed more awareness than Franklin of the possibility that work as such could be psychologically beneficial and rewarding.[84] It was essential to control "the animal appetites"—in this connection Channing endorsed the temperance movement. From private morality he was led into a discussion of relevant public issues. He defended an unpopular state law recently enacted making liquor by the drink illegal and limiting legal purchases to very large amounts for consumption at home. He praised the formation of a state Board of Education and the establishment of a Normal School to provide teacher training. He also called on his audience to support selling the public lands in the West and using the money to fund public education, instead of giving the lands away as homesteads to settlers. Although Channing went out of his way to deplore political partisanship, it is worth noting that all the political policies he endorsed were Whig measures. While self-improvement in antebellum America would be no means be limited to Whigs, the Whig party would retain a special concern with its promotion.

In "Self-Culture," Channing had delivered himself of a seminal discourse, one that not only laid out a social agenda but suggested how it could be carried out on an individual basis. It deserves to rank as a minor classic of American culture and the Protestant ethic, bridging the worlds of Benjamin Franklin and Horatio Alger, popularizing faculty psychology, and synthesizing the Enlightenment with Christianity. Although Channing himself had carefully avoided appeals to getting ahead in the world, in practice his version of self-culture merged with popular manuals on "how to succeed" into a generalized message of self-improvement.[85] How the project of self-improvement was actually pursued in two famous cases will be the subject of the next chapter.

Self-Made Men: Abraham Lincoln and Frederick Douglass

Few expressions in our language have shriveled as badly as the term "self-made man." Today, it would rarely be applied to anyone other than a successful entrepreneur. Among intellectuals, at least, it is widely regarded as the platitudinous expression of an obsolete individualism. Once upon a time, however, the self-made man represented a heroic ideal, with significance to millions as an expression of the meaning of life, an ideal in which making money was incidental to self-fulfillment. Henry Clay has been credited with inventing the term, and it was often applied to him by others.[1] As Clay and his contemporaries used the expression, a self-made man was one who had attained eminence by his own efforts in any walk of life, not necessarily in business and not just in monetary terms. The process of becoming self-made was understood as the development of human potential broadly conceived. Finally, what distinguished the self-made man was that his identity was a voluntarily chosen, conscious construction, not something that had to be achieved by an individual in isolation.

When Charles Seymour published his collection of biographical sketches in 1858, under the title *Self-Made Men,* his sixty subjects included very few businessmen or examples of the newly rich, but consisted primarily of scientists, inventors, and statesmen. Forging their own identities out of the raw material of human nature was one manifestation of the innovative energy that made Seymour's subjects fit models for imitation.[2] When the famous novelist Harriet Beecher Stowe published *The Lives and Deeds of Our Self-Made Men* in 1872, her chosen subjects consisted of antislavery crusaders and Union war heroes; they did not include a single businessman.[3] As these examples indicate, the nineteenth-century ideal of the self-made character was concerned as much with social utility and personal fulfillment as with social mobility. To be self-made was to have made, not money, but a self. Our own image of the self-made man represents a corrupted version of the ideal, after it became identified more narrowly with entrepreneurship and money-making. How the generalized term became more restricted in application is a subject that would repay further inquiry.[4] Perhaps the change is related to a corresponding change in the meaning of the expression "to make one's fortune"—from "make one's destiny" to "make one's wealth."[5]

The most famous of American writers to celebrate the self-made man was, of course, Horatio Alger, Jr. Alger, a Unitarian minister, wistfully defended the antebellum ideal of individual character in a postbellum world of ruthless corporation competition. In this alien new environment, Alger realized that only by tacking on some providential good luck as a *deus ex machina* could he give his stories a happy ending. His fictional portraits of poor but honest boys were intended to provoke the compassion of the middle class as much as to encourage the poor. Notwithstanding his reputation today, Alger actually celebrated neither millionaires nor acquisitiveness.[6]

The self-made man in the antebellum era was ideally one who had successfully pursued self-improvement and had attained an appropriate balance of character. This in turn—the world being at least somewhat just—would usually lead to a temporal reward: economic security and the esteem of others. The self-made man could also be an instructive example to others of what human nature should be like, and an inspiration to their own efforts at self-improvement. An exemplary individual of this sort was a "representative man," as that term was used by Ralph Waldo Emerson and others.[7] This chapter will examine two famous self-made Americans of the nineteenth century, Abraham Lincoln and Frederick Douglass. Each expressed *ideas* about the construction of the self, while at the same time exemplifying the *practice* of self-construction. They were advocates of self-construction as well as analysts of it. I take them, in something like the Emersonian sense, as representative.

ಶ್ಠ ABRAHAM LINCOLN

Abraham Lincoln never dwelt upon his humble background. "It is a great piece of folly to attempt to make anything out of my early life," he is reported to have told a campaign biographer who approached him for information. "It can all be condensed into a single sentence and that sentence you will find in Gray's Elegy—'The short and simple annals of the poor.' "[8] It was left to others to celebrate the log-cabin birth and lowly origins of the Great Emancipator.[9] Although Abraham Lincoln fondly recalled his stepmother, Sarah Bush Johnston Lincoln, he had remarkably little to say about his natural mother, Nancy Hanks Lincoln, who died when he was nine. He seems to have felt ashamed of her, not only because he believed her illegitimate, but also because he feared (wrongly) that she was not legally married to his father.[10] The little that has come to light about Abraham's relationship with his father, Thomas Lincoln, does not indicate that it was a close one. When Thomas lay dying in 1851, Abraham refused to visit him and did not attend the funeral either.[11] Lincoln's biographer David Herbert Donald notes, "In all of his published writings, and, indeed, even in reports of hundreds of stories and conversations, he had not one favorable word to say about his father."[12] What distanced Abraham from his parents was probably his hunger for education. Thomas, Nancy, and Sarah were all functional illiterates, and Abraham complained that they had offered their children "absolutely nothing to excite ambition for education."[13]

A recent historian of the Lincoln family, Jean Baker, contrasts the "rustic traditional mentality" of Abraham's parents' world with the "bourgeois" outlook, based on self-improvement, that he embraced after the age of twenty-two.[14] Abraham's cousin John Hall recalled young Lincoln declaring that "he intended to cut himself adrift from his old world."[15] Doing so required remaking himself, a project he pursued first in New Salem and then in Springfield, through self-education, professionalization, and his socially advantageous marriage to Mary Todd. At the Todd-Lincoln wedding, the groom invited no one from his own family.[16]

Abraham Lincoln's distancing himself from his parents, particularly from his father, apparently fits into a pattern common among American self-made men of his generation. The historian Joyce Appleby has studied 188 autobiographies of people born between 1765 and 1805 who became culture heroes during the antebellum era. "Their lives served as models of innovation in a society losing all desire to replicate past ways of doing things." She finds that the key to success was usually presented as a break with family expectations. "The son's ambition juxtaposed against the father's failure" was a typical feature of these accounts. "The opportunity to quit the family farm is presented as a deliverance," she notes.[17] Clearly, Lincoln was acting out a paradigmatic role. His life, when retold later as heroic legend, lent itself perfectly to the genre Appleby has identified.

Lincoln's political vision for America mirrored his personal ambitions. His support for the economic program of the Whig party dovetailed nicely with his desire to encourage upward social mobility, for others as for himself. The Whigs tried to promote economic development and diversification, which Lincoln believed would open up new opportunities for individual economic advancement.[18] "Improvement" was necessarily a collective as well as an individual project for Whigs like him. As one historian has summed up the differences between the parties of the day: "The Democrats saw themselves as the party of liberty, while the Whigs claimed to be the party of improvement. Whether the subject was a bank, a road, or a school for the deaf, Whigs usually lined up in favor of a systematic program for social uplift, while Democrats worried that such projects might limit personal freedom or serve paternalistic purposes."[19] This is not to say that the impulse toward self-improvement was confined to Whigs; Andrew Jackson himself aspired to gentility (though he never went so far as to learn how to spell).[20] But the collective version of that impulse, the desire to reshape the nation as a whole so as to facilitate the improvement of the population within it, was characteristically Whig.

The creation of economic opportunities was but one facet of Lincoln's program for the conscious reconstruction of individual selves. Lincoln found the Whig party's cultural agenda congenial too. In another historian's words, "Whiggery stood for the triumph of the cosmopolitan and national over the provincial and local, of rational order over irrational spontaneity, of school-based learning over traditional folkways and customs, and of self-control over self-expression."[21] The internal improvements that the Whig party favored were human as well as material.[22] As a Whig, Lincoln worked to create a social order that would facilitate individual self-realization as he understood it.

Not only economics and culture, but character itself has been been seen as differentiating the two parties of the Whig/Jacksonian era. A historian of the second party system argues that the Whigs were the party of those who had left behind the values of their traditional communities to embrace the modern world. Conscious of their emancipation from the restraints of tradition, the Whigs were more aware than the Democrats of the need for a new self-control, especially control of passion, to prevent individualism from turning into anarchy.[23] Lincoln, as we shall see, displayed just such a concern with character. He did not think America's free institutions could work without a firm inner sense of personal moral responsibility.

More and more, in Victorian America, the attainment of polite culture was added to, and integrated with, the desirability of a balanced character. Balance of character was the first priority, but the additional acquisition of politeness would convert the self-made man into a self-made gentleman. Under the tutelage of Mary Todd Lincoln, Abraham Lincoln pursued this objective too.

The late political scientist David Greenstone, in his last and uncompleted book, *The Lincoln Persuasion,* distinguished two kinds of American political thinkers: "humanist liberals" and "reform liberals."[24] Humanist liberals believe the purpose of the state is to satisfy human preferences; reform liberals believe the purpose of the state is to develop human potential. Humanist liberals shrink from prescribing The Good that we should prefer and toward which the state should point; reform liberals do not. Both humanist and reform liberals approve of individual autonomy and believe that they are fostering it. Attempting to elaborate on and clarify Greenstone's model, I would propose that humanist and reform liberals both believe that people have a *right* to self-realization, but only reform liberals believe that people have a *duty* to self-realization.

Greenstone calls the antebellum Democrats humanist liberals, and the Whigs reform liberals. A familiar way to describe the difference between the two parties is to say that the Democrats believed in laissez faire and the Whigs in government intervention. Greenstone shows that these different policies were rooted in different attitudes toward human nature. The Democrats, as humanist liberals, believed that people could be trusted pretty much as they naturally are; the Whigs, as reform liberals, believed that people could be trusted only if their character had been consciously improved. Contemporaries were quite aware of this distinction; as a Whig editor remarked to Henry Clay, the long-standing difference between Whigs and Democrats "was, that the former dealt with man *as he should be,* while the latter appealed to him *as he is.*"[25]

Typically, Democrats praised the innate powers of humanity; Whigs, the acquired ones. In the language of the time, Democrats celebrated the "natural man"; Whigs, the "cultivated" one. John William Ward's *Andrew Jackson: Symbol for an Age,* accurately portrays the spirit of the Democratic homage to the natural man.[26] In Abraham Lincoln, the Whig-Republican tradition found its own hero, the self-constructed or self-made man. The character type that Lincoln pursued in private and endorsed in public was the conscious, willed creation of the individual. But Greenstone believes that after he became a Republican, Lincoln achieved a synthesis and reconciliation of the humanist and reform sides of liberalism. Emancipation, by removing the weight of chattel slavery from African-Americans, represented a massive act of humanist liberalism. At the same time, the Republican party continued a Whiggish tradition of reform liberalism: it sought to construct a balanced and diversified economy within which diverse talents could find fulfillment and balanced characters be constructed.

As we have seen, Henry David Thoreau thought in 1854 that the *res publica* had been well settled, and it was time to turn toward the *res privata.*[27] If Abraham Lincoln had ever thought so, the passage of the Kansas-Nebraska Act in that year changed his mind. Lincoln decided it had become necessary to rededicate the nation to its original principles as he understood them, which meant to make it a place where people could make themselves. As he put it after the war for the Union had begun: "This country, Sir, maintains and means to maintain, the rights of human nature and the capacity of man for self-government."[28] In Lincoln's philosophy, the capacity of human beings to govern themselves individually was what enabled them to govern themselves collectively. And the purpose of collective self-government was to facilitate individual self-government.

❧ LINCOLN AS ADVOCATE OF SELF-CONSTRUCTION

Abraham Lincoln preached what he practiced. Four of his public speeches may be taken as illustrations of his views on the purposeful construction of the self: his Lyceum Address, his Temperance Address, his Eulogy for Henry Clay, and his Address to the Wisconsin Agricultural Society. A fifth speech, the celebrated one at Gettysburg, shows how (like the Founders themselves) he discussed the purposeful construction of the nation using metaphors drawn from the individual self.

In an 1838 address to the members of the Young Men's Lyceum of Springfield, Illinois, Lincoln warned that since American democracy could never be overthrown by a foreign invader, the only enemy to be feared was one within: undisciplined passion. Pointing to several recent examples of frontier lynchings, Lincoln deplored "the increasing disregard for law which pervades the country; the growing disposition to substitute the wild and furious passions, in lieu of the sober judgment of the Courts; and the worse than savage mobs, for the executive ministers of justice."[29]

The model of faculty psychology that Lincoln was invoking derived from the Scottish Enlightenment and, before that, the natural law tradition. It received its fullest exposition in the moral philosophy taught in American colleges in the eighteenth and nineteenth centuries. In this paradigm, the "passions" were both dangerous and strong; it was the task of responsible individuals, allied with political institutions, to keep them under control. This was what the authors of *The Federalist Papers* had explained when calling for the establishment of the Constitution in 1788; now, fifty years later, Lincoln was employing the same language in calling for the preservation of that Constitution. The goal was the maintenance of rational balance, both in the individual character and in the body politic. To let undisciplined passions gain dominance would open the door to mob rule. Lincoln's use of faculty psychology in speaking to an unsophisticated audience on the American prairie illustrates the pervasiveness of that conception of human nature in American culture. Lincoln had not been to college, but he had made the moral philosophers' model his own and expounded it with lucidity and power.

Lincoln warned the young men of his home town that during the generations to come ambitious demagogues would seek to prey upon the passions of the people, unless these were kept under stern control. "Passion has helped us" in rallying the people to the cause of the Revolution, Lincoln acknowledged, "but can do so no more. It will in future be our enemy." He cautioned: "Reason, cold, calculating, unimpassioned reason, must furnish all the materials for our future support and defence." Only by the control of passion could American democracy keep from degenerating into anarchy or demagogy. When Lincoln declared that America would stand or fall by *"the capability of a people to govern themselves,"* he meant this in both a political and a psychological sense.[30]

A few years later, in 1842, in an address to a local temperance society called the Washingtonians, Lincoln renewed his endorsement of self-discipline. (The Washingtonians were the working-class wing of the temperance movement; they took the name of a wealthy plantation owner because George Washington was famous for his self-control. Women members organized separately as Martha Washingtonians.)[31] Lincoln's own teetotal position was unambiguously stated at the outset: "the world would be vastly benefitted by a total and final banishment from it of all intoxicating drinks." Once again, Lincoln drew analogies between the psychological and the political. Comparing the American Revolution with what he termed "the temperance revolution," Lincoln declared that in the latter, "we shall find a stronger bondage broken; a viler slavery, manumitted; a greater tyrant deposed." Lincoln was speaking to reformed alcoholics, people who had succeeded in retaking control over their own lives and passions. "Even though unlearned in letters," they exemplified the virtues of self-control that society so sorely needed, and hence "for this task, none others are so well educated." For Lincoln, as we have seen, education meant self-realization. A whole society of such self-constructed characters would be an exciting prospect. "Happy day, when, all appetites controled [*sic*], all passions subdued, all matters subjected, *mind,* all conquering *mind,* shall live and move the monarch of the world."[32] This was as close as Lincoln ever got to millennial metaphor. His vision of a good society built upon disciplined control of the passions was shared by other prominent Whigs of that generation, such as Dorothea Dix, Horace Mann, and Lincoln's own idol, Henry Clay.

Lincoln's youthful Whiggery was bound up with his admiration for the Kentuckian Henry Clay, "my beau ideal of a statesman," as Lincoln called him.[33] As a self-educated, self-made man, Clay was a role-model as well as a political leader for Lincoln. When Clay died in 1852, Lincoln delivered a eulogy, although it was the kind of speech he seldom gave.[34] In some ways it was a very ordinary speech and much like many other eulogies for Clay. These tended to treat him as a nationalist, a mediator of conflict, a man who had risen from humble origins, and one who had learned to control his passions.[35] Lincoln's eulogy shares some of these characteristics but is also distinctive. To us, the eulogy reveals as much about the speaker and his values as it does about the subject. As Jonathan Edwards had offered David Brainerd as a model character for imitation, Abraham Lincoln offered Henry Clay.

Henry Clay had had to educate himself as best he could throughout his life, Lincoln noted. "Mr. Clay's lack of a more perfect early education, however it may be regretted generally, teaches at least one profitable lesson; it teaches that in this country, one can scarcely be so poor, but that, if he *will,* he *can* acquire sufficient education to get through the world respectably."[36] For Lincoln, Clay illustrated the power of self-determination, the relationship between *"will"* and *"can."* Yet Lincoln did not devalue booklearning (as many self-educated people have done): to lack formal education was in itself regrettable, even if one could partially compensate for it through willpower.

Lincoln identified the dead statesman with America itself. Only by perpetuating the personal and political virtues Clay had embodied would the Union be perpetuated. Clay's character illustrated the virtues of balance. "He owed his preeminence to no one quality, but to a fortunate combination of several," Lincoln explained. Clay put his talents at the service of the Union, and balanced its components as carefully as he did his own. "In the construction of his measures he ever carefully surveyed every part of the field, and duly weighed every conflicting interest." The connection between Clay's personal efforts to subordinate passion within a balanced character and his role as a sectional moderator and compromiser was one that his admirers often noted.[37] Yet the American nation was not an end itself, any more than Clay's personal ambition was mere self-aggrandizement. "He loved his country partly because it was his own country, but mostly because it was a free country," Lincoln declared; "he burned with zeal for its advancement, prosperity and glory, because he saw in such, the advancement, prosperity and glory, of human liberty, human right and human nature."[38]

Henry Clay was a good man and a heroic model, Lincoln showed, because he had devoted his life to the service of his country. But the country, for its part, was good because it served the people who lived in it. And it was free, but even freedom was not entirely an end in itself. Freedom was good, Lincoln suggested, because it was a necessary condition for the advancement of "human nature." A free country provided people with an opportunity to pursue self-development. This, for Lincoln, was the ultimate political good.

Lincoln identified himself with Clay, and in his description of Clay's patriotism he had perfectly described his own. Lincoln, too, loved America mostly because it was a country dedicated to freedom. Even some of the specific issues that Lincoln would have to deal with in the future are prefigured in this remarkable oration. The eulogy credits Clay with taking a constructive interest in resolving the problem of American slavery. It especially praises Clay's great Missouri Compromise of 1820, and before long Lincoln would be defending that very compromise, first against the Kansas-Nebraska Act and then against the Dred Scott Decision. The issues of race and slavery, which the humanist liberals had avoided by tolerating white racism as a politically acceptable preference, were finally confronted by the reform liberals as constituting a barrier to the fulfillment of human potential.

Lincoln's conversion from the Whig to the Republican party did nothing to weaken his dedication to the ideal of self-improvement, as is demonstrated by his address to the Wisconsin Agricultural Society at the state fair in 1859. This seldom-noticed speech is in fact one of the most revealing of Lincoln discourses.[39] Lincoln began by refusing to "flatter" his farming audience with assurances of the peculiar virtue of their occupation (such as Democratic politicians often made); farmers "are neither better nor worse than other people" on the average, he declared. He did have good words for the institution of state fairs, because they overcame local prejudices and distrust of "strangers," while promoting "civilization" in general and scientific agriculture in particular. Lincoln's preference for cosmopolitan values over provincialism, like his endorsement of scientific agriculture, put him in the mainstream of the Scottish-American Enlightenment. He associated scientific agriculture with the wisdom of the Founders in providing a patent clause in the Constitution and a patent office to enforce it. Disclaiming any personal knowledge of farming, he nevertheless urged his audience to try to increase yields on the acres they already owned rather than simply acquiring as much land as possible; to this end he urged that they experiment with new technology, such as the possibility of steam-powered plows.[40]

From Lincoln's own point of view, no doubt the heart of his address was its endorsement of the "free labor" ideology of the new Republican party over the "mud-sill" theory of southern elitist spokemen. The latter had held that since most people had nothing to sell but their labor, they were better off in a system such as slavery, where their employers had a stake in their long-term welfare, rather than in an impersonal marketplace where they were forced to sell their labor.[41] Lincoln tells his audience that arguments claiming labor must necessarily be subservient to capital are false to their experience of life; most of them mingle their own labor with their own modest capital in family enterprises. Wage labor is ideally but a temporary stage of life for young people who have not yet set up households. Intimately linked with this vision of democratic capitalism was Lincoln's vision of democratic education. Both are part of the "free labor" ideology as he defines it. In traditional society, he points out, the educated were exempt from work; in America, where all are educated, education is no longer the mark of a leisure class. Instead we must ask, "How can *labor* and *education* be the most satisfactorily combined?"[42]

The answer to this question brings Lincoln back to agriculture and what makes it special. Thomas Jefferson had seen family farms as guarantors of their cultivators' personal independence and virtue.[43] Lincoln chose to make a different point. "No other human occupation opens so wide a field for the profitable and agreeable combination of labor with cultivated thought, as agriculture." Book-learning is helpful to the farmer, not only for its substantively useful information, but also for its mental discipline; "it gives a relish and facility" for problem-solving. The wise farmer sees the need to educate himself. In the end, education and farming alike teach the same life-lesson of character development: that "careless, half-performed, slovenly work" gets one nowhere.[44]

Lincoln concluded his speech with an exhortation against fatalism and the belief that all things are transitory. Amid the trials of life, he noted, it is tempting to take refuge in the maxim, " 'And this too shall pass away.' " Yet, Lincoln insisted, it is ultimately better not to allow ourselves such solace but instead to work for the permanent improvement of our selves and our lot. "Let us hope, rather, that by the best cultivation of the physical world, beneath and around us; and the intellectual and moral world within us," we can secure individual and collective "prosperity and happiness" which, "while the earth endures, shall not pass away."[45] As a nineteenth-century reform liberal, Lincoln believed in the permanence of progress. And, careful rhetorical craftsman that he was, he had not ignored the double meaning of the word "cultivation."

One more Lincoln speech will repay examination here, and that is the famous brief address at Gettysburg Cemetery in November, 1863.[46] Once again, he was concerned with the construction of the self, but this time as a metaphor for the construction of the nation. Like the Founders of the republic whom he so greatly admired, Lincoln personified the nation as if it had been an individual. But while Publius had written about the nascent Union in psychological metaphors, Lincoln at Gettysburg used biological ones. The nation was born; it lives; it is in danger of perishing. Its life has a moral dimension, just like a person's. The nation is dedicated to the fulfillment of a moral purpose; "under God," it can experience a spiritual "new birth."

"Fourscore and seven years ago." Lincoln began with a conscious archaism that evoked the King James Bible. It was appropriate to do so, since the speech that followed would be cast in terms which, if not overtly Christian, were ultimately religious in significance. Counting back eighty-seven years from 1863 we come to 1776, not 1789. Lincoln was referring to the Declaration of Independence, not to the ratification of the Constitution, as the foundation of the American nation.

"Our fathers brought forth on this continent a new nation." To bring forth is, of course, to give birth. Here, at the very outset, the metaphor Lincoln so carefully sustained throughout the Address rings false: it is not fathers, but mothers, who bring forth children. But Lincoln was operating within a patriarchal culture that traced inheritance through the male line (and, of course, all the signatories of the Declaration *were* men). Another problem with the metaphor is that eighty-seven years is too long ago for "our fathers" to have been involved; literally, it would have been the grandparents' generation, if not earlier. But Lincoln preferred the evocative emotional power of "fathers." In doing so, he was defining the "Founding Fathers" not as the framers of the Constitution but as the authors of the Declaration of Independence.

"Conceived in liberty and dedicated to the proposition that all men are created equal." While newborn humans were conventionally described as "conceived in sin" (the Christian interpretation of Psalm 51:5), the newborn nation had been conceived in a more positive state of grace. Infant baptism is a form of dedication at birth for individuals;

Lincoln attributed such a dedication to the nation. Taking over a phrase Jefferson had used as a logical postulate to justify government by consent ("all men are created equal"), Lincoln reinterpreted it as a goal for the new nation to fulfill. Just as a baptized person needs to grow in the faith to fulfill the promises made on his/her behalf—or, in Lincoln's secular reform liberalism, just as an individual needs to work for self-improvement—so the young nation needed to grow toward the fulfillment of its promised principle of equality.

"Now we are engaged in a great civil war, testing whether that nation, or any nation so conceived and so dedicated, can long endure." Of course, the secessions of 1860–61 had threatened the permanent breakup of the Union (and perhaps, its further fragmentation by future secessions of disaffected states.) But by November 1863, the Union war aims had come to include not only the restoration of the Union as it had been, but also the emancipation of the slaves in rebel hands. To win the war would not only be to preserve the Union itself, it would also be to vindicate the moral mission to which the Union was dedicated, the realization of human equality. As Lincoln had said in Peoria in 1854, if the nation breathed new life into the principles of the Declaration of Independence, "we shall not only have saved the union, but we shall have so saved it as to make . . . it forever worthy of the saving."[47] What was at stake was not simply the future of the United States of America, but the future of *any* nation that might aspire to liberty and equality. The Emancipation Proclamation is not mentioned explicitly, but it does not need to be: the war is being fought, Lincoln tells us, for "liberty," "freedom," and "the proposition that all men are created equal." These phrases were well understood at the time in an antislavery sense; indeed they had been the subject of a spirited debate at the Republican National Convention of 1860, when the arch-critic of slavery, Joshua Giddings, insisted that an endorsement of the principles of the Declaration be included in the Republican party platform.[48]

Invoking religious ideas, Lincoln went on to pay tribute to the blood sacrifice that had been made on the field where his audience was gathered, "to those who here gave their lives that that nation might live." Elsewhere he interpreted the loss of life in the war as a kind of atonement for the collective guilt of American society in the sin of slavery.[49] Now, it was up to the living members of his audience to make a decision ("highly resolve") to take upon themselves the redemption offered by that massive sacrifice, and as a redeemed people, to see to it that the nation had "a new birth of freedom." To triumph over the slave power would be an experience in the history of the nation analogous to the "new birth" of a Christian who has undergone an adult conversion experience. If the triumph were attained, "these dead shall not have died in vain," and (recurring to Jeffersonian principles of government by consent as amplified by nineteenth-century romantic democracy): "government of the people, by the people, for the people shall not perish from the earth."

Lincoln was not an orthodox Christian himself, but he had had plenty of experience from his wife and others who were, and he had engaged in theological disputations in his youth. In the Gettysburg Address, as in several other examples of his finest rhetoric, he put to good use the spiritual insights he had absorbed from Christianity.[50] They provided a powerful complement to his deeply felt dedication to the intellectual and moral growth of the individual, and to the development of a political order that would support such growth.

✌ FREDERICK DOUGLASS

"You have seen how a man was made a slave; you shall see how a slave was made a man." Such was the avowed purpose of the *Narrative of the Life of Frederick Douglass, an American Slave, Written by Himself,* published in 1845. Frederick Douglass was arguably the most thoroughly self-constructed person in the whole nineteenth century. He not only made his own identity, he made his own legend. Over a period of forty-seven years, Douglass published three autobiographies—four, if you count both versions of the last one.[51] Together, Douglass and Lincoln became two of the greatest mythic self-made heroes of a time and a country that idealized self-made men. (It is no mere coincidence that the same generation also saw the first publication [in 1868] and wide popularity of Franklin's *Autobiography.*) But while the legend of Lincoln was the posthumous creation of other people, that of Douglass was his own.

Frederick Douglass's self-definition was a life-long process, and the autobiographies show how it evolved. As the editor of one of them has aptly put it, they reveal Douglass not as a finished self-made man but as "a man still in the making."[52] The transition from chattel to man was not simple and was not completed all at once. Significantly, Douglass changed his name several times during his flight from slavery and did not resume his original one even after it would have been safe to do so. Looking back in old age, he observed accurately, "I have lived several lives in one."[53]

Chief among the reasons for Douglass's eventual estrangement from the Garrisonian abolitionists who initially befriended him was that they would not let him control his own *persona*. They wanted him to retain "a little of the plantation" in his speech, because it would make him more convincing to audiences as a former slave. This was not the identity the fugitive himself was cultivating. "I was growing and needed room," he explained; yet his personal growth conflicted with the propaganda needs of abolitionist agitation. "People doubted if I had ever been a slave. They said I did not talk like slave, look like a slave, or act like a slave."[54] Douglass's critics still voice the same reproach: that he alienated himself too much from his origins.[55] But (as he complained to James Redpath in 1871) he always wanted to be *more* than "Fredk Douglass the self educated fugitive slave."[56] What he wanted was to develop his own potential to the fullest, demonstrating thereby the falsehood of racism.

Like Lincoln, Douglass needed to "cut himself adrift from his old world." Douglass was even more irretrievably cut off from his parents than Lincoln; he knew his mother but slightly and could only speculate on who his father had been. The world the two men embraced was that of literacy and formal orations. Both learned to read by digesting the wisdom of a few precious books; in Douglass's case a seminal text was *The Columbian Orator,* edited by Caleb Bingham, which taught rhetoric and elocution in the neoclassical, sentimental school of Hugh Blair and Scottish moral philosophy.[57] Most of the volume was filled with sample orations to memorize and deliver for practice. The selections affirmed Enlightenment liberalism along with classical virtue, celebrated America as a land of equality and opportunity, deplored slavery and the slave trade, and endorsed mutual understanding between different races.[58] (The 1832 edition, which young Frederick bought and used, had more selections from the American Whig orator Edward Everett than from any other author.) Douglass immersed himself in this oratorical language and the value system it implied. While it opened up a new world for him, it also somewhat closed off the old one. When Douglass was urged, after the Civil War, to go South and run for office (as some black carpetbaggers did), he demurred. "I had acquired a style of speaking which in the South would have been considered tame and spiritless," he explained; "consequently he who 'could tear a passion to tatters and split the ear[s] of the groundlings' had a far better chance of success with the masses there than one so little boisterous as myself."[59]

There is no single moment of "new birth" in Douglass's life story. Throughout the accounts he gave of his life, there are recurrent epiphanies, generally the discovery of some new power by the author, some hitherto unused faculty of his nature. For example, his religious conversion is described as the awakening of his "religious nature."[60] (This is just the way Channing would have described it; an evangelical Christian would have spoken of an encounter with the Risen Christ.) Douglass calls his successful resistance to the slave-breaker Edward Covey a triumph for "my spirit," a "resurrection from the dark and pestiferous tomb of slavery."[61] It is Douglass's vindication of the power of his faculty of free will. Douglass's most recent biographer, William McFeely, is troubled because Douglass gives insufficient credit for his victory to the help he received from his fellow slaves.[62] But Douglass was not really interested in the issue of individual versus collective effort; he was interested in the triumph of the human will over brutishness. Contemporary audiences would not have missed Douglass's conscious irony: it is the black slave who embodies the freedom of the human will and the white master who personifies the brute.

Another pivotal moment of self-discovery for Douglass was his first public speech, in Nantucket in 1841. "I spoke but a few moments, when I felt a degree of freedom, and said what I desired with considerable ease," Douglass recalled in his *Narrative* of 1845. "From that time until now, I have been engaged in pleading the cause of my brethren."[63] In later versions of his autobiography, Douglass emphasized his initial embarrassment more; by then, he could afford to admit it.[64] There is no doubt that telling about himself helped Douglass to construct himself. His ability to use the word elevated him above the merely physical, the slavish, the passive. Speech was an instrument of will overcoming doubt and fear.[65]

Like Lincoln, Publius, and the moral philosophers, Douglass subscribed to the hierarchical paradigm of faculty psychology, which taught the supremacy of reason over passion and mind over matter.[66] He conceptualized his struggle not in racial terms, but in psychological and spiritual ones: "The forces against us," he declared, "are passion and prejudice, which are transient, and those for us are principles, self-acting, self-sustaining, and permanent."[67] Douglass's commitment to civilization, rationality, and principle never blinded him to the power of the passions opposing them. There is still "enough of the wild beast left in our modern human life to modify the pride of our enlightenment and humanity," he acknowledged.[68] Perhaps one reason why Douglass and Lincoln were both less indulgent of the emotions than some of their Victorian contemporaries is that both were upwardly mobile men, who had had to work hard to (re)make themselves, and who therefore knew the emotional cost of the enterprise and valued the outcome accordingly.

Faculty psychology provided Douglass (and other abolitionists) the basis for a powerful critique of slavery. "God had given the slave a conscience, and freedom of will, but the slaveholder took that from him, and said he should not be governed by conscience and his religious aspirations."[69] The profound evil of slavery lay in the way it subverted the proper order of creation and corrupted the character of whatever people came in contact with it. Slavery was "demoralizing and debasing" for the African-Americans; as for the whites, it had a "brutalizing, stupefying, and debasing effect upon their natures."[70] "There could be no relation more unfavorable to the development of honorable character" in either party than slavery; as Douglass put it, "Reason is imprisoned here, and passions run wild." It was the same indictment of slavery that Thomas Jefferson had made.[71]

Unlike Jefferson, however, Douglass extended his critique beyond slavery to include other forms of racial oppression. He observed that northern racism, like southern slavery, undercut the just claims of moral meritocracy. "In our case [as African-Americans], vice and virtue are often treated with equal disfavor by our oppressors," Douglass protested. "In many of the Northern States of the Union, a low, idle, vicious white man stands higher in the social and political scale . . . than the most refined and virtuous colored man."[72] And even after emancipation came to the South, he recognized that the legacy of slavery continued to have brutalizing effects in the region.

The combination of self-respect and self-improvement that Douglass promoted was by no means unusual within the free black communities of the North. "In 1838, there were 80 mutual aid and self-improvement societies among black Philadelphians and there were more than 100 such organizations ten years later."[73] Indeed, the terrible Philadelphia race riot of 1844 had originated in a white mob's attack on a black temperance parade. Douglass, like Lincoln, supported temperance and saw it as a symbol of the triumph of rationality over passion. "If we could but make the world sober, we would have no slavery," he went so far as to declare. *"Mankind has been drunk."* "If the slaveholder would be sober for a moment—would consider the sinfulness of his position—hard-hearted as he is, I believe there is humanity enough if we could get him sober—we could get a public opinion sufficiently strong to break the relation of master and slave. *All great reforms go together.*"[74] Temperance and antislavery had in common the object of redeeming people who were not fully realizing their humanity. Sir Charles Lyell, a British geologist, had returned from a visit to the United States commenting on "the contentment and happiness of the slaves." "He might as well speak of the happiness and contentment of a drunkard lying in the ditch," Douglass noted scornfully. "Why such a man would not be said to be a man. Show [me] a man contented in chains, and [I will] show that his manhood was extinct."[75] The common reform goals of self-improvement and redressing the wrongs of racism were stressed by many African-American leaders of Douglass's generation; they were subsumed together within the objective called "elevating the race."[76]

Douglass cast himself as a representative man in the Emersonian sense, using himself to construct a positive image of human nature in which the Negro race participated. Today we have a problem seeing him as representative, because we think representative means "typical." But for Douglass, a representative man was one who illustrates potential, an example *to,* not an example *of,* the generality of mankind. His writings and speeches celebrated many black heroes whose achievements made the same point his own life did; his periodicals commended books like Wilson Armistead's *A Tribute for the Negro* and William Wells Brown's *The Black Man: His Antecedents, His Genius, and His Achievements.*[77]

The fullest exposition of Douglass's theory of the function of representativeness is his oration on "Self-Made Men." This was his most popular speech on the lecture circuit, delivered before more than fifty audiences in the United States, Canada, and Britain, beginning in 1859 and continuing until at least 1893. Yet except for Waldo Martin, most Douglass scholars have ignored it or downplayed its importance.[78] It underwent many mutations over the years, to suit different audiences, in keeping with Douglass's practice that his writings were subject to continual revision; the first and last versions of it are virtually different speeches. The core of the message, however, remained the same.[79]

Douglass announced his subject as "manhood itself, and this in its broadest and most comprehensive sense." Self-made individuals are of interest because of their "universal" significance: they show "what man, as a whole is; what he has been; what he aspires to be, and what by a wise and vigorous cultivation of his faculties, he may yet become." The faculties are present in everyone, but we can best observe them in examples where they are marked.[80]

Douglass readily acknowledged that, strictly speaking, there are no *self*-made men; we are all interdependent. It is the conscious development of the faculties, not the issue of individualism, which is important to him. Self-made men, he explains, are those who show it is possible, even without formal advantages, to attain knowledge and usefulness, to learn the true ends of living, and "to build up worthy character." Such people demonstrate "the grandest possibilities of human nature." They can be found in every race and every walk of life. "Every instance of such success is an example and a help to humanity."[81]

Douglass rejects chance and Providence as determining people's lives; he is particularly explicit in dismissing the efficacy of religious faith and prayer. Men make themselves by self-discipline and honest work.[82] The present-day reader will at once reflect that these qualities do not necessarily make for worldly success, but the reflection misses Douglass's point. Self-discipline and honest work were important to Douglass not because he thought they make for worldly success, but because they build character. To be a self-made man in his terms was not the same thing as to be successful or rich. John Brown was a drifter, a failure in everything he attempted, an executed criminal. But Douglass considered him a heroic self-made man because he held the right principles and was true to them.[83] Douglass himself, after all, was not deemed a hero because he attained wealth or wielded great power; other African-Americans gained more wealth and higher office than he in the nineteenth century. Douglass's peerless influence and achievement derived from his self-constructed character and his ability to articulate great principles.

At the same time, it would be wrong to think that Douglass was interested only in the individual, and not in collective action. He embraced the political version of abolitionism and criticized the Garrisonians for their preoccupation with impractical individual virtue. He argued that the Constitution, if properly interpreted, could be put to antislavery purposes.[84] Douglass's political thought illustrates beautifully David Greenstone's conception of reform liberalism as a philosophy dedicated to national regeneration.[85] Douglass believed that society as a whole replicates the process that the self-made individual undertakes, as it consciously labors to progress from barbarism to civilization.[86]

Emancipation Douglass considered but the first step toward the realization of the full humanity of the freed people. Political participation was another stride forward. But education was probably the most important. "With all my admiration for self-made men, I am far from considering them the best made men," Douglass pointed out. "There never was a self-educated man, however well educated, who, with the same exertion, would not have been better educated by the aid of schools and colleges."[87] At the dedication of the Douglass Institute in Baltimore, the hero of the day proudly proclaimed: "A people thought incapable of anything higher than the dull round of merely animal life, . . . deprived of the social incentives to excellence which everywhere act upon other men, dare here and now to establish an Institute devoted to all the higher wants and aspirations of the human soul."[88] It was a direct challenge to the legacy of Thomas Jefferson, who with all his enthusiasm for education had shown not the slightest interest in the education of African-Americans. As far as Jefferson was concerned, emancipated slaves should be deported, not educated. In the phrase "incapable of anything higher than the dull round of merely animal life" Douglass had perfectly captured Jefferson's attitude toward black people.

In the end, Douglass saw himself more as a human being than as a black man. It is this which explains his attendance at the Seneca Falls convention for women's rights and his support for the political version of feminism. It explains his sympathy for the Chinese immigrants in California and for the temperance movement. It also explains his integrationism and insistent affirmation of racial equality. "I see no superiority or inferiority in race or color," Douglass told a black audience in 1889. "Our color is the gift of the Almighty. We should neither be proud of it nor ashamed of it. But we may well enough be proud or ashamed when we have ourselves achieved success or have failed of success."[89]

As the creator of his own legend, Douglass built better than he could have known. His biographers have often taken him as a (or the) representative African-American, and tried to claim him for their own vision or, failing that, have argued with him as if he were still alive.[90] Douglass applied the lesson of "Self-Made Men" to his own people: "Give the Negro fair play and let him alone," he declared.[91] But he went on to say what fair play would entail: he thought it would take a major national commitment, including a massive expenditure of public funds, to level the playing field for black competitors. Douglass can speak to the issues of today if we want him to: compensatory education, head start, measuring how far students have come instead of what point they have reached—these contemporary issues find an advocate in Frederick Douglass. But it is time for historians to stop trying to *evaluate* Douglass by the standards of the twentieth century and instead work to *understand* him in the context of his time. The context of Douglass's thought was that of nineteenth-century reform liberalism, the self-conscious nurture of the human faculties, and the realization of human potential.

To sum up: Abraham Lincoln and Frederick Douglass were both models and advocates of self-improvement. Exemplary self-made men, what each of them had made was not money but a self. They were representative types of a new ideal—the notion that individuals did not have to live with the identity to which they had been born, but had the power to redefine themselves. Beyond this, both Lincoln and Douglass espoused a specific theory of self-improvement based on a paradigm of the human faculties and how these should be disciplined. In particular, this paradigm—the prevailing one of their age—emphasized the need to subordinate the passions to reason and conscience. A normative model of human nature propagated in the eighteenth-century Enlightenment came by the nineteenth century to saturate antebellum American culture so thoroughly that even autodidacts like Lincoln and Douglass became exposed to it, absorbed it, and made it their own. If we want to recapture a sense of the world Abraham Lincoln and Frederick Douglasss lived in, the world of nineteenth-century America, we need to recapture an appreciation for the enterprise of self-improvement and the model of human nature on which it was predicated.

ेॐ CHAPTER 6

Shaping the Selves of Others

"**M**en must be subjected to some law," William Ellery Channing observed, "and unless the law in their own breast, the law of God, of duty, of perfection, be adopted by their free choice as the supreme rule, they will fall under the tyranny of selfish passion, which will bow their necks for an outward yoke."[1] Concern with self-improvement, that is, making one's own character, led quite naturally to a concern with the improvement of the characters of others. Since a failure to subdue the passions in human nature posed a political threat, there was a collective, as well as an individual, impulse toward the imposition of self-control. This was a generation whose reformers were extraordinarily successful in embodying their values in institutions that were designed to shape human character. Common (public) schools for children, professional schools for adults, penitentiaries, workhouses, insane asylums, Indian reservations—all professed didactic objectives. Even the age-old institution of the family came under renewed examination as the locus for character-formation.

But all of the impulse to discipline or redeem the characters of others cannot be attributed to prudential self-interest; much of it was humanitarian or religious in motive. The following examples illustrate some of the forms that this concern with constructing the selves of others took in early Victorian America. They show how faculty psychology formed the basis of attempts to shape the selves of others, and how classical republican political ideas continued to be important even in a country long since dedicated to Lockean liberal principles. The examples of Horace Mann and Dorothea Dix show how their objectives led them away from a preoccupation with the universals of human nature and toward manipulating the environment in which human nature was shaped. In contrast, the example of Horace Bushnell shows that a recognition of the malleability of human nature could lead, not to optimistic perfectionism, but to a new form of conservatism.

?● HORACE MANN

Of the thinkers who applied faculty psychology to American institutional life, perhaps the most influential was Horace Mann (1796–1859). Mann was the guiding spirit of the first statewide board of education and the first normal schools (teacher-training colleges) in the United States. Later, as president of Antioch College, he pioneered coeducation. His ideas were taken up and disseminated by important coadjutors like George B. Emerson and Henry Barnard, but Mann remained the premier theoretician and publicist of the public school movement, an authority recognized not only in North America but in Europe as well.[2]

Mann grew up in the Yankee Calvinist world of rural New England. When Horace was fourteen years old, his beloved brother Stephen accidentally drowned. Stephen Mann had not been a converted church member, and he had been profaning the sabbath by swimming on Sunday when he died. The town minister, Nathaneal Emmons, a rigorous Calvinist of renown, offered not a crumb of consolation to the bereaved family in his funeral sermon but used the opportunity to treat the boy's death as a cautionary lesson in the dangers of postponing preparation for grace. Young Horace was left permanently estranged from a theology that could be so cruel and condemnatory. After years of religious doubt and questing, exacerbated by further personal tragedies including the death of his first wife when she was but twenty-three, Horace Mann fell under the spell of William Ellery Channing's humane and evocative preaching. He embraced Unitarian Christianity and Channing's views on the cultivation of the faculties as humanity's reasonable service to a loving God.[3] Even so, some of Nathaneal Emmons's preaching seems to have stayed with Mann, for he retained a vivid sense of the depravity lurking within human nature. Unitarianism conceived of this evil element not as original sin, but as dark and irrational passions that should be subordinated to reason and the moral sense.

In 1837 Horace Mann was a prominent Massachusetts attorney and rising Whig politician who had recently become the presiding officer of the state senate. Having guided through to passage a law establishing a state Board of Education, Mann took the surprising step of leaving the legislature for membership on the new Board. Shortly after becoming the Board Secretary, he founded and edited *The Common School Journal* to provide an additional forum for the advancement of his ideas; the opening of several state normal schools, beginning with one at Lexington in 1839, manifested his efforts on behalf of teacher training.

Horace Mann and the other members of what has been called the "New England school of pedagogy" (though its influence extended far beyond New England) envisioned the public school system as an institutional embodiment of faculty psychology. Within its framework, they drew upon educational ideas of John Locke, Johann Heinrich Pestalozzi, and the Scottish moral philosophers. The Scottish phrenologist George Combe, who tried to link faculty psychology with physiology by identifying each faculty with its location in the brain, exerted a particular influence on Mann. The education of the faculties of human nature was based on the principle of natural law: the powers of human nature are God-given; they have a proper use; and their existence creates a moral imperative to use and develop them properly. It follows that one has moral duties to oneself: for example, "self-knowledge, self-control, and self-culture." Public education represents the collective commitment of society to the enterprise of self-improvement, the goal being the creation of a balanced character.[4] Formal schooling was not an alternative to self-improvement but preparation for it.

Good teachers, according to Mann, make themselves redundant by training their pupils for self-improvement and self-control. What teachers need to do their job properly is to have "knowledge of the human mind, as the subject of improvement; and a knowledge of the means best adapted wisely to unfold and direct its growing faculties."[5] In the sequence of human faculties, the lower ones develop first, beginning with hunger and basic emotions like anger and fear, but we should end our lives at the top of the "ladder" of moral development—a ladder which, like that of Jacob or Plato, leads to heaven. The wise teacher can lead a student gradually up the ladder of the faculties to nurture the development of religion and morality in the personality.[6]

According to this model, young children needed to develop their physical and emotional faculties while their mental and moral ones were still maturing, and Mann carried out this implication consistently. He devoted much attention to the health and comfort of the children in public schools, to improving the physical facilities of the schools, as well as to promoting physical education and the teaching of human physiology.[7] Affective learning was also stressed; teachers were instructed to foster empathic feelings among the children as well as between student and teacher. Children should learn to appreciate the beauties of nature and, especially, the emotional gratifications of learning, so they would derive intrinsic, rather than only extrinsic, rewards from their studies.[8] Mann's interest in the benefits of physical and emotional education was not unusual among his generation of reformers, some of whom promoted "the manual labor movement" in schools and colleges for that purpose.[9] Because of his belief in the proper nurture of all the faculties, it is not unreasonable to see in Mann a precursor of John Dewey's concern with the education of the "whole child."

When the human personality was fully formed, however, there could be no doubt that the emotions needed to be subordinated to reason and conscience in the interest of a well-balanced character. Within human nature, after all, were "appetites more ferocious than those which madden the wild beasts of the forest" and "passions more relentless than the vulture's when she swoops upon her prey." Schoolteachers must learn to control these, and show the child how to do so for himself. The goal was usually termed "self-government," defined as "a voluntary compliance with the laws of reason and duty."[10]

Self-government, of course, had a political as well as a psychological meaning. Mann wanted to preserve the constitutional legacy of the Founders and shared their view of human nature. The framers of the Constitution had relied upon institutional checks and balances to limit the amount of damage that passion and selfishness could wreak. But Mann felt that the adoption of universal white manhood suffrage had created an altogether new situation, one in which there were no longer any effective limits on the power of the numerical majority. In this new mass democracy, nothing but mass education could save the polity.[11] By appealing to prudential fears for the future of the republic, Mann regularly supplemented his appeal for the support of education as a humanizing project, an end in itself.

Two of Mann's seminal public addresses show how he marshaled conservative arguments on behalf of humanitarian policies. In 1838 he delivered his lecture on "The Necessity of Education in a Republican Government." Like Abraham Lincoln and Frederick Douglass, Horace Mann was convinced that the perpetuation of free institutions depended upon the subordination of the dangerous passions to the faculties of reason and morality. But in America's fluid society, the inflammatory press, unreasoning political partisanship, and the opportunity for financial speculation all served to excite the passions of the populace, especially "the love of gain and the love of place." Only through universal public education could the people be trained to self-control.[12]

In his Fourth of July Oration of 1842, Mann pursued the same theme with rotund eloquence. "The great experiment of Republicanism,—of the capacity of man for self-government,—is to be tried anew," he observed; but "wherever it has been tried—in Greece, in Rome, in Italy—[it] has failed, through an incapacity in the people to enjoy liberty without abusing it." Latin America offered him other examples of independent republics in which real self-government had proved unable to take root among an uneducated populace. Public education was the only hope. The illiterate, the prejudiced, and those swayed by unreasoning passion were not capable of self-government. Mann's Independence Day address concluded with this ominous peroration: "Licentiousness shall be the liberty; violence and chicanery shall be the law; superstition and craft shall be the religion; and the self-destructive indulgence of all sensual and unhallowed passions shall be the only happiness, of that people who neglect the education of their children."[13]

Mann's devotion to the cause of public education disposed him to admire strong, paternalistic governments that assumed responsibility for the intellectual, moral, and physical welfare of their citizens. A wise statesman was "like a father" to his people; his functions were "not confined to a superintendence and management of the pecuniary or worldly interests of society." "There is a science of moral economy, as well as a science of political economy," Mann declared, "and he is no statesman who has not studied and mastered the former as well as the latter."[14] Mann toured Europe in search of ideas to implement and came away most favorably impressed by the Prussian educational system; his critics suspected him of admiring the Prussian political system as well, though he denied it. Yet if forced to choose between "anarchy and lawlessness" on the one hand and "a government by mere force, however arbitrary and cruel" on the other, Mann did think the latter preferable. But, of course, to educate people to self-government of their "animal and selfish natures" was best of all.[15]

For the past generation, historians have been investigating the relative importance of Lockean liberalism and classical republicanism in American thought. If we analyze Horace Mann's pedagogy and political thought in these terms, we find that he drew on both. Mann's pedagogical methods owed much to Locke. He subscribed to Locke's dictum that "a sound mind in a sound body" expressed the goal of education and emphasized, as Locke did, the importance of early education in providing a wholesome environment to develop human potential in the right directions. He preferred, as Locke did, affectionate authority to corporal punishment.[16] His pedagogical conception of "virtue" included respect for the rights of others (including property rights) and did not emphasize, as classical republicanism did, the martial virtues. Mann's search for a nondogmatic, interdenominational form of Christianity to teach in the public schools bore a striking resemblance to Locke's Latitudinarianism.[17]

Turning from educational to political thought, we find that Mann is very close to classical republicanism in a number of ways. Of course he accepted government by consent, but he regarded it as a problem to which public education provided the solution. He saw education as the responsibility of the state, virtue as the end of education, and citizenship as a crucial aspect of the virtue that education should nurture. His concept of virtue emphasized self-transcendence (unselfishness and love of God) rather than enlightened self-interest. Most conspicuously of all, he shared the classical republicans' preoccupation with safeguarding the polity against the danger of corruption and decay. On the whole, then, Mann seems closer to classical republicanism than were the framers whose handiwork he was trying to preserve.

But it would not have occurred to Mann himself to address the question we have just been considering. The intellectual paradigm he was concerned to implement was neither liberalism nor republicanism, but faculty psychology. He made free use of both Locke and the classical republicans in the pursuit of his objective, and he did not see the two as incompatible alternatives. Whether one looked at the matter from a liberal or a republican point of view, only an educated citizenry could make free institutions work. As this examination of Mann's position shows, Americans did not move smoothly from republicanism to liberalism in a unilinear progression, nor was the process completed by 1789 or even 1815. The sources of American social thought were not confined to Lockean liberalism and classical republicanism, but prominently included faculty psychology.

Massachusetts was undergoing substantial changes during Horace Mann's lifetime, and his attitude toward these changes has been evaluated rather differently by historians. Michael Katz, in a well-known work, has interpreted Mann as supporting industrial capitalism. It is true that Mann welcomed the growth of big business, because he thought that large industrial employers would provide equality of opportunity, reward educated workers, and foster meritocracy. But it is also true, as David Hogan has pointed out, that Mann promoted the Protestant ethic rather than the spirit of capitalism—that is, he believed in character-building hard work but distrusted speculation and tried to discourage competition and cupidity.[18] On the whole, Mann showed less concern over industrialization than he did over immigration. He regarded the need to educate the incoming flood of poor Irish children as a matter of grave urgency: "a foreign people, born and bred and dwarfed under the despotisms of the Old World, cannot be transformed into the full stature of American citizens merely by a voyage across the Atlantic." He worked particularly hard to place the children of migratory immigrant laborers (who moved along with the railroad, canal, and turnpike construction projects) into schools.[19] The personal motives behind Mann's educational crusade were more political than economic—and probably more humanitarian than either.

Among those whom Mann's innovations antagonized were partisan Democrats, some orthodox Christians, some local school boards, and a group of pedagogically conservative schoolmasters. The original Massachusetts Board of Education was appointed by a Whig governor, Edward Everett, and all but one of its members were Whigs. The Board's novel efforts on behalf of statewide standards for school facilities, textbooks, pupil attendance, and teacher qualifications were resented by many local authorities. When the Democrat Marcus Morton was elected governor of Massachusetts in 1839, he encouraged the General Court (state legislature) to abolish both the Board of Education and its new normal schools, but the measure was rejected by the lower house, 245 to 182. At the next election, the Whigs regained their customary control of the statehouse, and Mann could breathe easier.[20]

The opposition to Mann drew much of its strength from resentment against his policy regarding the teaching of religion in the public schools. The Massachusetts Board of Education began with a Unitarian majority; eventually it became somewhat more representative of the religious composition of the state, although in Mann's time all its members were Protestants and several were ministers. Mann never doubted that religious instruction, which was then customary in the public schools, should be continued; it played a central role in the education of the moral sense as he envisioned this.[21] However, Mann, supported by most of the Board, adopted a policy intended to reconcile the need for religious instruction with the diversity of Protestant religious doctrine. This policy prescribed that only those beliefs should be taught in the public schools on which all Protestants were agreed; it resembled the sort of instruction that Franklin had advocated. In the days of more local autonomy, communities had been accustomed to teaching the religion of the local majority in their schools. Now, some resentful religious groups noticed that teaching the religion of the least common denominator was virtually equivalent to teaching Unitarianism; among those complaining were both orthodox Congregationalists and Episcopalians. Mann overcame their protests with the aid of moderate non-Unitarian Protestants.[22] Within a few years of Mann's departure from the Board, this intra-Protestant conflict was overshadowed by another one he did not have to face: the rising dissatisfaction of the Catholic Irish immigrants with nondenominational Protestant public schools. Eventually, of course, the Irish-Americans created a Roman Catholic parochial school system and the public schools became secularized.

Controversies with fellow educators over pedagogy dragged on even longer than political and religious ones. Mann believed in an authoritative, rather than an authoritarian, style of teaching. He wanted the classroom to be a little commonwealth in which students were prepared for republican citizenship; he felt this meant treating them with some measure of respect for their own personhood. Ideally, Mann wanted children to learn because learning was made interesting and became its own reward. In the teaching of reading, he favored recognizing whole words over sounding them out phonetically, partly because it was less tedious and led to quicker satisfactions. Subjects like drawing and music were good for encouraging affective expressiveness. "Emulation," as a system of competitive prizes or incentives was called, he disliked. Corporal punishment he discouraged without ruling it out entirely; it should be an exceptional last resort.[23]

All of these pedagogical views were denounced in two pamphlets published by Mann's critics among the Boston schoolmasters—each of which elicited a pamphlet reply from him.[24] The critics shared Mann's belief in faculty psychology and mental discipline, and they also took as their aim the creation of a "well-balanced character." But, they charged, Mann seemed disposed to coddle children emotionally, leaving them "the weak subjects of passion, rather than rational freemen."[25] This well-documented pedagogical controversy is useful in showing Mann's relation to the spectrum of contemporary educational opinion. If Mann's pedagogy showed the influence of Unitarian ideas of culture, that of his critics displayed the spirit of Calvinist discipline.[26] The critics also complained that by founding the normal schools, Mann had cast doubt on the competence of the existing teachers. The masters noticed with concern that the normal schools intended to recruit more women into the profession; women, since they were paid less than men, were feared as competitors.[27]

In 1848 the grand old statesman of Massachusetts, John Quincy Adams, died of a heart attack while speaking on the floor of the U.S. House of Representatives. To fill the congressional seat that he vacated, the Whig party turned to Horace Mann. Mann won the election and began a new phase of his career. As Secretary of the Board of Education, he had enjoyed the support of both the reform and conservative wings of the Massachusetts Whig party: his universal uplift and humane pedagogy appealed to the reformers, while his classical republicanism reassured the conservatives. In Congress, however, when confronting the issues raised by the proposed Compromise of 1850, Mann sided emphatically with the reformers, the Conscience Whigs, against the Cotton Whigs led by Daniel Webster. Mann's antislavery convictions were also manifested in his legal work of defending, through several prolonged and bitter trials, two white men who had aided the attempted mass escape of seventy-six slaves from the District of Columbia.[28]

Mann's opposition to slavery grew directly out of the same ideological commitments as his views on public education. In his maiden speech to the House of Representatives, after canvassing with a lawyer's thoroughness the legal arguments for the authority of Congress to abolish slavery in the territories, Mann declared that slavery was contrary to human nature: "Enslave a man, and you destroy his ambition, his enterprise, his capacity. In the constitution of human nature, the desire of bettering one's condition is the mainspring of effort." As a result, slavery undermined the work ethic and the ideal of self-improvement. By its unproductivity, slavery kept population density low and thus inhibited the growth of common schools, even for white people.[29]

The congruence between antislavery and Mann's educational philosophy was underscored in the introductory essay he wrote in 1851 for a one-volume collection of his writings and speeches against slavery. The volume is dedicated, and the essay addressed, to "the young men of Massachusetts." The author exhorts the youths to pursue moral principle, not wealth or transitory pleasures, and in this spirit to support the antislavery cause. He concludes with a quotation from Seneca on the nobility of suffering in the cause of virtue. In this document of New England didacticism, waging the crusade against slavery becomes a vehicle for self-improvement.[30]

Because of Mann's opposition to the Compromise of 1850, the Webster faction denied him renomination by the Whig party. He responded by joining the Free Soil party and running for governor on that ticket in 1852. Mann lost, ending his political career. But he was ever ready for a new challenge and assumed one as the first president of the newly founded Antioch College in Yellow Springs, Ohio. There he battled with an inadequate and impractical financial structure, while trying to implement an elective curriculum and coeducation, both of which were controversial innovations. He continued to expound and elaborate his educational philosophy. Amidst these labors, in which he had driven himself to exhaustion, Horace Mann died of an infection in 1859.

Antioch's introduction of coeducation was a logical consequence of Mann's educational philosophy. His ideal for the education of women was essentially the same as that for the education of men: the creation of a balanced character. But just as a balanced character required the improvement (use and development) of the faculties within it, so society as a whole needed the balanced improvement (use and development) of whole individuals composing it. If men were educated and women were not, the social organism would be imbalanced. This was not to say that men and women were interchangeable. Mann believed that women could supply in abundance those aspects of human nature he thought Calvinism had repressed: the kindly, nurturing, and expressive qualities. Society stood in need of these. Some occupations were especially well suited to people with such qualities, and teaching school was one such. The "elevation" of women in modern society brought with it "new duties" as well as new "privileges." Coeducation provided an efficient means of educating women for their personal fulfillment and social service; it benefited the male students as well by exposing them to the civilizing influence of the women.[31]

Mann could rehearse the historic injustices—political, economic, and educational—that women had suffered at the hands of men. He drew the line at extending women the suffrage; still, "the first step which a community desiring most rapidly and certainly to improve itself is bound to take is to improve the physical, mental, and moral condition of its daughters." When this is done, it will "give to the forces of civilization a power superior to [that of men]."[32]

As Mann saw it, education—for women and girls as for men and boys—was the ultimate good cause: while all other reforms were remedial, public education was preventive and would forestall the need for other reforms. In the same spirit that Woodrow Wilson would later wage a war to end wars, Horace Mann crusaded for education as the reform to end reforms. Public education could be the means designed by Providence to usher in the millennium, the promised Kingdom of God on earth.[33]

?◦ DOROTHEA DIX

Dorothea Dix (1802–1887) personified the role that Horace Mann envisioned for the enlightened educated woman. She raised the moral level of society by promoting redemptive institutions: asylums for the mentally ill, where they might be restored to their proper balance of character. To maximize her own effectiveness, Dix self-consciously constructed a public image for herself. She took as her model the uplifting, nurturing image of womanhood effectively portrayed for her generation by the moral philosopher of domesticity, Catharine Beecher.[34]

Dorothea Dix's vision of the social role of women was predicated on a distinctive view of female human nature that was coming into acceptance during the nineteenth century. The historian Nancy Cott has named this Victorian vision of womanhood "passionlessness," because it held that the dangerous passions were weaker in women's nature than in men's. This model of woman's character stands in marked contrast to the older, traditional image of women as passionate and corrupting. "The positive contribution of passionlessness," Cott points out, "was to replace that sexual/carnal characterization of women with a spiritual/moral one, allowing women to develop their human faculties and their self-esteem."[35] The model also gave women a special role to play in the social subordination of passion to reason. Dorothea Dix took up this challenge.

The public *persona* that Dix cultivated did not entirely correspond to the woman behind it. Dix was not simply the mild, nurturing figure representative of the "passionless" ideology. No one could have been, who achieved what Dix did: to challenge custom and publicize a widespread injustice, to lobby successfully with some twenty state legislatures, to found or substantially expand some thirty-two insane asylums across the United States and Canada. She also toured thirteen European countries on behalf of her cause. Her friend and admirer Horace Mann described her accomplishments in a way that hinted at her toughness while celebrating what Victorians would have called her true womanhood. "Miss Dix has won as many legislatures as Napoleon ever subdued kingdoms; and her sweet voice, thrilling from that deep heart in whose sacred recesses all the moanings of the insane are echoed, translates the celestrial languages of benevolence and duty to men, and thus accomplishes what imperial guards and Pretorian Cohorts could never achieve."[36]

The woman who embraced the ideal of "passionlessness" had powerful passions of her own which she successfully sublimated into devotion to her cause. Stern, bossy, and tenacious, she nevertheless knew how to exploit the conventional image of meek womanhood for political advantage.[37] Both in the mental health profession and in the Civil War Army nurse corps, plenty of men and women were intimidated by Dorothea Dix's dominating personality and influential political connections. Yet she remained scrupulously aloof from all women's rights and antislavery agitation, and hewed to a strict standard of feminine modesty that has made it difficult for biographers to find out about her personal life.[38]

Dorothea Dix was the neglected daughter of an alcoholic Methodist circuit-riding preacher and an invalid mother; from the age of twelve on, she was reared by her paternal grandparents. While still a teenager, she got a job as a schoolteacher; a former pupil remembered her as a disciplinarian quick to resort to the birch.[39] Like many other women of her day she poured out her feelings in letters; Dix's epistolary friendships with Anne Heath and Elizabeth Palmer Peabody provide much of what we know about her life.[40] Peabody was the private secretary of William Ellery Channing, and through her Dix came into contact with the eminent Unitarian divine.

In 1827 Dr. Channing invited Dix to tutor his children. Before long he had become her friend and religious mentor as well as employer. Unitarian Christianity provided Dix with an orderly universe where she could begin to feel secure and accepted; God cared about her and the development of her potential. But if Unitarianism was reassuring, it also entailed an ideology and sensibility of emotional control different from her father's Methodist enthusiasm. Dix became part of the circle of Unitarian reformers that included Horace Mann and his wife Mary Peabody Mann (Elizabeth Peabody's sister), as well as Charles Sumner and Samuel and Julia Howe. All were concerned to foster the improvement or perfection of the individual by means of social reform.

Dix tried her hand at writing—hymns, poems, meditations, a reference work for schoolteachers, didactic children's stories, even a compilation of quotations about flowers—but found nothing that really engaged her. She suffered from illness and recurrent depressions. In 1836 she took a trip to England on the advice of her physician and friends; there she stayed with the wealthy, philanthropic family of the Liverpool Unitarian William Rathbone. The Rathbones nursed Dix back to emotional health and introduced her to their own circle of reformers, among whom was Samuel Tuke, a Quaker known for his work with the insane at an asylum called York Retreat. Tuke offered her intellectual inspiration, and the Rathbones, a practical example of how "moral treatment" for emotional problems could help a patient like herself.[41]

Once she was back in America, Horace Mann considered appointing Dix to an administrative post at his new Lexington Normal School, but her proposed regimen of rules looked unworkably strict, so he withdrew the offer.[42] Dix externalized her concern with controlling and redeeming herself into a virtual obsession with controlling and redeeming others. The mentally ill were better suited to be her clients than college students were.[43]

In 1841, following a first-hand observation of conditions in the East Cambridge Jail, where insane inmates were incarcerated along with criminals, debtors, and vagrants, Dix publicly took up the cause of hospitalization for the mentally ill. After she had presented the prototype of her many famous memorials, graphically depicting the deplorable conditions under which some of the insane were confined, and following spirited debate in both the legislature and the press, the Massachusetts General Court (state legislature) passed in March of 1843 an appropriation to expand hospitalization and therapeutic work with the insane.[44] The Napoleon of reform had won the first of her campaigns.

Dorothea Dix was a publicist and what we would call a lobbyist, not a physician or psychiatric researcher. But she had ideas about the nature of madness. In her approach to the subject, she relied on the conventional faculty psychology of her day, derived from Scottish-American moral philosophy. This was not actually very different from the description given more than a century before by the versatile authors of *Cato's Letters,* who had attributed madness to disordered passions. More immediately, Dix's model resembled that presented by her contemporary Thomas Cogswell Upham, the Bowdoin College moral philosopher who wrote about mental disease for the lay public.[45] The causes of insanity were seldom organic, Dix believed, but more commonly a breakdown of the proper relationships among the mental faculties. Mental health was dependent on the integration of the faculties; mental illness was a condition of "shattered harmonies."[46] Sometimes the overindulgence of a passion could lead to the consumption of harmful substances like alcohol and tobacco, in which case physical harm compounded the psychological difficulties. Dix campaigned energetically against both alcohol and tobacco as contributing to mental illness.[47]

Like her friend Horace Mann, Dix worried about the psychosocial costs of America's free enterprise capitalism and fascination with social mobility. She believed that anxiety induced by competition was responsible for much insanity. She offered what she thought was evidence for this: "politicians and merchants are peculiarly liable to insanity," as were immigrants, exposed to American competitive capitalism for the first time. On the other hand, she believed that American Indians and slaves, who stood outside the competitive system, suffered less. In attributing insanity to anxiety over competition, Dix was following the respected American physician Amariah Brigham.[48]

Orthodox eighteenth-century therapies for madness had been generally somatic and (as Alan Bennett's historical drama *The Madness of George III* recounts) often horrific. The newer interpretation of madness that Dix endorsed, derived from faculty psychology, emphasized psychic rather than physical causes, laying the basis for new therapies. The problem was often seen as an excess of passion. (Sometimes religious enthusiasm was blamed.)[49] Since the faculties of insane persons were out of order, for them the issue of self-improvement came down to that of self-control. "Much of the essential difference between sanity and insanity consists in the degree of self-control exercised," declared the administrators of a Kentucky asylum that Dix supported.[50]

Therapeutic methods with which Dix sympathized tried to create psychological controls within the patient. Dix learned about the methods from the English Quakers at the York Retreat; they in turn were following in the footsteps of the famous French psychiatrist of the Revolutionary era, Philippe Pinel (1745–1826). Pinel had developed his ideas on the treatment of the insane within a framework of faculty psychology similar to that of his Scottish contemporaries. The techniques were called "moral treatment" because they derived from moral philosophy and addressed what the moral philosophers defined as the "active powers" (that is, motives, especially emotions) rather than the "intellectual powers" (that is, faculties of perception and memory).[51] The most important therapeutic principle followed was that of balancing the passions. Therapies for opposing and balancing the disordered passions were elaborated by Pinel's student Jean-Etienne-Dominique Esquirol. For example, the therapist might try to make a depressed patient happy or teach a jealous one trust. Patients were managed by giving and witholding privileges; coercive restraints like straitjackets were used only occasionally as a means of teaching the patient self-control.[52] In America, the methods of moral treatment were being promoted by Dix's contemporary Edward Jarvis, a well-known alienist.[53]

Practitioners of moral treatment preferred to have their therapy carried on in an institutional setting where the patient would be isolated from the anxieties that had presumably disordered the faculties.[54] The word "asylum," of course, means "refuge." The asylum was ideally intended to be a home away from home. The setting would resemble that of a family, in which the therapists played the role of parents and the mentally ill patients that of children. (Michel Foucault, in a typically elliptic turn of phrase, has commented that Tuke's York Retreat "isolated the social structure of the bourgeois family, reconstituted it symbolically in the asylum, and set it adrift in history.")[55] In such an environment, it was hoped that even those residents who could not be cured would at least benefit from caring. Even well-to-do families of patients were willing to commit mentally ill loved ones to asylums where moral treatment was practiced, since they felt reassured that domestic values would be preserved.[56]

Dix and the reformers of her persuasion preferred to have their asylums located in rural areas, partly for the sake of isolation and calm, but also in order for the patients to be able to engage in agricultural work as a form of therapy. "No form of labor appears so well calculated to promote the comfort and restoration of such patients as have had habits of employment, as working on a farm."[57] The therapy of agricultural labor encapsulates perfectly the ambivalence with which the reformers regarded the industrial revolution. On the one hand habits of steady work were a means to self-improvement. (An historian of British psychiatry in this period comments aptly: "The ideas most closely related to those of the moral managers were popularized by Samuel Smiles," the author of *Self-Help*.)[58] On the other hand, industrial capitalism seemed anxiety-provoking and dehumanizing. Like Horace Mann and the writers of the self-help manuals, Dorothea Dix looked for salvation to the Protestant ethic rather than to the spirit of capitalism.

The best-known work on nineteenth-century American insane asylums is David J. Rothman, *The Discovery of the Asylum,* first published in 1971 and reissued with a new introduction in 1990. In it Rothman rightly pointed out that the founders of insane asylums were preoccupied with issues of order and control; he usefully related asylums to the other correctional institutions that were being founded at the same time, such as penitentiaries, reform schools, and workhouses. With regard to several important issues, however, the book has been superseded. As Mary Ann Jimenez makes clear, the colonial policy of laissez-faire toward mental illness had already come to an end around the start of the nineteenth century. By Dix's day, the issue was not whether the insane should be incarcerated; they already were. The question had become whether they should remain confined in places that were merely custodial (and often brutal) or be relocated in institutions offering some hope of treatment and cure. Also, despite Rothman's insistence that American asylums were a response to distinctively American social conditions, David Gollaher has demonstrated that Americans like Dix drew heavily on transatlantic ideas and experience in implementing their own belated reforms.[59] Finally, Rothman's book gives no hint that the founding of the asylums was a controversial political issue.

Dix's asylum program was readily compatible with the reform agenda of the international evangelical movement and the government activism of the Whig party. Jacksonian Democrats, in contrast, looked upon such plans as the creation of paternalistic elitists, threatening to American customs of low taxes and local autonomy. Ralph Waldo Emerson, a perceptive if detached observer of the American political scene, satirized the Whig outlook as that of an officious physician "whose social frame is a hospital." He dresses everyone in "slippers & flannels, with bib & pap spoon," and prescribes "pills & herb tea, whig preaching, whig poetry, whig philosophy, [and] whig marriages."[60] In Dorothea Dix, Emerson's metaphor of Whiggery attained something like literal truth.

For years Dorothea Dix traveled about the United States, lobbying with one legislature after another to create or expand asylums for the insane. Because the mentally ill were being housed in a variety of institutions, Dix was occasionally drawn into addressing problems of prisons and almshouses as well as asylums. Each legislature in turn received her concentrated attention and increasingly well organized publicity campaign. A Unitarian herself, Dix crafted her religious rhetoric to appeal to evangelicals of every theological stripe: "Raise up the fallen, console the afflicted, defend the helpless, minister to the poor, reclaim the transgressor, be benefactors of mankind!"[61] But religion was not the only weapon in her arsenal. The rhetoric of her memorials ran the gamut of sensationalism, statistics, and appeals to both morality and practicality, leavened with self-deprecating references to her own weak womanhood.[62]

By 1848 Dix felt ready to take on Congress. She set up headquarters in Washington and petitioned for a bill that would grant 5 million acres of federally owned public land to the states, with the provision that the proceeds from their sale should go to finance insane asylums. On June 27, 1848, she formally presented her memorial to Congress, a powerful recapitulation of the arguments she had been developing over the years.[63] The contents of her bill embodied Whig principles of federal intervention, internal improvement projects, and relatively high prices for public lands. Dix did not write off Democratic members, however; she lobbied them with appeals on behalf of the weak and powerless.[64]

Congress proved a tough nut to crack, and for several years Dix was forced to divide her time between her national effort in Washington and trips to various southern legislative capitols to keep up the pressure at the state level. By staying well away from antislavery and women's rights issues, she preserved her credibility in the slave states, though she endorsed such causes as temperance, prison reform, and care for the deaf-and-dumb. (As a prison reformer Dix endorsed solitary confinement—the Philadelphia System—as a means of overcoming criminals' "outbreaks of passion.")[65]

But Dix's efforts to help the insane at the federal level were doomed to failure. Even the succession of her close personal friend Millard Fillmore to the presidency in 1850 did not bring Dix her looked-for success; though her bill passed the Senate in Fillmore's first Congress and the House in his second, her opponents took advantage of the sectional debate to sidetrack it. (Fillmore did at least get an insane asylum established in the District of Columbia.) Finally, in 1854, with traditional party lines crumbling and many northern Democrats grown less unsympathetic to internal improvements, enough Democratic votes could be added to the core of Whig support for the measure. A bill providing 10 million acres for Dix's purposes passed both houses of Congress, only to be vetoed by Franklin Pierce, a self-styled neo-Jacksonian strict constructionist. "I can not find any authority in the Constitution for making the Federal Government the great almoner of public charity throughout the United States," the Democratic President declared in his veto message. Dix herself, a canny political analyst, laid the blame on Pierce's confidant and Secretary of War, Jefferson Davis.[66] Few Democrats were willing to defy their President once Pierce had taken a position, and the veto could not be overridden. Care and treatment of the mentally ill would remain a responsibility of the states.

When the Civil War came, Dix was called into service as Superintendent of [female] Nurses for the Union Army, a post that involved both recruiting and administrative responsibilities. To the last, Dix had hoped the war could be avoided, and when it came she grieved for the men under her care. Dix worried about the moral standards of the women she recruited, and insisted on "matronly" women over 35, with "habits of neatness, order, sobriety, and industry."[67] Partly because her own authority was ill-defined, she quarreled constantly with other authorities, whether doctors, military commanders, or the civilians of the U. S. Sanitary Commission. Her talents for exposing horrors came back into play when when she investigated the condition of returned Union prisoners of war and reports of atrocities in Confederate prison camps.[68]

It could be argued that Dix was too successful for the long-term good of her insane clients. Earlier philanthopists had concentrated their attention on particular groups of the insane, but Dix generalized her efforts, just as Mann worked for the education of all children. By promoting a climate of opinion in favor of hospitalizing all mentally ill patients, she helped create a situation in which mental institutions became overcrowded with people whom the authorities had little hope of curing and in whom they took little interest. And once the insane were out of sight, it suited the convenience of society to keep them there whether they were benefiting or not. Dix lived long enough to witness some of these problems for herself. She ended her days residing, "more as guest than patient," at an asylum in New Jersey she had helped to found.[69]

In the long run, the institutions Dix promoted tended to deteriorate into merely custodial situations not unlike the ones from which she had rescued people decades earlier. Physically, the asylums came to resemble warehouses more than rural havens of domestic care. This irony should not lead us into confusing Dix's original reform impulse with its later corruption. Responsibility for the declining quality of mental care in the postbellum era probably rests more with par-simonious legislatures and the harsher outlook of the mental health professionals of that generation than with flaws in Dix's own human-itarianism.[70]

❧ HORACE BUSHNELL

Among the most profound of all the thinkers who pondered the con-struction of the self in antebellum America was Horace Bushnell

(1802–1876), Congregational minister in Hartford, Connecticut. Bushnell was a leader in a massive shift of attention among American social thinkers away from the universal aspects of human nature and toward the particular effects of nurture. But he was not without interest in human nature itself; he developed a new paradigm for conceptualizing human nature in which the unconscious played a major part. Long before Freud, he recognized the importance of early childhood and the power of parents over the personalities of their children, as well as the turbulent depths of the unconscious mind. And although his contemporaries considered his theology liberal, his social thought was that of a Burkean conservative.[71]

Bushnell had much in common with Horace Mann and Dorothea Dix, since like them he was concerned with the construction of other selves.[72] However, unlike the other two, he worked not from a basis in the Unitarian humanism of Massachusetts Bay, but out of the Calvinist Connecticut Valley tradition that had included Jonathan Edwards. While the evangelical Calvinist moral philosophers would have agreed with the need to train the human faculties, they had tended to put more emphasis upon controlling them, that is, on self-discipline. The Unitarian thinkers emphasized the positive development of the faculties: in Channing's term, self-culture. As John Witherspoon had reconciled the Calvinist tradition with faculty psychology, Bushnell reconciled the Calvinist tradition with the nurture of the faculties. In doing so he also considerably modified the inheritance of the Scottish moral philosophers.

The starting point of Bushnell's line of thought was his critique of revivals of religion. Bushnell believed that revivalism, intended to elicit decisions for Christ, overemphasized individualism and conscious choice as the basis of personal religion. "The Holy Spirit works by indirection," he declared, "by siege, not by fiat." Although his line of argument forced him to dissent from the great Edwards, Bushnell accepted this necessity.[73] He was convinced that religious attitudes were more effectively transmitted as part of a total cultural heritage and personality structure, acquired by imperceptible degrees and without conscious reflection during childhood. The proper context for winning souls to Christ was therefore not the revival tent but the family hearth. The objective of Bushnell's most famous work, *Christian Nurture,* was to show how early conditioning, accomplished before the development of independent judgment, could effectively preempt the need for revivals. "The child is to grow up a Christian, and never know himself as being otherwise."[74]

Of course, Channing and his Arminian precursors had long criticized revivals too. Channing's ideal of "self-culture," the gradual development of character by the individual himself, had also been intended as an alternative to dependence on sudden conversion experiences induced by revival preaching. Horace Mann too thought it was not safe to let children grow up sinful, while waiting for a preacher to convert them.[75] Bushnell shared the Unitarians' distrust of enthusiasm in religion. But he realized that the shaping of character begins far earlier than they had suspected, that much of it is unconscious, and that it is largely determined by the parents of children. So, while the Unitarians looked to the school, or to remedial institutions for adults, Bushnell emphasized the nursery at home.

The Unitarians' rejection of the evangelical model of conversion did not entail a rejection of evangelical voluntarism, but Bushnell's argument against revivalism was strongly antivoluntaristic. The essence of religion was conveyed in early childhood, he believed, before people ever acquired free will or moral responsibility. As a result, a Christian character was truly a divine gift that the individual did not earn on his or her own. Human beings stood in need of divine regeneration, but the channel of grace through which this intervention came was not the revival preacher but their parents.[76] In this way, Bushnell remained loyal to the Calvinist doctrine of original sin and the theological tradition of the Connecticut Valley, despite his criticisms of Edwards. One difference between him and Edwards was that Bushnell could explain saving grace without recourse to supernatural agency.

Like Edwards before him, Bushnell devoted considerable attention to criticizing the doctrine of free will. But whereas Edwards attacked free will with formal logic, Bushnell attacked it with psychology. Bushnell minimized the power of conscious choice in our lives. Actions that people take in adulthood, apparently out of conscious choice, often have their ultimate origins in unconscious attitudes acquired during childhood. "What they do not remember remembers them," he wrote. "What was before unconscious flames out into consciousness."[77]

Bushnell had been deeply influenced by Coleridge's *Aids to Reflection in the Formation of a Manly Character, on the Several Grounds of Prudence, Morality, and Religion* (1825). As the title indicates, this was a work of moral philosophy, but presented in the form of cryptic "aphorisms" that rejected Lockeanism in favor of a modified Kantianism. Samuel Taylor Coleridge (1772–1834) drew a distinction between Understanding, a faculty that comprehended empirical knowledge, and Reason, a faculty that intuited moral principles. Through the fragmentary poetic utterances of the *Aids,* Coleridge taught that religion belonged to the realm of Reason rather than to that of Understanding. It is difficult, at this remove in time, for us to appreciate the powerful impact of these aphorisms in a cultural context in which moral philosophy was central to intellectual life. The Vermont moral philosopher, James Marsh, reprinted Coleridge's book in America with a long interpretive introduction that adapted the Anglican poet's reflections to the needs of American Calvinists.[78] Inspired by this new philosophical Romanticism, Bushnell proceeded to elaborate it into an even more adventursome reinterpretation of the Christian tradition and a new theory of the construction of human identity.

Bushnell embraced a metaphysical dualism of mind and matter. Understanding gave us knowledge of the material world; Reason, that of the spiritual. Conventional logic was limited in its applicability to the realm of Understanding. Theology was poetry; doctrine was meant to be interpreted symbolically.[79] Orthodox Calvinists were horrified; some attempted to have Bushnell tried for heresy before an ecclesiastical tribunal but were frustrated in this intention.

Bushnell asserted that because religion was known to Reason and not to Understanding, it did not have to be taught as a set of doctrines; indeed, it did not even need to wait upon the development of language. One could begin to inculcate religion as early as infancy, as a set of emotional responses—faith, trust, love—antedating any formal verbal instruction. Bushnell divided childhood into two stages, the early "age of impressions," and the "age of tuitional impulses," which came only after language comprehension. The first was the more important. "Let every Christian father and mother understand, when their child is three years old, that they have done more than half of all they will ever do for his character."[80]

According to Bushnell's epistemological doctrine, the power of the unconscious mind was exerted through Reason, while Understanding was limited in its scope to that of which we are conscious. All our lives are lived in two societies, using two different languages, he explained. There is "voluntary society," in which we are conscious of our purposes and say what we mean. But there is also an "involutary society," in which we are unconscious of our motives and communicate through "the look, the gait, the motion, the tone or cadence." Through the language of involuntary society, those with whom we come in contact are ever influencing us without either party being necessarily aware of it.[81]

Bushnell's *Christian Nurture* was the most sophisticated of many child-rearing manuals and other books for or about children published in the generation leading up to the Civil War. Some of these writings were religious, some secular; some were fiction, some poetry; some directed to parents, some to educators. The flow of this river of print was in the direction of treating children less harshly and respecting their personhood more. Bushnell's *Christian Nurture* provided a comprehensive, sophisticated rationale for this vast, inchoate shift in attitudes.[82] The book propounded a comprehensive theory of the socialization of the child and the inculcation of values. It is not enough to say that parents can "influence" their children, Bushnell insisted: parents possess "organic power"—a determining force that they exercise whether they try to or not. "A power is exerted by parents over children, not only when they teach, encourage, persuade, and govern, but without any purposed control whatever. The bond is so intimate that they do it unconsciously and undesignedly."[83]

Bushnell's advice to parents on how best to discharge their awesome responsibility resembled Mann's advice to teachers: be authoritative but not authoritarian. Bushnell did not want the family run like "a little popedom," that is, autocratically. In his emphasis upon the need for discipline, he showed a firm commitment to social and psychological control, but in his advice on the form that discipline should take, he consistently opposed overt repression or coercion. While continuing to believe in original sin, that is, that children needed redemption from evil propensities, Bushnell felt redemption came best in a gradual, unobtrusive way that respected the autonomy of the subject. The purpose of Christian nurture was to control the child, and to do so in such a way that when he grew up he would control himself. If the parents conditioned the child properly, he would grow up feeling "a ready delight in authority."[84]

When it came to religious training, Bushnell believed that parents should try to convey a "feeling" rather than a "doctrine." Example is far more important than precept, he insisted over and over again. The parental image itself imparted the germ of religion in the mind of the child, "personating God," so it was important that the authority figure should be loving. Then, "when the unseen Father and Lord is Himself discovered, there is to be a piety made ready for him."[85]

Bushnell included an extensive defense of the practice of infant baptism in his book. The American evangelical tradition, in its preoccupation with a conversion experience in adulthood, had long obscured the significance of infant baptism. Many Protestants had come to believe that only fully consenting adults should be baptized; indeed, this was the distinguishing mark of the Baptist denominations. Bushnell, however, could justify baptizing infants into the faith of their parents in view of the "organic unity" between them. He rejected any "superstitious" belief that the rite opened the gate of heaven, but he did feel it constituted an appropriate solemnization of the parents' responsibility toward their new child.[86]

If one can identify a single overall objective of Bushnell's theology, it would be *comprehensiveness*. He wanted to transcend the sectarian divisions and dogmatic debates that have plagued Protestantism since the Reformation. The point was to affirm the social order and make the church reinforce it—a task a divided church could not perform. Bushnell conceived of Congregationalism as a kind of American national church, not enmeshed with the government as was the Church of England, but nevertheless embodying, as Coleridge claimed Anglicanism did, the national character in its sacred dimension.[87] Because the family (rather than the individual) was the true unit of society, he envisioned both church and state as the family writ large. The church would nurture the adult's continued growth in character as parents had done earlier; "the church is to her disciples a perpetual school of character." Acting together, church and state should assume responsibility for the corporate nature of national life and nurture a national culture and a national character.[88]

Where the political tradition of Jefferson and Jackson had focused on the most self-sufficient persons—adult white males—Bushnell took as the center of his own attention the person who was most obviously dependent on the social matrix: the child. For him, the child was symbol of the man; the extreme dependence of the infant, "a type of universal want." Instead of considering society to be the creation of individuals, as the dominant social contract theory did, Bushnell saw the individual as the creation of society. The family was the locus where individual personalities were socially determined.[89]

In Bushnell's thinking, society was as much a unified organism as the family, and in need of constant moral "improvement" just as the individual was. In the same way that an individual should try to order his faculties and be thrifty and productive, so a community should strive to be well regulated, moral, "enterprising, hopeful." The goal of national life and therefore of government should be the nurture of the whole personalities of the citizenry, not simply their virtue narrowly defined, still less their mere economic prosperity. Taken together, these whole personalities created a social organism. The state should promote the development of *"the total value of the people"* (his italics). The end of government "includes the natural capacity, the industry, the skill, the science, the bravery, the loyalty, the moral and religious worth of the people."[90]

But far from being an easy optimist about social progress, Bushnell thought that progress was highly problematic and degeneration a very real threat. Indeed, one of his most provocative essays on American society bears the title, "Barbarism the First Danger."[91] In his concern with preserving national virtue against barbarism, Bushnell perpetuated the Atlantic republican tradition, though he is even closer in spirit to Romantic nationalists such as Edmund Burke, J. G. von Herder, and the American Rufus Choate (who combined his own conservative Romanticism with civic humanism.)[92] Institutions of balanced government were no safeguard against degeneration; Bushnell looked instead to religion, patriotism, virtuous manners, and the strength of the family.

The central figure in the family was the mother. To Bushnell, it was obvious that the lion's share of parental responsibility rested with her. The Christian nurture she provided was essential to proper character-formation. She was the guardian of cultural and moral values, their transmitter to the next generation. Like Horace Mann and Dorothea Dix, Bushnell accepted Catharine Beecher's definition of what constituted woman's sphere.

One important part of women's sphere as thus defined was polite culture, which included both good manners and good taste. These were moral imperatives and even spiritual qualities for Bushnell. In Victorian America, as Richard Bushman has pointed out, "refinement was less and less experienced as an artificial imposition, at war with the natural person hidden behind the masquerade of fashionable dress. Refinement was a personal quality like courage or kindness, ingrained in one's character and among the most admirable of virtues."[93] Women were the refiners of society, who nurtured good manners and good taste in the next generation.

Bushnell sharply distinguished "taste," a love of beauty that humanity shared with God Himself, from mere "fashion," a proud, snobbish, and exclusive attitude. While "fashion" was "unrepublican," "taste" was a divine quality. In ascribing aesthetic taste to God, Bushnell was following in the footsteps of Jonathan Edwards. In distinguishing "taste" from "fashion," he showed how far middle-class polite culture had come from its remote origins in the royal courts of Europe, and how democratized it had become. Like David Hume, Bushnell saw good manners and good taste as indices of the progress of society.[94] If they discharged their role as custodians of manners and taste, women could lead society to ever higher levels of civilization and away from barbarism.

Bushnell's logic was clear. The family was all-important to the progress of the human race, and the mother was all-important to the family. That was why women had to remain primarily domestic in their concerns—even though he was willing to define this domesticity broadly, to include participation in moral reforms. Bushnell endorsed Mann's experiment with coeducation and even supported women's entry into some of the professions (for example, all medical specialties except surgery). He showed considerable sensitivity to the legal wrongs women endured and supported their claims to equal property rights in marriage. But women's suffrage he declared "a reform against nature," which would pervert the faculties of women's nature and threaten to plunge society into a new Dark Age. Of course, he rejected the natural rights philosophy on which the Seneca Falls Convention based the claim to women's suffrage.[95]

Bushnell did not think of the family as a simply a "haven in a heartless world." He thought of it as the nursery of the next generation, and thus the source of whatever stability or improvement or redemption the world could expect.[96] By contrast, electoral politics were corrupting. Like many American intellectuals of his day and since, Horace Bushnell despised partisan politics and the deals struck by politicians.[97] For women to compromise their civilizing role in order to participate in electoral politics would transform them, in his eyes, from part of the solution to part of the problem.

For Bushnell, American institutions, like Americans themselves, were the products of history and culture; in fact, they drew their legitimacy from this. The Constitution of the United States, he argued, embodied the nation's historical experience and owed its authority to this, not to popular sovereignty or the consent of the majority. It would be just as legitimate if it were unwritten, like the British Constitution. Government "may be hereditary, or elective, parliamentary, or imperial; it has a divine right in one form as truly as in another, if only it rules historically, and not mechanically."[98]

When the Civil War erupted, Bushnell interpreted secession as demonstrating the anarchic implications of Jefferson's contractual political theory. The suffering of the war itself he viewed as a form of national redemption for collective guilt—much as Lincoln also did.[99] Bushnell welcomed the rise of the Republican party, which by taking a tough stand against the arrogance of the slave power awakened in him a new interest in politics. He remained a loyal supporter of Grant when many other intellectuals were supporting Greeley in 1872.[100] Even so, the corruption of the Grant administration did not encourage Bushnell to revise his low estimate of the quality of American political life.

For all his distinctiveness, Bushnell still displays essential continuities with the tradition we have been examining in this book. He had been trained at Yale in the philosophy of the Scottish Enlightenment and shared many of the concerns of its thinkers. They too had felt somewhat disillusioned with politics and looked to cultural influences as an alternative means to accomplish their social goals. They too had stressed the power of manners and culture as opposed to that of conscious policy-making. They too had valued the importance of women as shapers of manners and culture. They had been moving toward an organic conception of society such as the one he adopted. Kames, like Bushnell, had taught that culture was prior to personality and shaped decisions that the individual imagined were freely chosen.[101] What we find in Bushnell is the pressing of such tendencies within the Scottish tradition to the point where they merge into Romanticism; this is why he found Coleridge so stimulating.

Although Bushnell came to reject altogether the possibility that conscious reason could ever control the emotions, he did not abandon faculty psychology. Surprisingly enough, in view of his recognition of the importance of the unconscious, Bushnell continued to endorse balance of character as an objective and to warn of the danger of uncontrolled passion. One of his objections to the conduct of American politics was the frenetic emotionalism of election campaigns, which he disliked for the same reason he disliked religious revivals, and which he feared was unbalancing the national character.[102]

Although Bushnell rejected the doctrine of natural rights and the social compact, he by no means rejected the Enlightenment altogether. Indeed, he defined religion as nonrational (in the usual sense of the term) precisely in order to avoid a conflict between it and secular thought. By endorsing the Coleridgean division between Reason and Understanding, he liberated secular thought from the control of biblical or creedal literalism. Most importantly, Bushnell preserved the Enlightenment's high value on the worth of the individual. It was to free individuals from evangelical humiliation and from the passions of revivalism that he undertook his project of Christian nurture. His solicitude for children and his humane program of child-rearing formed part of the expanding nineteenth-century concern with kindness and sympathy for the weak.[103] Bushnell, like Mann, represents one aspect of an American tradition of humane concern with education and child-rearing that eventuates in John Dewey.[104]

Bushnell is best viewed as working out of the same set of preoccupations as John Witherspoon, who sought to reconcile Reformed religion with Enlightenment rationalism and polite culture. Whereas Witherspoon tried to effect that reconciliation through *synthesis,* Bushnell tried to effect it through defining *separate spheres* for religion and the Understanding (analogous, in some ways, to the separate spheres of the two genders). But like Witherspoon, Bushnell saw the formation of Christian and polite character as central to the project.

While he cannot be termed either an individualist or a political liberal, Bushnell continued the typically American preoccupation with the conscious construction of character. Like Franklin, he believed in the importance of habit and early conditioning—carrying these beyond anything Franklin would have imagined. But Bushnell shifted the focus of the undertaking by one generation. Addressing a predominantly middle-class audience of people who had successfully made themselves, he showed them how to continue the process of self-formation into the formation of their children's personalities. Indeed, since so much of character-formation occurs in early childhood, one can do even more to shape one's child's character than one's own.

The intended outcome of Bushnell's educational project was much the same as that of Horace Mann or indeed of Thomas Jefferson: a morally responsible, emotionally stable, good Christian citizen.[105] The ultimate paradox in Bushnell's thinking, then, is that he uses nonrational techniques of emotional conditioning in early childhood to create adults who will be rational, responsible beings.

Dorothea Dix, we have seen, was a humanitarian reformer whose life-work later took on repressive forms that she had not intended. Bushnell's ideas too were put to uses that he did not intend. Although he was largely uninvolved in the social reforms of his day, the "social gospel" preachers of the next generation found Bushnell's writings on the organic nature of society a welcome resource in their efforts to mitigate laissez-faire and foster a sense of corporate responsibility for the unfortunate.[106] Still more ironically, the argument that personality is largely shaped in early childhood would be used in later generations to undercut individual moral responsibility, an implication from his work that Bushnell himself would have deplored and resisted.

✺ PART III

The Cultivation of the
Self Among the
New England Romantics

The Platonic Quest in New England

This chapter is about a particular kind of self-cultivation: the pursuit of spiritual self-transcendence. Unlike many other mysticisms, this one did not despair at the corruption of the world but expressed rather the opposite attitude: a boundless optimism that believed all things possible—even the attainment of the divine. Still more remarkably, it appeared where one might least expect to find mysticism: in a prosperous young nation, within a region where the market revolution was far advanced, and among members of a religious denomination dedicated to thoroughgoing rationalism.

The closest thing to a modern intellectual community in the antebellum United States was a little group of writers and lecturers living in the northeastern corner of Massachusetts. In Boston they had connections with business, politics, and organized religion; in Cambridge, with Harvard University. In the village of Concord they approximated a tiny intelligentsia. To a person, the members of the group were either Unitarians or former Unitarians. Some of them would also have called themselves Transcendentalists, because they sought to transcend the material world in communion with the divine. The group are of historical interest as social critics, opinion leaders, and reformers, but above all for their literary achievements, their contributions to what has been called an American Renaisssance, a body of artistic work that has not ceased to engage the American literate public from their day to ours.

Two of the most salient characteristics of the literature created by
the New England Transcendentalists are its Romanticism and its
endorsement of democracy. Romanticism as a self-concious movement
came to America belatedly and from outside (one of its leading
importers and proponents was Margaret Fuller); it taught Americans to
value qualities of intuition and feeling that the conventional rationalist
model of faculty psychology had generally subordinated. Sometimes, as
in Fuller's case, American Romantics significantly altered the model of
faculty psychology they had inherited from the Enlightenment. More
often, however, they retained the model but emphasized the role of the
emotions within it. The emotions they most favored were the sentiments—that is, feelings of attachment to abstract principles like patriotism, honor, and religion—and the affections—that is, benevolent
feelings toward other persons, including God.

The democratic character of American Transcendentalism was evident not only in its celebration of the emotions with which everyone
was endowed but also in its celebration of the potential for self-
development possessed by everyone. To understand this body of literature, it is essential to understand the importance that its creators
attached to individual self-definition and self-expression. F. O.
Matthiessen captured the point when he chose the daguerrotype of
Donald O. McKay, master shipbuilder, for the frontispiece of his great
literary history, *American Renaissance.* McKay, Matthiessen wrote, typified "the common man in his heroic dimension." (As a designer of
clipper ships for the China trade, McKay also typified the market
revolution going on at the time.) McKay was, in his own way, as much
a creative artist as were the Concord intellectuals—and they knew it.[1]

The community of which the Transcendentalists were members
intensified the concern with self-improvement that was widespread in
the America of their time, placing it at the very center of both their
personal lives and their art. Ralph Waldo Emerson's Phi Beta Kappa
Address of 1837, "The American Scholar," which may be considered
their manifesto, attempts to define the identity to which they themselves aspired. Recognizing "the new importance given to the single
person," the address is concerned with "the upbuilding of a man," the
construction of a personal identity as a whole being. Emerson's ideal
"Man Thinking" is a creator of new thoughts, one who does not merely
read books, but who "can read God directly." The ultimate goal is a
democratic mysticism: "A nation of men will for the first time exist,

because each believes himself inspired by the Divine Soul which also inspires all men."[2] Because Emerson and his circle were so deeply involved with the issue of self-construction, and carried it to such a religious extreme, they provide an appropriate climax for our study.

Among the faculties of the self the New England writers sought to cultivate were not only reason but also certain kinds of emotion, especially religious and moral feelings. In this respect both the Unitarians and the Transcendentalists were the heirs of theologically liberal pietists of the seventeenth and eighteenth centuries. The Unitarian Christians shared with evangelical revivalists the goal of awakening the religious affections.[3] Yet the Unitarians disapproved of much of what went on in revivals as superficial, manipulative, and anti-intellectual. The principal alternative vehicle they developed for the nurture of religious and moral sentiments was literature. From the Christian Unitarians came the didactic and sentimental writing we call the genteel tradition in American letters. From their iconoclastic offspring in the village of Concord came the outburst of literary creativity we call Transcendentalism: no longer Christian, but every bit as concerned with spiritual and moral objectives.[4]

The enterprise of self-culture was conducted by Unitarians and Transcendentalists to a surprisingly large extent through Neoplatonic categories, which give it its particular intensity and spiritual quality. For these thinkers, self-culture became a religious undertaking, a quest for the divine. It is thus useful to begin this section by exploring the history of Neoplatonism as that tradition was known and exploited in early New England.[5] This exploration will require excursions into mystical philosophy by little-known writers. What these writings provide, however, is an account of one form of self-culture that came to powerful expression in the golden age of American Romantic literature.

℘ THE CAMBRIDGE PLATONISTS OF OLD AND NEW ENGLAND

In 1875 the prominent Unitarian minister and local historian Henry Wilder Foote preached a eulogy for his late colleague, the philosopher and former president of Harvard University, the Reverend James Walker (1794–1874). It was an appropriate occasion to define the

achievement of the antebellum generation of Harvard Unitarian leaders
that Walker represented. "They were much more than mere denomi-
nationalists or founders of a sect," Foote declared. "The whole tone of
their teaching was profoundly positive in its moral and religious
quality. Trained at our American Cambridge, they were really the
legitimate heirs of that noble group of men nurtured at the Cambridge
of England—the Latitude Men, as they were called—who blended
culture and piety and rational thought in their teaching."[6] As we shall
see, Foote's perceptive characterization illuminates not only the classical Unitarian Christianity of Walker and William Ellery Channing
but the literary Transcendentalism of Emerson, Fuller, and Thoreau
as well.

The group of seventeeth-century English intellectuals called the
Cambridge Platonists was centered at Emmanuel and, later, at Christ's
College of Cambridge University. It included Benjamin Whichcote
(1609–1683), its founder; Ralph Cudworth (1617–1688); Henry More
(1614–1687); and John Norris (1657–1711). All came out of Puritan
backgrounds which they to some extent rejected. The Cambridge Platonists occupied a difficult position, resisting most of the trends of
their time. They were moderates in an age of polarization; sympa-
thizers with the Dutch Remonstrants, or Arminians, after these had
been repudiated by the Reformed community at the Synod of Dort;
and advocates of toleration in an age of religious warfare.[7] They were,
however, by no means without influence, and among those in the next
generation who respected their views and shared many of their values,
even while disagreeing with their doctrine of innate ideas, was John
Locke.[8]

The favorite biblical text of the Cambridge Platonists was Proverbs
20:27: "The spirit of man *is* the candle of the LORD" (KJV). The
Hebrew "spirit" here mentioned they interpreted to mean *psyche* in the
Greek sense, usually translated in English as "soul" or "mind," but
typically called by them "reason." The mind or reason was the "candle
of the LORD" because it was the divine light vouchsafed to guide
humanity through the pitfalls of this life. The good life was the rational
life, a quest for wisdom and virtue, freely undertaken. The Cambridge
Platonists were humanists in both senses of that word: they practiced
Renaissance classical scholarship, and they believed that the proper
destiny of humanity could be defined in terms of the full development
of human powers. "In the use of reason and the exercise of virtue we

enjoy God."[9] Thus were Christianity and the Greek philosophic ideal synthesized by these engaging Christian Platonists.

There are many analogies between the English Platonists of seventeenth-century Cambridge and those of nineteenth-century New England Unitarianism. To begin with, they found themselves in similar situations. Both groups were intellectual elites, lacking any substantial popular following. Dependent to some extent on the favor of the powerful, they nevertheless faced up to the duty to criticize power when necessary, whether that of Archbishop Laud in the seventeenth century or Daniel Webster and the cotton-mill owners in the nineteenth. Both conceived of themselves as defending rational Christianity on two fronts: against Calvinism on the one hand and infidelity on the other. Both espoused the virtues of tolerance and inclusiveness—and, truth to tell, these virtues worked to their advantage, as groups that had little coercive power save that of their arguments.

In describing the relations between the nineteenth-century American Unitarians and the Cambridge Platonists of Renaissance England, it may seem convenient to speak in terms of influences. But it would be a mistake to invest the term "influence" with a *causal* meaning. We should not for a moment suppose that William Ellery Channing or James Walker or A. A. Livermore began by making a decision to subscribe to a set of Neoplatonic doctrines and thus was somehow compelled to follow out this logic. A more accurate understanding would be that the Unitarians were aware of this tradition and *made use* of it because it helped them formulate and legitimate what they wanted to say. The many parallels in situations gave rise to analogies in attitudes, so that the earlier Cambridge thinkers provided a ready resource for these later ones. In this respect the use that New England intellectuals made of Neoplatonism may be compared with the use the framers of the Constitution made of the Scottish Enlightenment.

One reason, and a necessary one, why the nineteenth-century Unitarians were able to make so much use of the Platonic tradition is that they were still trained in classical scholarship. Indeed, classical studies remained the backbone of the standard curriculum in both secondary and higher education in nineteenth-century America.[10] Under the leadership of George Ticknor, Harvard pioneered in the teaching of modern foreign languages, but this does not mean the Harvard Unitarian intelligentsia of his time devalued the ancient languages or their educational role. Even after President Charles W. Eliot introduced the elective system, Greek and Latin requirements dominated the Harvard College admissions procedure until the end of the century.[11] The traditional classical curriculum and the pedagogical innovations of nineteenth-century Harvard were both defended as providing the proper development of the human faculties, in terms of an educational theory not altogether different from the Renaissance humanism of Ralph Cudworth.[12]

Both the seventeenth-century Platonists of the Cambridge in old England and the nineteenth-century Platonists of the Cambridge in New England made use of many classical thinkers in addition to Plato. In particular, they borrowed from Plotinus (205–270 A.D.), the founder of Neoplatonism. Six hundred years after Plato, the Alexandrian Plotinus elaborated his predecessor's philosophy into a system for seeking God within one's own *psyche,* working through the essential identity between the spirit or reason within and the universal Spirit or Reason, the *Nous,* that controlled the Universe.[13] Many Christian thinkers across the centuries have found the spiritual program of this pagan philosopher congenial. The seventeenth-century Cambridge Platonists might more accurately be called Neoplatonists, because of their fondness for Plotinus, but since the term Cambridge Platonists has become conventional, I use it.

The history of self-cultivation among New England intellectuals begins with their interest in what Christians call natural religion, that is, God's revelation to humanity through nature rather than Scripture. Of particular relevance to them was a form of natural religion that looked inward toward human nature itself rather than outward toward the external world. This inward form of natural religion not only contemplated the human faculties as evidence of divine workmanship but undertook to cultivate those faculties (conscience and religious sentiment) that provide access to divine truth. From Plotinus, Christian Neoplatonists derived a mystical natural religion of the soul. This kind of inward natural religion was prominent in the pietistic side of the New England liberal Christians. Through the exercise of reason, they pursued Perfection; through knowledge, they sought communion with the Unknowable.

Of course, Neoplatonism was not the only philosophical system employed by the nineteenth-century Unitarians. What may be called the classic form of New England Unitarianism, as stated by Channing, fitted its Platonic heritage into a framework of Scottish moral philos-

ophy and revealed Christianity.[14] Surprisingly enough, the philosophy
of the Scottish Enlightenment lent itself to accommodation with elements of Platonism. Scottish philosophy had originated in a synthesis
of seventeenth-century rationalism with Lockean empiricism. It was
intended to respond to Hume's skepticism by providing rational justification for both moral judgments and empirical science.[15] The Cambridge Platonists had shared a similar purpose, seeking to validate both
morality and modern science within a Christian context. Also like the
Platonists, the Scottish philosophers located *a priori* principles of reasoning in the structure of the human mind itself. The dominant school
in Scottish philosophy taught that the structure of the mind included
certain principles (Thomas Reid called them the principles of "common sense") that provided intuitive, yet rational, validation for trusting
our five external senses as well as believing in our own free will and
continued existence from moment to moment. In Reid's version, which
the New England Unitarians followed, the philosophy also continued
the ethical rationalism of Cudworth and More. Most important of
all, the Scottish moral philosophers shared with Platonism a dedication
to faculty psychology and to affirming the supremacy of some
parts—the rational and moral aspects—of humanity's complex nature
over the others.[16] This explains why it was possible for the New
England Unitarians to find room within their Enlightenment world
view for the Neoplatonic natural religion of the soul.

Classic Unitarianism (as distinguished from its Transcendental offspring) was consistently dualistic in metaphysics, affirming the existence of both mind and matter. So was the Scottish common-sense
realism that the Americans took as their guide in matters of metaphysics.[17] But within this framework, mind was exalted over matter.
No one explained the attitude better than Channing: "From the very
dawn of philosophy there have been schools which have held that the
material universe has no existence but in the mind that thinks it. I am
far from assenting to these speculations. But I recur to them with
pleasure, as indicating how readily the soul passes above matter, and as
manifesting man's consciousness of the grandeur of his spiritual nature."[18] The Platonic-Neoplatonic philosophical tradition is, of
course, accounted as idealist in general; nevertheless there are passages
in the writings of the seventeenth-century Cambridge Platonists that
accord an independent, but inferior, existence to matter.[19] The Cambridge Platonists were actually metaphysical dualists who were ini-

tially attracted to Cartesianism until they came to the conclusion that its sharp separation between mind and matter did not lend itself to the kind of Plotinian natural religion that interested them.[20] Centuries later, the shared desire to accept the reality of both mind and matter while according mind supremacy *over* matter is what drew the New England Unitarians to the Cambridge Platonists.

In this dualistic outlook, mind was the active force in the universe and matter, passive. The power of mind over matter was mirrored in the human character by the authority of reason over passion, for the passions represented what was merely animal in our nature. The impulse to subject matter to mind in the world at large was accompanied by the injunction to subject passion to reason in the world within. The analogy between mind-over-matter and reason-over-passion was by no means confined to Unitarians but had originated with Plato and his followers.[21] During the nineteenth century the analogy was both widespread and commonplace. Lincoln used it in his speech to the temperance society: "Happy day, when, all appetites controled [*sic*], all passions subdued, all matters subjected, *mind,* all conquering *mind,* shall live and move the monarch of the world."[22] What seems at first, therefore, a metaphysical issue remote from everyday experience turns out to have had, for contemporaries, significance for the practice of self-improvement.

A fine example of the Neoplatonic natural religion of the soul as practiced by New England Unitarians is James Walker's 1858 sermon entitled "Man's Competency to Know God."[23] Walker quotes both Henry More and John Smith of the Cambridge Platonist school in the course of proving that we do possess a measure of reliable understanding of the divine perfections: "When we say that God is wise and just and benevolent, we know what we mean; we mean that he is wise and just and benevolent as men sometimes are, only in an infinitely higher degree." It is essential to both the Christian Gospel and any meaningful form of theism that one be able to attribute intelligible moral qualities to God, Walker affirms. But this is not to abandon a sense of mystery and awe and reverence. Precisely because of the commonality between the human and the divine, our natures reach out for His, and religion "addresses itself to our aspirations," Walker declares—"not so much to the curiosity of men and the speculative understanding, as to the sentiments, and especially to that mystical but most characteristic sentiment in human nature, the desire in man to raise himself above himself." Religion "is the instinctive sentiment of the infinite, struggling after an object with which to be satisfied and filled."

> Why then should we be unwilling to admit, as the final and crowning source of our knowledge of God, a practical, a direct, or if you will a mystical, insight into divine things? . . . I speak not now of that false mysticism from which the world and the Church have suffered so much and so long. . . . I mean a true mysticism, which is favorable if not necessary to the life and warmth of a sober and rational piety,—a mysticism which supposes a real communion of the soul with its Maker.[24]

Walker's "true mysticism" represented the way in which Unitarian self-culture would lead to the pursuit of self-transcendence (and hence, as the name implies, to Transcendentalism).

‏‮ UNITARIAN PERFECTIONISM

Just as they appreciated the wisdom and benevolence of God in the order and beauty of external nature, New England Unitarians saw the same divine qualities manifest in the design of the human mind or soul (words they used synonymously). In accordance with the familiar model, they saw the human mind as composed of a number of faculties, arranged in sequence from conscience at the top to the animal passions underneath, with various rational and emotional springs of action in between. Thus both the macrocosm without and the microcosm within displayed the principles of order and hierarchy. The principles of natural religion, the revelation of the divine in nature, applied equally to the external world and human nature within.

"Will the day ever come," demanded the Unitarian Henry W. Bellows (1814–1882), rhetorically, "when the sacredness we now superstitiously confine to the Scriptures shall be extended to the soul of man, his reason, his affections, his conscience; and to Nature herself—each of them a book of God, all volumes of one work, truly coherent, equally divine, and not intelligible except in connection and harmony with each other?" Bellows went on to declare that "the faculties of man are divine seeds sown in the soil of his nature and circumstances . . . Men, no doubt, are arbitrary and capricious, but reason and conscience are never so. It is by acting against reason and conscience that we exhibit our wilfulness and folly."[25]

The Cambridge Platonists of the seventeenth century had commended the practice of religion as helping an individual maintain the proper harmony within his mental faculties, particularly the supremacy of conscience and the subordination of the passions.[26] Suprisingly little had changed for the author of an article in the Unitarian *Monthly Religious Magazine* in 1867, who endorsed the Great Chain of Being, the authority of conscience over the other faculties, and the primacy of mind over matter in the course of demonstrating "the personality of God."[27] Even the scientific study of external nature required some attention to the scholar's inward harmony and benefited from "a devout spirit," explained Andrew Preston Peabody. The scientist's mind "must be stable, calm, self-collected, released from the tyranny of the lower appetites and passions."[28]

Unitarians called the process of creating and maintaining the proper order among the faculties of the mind or soul "the cultivation of a Christian character."[29] It was the most important purpose of living. In a typical Unitarian statement, "Life is then the education of the soul, the discipline of conscience, virtue, piety." The process was undertaken in a devotional spirit, just as the Cambridge Platonists had enjoined centuries before: "religion is the mind's good health," Benjamin Whichcote had declared.[30] The gradual development of harmony and order in the soul prepared one in this life to enjoy the spiritual blessings of heaven, which would otherwise be meaningless. Thus, Convers Francis explained in 1833, "we are saved when we become capable of salvation." The role of divine grace was to provide mankind with "the means of salvation, or, which is the same thing, the means of spiritual improvement and spiritual happiness."[31] Neither grace nor salvation was treated in supernatural terms by classic Unitarianism.

A striking argument that the fulfillment of our own identity as religious beings affords grounds for theistic belief was made by James Walker in *The Philosophy of Man's Spiritual Nature in Regard to the Foundations of Faith.*[32] Walker began with the conventional assertions of Scottish philosophy and Cambridge Platonism. People have natural religious "faculties," which include a moral sense, an inclination toward veneration, and an ideal of perfection. A person ought to develop the full range of human faculties in order to realize full humanity, and this includes the religious faculties. The philosophical principle of common sense, which justifies trusting that the faculties of sensation reveal an objectively existing material universe, also legitimates, Walker claims, trusting that the religious faculties reveal objective spiritual truths. Analysis of Walker's argument shows that it is a composite of several. Beginning with an argument for God from the design of the human faculties, he constructs next an argument that the full development of our nature requires religious expression even for humanistic reasons. He complements this with an objective justification for religious faith that synthesizes arguments from Thomas Reid and Immanuel Kant, among others. Finally, in discussing the sentiment of veneration, Walker gives us the argument from religious experience. An astonishing range of theistic reflection, from Plotinus to William James, finds resonance in this remarkable lecture/essay.[33]

Classic Unitarianism expressed in its own distinctive way the perennial strivings of Christian perfectionism, in the words of William Ellery Channing, "the desire of an excellence never actually reached by humanity, the aspiration toward that Ideal which we express by the word *perfection*."[34] A carefully chosen selection of Channing's finest sermons on this theme was published after his death by his Transcendentalist nephew, William Henry Channing, under the title *The Perfect Life*. The discourses typify the aspect of the Unitarian heritage that Transcendentalists most admired: "Man may entirely trust the revelation of God given in human nature,—in conscience, reason, love, and will,—in reverence for the sublime and joy in the beautiful,—in the desire for blessedness such as the earth cannot appease,—in the ideal of perfection,—and above all in the longing for oneness with the Infinite Being by affinity and fellowship."[35] In emphasizing this theme in William Ellery Channing's thought, his nephew was not misrepresenting him. The sermons included some of the elder man's favorites, delivered repeatedly under various auspices and in some cases already in preparation for publication before his death.[36] Taken together, the discourses outline a complete theory of human nature and achievement. They posit a "religious principle" in human nature from which the author derives all artistic and philosophical efforts as well as all efforts at social reform. For Channing, civilization itself represents the result of human religious striving. Ultimately, only union with Divine Perfection can satisfy the religious impulse, though its by-products in civilization are not devalued.

Although they did not think it could be easily fulfilled, Channing and his Unitarian colleagues had an exalted conception of ultimate human potential. The more a person developed his or her potential,

Channing believed, the closer he or she approached to God. This was what Jesus Christ had manifested. Christ was divine only in the sense that He was fully successful in developing qualities of excellence all people possessed. Thus the Unitarian doctrine of self-fulfillment found theological expression in their Christology.[37]

The formation of a Christian character could be expressed as the formation of a Christ-like character, and, at last, of a God-like character. "The idea of God, sublime and awful as it is, is the idea of our own spiritual nature purified and enlarged to infinity. In ourselves are the elements of the Divinity," declared Channing in one of his most famous sermons. Only because of this likeness can we "enjoy" either God or the universe. Human likeness to God resided solely in the "higher or spiritual nature," and so the pursuit of the Godlike involved the cultivation of the higher faculties and the subordination of the lower. "Whenever we invigorate the conscience by following it in opposition to the passions; . . . whenever we lift up the heart in true adoration to God; whenever we war against a habit or desire which is strengthening itself against our higher principles; . . . then the divinity is growing within us, and we are ascending towards our Author." "God becomes a real being to us in proportion as His own nature is unfolded within us," announced Channing. "To a man who is growing in the likeness to God, faith begins even here to change into vision."[38] In daring to avow such an aim, Channing was manifesting the glorious optimism, the unlimited perfectionism, of early-nineteenth-century America.

Nor was Channing unusual among the Unitarians of his generation for his interest in Christian perfection, as some historians have thought.[39] The aspiration was common to the whole range of classic Unitarian literary and religious production, from the *Monthly Anthology* of Joseph Stevens Buckminster (published 1803–1811) to the *Monthly Religious Magazine* of Edmund H. Sears (published 1844–1874). Even after the Transcendentalist controversy had divided the denomination, Unitarian conservatives did not renounce this perfectionist tradition.[40]

Of course it is inconceivable that Neoplatonic perfectionism should have undergone no transformations across the centuries from Plotinus to the Cambridge school to the New England Unitarians. The major changes, however, were all in the same direction: they all had the effect of making the Neoplatonist tradition more optimistic. The goal remained that of human communion with the Divine Mind; it came to seem more attainable when Neoplatonism was synthesized with the

Judeo-Christian concept of a God who reaches out to mankind, and was made more attainable still by the Renaissance, the Enlightenment, and nineteenth-century humanitarian liberalism. And so we come to a time when the two Channings could think in terms of human "affinity and fellowship" with the Infinite Being.[41]

An apt illustration of how Neoplatonism was reinterpreted in nineteenth-century dress is provided in *Union with God and Man,* by the Unitarian biblical scholar Abiel Abbot Livermore (1811–1892). Livermore begins with a conventional statement of Christian Neoplatonism: *"To be made perfect in one*—one with God and one with each other—is the perfection and happiness of mankind." In Newtonian fashion, he applies this to the physical universe, where "seemingly lawless" phenomena are "but more dazzling demonstrations of [God's] eternal truth."[42] To this harmonious but essentially static vision of divine order, Livermore adds a nineteenth-century faith in progress. It reinforces his optimistic world view, to be sure; any seeming disharmonies can be interpreted as "only a temporary transition to a new and better union." If there be a contradiction in having something that is perfect becoming continually more perfect, Livermore takes no notice of it. (Very likely he would argue that perfection is the law of spirit and progress the law of matter.) "The whole creation, physical, mental, and spiritual, has in truth been constructed to bring us into contact with God at every point, to impart to the mind the light, and to pour into the heart the life, of this blessed union." Mystic or not, Livermore is no medieval ascetic: "St. Simon Stylites dwelt thirty-seven years on the tops of pillars in the open air . . . that he might crucify the body by this lingering martyrdom and be perfectly joined to the Divine Being." But Simon isolated himself from humanity, and "however faithful his struggle and his self-sacrifice to be one with God, he lost the other blessedness of being one with mankind."[43]

The year was 1848, and slavery was still entrenched in the American Union. Yet Livermore denounced all slavery and racial oppression as incompatible with his spiritual vision. "The human soul is the greatest thing on earth. It transcends all cultures, or races, or colors. Mankind are one." The true historic role of the Gospel, he declared, is to introduce a unified state of human civilization that will bring the world of affairs into correspondence with this spiritual unity and grandeur.[44] Livermore's postmillennialism synthesized an ancient philosophy with Renaissance humanism and nineteenth-century humanitarianism.

Just how creative Unitarian Christian Platonism could be is demonstrated in "The Appeal of Religion to Human Nature" by Orville Dewey (1794–1882). First published in 1846, it is a sermon on Proverbs 8:4: "Unto you, O men, I call; and my voice is to the sons of men." Dewey asks what it is in human nature that God's voice addresses, and answers, our moral nature. "The voice of religion, then, must be as the voice of goodness." God must be good because if He were not, He would not deserve our worship. So far, the seventeenth-century Cambridge Platonists could go. But now Dewey begins to sound like a nineteenth-century religious liberal: "Whatever of the holy and beautiful speaks to you, and through what medium soever it comes, it is the voice of religion. All excellence, in other words, is religion."[45] He then takes a series of logical steps that introduce a view of religion as a postulate of human reason in a manner suggesting the influence of Kant:

> Whatever your conscience dictates, whatever your mind clothes with moral beauty, that, to you, is right; be that, to you, religion. Nothing else can be, if you think rationally. . . . Nay, if I knew a man whose ideas of excellence were ever so low, I should still say to him, "Revere those ideas; they are all that you can revere." . . . All that you can worship, then, is the most perfect excellence you can conceive of. Be that, therefore, the object of your reverence.

Dewey would seem to be saying that we cannot be sure whether the voice within is really the Divine Reason or only our image of it; we cannot therefore tell whether we are truly in contact with God Himself or only with our notion of Him. But in the last analysis this does not make any difference; we are still obliged to worship as best we can. Dewey's ontological agnosticism did not weaken in the slightest his commitment to religion as an activity. In this remarkable discourse, the construction of the self has been transformed into the construction of God in our own image.

?◦ TRANSCENDENTALISM AND THE NEOPLATONIC TRADITION

What the Transcendentalists took from the Anglo-American Platonic tradition was twofold: a way of looking at nature, and a way of looking at human nature. Like the Cambridge Platonists and such successors of theirs as Joseph Butler and Lord Herbert of Cherbury, the New England Transcendentalists regarded external nature as a gigantic system of analogy. The cosmos taught moral and spiritual principles in the guise of physical ones. The Transcendental artist interpreted the ideal realities behind these physical superficialities. He or she was a combination of poet and priest, the inheritor of the role of the New England clergy and as much a conduit of divine Revelation as any ancient prophet.[46]

But the continuity between Transcendentalism and the Platonic tradition was even stronger in the internal natural religion of the soul than in that form of natural religion which contemplated the external universe. As others had done for centuries, the Transcendentalists looked on human nature as a microcosm, a world within. This microcosm was an even more trustworthy source of Revelation than the macrocosm. Of Kant's two objects of wonder, the Transcendentalists found "the moral law within" more wonderful than "the starry heavens above." John Smith of seventeenth-century Cambridge had discovered "God's own breath within him."[47] So did the Unitarian of the nineteenth-century American Cambridge and the Transcendentalist of nineteenth-century Concord. Frederic Henry Hedge (1805–1890), the Unitarian minister who was the prime mover of the Transcendental Club (or Hedge Club) that helped give the new movement impetus and definition in the 1830s, put it this way: "The first monotheist was one who withdrew his gaze from the starry heaven and the creaturely earth, and found in the secret of his own thought the divine 'I am.' "[48]

The continuity between Unitarian Platonism and Transcendental Platonism is most readily traced in the writings of Ralph Waldo Emerson (1803–1882). Historian Sydney Ahlstrom has observed that "the Emersonian message was first of all a Hellenic revival," a revival of Neoplatonism. Earlier, F. O. Matthiessen, in his classic characterization of the golden age of our literature as an American Renaissance, pointed out Emerson's familiarity with the Cambridge Platonists as well as other seventeenth-century metaphysical writers.[49] Emerson's journals and notebooks, both before and after his break with institutional Unitarianism, amply confirm the extent to which he drew upon the tradition of Plato, Pythagoras, Plotinus, and Cudworth as he searched for what he called "a vocabulary for my ideas." "I want a spermatic book," he confided in 1841; "Plato, Plotinus, and Plutarch are such."[50] While an undergraduate at Harvard College, Emerson won the Bowdoin Prize for an essay on "The Present State of Ethical Philosophy," praising Cudworth and his successors in the school of ethical intuitionism.[51] It was a conventional point of view at a college where Cudworth was a standard authority on both ethics and natural theology. In his youth as a classical Unitarian, Emerson echoed the Cambridge Platonist interpretation of human reason as "a prior revelation."[52] Later, of course, he would carry this a step further and decide that reason was sufficient revelation.

Emerson's brief sermon on "Self-Culture," preached while he was still minister to the Second Church in Boston, illustrates the Platonism he inherited. The text, Romans 12:1, reads: "I beseech you therefore, brethren, by the mercies of God, that ye present your bodies a living sacrifice, holy, acceptable unto God, which is your reasonable service." Emerson unhesitatingly declares that "the duty to which we are called is nothing less [than] an unceasing effort at self-culture," interpreting self-sacrifice as self-improvement.[53] Of course this is a triumph of nineteenth-century Arminianism over Pauline theology. But the sermon is also a late example of a tradition of Platonic Christian humanism going back at least as far as the Renaissance. God's service is perfect freedom, perfect rationality, and the perfect development of the human faculties.[54]

An awareness of the Neoplatonic tradition behind Transcendentalism helps illuminate not only the continuities but also the distinctions between Transcendentalism and classical Unitarianism. Renouncing the dualistic compromises made by the New England liberal Christians and their seventeenth-century predecessors at the English Cambridge, the Transcendentalists returned to an idealist monism closer to that of the ancient world, of Plotinus and Plato.[55] Emerson's journal records his observations that Cudworth is more valuable as a vehicle for Plato's thought than for his own sake; that the Platonists represent a decline from Plato.[56] Thoreau seems to have used Cudworth in much the same way.[57]

Classical Unitarianism, like the Scottish philosophy on which it was based, had embraced both empiricism and idealism. The Transcendentalists rejected the empiricist half of classical Unitarianism. Not nature itself, but the human emotional and moral response to nature, interested them. Where the Unitarians had been wont to respect both Cudworth and Locke, both Butler and Paley, both Plotinus and Thomas

Reid, the Transcendentalists admired only the former of those pairs. Along with other Protestants, the Unitarians had long been accustomed to employing Locke's empiricist methodology to legitimate Scripture. They had applied a technique called supernatural rationalism to developing evidences for the truth of Scripture.[58] This technique, pioneered by Locke himself, authenticated purported revelations by means of miracles and fulfillments of prophecy. (If the messenger could tangibly demonstrate his power, then his message must be credible.) When the Transcendentalists lost faith in the relevance of such empirical proofs, the supernatural rationalist demonstration of biblical authority ceased to convey conviction. In his debate with Andrews Norton, a centerpiece of the Transcendentalist Controversy that divided Unitarians for a generation, the Transcendentalist George Ripley did not deny that the miracles had occurred; he denied that empirical evidence was relevant to deciding a religious issue.[59]

What was new about Transcendentalism was not its pietism or its spiritual interpretation of experience, but its rejection of all authority outside the individual. Neither empiricism nor Scripture, nothing, in fact, that was publicly verifiable, was accepted as a religious authority by the Transcendentalists. Theodore Parker's distinction between the "transient" and the "permanent" in religion reserved nothing save the conscience of the individual to the religious category of the "permanent." Jesus, like Plato, had taught the supremacy of the conscience, though his followers had perverted the purity of the message. "The difference between the Christianity of some sects, and that of Christ himself, is deeper and more vital than that between Jesus and Plato."[60]

Although the Transcendentalists seem to have espoused a philosophy closer to that of Plotinus than to that of Cudworth, they were neither unaware nor unappreciative of the Cambridge Platonists as precursors. The fullest and most explicit expression of their attitude toward Cambridge Platonism is presented in a review essay of a new edition of Cudworth's works, written by Theodore Parker (1810–1860).[61] Parker devoted most of his attention to Cudworth's *True Intellectual System of the Universe,* a work well known to Harvard students of Parker's generation.[62]

Parker describes the Latitude Men, Cudworth's circle, as "foes to fanaticism, to irreligion, and to superstition." They stood in opposition to the "profligacy" of Charles II's court and to the atheism of Hobbes, which Parker feels was the inevitable consequence of that profligacy.

Cudworth's *True Intellectual System* is organized as a refutation of Hobbes's false one. In his presentation, Cudworth sets forth the atheist's arguments (with a fullness and candor that Parker and most other commentators have found commendable), then rebuts them. Parker summarizes Cudworth's own position as follows: "1. There is a self-conscious God, ruling over all things. 2. God is good, and there is an eternal distinction between Good and Evil. 3. Men are free agents, and therefore accountable Beings." This is, of course, also the position of classic Unitarianism. Whether Parker himself conceived of God as self-conscious is doubtful, but he chose not to raise the issue here.[63]

Yet Parker did not shrink from criticizing Cudworth, and his criticisms are revealing of the Transcendentalist position. He believed that "Cudworth would have been more convincing" in his defense of theism if he had placed more stress on Parker's own two favorite arguments for the existence of God: (a) the existence of necessary truths, such as those of logic and morality, which "supposes the existence of an eternal mind, from whence they come, and in which they reside"; and (b) the argument from personal religious experience. Parker also rejects Cudworth's conception of "plastic nature," the unconscious power of nature itself, which, created by God, blindly carries out His purposes. Parker finds this concession to the autonomous functioning of nature an unnecessary hypothesis; it creates a dualism where monism will suffice. To the New England Transcendentalist, the workings of the universe displayed the mind of God directly, not indirectly through a mediating power.[64]

For the most part, the Transcendentalists valued the writings of Cudworth and his Cambridge school as introductions to the Platonic and Neoplatonic tradition rather than as authorities in their own right. Emerson's essay "The Oversoul" (1841) illustrates the point. It begins with an epigraph from Cudworth's friend Henry More:

> But souls that of his own good life partake,
> He loves as his own self; dear as his eye
> They are to Him: He'll never them forsake:
> When they shall die, then God himself shall die:
> They live, they live in blest eternity.

Once Emerson begins to discuss his theme, however, it becomes apparent that his conception of the Oversoul is closer to that of Plotinus than to that of the Christian More, whose lines he quoted, it would seem, to ease the reader into an unfamiliar frame of reference. Here is Plotinus, sixteen centuries before, speaking in the name of the cosmos itself:

> It is God who made me [the world], and from Him I came perfect. I include all living beings, and I am self-sufficient, for I contain all creatures, plants, animals, and everything that may be born. I have within myself many gods, hosts of daemons, lofty souls, and men who find happiness in virtue. . . . All that is within me desires the Good, and each attains it according to its ability. From that Good all the heavens depend, as do my whole soul, the gods within me, and all the beings I contain, both animate and seemingly inanimate.[65]

This is a vision of a divine wholeness, a perfect plenitude. And here is Emerson, addressing the subject from the human point of view:

> Man is a stream whose source is hidden. Our being is descending into us from we know not whence . . . that Unity, the Over-Soul, within which every man's particular being is contained and made one with all other. . . . We live in succession, in division, in parts, in particles. Meantime within man is the soul of the whole; the wise silence; the universal beauty, to which every part and particle is equally related; the eternal ONE. . . . We see the world piece by piece, as the sun, the moon, the animal, the tree; but the whole, of which these are the shining parts, is the soul.[66]

Strikingly similar as these conceptions are, the intellectual history of sixteen centuries has wrought its effect on them. Plotinus had taught that only by long discipline could one travel up the mystical ladder to attain a vision of the wholeness. Emerson, as a post-Christian, post-Enlightenment Romantic, believes the process is one of opening up the self to an inborn genius. In his poem "The Snow-Storm," written the same year as "The Over-Soul," Emerson displays—with greater artistic success than the essay achieves—his belief that the highest human genius lies in the self's receptivity to the impulses of nature. The snow storm serves him as the perfect symbol for a wild, ecstatic artistry that is our model and yet beyond our reach. (Plato too said we should imitate an ideal beauty, but how different is Emerson's snow storm from Plato's geometry!)[67]

In *Representative Men* (1850), Emerson directly confronted the ultimate fountain of Platonism, Plato himself. On the one hand, Plato was *The* Philosopher. "It is impossible to think, on certain levels, except through him. He stands between the truth and every man's mind." On the other hand, Plato was "a great average man" who simply realized the potential in all of us. He was the personification (the "representative man") of the maturity of Greek civilization. Yet, because of his travels abroad, he also synthesized the European (scientific) and Asian (mystical) approaches to knowledge, the Understanding and the Reason. "No man ever more fully acknowledged the Ineffable," Emerson noted, but "he cries, 'Yet things are knowable!' " Out of these seeming contradictions, Emerson constructed a portrait of Plato, not as a man of paradoxes, but as a "balanced soul."[68] What interests Emerson in the essay is not philosophy as such but the nature of genius and its relationship to its context and to posterity. As a result there is practically nothing to distinguish his treatment of Plato's philosophy from one that a Unitarian of the classical school might have written.

❧ CONCLUSION

In 1876 Octavius B. Frothingham (1822–1895) published an account of *Transcendentalism in New England.* Frothingham was still close enough to the issues involved to write as something of a partisan. He accused the classical Unitarians of having neglected an important aspect of their heritage. "The [prewar] Unitarian divine was more familiar with Tillotson than with Cudworth, and more in love with William Paley than with Joseph Butler," he complained. It had been left to the Transcendentalists to reinvigorate the tradition of the Cambridge Platonists, Frothingham declared.[69]

In 1940 Perry Miller published his essay "From Edwards to Emerson," by now a classic of American literary studies, which adopted a similar interpretation. "In Unitarianism one half of the New England tradition—that which inculcated caution and sobriety—definitely cast off all allegiance to the other," the mystical half. When Emerson embraced idealism, Miller believed, he was reaching back over the heads of his classical Unitarian parents' generation to recover a lost Edwardsean mysticism.[70] Miller was quite correct to recognize a strain of mysticism within the New England tradition. (In this essay he was not interested in its Neoplatonic origins.) But he erred in believing that this strain had gone into some sort of cultural hibernation during a cold winter of rationalism.

The prominence of Cambridge Platonist and other Neoplatonic themes in classic Unitarian thought helped lay the groundwork for the reception of the philosophy of Immanuel Kant (1724–1804) by the Transcendentalist Unitarians. Although the emergence of New England Transcendentalism is usually traced to the impact of Kant and the post-Kantians, it is possible to tell the story (as we have done) with surprisingly little reference to Kantianism, simply in terms of the reactivation by the Transcendentalists of idealist themes going back through Unitarianism to Platonism. Indeed, it is possible to view Kant himself as "the continuer of the modern Platonic tradition."[71] Emerson and the Transcendentalists co-opted Kant into the service of an intellectual tradition that included Cudworth and Coleridge, as well as James Marsh, the Transcendentalists' Calvinist contemporary who mediated Coleridge to Americans.[72] In fact, the Transcendentalists' enthusiasm for the philosophy of Kant would not have been controversial if it had confined itself to affirming that what Kant called the "practical reason" testified to the existence of God. It was Kant's negative, or critical, assertions, his rejection of the traditional arguments for the existence of God and the authenticity of revelation, which made his philosophy and that of his Transcendentalist followers shocking to New England's Christians, liberal and orthodox alike.

In the course of exploring the importance of self-construction to Unitarians and Transcendentalists, this chapter has also helped define the relationship between these two closely connected movements. Emerson and the Transcendentalists received their idealist inspiration from liberal precursors—principally the Cambridge Platonists, classical New England Unitarians like Joseph Stevens Buckminster, the Channing brothers, and Edward Everett—and from European post-Kantians. Of course the Transcendentalists also encountered New Light pietism—for example, we know now that the young Ralph Waldo Emerson was exposed to this through his intellectually eclectic aunt, Mary Moody Emerson.[73] If the Transcendentalists had read Jonathan Edwards, they would have found him an admirer of the Cambridge Platonists (despite what he regarded as their Arminian heresies).[74] But in fact the Transcendentalists turned to reading Plotinus and Plato themselves, without making any significant philosophical detour through Edwards. The New England Transcendentalists found Coleridge and Kant congenial insofar as they interpreted them as contemporary restatements of an enduring idealist tradition.

An overview of the Cambridge Platonists and their relation to New England religious thought illuminates the controversy between the Unitarians and the Transcendentalists by showing what was, and what was not, at stake. Both sides in the controversy were convinced of certain principles they had each inherited from Cambridge Platonism. Neither doubted the power of the "candle of the LORD" within the individual to illuminate the objective divinity that ruled the universe. Both believed in the paramount importance of self-construction, leading toward self-transcendence in communion with the divine. The issue in the controversy concerned whether there was there any authority *external* to the individual to which one could look for guidance in religion. Classical Unitarianism affirmed that both Scripture and empirically known nature constituted such authorities. Transcendental Unitarians, for all that they delighted in the poetic inspiration external nature could provide, denied that either it or Scripture constituted a religious authority binding on the individual. For the Transcendentalists, self-construction had attained an epistemological function: the self-made person could make his or her own truth.

During the years after the Civil War, Platonism continued to occupy a central place in the intellectual history of Unitarianism. Benjamin Jowett's translation of Plato reached the United States in 1871, providing a more accessible English version than ever before. In the complex interweaving of Transcendental and Christian elements that occurred in the work of thinkers like Frederic Henry Hedge, William Rounseville Alger, and A. A. Livermore, Platonism played a central part. It provided an intellectual basis for the eventual reconciliation between Transcendentalism and the Unitarian establishment. The postbellum writings of Edmund H. Sears (1810–1876) demonstrate such a synthesis. Sears's impressive study of the Gospel of John drew upon Cudworth and Plato to transcend the debate between Ripley and Norton over the authority of Scripture and miracles.[75] He accepted the position Ripley and the Transcendentalists had maintained, that religion must commend itself to the human heart, but he argued that the Gospels satisfied this criterion. And in his *Foregleams and Foreshadows of Immortality,* Sears produced what was perhaps the greatest of all Unitarian works of Plotinian natural religion of the soul.[76]

The Platonic idealist tradition proved both a strength and a weakness for New England Unitarian culture. The Unitarians of the pre-Civil War period, one must admit, lacked appreciation for carnality. Their forms of expression, spoken and written, dealt in spirituality. Even when Transcendentalists like Thoreau took note of concrete reality, they did so to capture its symbolic and ideal meaning. The whole thrust of Unitarian, including Transcendentalist Unitarian, intellectual and artistic activity was to go beyond the material in search of the ideal, in short, the Platonic Quest. The strength of this cultural tradition lay in its invocation of moral and spiritual values through oratory, poetry, and prose. Conversely, art forms that emphasize carnality, like drama, dance, and sculpture, remained alien to it. In the next chapter we shall look at a person who worked to remedy this deficiency and others in New England culture: Margaret Fuller.

CHAPTER 8

Margaret Fuller's Heroic Ideal
of Womanhood

W hen Margaret Fuller (1810–1850) was fifteen years old, a famous hero came to town. Hoping to meet him, she made bold to write a letter to the Marquis de Lafayette. "Sir, the contemplation of a character such as yours fills the soul with a noble ambition. Should we both live, and it is possible to a female, to whom the avenues of glory are seldom accessible, I will recal [sic] my name to your recollection."[1] Alexander Hamilton or Benjamin Franklin would have understood such feelings of virtuous ambition in a young person—but, as this writer acknowledged, the path to fame would be countless times harder for a girl. The young Margaret Fuller derived her heroic ambition in part from the classical republicanism in which she was educated but also from Neoplatonic and Romantic aspirations that would have been alien to Hamilton and Franklin. Her goal was no mere passing adolescent phase; at the age of thirty she shared her deepest feelings with a friend: "I must die if I do not burst forth in genius or heroism."[2] The juxtaposition of "genius" and "heroism" suggests the blending of Romantic with classical ideals in her mind.

As a woman, Margaret Fuller had to do more than struggle against odds to achieve her heroic ideal; she had to redefine the ideal itself, which was traditionally masculine. Fuller was convinced that theory had to precede and inform practice; hence before women could be truly free, they had to understand their goals, to know what they were free to become. Margaret Fuller ransacked history, literature, and classical mythology for positive feminine images, not only for pedagogical purposes but also to apply to her own life. She identified and re-created representative women in the same sense that her friend Ralph Waldo Emerson identified archetypal representative men—in order to show the possibilities that individuals could realize. By her example she hoped to inspire later generations of women and girls, as Washington and Franklin were already being used to inspire young American males.[3]

Contemporaries and later scholars alike have raised the question whether Margaret Fuller should be remembered for what she wrote or for what she was.[4] Modern literary critics trained to regard texts as the focus of attention may feel that any attempt to look away from the text to the author or her context is a diversion, though the historian of ideas will not see things that way. It is a sensitive issue, because feminists have all too often been disparaged by shifting attention from the substance of their ideas to their person, sexuality, and appearance; Fuller came in for her share of such treatment, both before and after her death.[5] Actually, however, Fuller did not separate her life from her art. Like her friend Henry David Thoreau, she constructed her identity self-consciously, partly in the pages of her writings. Within her circle, people recognized Margaret Fuller as her own work of art.[6]

A perceptive characterization of the relationship between Fuller's life and writings came (perhaps surprisingly) from her contemporary Edgar Allan Poe: "Her acts are bookish, and her books are less thoughts than acts."[7] By Poe's own standards this was not a compliment, but Fuller was probably not offended by it. She believed that the artist should inspire doubly, through personal example as well as writings.[8] All who came in contact with Fuller, whether young or old, male or female, sympathetic or hostile, testified to her compelling presence and magnetism. Generations of biographers too have been fascinated by her personality and private life.[9] Our concern here, however, is not with these, but with the ideal heroic self that she devised and pursued. Fuller wanted both to write about the ideal she called "woman in the nineteenth century" and to exemplify it. "There are," she confided to a lover, "in every age a few in whose lot the meaning of that age is concentrated. I feel that I am one of those persons in my age and sex."[10]

Fuller's enterprise of self-construction led her into a highly original reconceptualization of the faculty psychology of her age. Instead of a character that was balanced in the conventional sense of reason super-intending passion, she espoused the ideal of a character that was balanced between male and female components. She arrived at this reconceptualization through the integration of the intellectual culture in which she had been trained with ideas she imported from European Romanticism. Among the resources she drew upon in developing her world view were classical learning, including Platonism and classical republicanism, the German Romanticism of Goethe and Beethoven, Jeffersonianism, Scottish moral philosophy, and the new Romantic moral philosophy of Coleridge, with its distinction between Reason and Understanding.

?◆ THE CLASSICAL HERITAGE

Of the classical and Romantic elements that composed Fuller's heroic ideal, the classical came first, in the rigorous education she received from an early age. Like another great feminist of her era, John Stuart Mill, Margaret Fuller was a precocious child educated by her father. A New England lawyer, Timothy Fuller held major political offices, including United States Representative and Speaker of the Massachusetts House. The knowledge of classical civilization he drilled into his eldest child far exceeded the education generally available to girls at the time. She gained not only a fluency in Latin and competence in Greek, but a universe of discourse that served her all her life. Margaret Fuller turned out to be the most formidably learned New Englander since Cotton Mather.

Timothy Fuller was a Jeffersonian Republican who was thoroughly devoted to the Jeffersonian ideal of developing human potential through education. He applied this ideal to his daughter with unusual rigor—in contrast to the relative indifference Jefferson himself showed on the subject of female education.[11] The education young Margaret received reflected her father's eighteenth-century taste: Latin prose, poetry, and composition, supplemented by Greek writings, including the Griesbach text of the New Testament, along with mathematics and natural philosophy. Later, he added moral philosophy of the Scottish school, including its ramifications in political economy (Adam Smith) and rhetorical theory (Hugh Blair and Lord Kames). Harvard's professor of logic and moral philosophy, Levi Hedge, was a family friend as well as an author Margaret studied. When she was nine, her father recommended/assigned *The Spectator, Paradise Lost,* Dr. Johnson, and Goldsmith. What was unusual, of course, was not the reading list but the youth, gender, and aptitude of the pupil.[12]

Timothy Fuller's canon was that of his generation of Harvard-educated New England Unitarians.[13] The Scottish moral philosophers whose views Harvard propagated had taught that women shaped the manners and morals of society through their domestic influence, and that the status of women was an index of social progress. These teachings were applied in America in the ideology historians have termed "republican motherhood," defining the appropriate place for women and the domestic role for which they were educated in the young republic.[14] Timothy Fuller shared these philosophical views but went beyond their conventional application to the education of women. He took the dignity of republican motherhood so seriously that he provided his daughter with an education the equal of any man's. Timothy was also aware of the writings of English Protestant Dissenters like Richard Price and Mary Wollstonecraft, whom he admired not so much for their Radical politics as for their dedication to rigorous rationality. Exponents of an orthodox eighteenth-century faculty psychology, they too influenced his thinking on the subject of female education.[15]

Timothy Fuller's curriculum perpetuated a world view in which passion was properly subordinated to reason, inclination to duty, and impulse to conscious resolve. To Margaret, this value system would be forever associated with the Latin authors who exemplified it, "the great Romans, whose thoughts and lives were my daily food during those plastic [i.e., malleable] years." "We are never better understood than when we speak of a 'Roman virtue,' " she noted; "every Roman was an emperor," for he governed himself. Even in childhood, Margaret was conscious that her own nature was different, more emotionally expressive. She found what she learned about the ancient Greeks more congenial to her natural proclivities. She identified them with idealism, imagination, and freedom; the Romans with practicality, logic, and "stern composure." Her father preferred the Romans, and under his Augustan discipline, Margaret recalled, "My own world sank deep within, away from the surface of my life. . . . But my true life was only the dearer that it was secluded and veiled over by a thick curtain of available intellect, and that coarse but wearable stuff woven by the ages,—Common Sense."[16] The eighteeth-century Scottish philosophers had used the term "common sense" to mean a faculty that revealed the truth; for Fuller, however, it hid the truth, by covering over the turmoil and excitement of her affective life.

Margaret Fuller's original heroic ideal was by convention a male one; she wanted to be virtuous, not in the Victorian sense of private female chastity, but in the classical republican one of public spirit and leadership.[17] "She was a citizen and a socialist," her sometime employer Bronson Alcott observed; "in this particular, she was less American than Greek."[18] Actually, Fuller saw herself as maintaining the political tradition of the American Founders, though she showed no interest in Locke's contractualism or his doctrine of natural rights. Clearly, she thought of America as a country dedicated to the fulfillment of individual potential.

Margaret Fuller's relationship to her Jeffersonian political antecedents was nuanced. In the words of Charles Capper, "not Jefferson the radical democrat, but Jefferson the intellectual republican" and educator interested her.[19] When the Republican party divided in the 1820s, the Fullers sided with its New England wing, the National Republicans led by John Quincy Adams, as opposed to the Democrats of Andrew Jackson. Margaret loved discussing the Adams-Jefferson correspondence with her father, and continued his loyal admiration for John Quincy Adams ("the Phocion of his time" in her words).[20]

Margaret Fuller's first publication was an affirmation of her family's orthodox classical republicanism. In 1834 the prominent Jacksonian intellectual George Bancroft published an essay in the *North American Review* deploring the effects of slavery in ancient Rome and celebrating Tiberius Gracchus and Julius Caesar, whom he portrayed as mobilizing popular sentiment against slavery. Bancroft was running for office at the time, and it is not difficult to read between the lines of this history his own politics, his hope that northern workingmen would rally to an antislavery version of Jacksonian Democracy. The Fullers had no quarrel with Bancroft's antislavery; while in Congress Timothy had resolutely opposed the admission of Missouri as a slave state. But Margaret refused to let this cryptic association between antislavery and what she thought of as demogogy go unanswered; she published a letter criticizing Bancroft for maligning the character of Caesar's assassin Brutus. Brutus was an honorable defender of the old republic against a usurping tyrant, she maintained. A rebuttal to Fuller in defense of Bancroft's interpretation followed. It was a debate over political values carried on in code, with Caesar standing for Jackson, and Brutus for his adversaries, the newly named Whigs.[21]

Such civic humanism was not the only imprint of classical education on Margaret Fuller; even more important was her thorough familiarity with Greco-Roman mythology. By treating the myths as archetypal forms, she made them a vocabulary in which to discuss human nature and gender issues in particular.[22] The most profound and wide-ranging influence of the classics on Fuller, however, came from Plato and his followers. So familiar was Plato's thought to her that after reading a new French edition of *Phaedrus* she could comment that it made her feel as if "returning to my native mountain air."[23] The use that Plato made of the material world as a source of spiritual meanings provided Fuller and her fellow Transcendentalists with their ultimate model. They worked within a version of Platonism adapted by his successors Plotinus and Proclus. Particularly relevant to their literary criticism was the teaching of Plotinus that what the artist imitates is not the appearances of the material world, as Plato had thought, but the eternal Forms themselves. Fuller's concept of human nature and its place in the cosmos encapsulates the Neoplatonism of Plotinus: "Man is a being of two-fold relations, to nature beneath him and intelligences above him. The earth is his school, if not his birthplace: God his object: life and thought, his means of interpreting nature and aspiring to God."[24]

Margaret Fuller was conversant with the modern as well as the ancient varieties of Platonic idealism. She knew the seventeenth-century Cambridge Platonists and the eighteenth-century neopagan Thomas Taylor. She admired the mystic Immanuel Swedenborg (though not the religious sect that bore his name) and wrote an imaginary dialogue between the metaphysical poet George Herbert and his brother, the philosopher Lord Herbert of Cherbury, to illustrate a kind of Platonic ecumenism between the Christian Platonism of the former and the deistic Platonism of the latter.[25] As a young girl, Margaret grew up in the intellectual capital of the Unitarian American Reformation, where variants of Platonic philosophy were a favorite resource of liberal theological critics of Calvinism. She knew the eminent Unitarian divine William Ellery Channing and other members of his family well; the Platonic elements in his thought enjoyed favor with the younger generation of his admirers, such as Fuller.[26] She must have been familiar with the Plotinian aesthetic theory of his brother, Edward

Tyrell Channing, which was elaborated in her own literary criticism
and that of her Transcendentalist friends. Most of all, she was exposed
to the Platonism of Emerson and Alcott.[27]

But though Fuller was thoroughly conversant with Plato, she was by
no means his uncritical follower. Here, as always, she used tradition as
a resource without letting herself be imprisoned by it. In some of his
passages Plato was the first feminist: among the guardians of his ideal
Republic a perfect meritocracy prevails, and women are included
within the public spirit of the *polis;* they receive the same education as
men and have equal opportunity to exercise political power. Elsewhere,
however, Plato compromised with and even legitimated the prevailing
subjection of women. Fuller accordingly rendered a mixed verdict on
Plato's philosophy of gender.[28] In metaphysics too she modified Plato
and Plotinus, preferring a mind-matter dualism typical of the
seventeenth-century Cambridge Platonists and the Unitarians of her
father's generation to the pure idealism of her Transcendentalist
friends.[29] Thomas Jefferson had been quite hostile to Plato, so perhaps
the Jeffersonian influences on young Fuller helped her preserve her
critical distance from the Athenian.[30]

Dualism of mind and matter occupied an important place in Fuller's
world view, because it represented for her the need to synthesize
thought and action. Like Plato and his followers, she thought of matter
as something inert, to be subjected to the control of the conscious
mind. Unlike them, however, she did not believe the goal of mind was
liberation from the world of matter. Identifying the Roman with the
material world and the Greek with the ideal, she honored both. Her
own country awaited the heroic deliverer who would integrate the two:
"no thin Idealist, no coarse Realist, but a man whose eye reads the
heavens, while his feet step firmly on the ground, and his hands are
strong and dexterous for the use of human implements." She went on
to describe how the American hero would exercise his faculties yet
discipline them, and why metaphysical idealism was inadequate for
him. The hero must be "a man of universal sympathies, but self-
possessed; a man who knows the region of emotion, though he is not
its slave; a man to whom this world is no mere spectacle, or fleeting
shadow, but a great solemn game to be played with good heed, for its
stakes are of eternal value."[31] Even Fuller was still conventionally
expressing the heroic in masculine terms when she wrote this in 1843,
though it was a universal human ideal independent of gender and, in

fact, described her own ideal self. The combination of idealism and realism she had in mind was not a compromise between radicalism and conservatism; when she encountered such evasion, Fuller condemned it, even in a friend. Rather, it was the ability to uphold ideals and work practically to implement them that she respected.[32] The career of Margaret Fuller is best understood as the self-conscious pursuit, ultimately successful, of such a synthesis in her own life and writing.[33]

✿ THE CULTURE OF THE FEMALE SELF

The literary historian David Robinson has demonstrated how Margaret Fuller adapted the Unitarian conception of self-culture, classically formulated by Channing, to feminist purposes. In doing so he has reaffirmed the judgment of her close friend James Freeman Clarke, who declared: "Margaret's life *had an aim,* . . . a high, noble one, wholly religious, almost Christian. It gave dignity to her whole career, and made it heroic. This aim, from first to last, was SELF-CULTURE."[34]

Although Fuller shared the aim of self-culture with other Unitarians and Transcendentalists, she developed it in her own way and, of course, in her own feminist direction. It seems appropriate that the New England liberals, having rejected the authority of Augustine and Paul with regard to original sin, should have rejected their misogyny as well. As put forward by Channing, Fuller, and others, the idea of self-culture was a version of the more general idea of self-improvement. As we have seen, the meaning of both terms was derived from agriculture, but culture had an organic, biological connotation as compared with the more mechanistic word "improvement."[35] The idea of self-culture fittingly enough expressed a nurture that was a *natural* development. In Fuller's conception, it consciously and legitimately fulfilled human nature, both male and female; it also sought a merger with the universal nature, which was divine. In the pursuit of this aim, Fuller pressed far beyond the Christian Unitarianism of Channing to a Romantic version of Neoplatonism.

Fuller's heterodox "Credo," recorded in her personal journal in 1842, summarizes her faith. The statement is thoroughly non-Christian (even by the standards of Unitarian Christianity), which no doubt explains why parts of it were felt by her self-appointed literary executors to be an embarrassment.[36] In it she describes a divine spirit, all encompassing yet not all powerful or all knowing: "Within it all manifestation is contained, whether of good (accomplishment) or evil (obstruction). To itself its depths are unknown. By living it seeks to know itself, thus evolving plants, animals, men, suns, stars, angels, and, it is to be presumed[,] an infinity of forms not yet visible in the horizon of this being who now writes." The generically Neoplatonic nature of her credo is evident. The wonderful vision of plenitude it contains leads Fuller not only to a reverence for nature but to a disavowal of a species-centered perspective: "I do not mean to lay an undue stress upon the position and office of man, merely because I am of his race, and understand best the scope of his destiny. The history of the earth, the motions of the heavenly bodies[,] suggest already modes of being higher than his, and which fulfill more deeply this office of interpretation" [of the divine purpose].

The consequences of Fuller's philosophy for human life we might call (without undue anachronism) a *process theology*. Life is a process of self-realization, Fuller repeatedly declared: "I believe in Eternal Progression. I believe in a God, a Beauty and a Perfection to which I am to strive all my life for assimilation." "I am deeply taught by the constant presence of any growing thing."[37] Fuller applied this creed to her life and work: for example, she regarded her writings as work in progress, never as finished products; she felt free to revise them, even after publication, just as she sought to correct the imperfections she recognized in her character.[38]

This developmental philosophy implied the central importance of education for human life. Margaret Fuller had plenty of experience as an educator, having taught school twice and led her celebrated educational "conversations" for adult women. As mentor to her younger brothers and sisters after the death of their father, she played out something like the role of republican motherhood for which he had so carefully prepared her. Her philosophy of education was a process of *drawing out* the students (of whatever age or gender) "to ascertain and fulfill the law of [their] being." From the existence of certain human faculties, or powers, she inferred the legitimacy of their cultivation: "The Power who gave a power, by its mere existence, signifies that it must be brought out toward perfection."[39] Education, for Margaret Fuller as for Horace Mann, included both the cultivation and the discipline of the human faculties. If she derived the former from Channing's philosophy of self-culture, she derived the latter from her classical training, especially the Latin studies. (Though discipline had been an important part of the New England way of life as practiced by Puritans and evangelicals, there is no evidence that Fuller was significantly influenced by Reformed Christianity.)

In Fuller's dualistic version of Platonism, the "search after the good and beautiful" did not entail a rejection of the material. The pursuit of the divine, while "drawing man onward to the next state of existence," should not "destroy his sympathies with the mineral, vegetable, and animal realms, of whose components he is in great part composed."[40] As mentor to her younger siblings, Fuller emphasized the material and practical, teaching "habits of industry," discipline, and thrift in ways Benjamin Franklin would have approved.[41] Later, when she taught for Bronson Alcott at the experimental Temple School in Boston, Fuller found herself in basic sympathy with his Neoplatonic goals but critical of the abstract, ethereal way he carried them out. Part of the problem, she felt, was his strict idealistic metaphysic: "you do not understand the reaction of matter on spirit," she wrote in an imaginary dialogue with him that she kept in her journal.[42] In public, however, she remained loyal to Alcott, especially after his school became the object of undeserved opprobrium. (Ironically, it was when Alcott addressed the carnal side of life as Fuller had wanted him to do—when he began to teach the children about the birds and the bees—that he brought down the wrath of the community upon his school.)

Education, of course, was not confined to learning from others, nor did it end with graduation ceremonies. Denied membership in any college or university by her gender, Fuller was not likely to have equated education with formal schooling. The most important education, she believed, was one a person gained through the experiences of life. Fuller's project of self-culture has been attacked as selfish and socially irresponsible, both in her own time and since, and otherwise sympathetic historians have argued that she achieved political relevance only through rejecting this undertaking and the New England Platonic philosophy behind it.[43] However, by cultivating her own intellectual faculties and personal autonomy while encouraging other women to follow her lead, Fuller was challenging the distribution of power in her society and to that extent making at least an implicitly political statement.[44] Like Emerson, she believed independence was a personal as well as a national goal; she set out to apply his principle of "self-reliance" to women. She brought society to the bar of justice to hold it responsible for the extent to which it developed or inhibited the human potential of all its members—female as well as male.[45]

The New England tradition of Platonic perfectionism strongly influenced Fuller's conception of friendship. Today we use the term "platonic" to mean nonsexual relationships; Fuller's ideal of a platonic relationship was one in which the partners were engaged in a common "pilgrimage"; the sexual dimension was irrelevant.[46] Whether friends, lovers, or spouses, of the same or different sex, the partners should help each other find fulfillment and realize their respective potentials. Superimposed upon all the other functions of human relationships, this platonic ideal added a layer of complication to Fuller's private life. Only by recognizing this ideal can we understand how Fuller conceived her various human relationships, the emotional intensity of her demands upon her associates, and the way their correspondence served as a form of self-construction and mutual criticism.[47]

One of the most successful of Fuller's platonic relationships, in this sense, was her friendship with James Freeman Clarke (1810–1888). Clarke was destined to become one of the leading exponents of the ideal of self-culture. Yet even he had shifting perspectives on Fuller's perfectionist strivings. In the collaborative *Memoirs* of 1852, while generally respectful of his late friend's self-culture, Clarke found some aspects of it disturbing. He complained that the ideal was, in principle, not altruistic, though he was fair enough to admit that the same criticism could be made of the ordinary Christian desire to save one's own soul. Along with Neoplatonic perfectionism he recognized in Fuller the classical pagan idealization of the hero as well as the new Romantic cult of genius, both of which seemed to him "idolatrous."[48] In 1880, however, when Clarke published his own book on *Self-Culture,* he made the development of one's faculties a specifically Christian responsibility (citing Jesus' parable of the talents) and held Margaret Fuller up, without reservation, as a prime exemplar of this virtue— along with John Milton.[49]

Margaret Fuller gave a public version of the ideal of mutual improvement that informed her concept of friendship in her famous "conversations" of 1839–1844. Such conversations, which we would call discussion groups, were familiar to her contemporaries. Thanks to Lawrence Buell, the importance of the discussion group for the Transcendental movement within which Fuller operated is now recognized by literary historians.[50] Like so much else about Transcendentalism, these groups had their origin in the Unitarian church. Their immediate precursors were the Unitarian "associations for mutual religious improvement," in operation as early as 1826.[51] And as Charles Capper has pointed out, "the ideal of the conversation as a critical intellectual method derives ultimately from Plato, whose Socratic dialogues Fuller reread and came deeply to admire in the months before she began her meetings."[52] In fact, the dialogue was a life-long favorite genre of Fuller's; she wrote dialogues not only for publication but even in her private journal. She also had before her the example of her sometime employer, the Platonist Bronson Alcott, who published his controversial *Conversations with Children on the Gospels* in 1836–37.

What was original about Fuller's conversations was that they were addressed to women. The principal published record we have of Fuller's conversations comes from Caroline Healey Dall (who also kept a record of Bronson Alcott's conversations); unfortunately the series Dall attended was also the only one that included men, which undoubtedly affected the nature of the discussions. Dall's record does show how Fuller used the Greek gods and goddesses as symbolic archetypes, mainly relating to the "human faculties." Thus, Jupiter symbolized the "will," and his conquest of the Titans represented the subjection of "the low and sensual passions." Minerva, goddess of wisdom, was the offspring of will; she showed her feminine nature in being "always ready for the fight if necessary, yet never going to it" as an aggressive male might do. Here, Fuller seems to identify Minerva with the rational moral faculty, the power of "seeing the relations and proper values of things."[53]

The women who attended these conversations were typically well educated and already held liberal to radical political and religious views.[54] Fuller took these things for granted and prescribed neither readings nor community involvement to them. The discussion sessions were intended to encourage the women to think for themselves, about themselves and their womanhood, and to express, clearly and confidently, what they thought. On occasion, Fuller tried to reach out to disadvantaged women, as when she held an impromptu conversation with some women inmates at Sing Sing penitentiary.[55] In the long run, she hoped the participants in her conversations could discover, collectively, "what pursuits are best suited to us in our time and state of society, and how we may make best use of our means for building up the life of thought upon the life of action."[56] Given Fuller's own powerful personality and strong opinions, it is remarkable that the sessions succeeded in drawing out the other participants as much as they did. After five years, when the last in the series of conversations was over, Fuller wrote in her journal that she had tried "to show them where the magazines of knowledge lie, and leave the rest to themselves and the Spirit who must teach & help them to self-impulse."[57]

Feminists of Fuller's generation typically discovered women's issues as a result of their involvement with other reform causes, such as antislavery or temperance. It was not so with Fuller: she addressed the situation of women first, as a philosophical and moral issue rather than as a political one. The priority of theory over practice was both logical and chronological in the case of Margaret Fuller. In David Greenstone's classification of American political ideologies, Fuller was a "reform liberal," whose politics was predicated on the duty of self-development.

From Margaret Fuller's point of view, the central problem of political life was that women were supposed to concern themselves only with the private, not the public, good. There seemed to her no reason why the good republican citizen could not be a woman. This was an issue of personal fulfillment as well as one of public policy. The orator who led by eloquent rhetoric was a role to which she particularly aspired. "If I were a man," she confessed, "the gift I would choose should be that of eloquence. That power of forcing the vital currents of thousands of human hearts into one current, by the constraining power of that most delicate instrument, the voice, is so intense." All her life she envied male friends who could speak in public; when Angelina Grimke and Abby Kelley showed that women could address audiences too, Fuller pointed to them with gender pride.[58]

In moving from theory to practice, Fuller showed more consistency of purpose than has generally been recognized. When she went to New York in 1844 to take up her job on Horace Greeley's newspaper, she became more overtly political in her concerns, but she was not breaking with her past. She had been recommended to Horace by his wife, Mary Greeley, who had attended the conversations. Fuller had long since identified herself with the progressive, antislavery wing of the Whig party that Greeley's *New York Tribune* represented. Her political views were a logical continuation of her father's political association with John Quincy Adams, as well as the complement of her philosophy of the development of human potential. While living in Providence, Rhode Island, she raised eyebrows by attending the Whig party caucus in 1837.[59] When the radical Democrat Thomas Dorr led his uprising there in 1842, Fuller remained aloof and unsympathetic—as did Greeley and other Whigs, whether conservatives or reformers.[60]

Like most of her Transcendentalist friends, Margaret Fuller deplored slavery yet declined membership in abolitionist organizations. Some of these organizations engaged in political activity and others did not (the Garrisonian wing); yet none suited Fuller's principles and temperament. The former alienated her by their ardent evangelical Christianity; the latter, by their stridency, factionalism, and moral condemnation of politics as corrupting. As one who believed in self-discipline and thought that social progress should be brought about by heroes, Fuller held the abolitionists to a high standard: "Those who would reform the world must show that they do not speak in the heat of wild impulse; their lives must be unstained by passionate error. They must be severe lawgivers to themselves."[61] Fuller defined her own concern as the cause of women and was not willing, as abolitionist-feminists were, to accord antislavery even a temporary priority over it.[62]

Margaret Fuller's writings do include repeated denunciations of slavery.[63] Her distance from organized antislavery was dramatized, however, by her conflict with the abolitionist Harriet Martineau. One of Britain's leading women intellectuals, Martineau met Fuller on a visit to the United States in 1835. Sharing a background in Unitarian religion as well as many common interests, the two quickly became close friends—only to become estranged later. The problem began when Fuller privately reproached Martineau for focusing her book on the United States too narrowly on the issue of slavery, as well as for its hostile depiction of Bronson Alcott's educational experiment.[64] Martineau's subsequent public attack on Fuller made it clear that fundamentally, their differences were philosophical: a follower of Joseph Priestley, Martineau was a metaphysical materialist, a determinist, and a utilitarian, for whom the Neoplatonism of Fuller and her Transcendentalist friends was "destructive of all genuine feeling and sound activity," being "fanciful and shallow."[65]

Like many other Americans of her generation, Fuller was fascinated by the writings of the utopian socialist Charles Fourier; of course it is hardly surprising that an admirer of Plato should take an interest in planned communities. Fourier proposed to match work with individual aptitudes, including new roles for women. Greeley's newspaper, through the efforts of Fuller's predecessor Albert Brisbane, had been the most important purveyor of Fourier's ideas to the American public. Fuller took a sympathetic interest in the utopian community at Brook Farm, but privately shook her head over its dogmatic impracticality—the same response she had had to Bronson Alcott's school.[66] She recognized the reciprocal relationship between institutions and human nature; her concept of the heroic in effect synthesized the two, by looking to the perfected person to embody the goals of society and lead it to them.[67]

੨☞ THE ROMANTIC SPIRIT

While Margaret Fuller's classical republican and Neoplatonic impulses were continuous with the New England tradition of her upbringing, Romanticism came to her later, via overseas models, and was associated in her mind with her attempt to rescue New England from cultural provinciality. The Germany of Goethe was the homeland of Romanticism as Fuller understood it. The German ideal of *Bildung* (education) provided Fuller with new insights into the process of self-culture. Having learned about German culture from mediators like Germaine Necker de Staël, Thomas Carlyle, Karl (Charles) Follen, and Frederic Henry Hedge, Fuller turned to the language with her usual gusto and soon could read the sources for herself. Applying the model of countervailing powers from faculty psychology to culture, Fuller argued that Germany provided the perfect "counterpoise" for America's cultural imbalances.[68] One of these imbalances, Fuller recognized, was that lack of appreciation for carnality mentioned at the end of the preceding chapter. To remedy this, she promoted art forms unfamiliar to New Englanders, such as sculpture and drama. Most concentrated of all were her efforts to promote an appreciation of German Romantic music, especially Beethoven.[69]

The titanic, frustrated, angry genius of Beethoven spoke directly to Margaret Fuller in a way that no other spirit ever did. After hearing a Beethoven concert, she poured out her soul to him in her secret journal, addressing the dead composer as "my only friend." On the one hand, the example of his achievement was overpowering. Although she possessed "a soul as deep as thine," she had not expressed herself in great art as he had done; so she begged, "forgive me, Master, that I have not been true to my eventual destiny." On the other hand, Beethoven's music communicated spiritual meaning from one genius to another, filling her with ecstasy. "Thou art to me beyond compare, for thou art all I want. No heavenly sweetness of Jesus, no many-leaved Raphael, no golden Plato, is anything to me, compared with thee."[70]

The Romantics whom Fuller admired taught her to broaden the traditional scope of heroic action beyond politics and war, to include literature and the other arts. Indeed, Romanticism taught a respect for the achievements of nonpolitical people that was altogether novel: armed with this insight, Fuller could declare that, in her own nation, "all symptoms of [artistic] invention are confined to the African race, who, like the German literati, are relieved by their position from the cares of government."[71] The Romantic concept of artistic genius made a heroic role more accessible to women, who were also outside the political community. Fuller used the New England tradition of didactic art to legitimate artistic endeavor in what she felt was a barren environment. The musician, the painter, the sculptor—they too, along with the orator and the poet, communicated spiritual truths. The Romantic ideal of heroic genius emphasized self-expression rather than self-discipline, but it retained a belief in universal human nature: if one could express one's deepest feelings, these would turn out to be the most important truths about everyone. For this reason, Fuller declared, "all true artists resemble one another."[72]

How Fuller's Romantic concept of genius subsumed older heroic and perfectionist ideals may be seen in a remarkable letter she wrote to James Freeman Clarke. "I have greatly wished to see among us such a person of genius as the nineteenth century can afford," she began, "a person endowed by nature with that acute sense of Beauty (i.e., Harmony or Truth) and that vast capacity of desire, which give soul to love and ambition." Echoing Plotinus, she hoped the genius would adore "the bright phantoms of his mind's creation, and believe them but the shadows of external things to be met with hereafter." With faculties strengthened by contemplation of the ideal, "I wished this being might be launched into the world of realities, his heart glowing with the ardor of an immortal toward perfection." After suffering and trial, the genius of the nineteenth century "would suddenly dilate into a form of Pride, Power, and Glory," becoming "a centre, round which asking, aimless hearts might rally."[73] Margaret Fuller applied this Romantic ideal to her own life. Through her conversation groups, she provided such "a centre" to rally the questioners and seekers among women.[74]

Like Horace Bushnell, Margaret Fuller and her fellow Transcendentalists seized upon the distinction between Reason and Understanding they learned from Samuel Taylor Coleridge. For them, Understanding was the faculty that perceived the physical world; Reason the faculty of introspection that discerned spiritual and moral truths. The Transcendentalists had come full circle: their Romantic use of the term "Reason" was also a revival of the way the Cambridge Platonists had used it. The difference between Understanding and Reason was a practical one for the Transcendentalists. The Understanding was the faculty they associated with materialism and self-seeking; Reason, with self-transcendence.[75]

Such a distinction between Understanding and Reason had not existed in eighteenth-century faculty psychology, which had followed the medieval schoolmen in distinguishing the understanding (all the powers of perception) from the will (motives). As we have seen, eighteenth-century writers such as Franklin had succeeded in dignifying prudential calculation as a rational power of the will. By the early nineteenth century the leading Scottish moral philosopher of the time, Dugald Stewart, and his followers at Harvard, Levi Frisbie and Levi Hedge, were clear that both prudence and the moral sense were rational powers of the will.[76] The Transcendental distinction between Reason and Understanding challenged this acceptance of prudence as fully rational; prudential motives belonged with Understanding. Reason, as distinguished from Understanding, represented a moral faculty untainted by self-interest.

Separating Reason from Understanding provided Transcendentalists with a lever for social criticism. In principle, of course, they admitted that the Understanding was a necessary and legitimate faculty; in practice, Transcendentalists felt it dominated American life at the expense of Reason. America's mercenary civilization, Fuller complained, "leaves the nobler faculties undeveloped."[77] Her account of *Summer on the Lakes* (1843) is a sustained critique of the failure of American commercial society on the frontier—its failure to respect nature, the alternative culture of the Indians, and the potential autonomy of the women settlers. The faculty of prudence, which Franklin had tried to nurture as an aid to conscience, had overreached itself.

As redefined, Reason was also an aesthetic faculty. Reason was in harmony with the feelings, especially such finer sentiments as the love of beauty and the love of truth. It could be nourished and strengthened by the artistic imagination. The literary historian Lawrence Buell has shown how, out of Unitarian aesthetic theory, came Emerson's image of the poet-priest.[78] Margaret Fuller pushed this tendency further; central to her Romantic aesthetic was the image of the genius-hero. This individual, guided by transcendent Reason, followed wherever it led, overcoming prejudice and fear, heedless of the consequences. Through artistic or other forms of leadership, this genius-hero would communicate to benighted humanity what Reason had revealed. In the end, such a person would attain a quality of vision which might be summed up in the most famous quotation attributed to Fuller: "I accept the universe."[79]

Supposedly Margaret Fuller said this to Thomas Carlyle, who responded, "By Gad, she'd better." The story is recounted by Perry Miller, but he terms it "legendary," and it does not show up in the sources. Just the same, the quotation is in character for Fuller, and it expressed a sentiment that would have been appreciated by Jonathan Edwards, if not by Carlyle. (Like Edwards's, Fuller's moral and aesthetic peace with the universe was hard won through existential struggle.) Although this anecdote has him poking fun at her, Carlyle recognized a kindred heroic spirit in Fuller.[80]

∂⊷ WOMANHOOD IN THE NINETEENTH CENTURY

Living in the generation that she did, Margaret Fuller was in a position to interpret the newly redefined Reason as a feminine faculty. By then, evangelical Christianity and the rise of polite culture had cooperated to emancipate women from some of the moral opprobrium with which they had long been stigmatized. To challenge the traditional image of women as slaves of their passions there had arisen a newer image of women as bearers of spiritual, moral, and aesthetic values. Instead of seductive threats to virtue, women could be considered its guardians. This was the basis upon which Catharine Beecher and Dorothea Dix, among others, constructed their model of the woman as reformer or redeemer of society.[81] The stage had been set—it would seem—for Margaret Fuller to proclaim that women were the superior disciples of Reason; men, the servants of mere Understanding. The argument Fuller actually made, however, was more accurate, subtle, and tough-minded.

Woman in the Nineteenth Century, Fuller's most important surviving work, was published in 1845; it was an expansion of an article published in 1843 entitled "The Great Lawsuit: Man *versus* Men, Woman *versus* Women." Although the reader expects the "lawsuit" to pit Woman against the oppressions of Man, Fuller constructs it as a struggle by imperfect individuals to realize the perfect ideal of Man or Woman. This ideal, which constitutes humanity's "inheritance" in the "lawsuit," is the Neoplatonic fulfillment of oneness with nature and the divine, as well as the ultimate expression of self-improvement. The key prerequisite for claiming the inheritance is to formulate an idea of what it would be like if we had it.[82]

In 1792, Mary Wollstonecraft had grounded her *Vindication of the Rights of Women* on eighteenth-century faculty psychology, arguing for the supremacy of reason and for the recognition that women share in this universal rational faculty.[83] In the 1840s, Margaret Fuller based her case for women on her adaptation of nineteenth-century Transcendentalist understanding of the faculties and their capacity for progressive growth.[84] The development of the faculties of *man* has been celebrated since time immemorial, she observed; now it is time to celebrate the development of the faculties of *woman.* The first step must be to forge a positive image of the potential of womanhood. In her effort to recover for the nineteenth century the full range of feminine possibilities that had ever been envisioned, Fuller mined her rich knowledge of literature, history, and myth. The archetypes of mythology were especially useful. As one scholar has put it, "In order to revise the self-estimation of women, Margaret Fuller had to transform the very gods that they worshipped."[85]

Woman in the Nineteenth Century stands in a traditon of Plotinian inward natural religion. It addresses a woman's quest for growth, fulfillment, and self-realization. Not only artists and philosophers, but everyone and everything in the universe are involved in such a quest, struggling by "divine instinct" to fulfill their destiny. "It is not woman, but the law of right, the law of growth, that speaks in us, and demands the perfection of each being in its kind, apple as apple, woman as woman."[86] In opposition to this ideal stood the prevailing practice, in which women's natures were developed only insofar as they were useful or pleasing to men. In its Neoplatonism, *Woman in the Nineteenth Century* presents a striking contrast with the Declaration drawn up by the women's rights convention at Seneca Falls in 1848. That document stands firmly in the tradition of Jefferson, Wollstonecraft, and Lockean contractualism. Fuller was out of the country by then; one wonders what role she would have played at the convention and how she would have brought her own very different feminist theory to bear.

The core of the problem of gender, as Fuller saw it, was the traditional belief that "the gift of reason, man's highest prerogative, is allotted to [women] in a much lower degree."[87] This faulty tenet of faculty psychology had been used to justify denying women autonomy and treating them in effect as "slaves," that is, instruments for goals defined by others. Once women were acknowledged to be possessed of the full range of human capacities—"intellect" as well as "affection" and "habits"—it would be clear that they exist and have value in their own right, not as means to the ends of men.[88] Recognizing women as whole personalities would entail widespread social transformations. Women needed "a much greater range of occupations than they have, to rouse their latent powers." ("Let them be sea-captains, if they will," she wrote.) Women needed to consent to the laws by which they were governed. In every human relationship, private as well as public, women should stop living for men and become more autonomous and assertive. Using virginity as a metaphor for self-sufficiency, Fuller concluded: "Would she [that is, Woman] but assume her inheritance, Mary would not be the only virgin mother."[89]

"There are two aspects of woman's nature, represented by the ancients as Muse and Minerva," Fuller explained. Although she nowhere made the identification explicit, the qualities she attributed to the Muse were those the Transcendentalists called Reason; those attributed to Minerva, the Understanding.[90] The urgent need for self-sufficiency dictated that, for the time being, women should cultivate their Understanding. The childishness and frivolousness women sometimes displayed were consequences of their constricting environment, not of their potential. The assertion of worldly self-interest had been denied them, leaving the faculty of Understanding stunted in women. To undo this harm required "in the present crisis, that the preference [be] given to Minerva." Once the effects of male oppression had been undone, however, women would be free to develop their true natures. Then the Muse of Reason would come into her own. "The electrical, the magnetic element in Woman has not fairly been brought out in any period. Everything might be expected from it; she has far more of it than man."[91]

In crediting women with more of Reason, Fuller was not embracing a doctrine of female superiority. "What Woman needs is not as a woman to act or rule, but as a nature to grow, as an intellect to discern, as a soul to live freely and unimpeded."[92] Unlike Emerson and Alcott, Fuller was not convinced that matter was inferior to spirit, or Understanding necessarily inferior to Reason. Her dualism stressed the coexistence of mind and matter, not the superiority of mind. It is typical of her practical sense of balance that she remained aware of the merits of Franklin's prudential maxims, even when criticizing American commercial culture. Indeed, to the surprise of her contemporaries, Fuller was not sure that even the passions should be subordinated.[93] She had moved beyond a hierarchical ranking of the human faculties to a concern with symmetry and complementarity.[94]

Fuller's ideas on race illustrate this synthesizing goal. In her review of the *Narrative of Frederick Douglass,* Fuller rejoiced that it illustrated "the powers of the Black Race" and expressed the opinion that the African and European races each had its own creative artistic "element," which might in American culture be synthesized with each other so as "to give to genius a development, and to the energies of character a balance and harmony[,] beyond what has been seen heretofore in the history of the world."[95] Like other feminists of her generation, Fuller found chattel slavery a powerful analogy and metaphor for the discussion of conventional relations between the sexes.[96]

Margaret Fuller sought to unify divided lives and overcome the mutual alienation of many polarities: art and life, idealism and realism, thought and action, passion and intellect, Greek and Roman, Reason and Understanding, female and male. Man and woman were "the two halves of one thought. . . . The development of the one cannot be effected without that of the other." "There is no wholly masculine man, no purely feminine woman," she wrote—consciously building upon Proclus but also anticipating one of the major insights of Freud. "The growth of man is two-fold, masculine and feminine," she concluded. No psychological "faculties have been given pure to either [sex], but only in preponderance," and each gender should be developed in every personality. "If these two developments were in perfect harmony, they would correspond to and fulfill one another, like hemispheres."[97] The heroic ideal had both male and female sides.

❧ CONCLUSION

This chapter has been about Margaret Fuller's heroic ideal, not about Margaret Fuller's heroism. In the end, of course, she lived out her ideal. Dispatched by Greeley's *New York Tribune* to cover the Italian revolution of 1848, she became America's first war correspondent. In this role she found at last the vocation she had been looking for all her life, an effective blend of idealism and activism. Some biographers have seen in Fuller's Italian career a repudiation of her New England past and its bourgeois, bookish sterility.[98] But the Italian years seem better to illustrate Fuller's successful resolution of her lifelong quest for identity, a fulfillment rather than a repudiation of her earlier goals.

Arrived in Rome, Fuller found life in the city she had always associated with discipline to be liberating. There she involved herself heroically in the way she had long dreamt of doing: reporting and participating in a revolution against oppression, tradition, and obscurantism, on behalf of republicanism and human potential. There too she met and loved a man, bore and loved their child. There, like the genius-hero she had described, she witnessed suffering, endured hardship, and grew personally as a result. On her way home, the woman who had written, "Let them be sea-captains," met her death heroically in a storm at sea.

Margaret Fuller's interaction with other feminists had been limited during her lifetime. Some of them came to their positions from ideologies with which she had little intellectual sympathy—for example, Frances Wright's Jacksonian anticlericalism or Sarah Grimke's evangelical abolitionism. In any case, women's rights as an organized movement did not appear until after Fuller had left for Europe. But after her death, Margaret Fuller's heroic ideal of womanhood exercised enormous influence. Elizabeth Cady Stanton, Paulina Wright Davis, Lucinda Chandler, Elizabeth Oakes Smith, Caroline Healey Dall, Ednah Dow Chaney, Georgiana Bruce Kirby, and many other feminist leaders and writers testified to this. Less well known are the thousands of rank-and-file nineteenth-century women who read her works and participated in the dozens of women's clubs, many of them named for her, that were self-consciously modeled on her ideals and example.[99] Even today, these have by no means exhausted their power.

At the conclusion of *Woman in the Nineteenth Century*, Margaret

Fuller had written, "What concerns me now is, that my life be a beautiful, powerful, in a word, a complete, life in its kind."[100] Although she was only forty when she died, Fuller's life was, in its way, a complete one. She had known political commitment, professional fulfillment, international recognition, a romance that defied convention, and the experience of motherhood. Is it too much to think that, in the end, she embodied her own heroic ideal: "the woman who shall vindicate their birthright for all women"?

The Constructed Self Against the State

When the news came to Concord of Margaret Fuller's death, Henry David Thoreau (1817–1862) hastened to Fire Island, New York, to comb the beach in hopes of finding her body or her effects, especially the manuscript of her book on the revolution in Rome. His efforts, like those of others, were in vain; the book and its author were lost forever. Margaret and David (as his family called him) had been friends and fellow Transcendentalists. The two provided each other with intellectual stimulation and mutual criticism; they reinforced each other's dedication to self-construction and self-culture.[1]

It would seem ironic today to apply the term "self-made man" to Henry David Thoreau. Thoreau was quite indifferent to the ideal of success as American society defined it. He despised the world of middle-class respectability that Abraham Lincoln and Frederick Douglass worked so hard to join. He dismissed the party politics that engaged them so deeply. The market revolution, which Lincoln sought to foster, held no allure for a man who deliberately set out to prove that one could get along without most of its new consumer goods. Polite culture he rejected along with the prudential rationale that justified it. Yet Thoreau was, in his own way, engaged in the same sort of enterprise as Lincoln and Douglass: consciously constructing an identity of his own.

Thoreau's greatest work, *Walden,* is a story about the quest for an authentic identity, a search the author pursues outside of society in an experimental communion with nature. This chapter, however, will examine a different work: the famous essay on what has come to be called "civil disobedience." Although widely read and taught, the essay has not been the subject of anything like the massive, intense scholarly examination that *Walden* has received.[2] I wish to show that the real subject of the essay is the construction of a moral self, to which the act of breaking the law is a means. In constructing this self, Thoreau worked within the framework of the faculty psychology of his age, to which, however, he gave a distinctive twist of his own. Thoreau refused to accept the conventional wisdom that conscience was a weak faculty, and undertook to illustrate, through precept and example, the potential power of conscience in everyday life.

Although Henry David Thoreau was not a member of any church and rejected orthodox Christian theological formulations, his essay is in its way a religious document, part of the literature of spiritual perfectionism. While earlier writers, such as Publius, had been concerned to show how virtue manifested itself in active citizenship, Thoreau saw the state as a potential threat to the good life. His essay on resisting state authority constitutes one of the boldest and most eloquent assertions of the right and duty to self-construction, and as such will provide an appropriate point at which to conclude our account.

Thoreau wrote in an arresting, epigrammatic style, deliberately provocative and paradoxical. A number of misconceptions have grown up about his famous essay: a lot of what "everyone knows" about it is not true, beginning with the title, "Civil Disobedience." There is no evidence that Henry David Thoreau ever used the expression "civil disobedience" in his life. "Resistance to Civil Government" was the title that Thoreau himself gave to his famous essay. After his death, the title was changed to "Civil Disobedience" in an 1866 edition of some of his shorter works. Very likely, Thoreau's editors felt "Resistance to Civil Government" smacked too much of the late Confederate rebellion. But their change tones down the assertiveness of Thoreau's original title. The changed title has fostered the misapprehension that Thoreau taught that acceptance of legal punishment was part of the duty of civil resistance. Actually, although he himself went to jail for the offense it discusses, the essay does not say that acceptance of legal punishment is a necessary part of a moral defiance of the law. Like Margaret Fuller, Thoreau suffered at the hands of his well-meaning literary executors.

Although most of those who have invoked his example have practiced nonviolence, Thoreau nowhere in his essay says that resistance to civil government should be nonviolent. And although many in America have invoked his authority to disobey laws they considered unconstitutional, Thoreau was completely unconcerned with issues of constitutionality. He subjected law to the test of morality, and regarded the Constitution of the United States as just one other form of human law to be brought to the bar of conscience. Finally, Thoreau differed from his twentieth-century followers in standing outside all organized movements of protest and reform.

Thoreau's critics have been no more accurate in their understanding of his essay than his professed followers. Contrary to some accusations, Thoreau did not espouse anarchy (except as a millennial ideal, the same way Karl Marx did). Nor was Thoreau unmindful of social responsibility. He respected the law enough to want to perfect it, to make it embody more closely what his generation called the higher law of morality and justice. And if he did not join any reform associations, he was nevertheless very conscious of his political context, and of writing for a particular audience whose political behavior he wished to influence.

✌ THE CONTEXT OF RESISTANCE

"Resistance to Civil Government" is demonstrably a major document, an inspiration to the human spirit that has transcended the limitations of time, space, and culture. It has been invoked by the Fabian Socialists in Britain, the anarchists in Russia, Upton Sinclair, Emma Goldman, Norman Thomas, and Martin Luther King in the United States, Mohandas Gandhi in India, the Danish resistance in World War II, and the early protesters against South African *Apartheid*.[3] Yet the essay hinges on a trivial episode: Thoreau spent one night in the county jail in his home town of Concord, Massachusetts, for nonpayment of a state poll tax.

Massachusetts had had a poll tax since colonial times. In Thoreau's day it was one dollar and fifty cents a year—about one percent of the earnings of an average New England farm laborer.[4] It was levied only on adult males. Uniform throughout the state, the poll tax was used for the support of local government. Fragmentary surviving tax records for

Concord indicate nonpayment of the poll tax was not unusual, especially among poorer people. Those who did not pay forfeited the right
to vote but were seldom otherwise pursued by the law.

In 1843, Bronson Alcott and Charles Lane refused to pay the poll tax
in Concord on ideological grounds. The two men were abolitionists
and anarchists; law-breaking for the sake of conscience had been advocated for years by people in their circles.[5] Both were arrested but
quickly released when another person paid the tax on their behalf.
When Henry Thoreau heard of their action, he made light of it in a
letter to a friend.[6] But Thoreau typically saw the comic and the serious
side of things simultaneously, and shortly afterwards he began refusing
to pay his own poll tax. In his case, however, the authorities took no
action against him for several years—perhaps because the village tax
collector and constable, one Sam Staples, was his hunting companion.

On the twenty-third or twenty-fourth day of July, 1846 (we cannot
tell which), Staples and Thoreau met by chance on the street. Staples
mentioned Thoreau's nonpayment of the tax, offering to lend him the
money or help him seek a reduced assessment from the selectmen.
Thoreau refused the offers. "Henry, if you don't pay, I shall have to
lock you up pretty soon," Staples is quoted as saying. "As well now as
any time, Sam." "Well, come along then."[7] Staples showed Thoreau to
a cell. Word of the arrest spread quickly in the village. Before nightfall,
an unknown party had paid Thoreau's tax for him. (The favorite suspect is Aunt Maria Thoreau.) Staples, who did not share Thoreau's
radical convictions and who was probably a bit peeved with his friend,
decided it was too much trouble to go back to the jail and release him.
So Henry David Thoreau spent the night in jail, though his tax bill had
already been paid, and was set free the next morning. The whole
business was irregular: legally, Staples should have proceeded against
Thoreau's property rather than his person, seizing a portion of his
library, for example, to sell at auction.[8] Whoever paid Thoreau's tax for
him cut short his gesture of protest and earned no gratitude; the
famous essay includes a bitter little paragraph accusing the unnamed
party of letting "their private feelings interfere with the public good."[9]

It is characteristic of Thoreau that he was able to turn this insig-
nificant episode into the basis of a great essay. He had a genius for
making even minor personal experiences (sometimes recast with poetic
license) into images of literary power. Henry David Thoreau is mem-
orable only for his writings, not for his deeds. In this respect he is

unlike Abraham Lincoln, Frederick Douglass, or Margaret Fuller. Unlike them too, Thoreau had no personal magnetism: he was neither heroic, nor temperamentally composed, nor considerate of other people. But he was able to create a literary *persona,* an authorial image, of power. The constructed self that interests us in his case is a purely literary invention. The narrator of the essay on "Resistance to Civil Government" is almost as much a literary construct as the pseudonymous author of *The Federalist Papers.* The historical Thoreau, the Thoreau of flesh and blood, is of interest to the extent that he helps us understand his constructed literary *persona.*

When Thoreau began withholding his poll tax he was probably protesting the complicity of his state in returning fugitives from southern slavery. An attempt to return a black man named George Latimer to slavery in the autumn of 1842 had aroused a storm of protest in Massachusetts. Early in 1843, the commonwealth responded by passing a "personal liberty law" that prohibited state officials from assisting in the capture of alleged fugitives. But the most committed abolitionists felt this did not go far enough; they demanded that Massachusetts refuse to recognize any property rights in human beings, regardless of what the federal Constitution might say. Thoreau associated himself with this position, at least by implication.[10] But at first he gave no public account of his reasons for not paying the poll tax; it was a private act on his part, as had been his earlier refusal to pay the tax for the support of the town church, a refusal the authorities had accepted.[11] In May of 1846, the United States and Mexico declared war on each other. Thoreau went to jail two months after this, and when drawing up his account of the episode, he cast it as a protest not only against slavery, but also against the war. The two were logically connected, since Thoreau, like many other northerners, regarded the war as aggression waged on behalf of slavery. In deciding to prepare a public statement, Thoreau was converting what had started out as a private act of conscientious refusal into what political theorists today call civil disobedience, that is, an attempt to influence state policy through publicized, principled law-breaking.

In June 1846, one month after the outbreak of war between Mexico and the United States, Thoreau published an antiwar statement in the *Boston Courier,* a newspaper that had been supporting the war effort. The statement (which did not come to scholars' attention until 1988) appeared under the title "Conflict of Laws":

In the conflict of laws, one law must be supreme. If our state laws conflict with our national, the state law yields. The higher law always renders the conflicting lower law null and void. Is it not so in all cases? If the national law bids me do what my conscience forbids, must not my conscience be supreme? Shall the law of conscience or the law of Christ be repealed by the Congress of the United States?[12]

Having staked out a moral claim to disobedience based on the analogy with American constitutional law, Thoreau then applied this principle to the existing war. He asserted that he would not serve in the army during the unjust war with Mexico, even if drafted. Since the United States did not conscript soldiers in the Mexican War, clearly Thoreau was raising the issue of civil disobedience as a vehicle for debating the morality of the war—not because a decision of conscience was actually forced upon him. Resistance to civil government, which Thoreau had initiated some three years earlier with his private conscientious refusal to pay the poll tax, would from this time on be part of an opposition to government policy both public and private, a tactic for reform as well as a matter of personal integrity. The war clearly precipitated this change in Thoreau's attitude. The next month, Thoreau chose to go to jail, escalating his level of protest.

The first version of "Resistance to Civil Government" was in lecture form; this was typical of the evolution Thoreau's essays underwent. The lecture was entitled "The Rights and Duties of the Individual in Relation to Government." No manuscript of the lecture survives, but the title implies that although he was addressing concrete political issues, slavery and the war, he was ultimately interested in general principles. The lecture was not given until January of 1848, by which time the war with Mexico was nearly over. The essay version first appeared in a Transcendentalist literary magazine called *Aesthetic Papers* in May 1849. In the essay, Thoreau briefly alludes to a third issue, besides slavery and the war, as justifying resistance to the American government of his day: the treatment of the Indian tribes.[13]

Why did Thoreau wait so long after his night in jail to lecture on the experience? The recently discovered newspaper statement helps us understand the delay. As that document testifies, Thoreau had attempted to preserve some of the conventional nonresistant attitude toward government. "I submit to loss, inconvenience, suffering, in obedience to law even if I conceive the law unjust," he declared, "but I cannot do wrong," even to obey the law. Attempting to apply this distinction, Thoreau expressed a willingness to pay federal taxes for the war effort, but not to serve in the army.[14]

The next month, Thoreau was arrested for his longstanding non-payment of the state poll tax. At some point—we cannot be sure when—he realized he could use this episode as part of his antiwar protest. Since refusing service in the army did not provide a way to resist the war directly, he would turn his earlier refusal to pay the poll tax to this new purpose. But it evidently took a while for him to figure out how to construct a new rationale for the protest, one that would justify refusal to pay a tax. The statement of June 15, 1846, had been composed hastily, in response to his feeling of outrage at the war. When he finally worked out his new position, he abandoned the commitment to "submitting to unrighteous laws" and the duty to paying war taxes that went with it.

Thoreau came from a family of committed abolitionists. The wing of the abolition movement to which they belonged was led by William Lloyd Garrison and was committed to total pacifism. Not even the government possessed the moral right to resort to violence, in their view—a position that led them to a version of anarchism. In order to avoid complicity in the evils of government, the Garrisonians refused to vote. Their position, termed "non-resistance" or "no-government," distinguished them from those abolitionists who engaged in politics, led by James G. Birney.[15]

Thoreau fully shared the Garrisonians' loathing for slavery. He felt that every person and institution sanctioning slavery, even passively, was corrupted by it. Like them he refrained from voting. But he never joined the Garrisonian organization, and he differed with both their nonresistant and no-government stands. In 1841, Thoreau challenged the nonresisters to debate in the Concord town lyceum and was congratulated afterwards for the skill with which he opposed Alcott.[16] Thoreau's original title, "Resistance to Civil Government," highlights his rejection of the principle of nonresistance. In the text itself, Thoreau acknowledged the validity of anarchy as an ultimate ideal when people have progressed morally to the point where they are ready for it. "But," he went on, "to speak practically and as a citizen, unlike those who call themselves no-government men, I ask for, not at once no government, but *at once* a better government."[17] By italicizing the words *"at once"* Thoreau was associating himself with the immediatism characteristic of abolitionists, who rejected as inadequate proposals for gradual emancipation. At the same time he was dissociating himself from Garrisonian anarchism.

Why did Thoreau turn to public lawbreaking as a vehicle for protest against the evil of slavery? Part of the answer lies in his sense of the failure of alternatives. Thoreau complains in his essay that legally provided remedies "take too much time, and a man's life will be gone."[18] This may well sound irresponsible, and it was meant to sound provocative. Yet it accurately reflected the virtual impossibility of eliminating slavery by the only legal means recognized at the time, Constitutional amendment. A Constitutional amendment requires ratification by three-quarters of the states, and if the fifteen slave states had all refused to ratify, not even the fifty-state Union of the twentieth century could have abolished slavery thus. As Thoreau put it, "in this case [continuing slavery], the State has provided no way: its very Constitution is the evil."[19]

In 1849, with the war over and his essay on "Resistance to Civil Government" finally published, Thoreau seems to have resumed paying his poll tax—for so the fragmentary Concord tax records, which show his 1849 poll tax "paid," are generally interpreted.[20] It possible that someone else was paying the tax for him. But it would have been quite characteristic of Thoreau to feel that he had made his point and "had other lives to live."[21] It was the literary delineation of the moral self that really engaged him, and the utility of defying the poll tax for this purpose was limited. Let us now examine Thoreau's conception of the moral self.

❧ THE ESSAY ON RESISTANCE

Henry David Thoreau declared that resistance to government was sometimes a moral obligation. When called upon to obey an unjust law, if the matter is important, if the incompatibility of the law with common moral standards is clear, and if a decision cannot be avoided, a person should disobey. In some circumstances this refusal will be a useful tactic for reform—and even if it is not, a government unresponsive to moral suasion is probably illegitimate and not entitled to obedience anyway.

Modern political philosophy distinguishes between conscientious refusal and civil disobedience. The former is performed as a matter of personal integrity when an individual is faced with a command he considers immoral. Any hope that constituted authority will change its mind is irrelevant, and frequently there is none. Conscientious refusal is often religious in motivation; pacifists who become conscientious objectors in wartime are a classic example. What modern political philosophers call civil disobedience, on the other hand, is undertaken as a reform tactic. Here, the refusal to obey the law is necessarily public, since the goal is to influence public opinion. Typically, modern civil disobedients organize their protest, commit themselves to nonviolence, and accept legal punishment. The disobedients demonstrate their profound moral repugnance for the law and hope to persuade the authorities or the electorate to reconsider it. Civil disobedience in this sense works only when dealing with authorities who are responsive to moral suasion, or who can be influenced by constituents who are.[22]

The distinction drawn by modern political science between conscientious refusal and civil disobedience is not made by Thoreau in the essay. He discusses resistance both as a matter of individual integrity and as a reform tactic, though there can be no doubt that he accords primacy to acting out of personal integrity. Action from principle may also be socially useful, but a duty is a duty, whatever the consequences: "This people must cease to hold slaves, and to make war on Mexico, though it cost them their existence as a people."[23]

Thoreau's essay assumes that he is dealing with a representative democratic government, of acknowledged legitimacy, enjoying the support of the majority of the population. He does not concern himself with tyrannical or colonial governments whose legitimacy is in question. In the latter cases, his task would have been too easy. His audience needed no persuading that the British colonial authorities of 1776, or the continental autocracies of their own 1840s, had no valid claim to necessary obedience.[24] Americans of Thoreau's day accepted as axiomatic the Lockean-Jeffersonian principle that governments derive their just powers from the consent of the governed, and Thoreau did not challenge this axiom. But he applied it in an unorthodox way. The unit that gives consent, he asserts, is not the majority but the individual. The reason, he explains, is that consent is a moral judgment, for which each individual is accountable to his own conscience.[25] The majority, on the other hand, is not a *moral* entity and its right to rule not a moral entitlement. As Bronson Alcott, who set Thoreau the example of resistance to civil government, aptly put it, "In the theocracy of the soul majorities do not rule."[26] The alleged right of the majority to rule, Thoreau declared, is based merely on the assumption that "they are physically the strongest."[27]

Thoreau begins his essay thus: "I heartily accept the motto,—'That government is best which governs least;' and I should like to see it acted up to more rapidly and systematically."[28] The motto appears to place Thoreau at the outset in the liberal tradition of Locke, Jefferson, and classical economics. Actually, his use of it is ironic. Thoreau took the motto from the masthead of a newspaper of the day, *The Democratic Review,* edited by John L. O'Sullivan. *The Democratic Review* supported the Democratic administration of President James Knox Polk and was a leading advocate of imperialism and the war. Thoreau is deliberately quoting from one of his political adversaries in order to use this adversary's own principles against him. (The judo tactic in debate, it is sometimes called.)[29] Thoreau would have been familiar with the motto because he had earlier published a book review in the paper. Although Democratic and pro-war, the *Review* was northern-based and in some respects antislavery. It seems unlikely, however, that Thoreau harbored any expectation that this piece too might find acceptance from O'Sullivan.

David Greenstone, in the course of distinguishing reform liberals from humanist liberals, decided that "what reform liberals all shared was belief in the possibility of a duty that transcended political commitments and institutions."[30] Was Thoreau then a reform liberal? I would argue that he was not any kind of liberal, but a Romantic religious perfectionist. Thoreau's orientation to political thought did not really come primarily from the liberal tradition. His extensive library included none of Locke's political writings and nothing at all by Jefferson.[31] He conceded the applicability of liberal premises to American institutions of government only in order to consign them to the inferior realm of the man-made, as opposed to the eternal moral principles of nature.

The coordinates of Thoreau's thinking about politics had been established by his study of moral philosophy as an undergraduate. The philosophers whom Harvard College took most seriously in his day were ethical intuitionists like the Scotsman Dugald Stewart. A favorite whipping-boy of Harvard moral philosophy was William Paley, Archdeacon of Carlisle and popularizer of "Christian Evidences."[32] Paley's eighteenth-century theological utilitarianism equated virtue with a prudential desire for a heavenly reward—a position that Thoreau regarded with contempt. As the title "Resistance to Civil Government" indicates, Thoreau framed his argument as a sarcastic commentary on Paley's chapter on the "Duty of Submission to Civil Government" in his *Moral and Political Philosophy.* Paley, a good English Whig, thought resistance to government sometimes justified, but only when a calculation indicated that, on balance, the government was doing more harm than good to the community and should be replaced.[33] (Paley only deals with the question of revolution, not with selective civil disobedience.) Thoreau comments sardonically: "Paley never seems to have contemplated those cases to which the rule of expediency does not apply, in which a people, as well as an individual, must do justice, cost what it may. If I have unjustly wrested a plank from a drowning man, I must restore it to him though I drown myself. This, according to Paley, would be inconvenient. But he that would save his life, in such a case, shall lose it."[34] Paley represented a tradition in Latitudinarian Anglicanism going all the way back to Archbishop Tillotson and John Locke, one that Benjamin Franklin had found congenial.[35] For Thoreau, Paley typified the shortcomings of the whole of bourgeois utilitarian liberalism, concerned with self-interest and expediency. It is no accident that Thoreau's essay, along with his other writings, gained a significant audience only when nineteenth-century liberalism was coming under widespread attack.

Thoreau's education had also familiarized him with the Latin and Greek classics. While writing his essay on "Resistance to Civil Government," he returned to Sophocles' *Antigone,* which he had read as an undergraduate, and translated passages from the heroine's defiance of civil authority.[36] But Thoreau cannot be identified with the tradition of classical republicanism. Classical republicanism assumed that man was essentially a political animal, and the good whole life necessarily a political one. Thoreau sharply disagreed. To him, the good man was not necessarily an actively engaged citizen.[37] Thoreau set Virtue and Commerce in opposition to each other on Romantic premises, not classical ones. Where the conventional American version of classical republicanism justified private property as a guarantor of political independence, Thoreau declared private property a hindrance to political independence.[38]

To understand Thoreau's purpose in the essay "Resistance to Civil Government," we must see it as an example of religious perfectionism.

Among the earliest and most consistently influential examples of the constructed self in American culture were religious identities. The distinguishing characteristic of the evangelical tradition is its insistence that a proper Christian must be born again, that is, must experience a transformation into a new identity as follower of Christ. The decision for Christ is generally conceived as a response to divine grace.[39] Henry David Thoreau's writings are also framed to provoke in his readers a conversion experience of a sort—or at least, as preparation for a transforming grace that will be encountered in nature. The objective is a new identity as a moral being, and this demands a conscious resolve.[40]

By Thoreau's time the Calvinist model of conversion through irresistible divine grace had come under serious attack by theological liberals. The liberals, who came eventually to embrace a Unitarian christology, conceived of conversion as a gradual process, natural rather than supernatural, moral as well as spiritual. Their theology was Arminian, that is, predicated on the belief that human beings had the free will to choose good over evil. Arminian clergy like William Ellery Channing and their academic counterparts, the Harvard moral philosophers, taught the cultivation of a Christian character as a lifelong process.[41] Henry Thoreau, like Margaret Fuller, received this heritage of religious thought and self-culture, elaborating it, as she did, in the direction of Transcendentalist perfectionism.[42]

The political tradition most relevant to Thoreau was Christian, or rather, Judeo-Christian, for his was a prophetic role. He was one of those who serve the state by recalling it to serve the eternal verities, "and so," he reminds us, "necessarily resist it for the most part."[43] His political predecessors were Protestants who pitted their consciences against the demands of constituted authority, like Roger Williams of Rhode Island. Particularly relevant was Jonathan Dymond (1796–1828), an English Quaker whose *Essays on the Principles of Morality* Thoreau studied in his student days. Dymond argued that the American colonists of 1776 could have made their point successfully and without bloodshed simply by massive noncompliance with the tax laws.[44]

Thoreau's essay on "Resistance to Civil Government" attempted to revive the spirit of Protestant Dissent in a former Puritan Commonwealth. His use of Christian imagery was invariably metaphorical, for in a literal sense Thoreau was not a believer, not even in the heterodox faiths common among Garrisonian abolitionists. But the ethical ideal he invoked could be authentically Christian: "Under a government which imprisons any unjustly, the true place for a just man is also a prison," he declared—"the only house in a slave-state in which a free man can abide with honor."[45] Like all his major works, the essay on "Resistance to Civil Government" concludes by looking forward to a millennial dawn. In this case, the new age would be a time when every human being had a fully developed conscience, and no coercive state would be needed.

The essence of Thoreau's message in all his writings is the same: the necessity for individual self-realization. He calls upon each member of his audience to obey the fundamental laws of his or her own being, without regard for neighbors, nation, church, or custom. Observing nature and reading great literature can help one discover these laws; the chief hindrance is society. (In defining society as the enemy of individual identity, Thoreau is, of course, the polar opposite of Horace Bushnell.) For Thoreau, *organized* society is especially dangerous: businesses, clubs, political parties, philanthropic associations, and, of course, the state. Even the family can be a problem, he notes.[46] The institution of slavery, which reduced human beings to living tools, was the ultimate denial of everything Thoreau stood for, and he correctly focused upon it his strongest hatred. Thoreau's biographer, Robert D. Richardson, has appropriately noted that "the earliest stages of Thoreau's move to Walden coincided with the emergence of Frederick Douglass, and the publication of Douglass's narrative of how he gained his freedom. *Walden* is about self-emancipation, but not at the expense of ignoring the problem of external, physical freedom."[47]

Thoreau believed that his American contemporaries lacked secure individual identities and were vainly pursuing them through socially defined but unsatisfying roles—a criticism recently repeated by the cultural historian Lewis Perry.[48] As he wrote in *Walden,* "We should not *play* life, or *study* it merely, . . . but earnestly *live* it from beginning to end."[49] According to Thoreau, one who engages successfully in the quest for personal authenticity will discover that his self-made identity is also his natural one. (He thus resolves the conflict between the Jacksonian celebration of the natural man and the Whig celebration of the constructed one.)[50]

While Thoreau's original act of not paying a tax was an assertion of private integrity, his public lecture and published essay on resistance to government were clearly intended to encourage others to take similar actions. In all his writings, Thoreau was in the somewhat self-contradictory position of one who exhorts his audience not to listen to others.[51] His way of resolving the paradox was to rely upon his own example, leaving others to apply it as they saw fit. His symbolic action of going to jail, which he makes the centerpiece of the essay on "Resistance to Civil Government," functions in this way, as does his symbolic withdrawal to a cabin in the woods in the book *Walden*. He typifies in extreme form the Romantic artist who proclaims that his art is a form of self-construction rather than a product produced for a patron, a public, or the market.

Thoreau was the ultimate Pelagian: whatever was important in life could only be achieved by an individual for himself. Most of the reformers of his day made the mistake, he felt, of trying to redeem others.[52] Thoreau was less optimistic than most of them were about average human nature. He expected only a handful of people to break free from the pettiness of ordinary existence and realize their human potential. The most important thing the few real *"men"* (as he called them) could do for their fellows was to set them an example of heroic independence.[53] This, civil disobedience accomplished. Resistance to government in the name of principle ennobles the one who performs it, and at the same time sets an example of authenticity in action—an example all are free to follow who can muster the moral courage. So committed was Thoreau to resistance as the best form of political protest that, not being able to find a suitable occasion for publicly violating a federal law, he used the violation of a state law to protest federal (as well as state) policies—though he as much as admitted this was stretching a point.[54]

The most important function Thoreau was willing to concede to the state was education. "To educate the wise man, the State exists; and with the appearance of the wise man, the State expires." So Thoreau's friend Ralph Waldo Emerson had written in his essay on "Politics."[55] Thoreau too believed that the good state, like all good educators, would end by making itself redundant. In the meantime, a few wise men could rightly be a law unto themselves. The best state "even would not think it inconsistent with its own repose, if a few were to live aloof from it, not meddling with it, nor embraced by it, who fulfilled all the duties of neighbors and fellow-men."[56] While continuing to fulfill their social responsibilities, these few do not require the coercion of the state. The enlightened state would permit them to serve as examples of voluntary harmony with self and others.

However much Thoreau had in common with Emerson's philosophy, in spirit he was closer to Thomas Carlyle (1795–1881). Both were tormented souls who passionately hungered after righteousness. Like Carlyle, Thoreau rebelled against bourgeois conformity and conventional religion. The two men appreciated each other's writing, and Carlyle exerted considerable influence on Thoreau. Most important of all, Thoreau shared Carlyle's admiration for the hero and the heroic.[57] Like Carlyle, Thoreau can be understood as a secularized version of a Calvinist saint. "Law never made men a whit more just," declared Thoreau, showing he retained his New England Puritan ancestors' contempt for a mere outward civility that lacked the conviction of the heart.[58] Jonathan Edwards would have said, "Amen."

In Thoreau's secularization of Calvinism, it was the individual conscience, not the Divine Word revealed in Scripture, that was the source of moral truths.[59] These truths were objective; they ought to be the same for all human beings. Though the negligence of most people sometimes impaired their vision, Thoreau did not worry very much about the problem of knowing the right. The problem that concerned him was getting people to *act* on the basis of their moral knowledge. Thoreau offers no guidance to resolving situations (such as the present debate over the morality of abortion) in which both adversaries claim a clear moral mandate. His concern was not to analyze, but to empower people with the courage of their convictions. Waiting on the opinion of others was folly. "Any man more right than his neighbors, constitutes a majority of one already."[60]

In the moral philosophy Thoreau had learned at Harvard, the powers of the human will were arranged in the sequence with which the reader of this book has become familiar. The highest faculty was conscience, or the moral sense; then came prudence, the faculty that calculated one's rational self-interest. Below these were ranged the passions, needing to be kept under rational control. Unfortunately, the motivating power of these faculties varied inversely with their rightful precedence.[61] All this was conventional wisdom to Thoreau's generation of college-educated Americans. Various solutions to the problem were also conventional. Education could strengthen the higher faculties, and the young could be trained to regard virtuous behavior as being in their own self-interest, thus allying prudence with conscience.

In America, it was widely believed that the country's wise Founders had contrived a set of republican institutions that limited the amount of harm passion or selfishness could inflict on the public.

Thoreau confronted the problem of human nature more directly than any of his contemporaries. He undertook to strengthen the weakest of the faculties, the conscience. He insisted that the individual conscience could and must be empowered to act, and not only for the individual himself, but also upon the body politic. Franklin had tried to strengthen conscience with prudence and good habits; Publius relied on institutional mechanisms; Edwards preached divine grace to the rescue. But Thoreau would have none of these. To achieve the goal of conscientious action there was nothing but the naked will power of the individual, unassisted by church sacraments or revival sermons. The few who could muster this power were truly heroes and an inspiration to others. "Action from principle,—the perception and the performance of right,—changes things and relations; it is essentially revolutionary," Thoreau explained. "It not only divides states and churches, it divides families; aye, it divides the *individual,* separating the diabolical in him from the divine."[62] In the contest among the faculties for control of the individual, to empower the conscience was to purge the will of baser impulses. The person who acted from conscience demonstrated his superiority to the weakness of the flesh and the inconstancy of the masses. Action from conscience was the ultimate assertion of self, which united the self with eternity, with nature, and with the Neoplatonic oversoul.

Society at large replicated the faculties of the individual, Thoreau observed: most men served unthinkingly with their bodies only; some served with their heads, making prudential calculations (such as "politicians, lawyers, ministers, and office-holders"); and a "very few" served in a prophetic role with their consciences.[63] Most of politics took place at the level of prudential calculations, where Paley's ethics of expediency legitimately applied. Seen from this "lower point of view" (as Thoreau called it), American democracy was a good form of government—it only became evil when it overreached itself and tried to subject moral values (rather than judgments about means) to the will of the majority.[64] Daniel Webster, his state's orator in the Senate, typified the good practical statesman, Thoreau explained; "still, his quality is not wisdom, but prudence."[65] Edwards could have uttered the same qualified acceptance of Franklin's promotion of socially useful schemes. A higher order of virtue than the politician's was displayed by the one who judged whether the political order was fulfilling its ultimate purposes.

Although the majority was not a moral entity for Thoreau, society as a whole most certainly was. The conscience of society consisted of its "wise minority."[66] When these people bore witness to principle, they were serving a social, as well as an individual, function: "It is not so important that many should be as good as you, as that there be some absolute goodness somewhere, for that will leaven the whole loaf."[67] Thoreau's ideal was not the recluse (as is sometimes supposed), but the moral leader who transforms society. This ideal had been shared by his Harvard mentors. Edward Tyrell Channing (1790–1856), the Boylston Professor of Rhetoric and brother of William Ellery Channing, taught that there existed in a society a moral elite who were "the only true radicals," because they were those "who aim at realizing great ideas, and who believe that much remains, and will ever remain to be learned and told." They were "true" radicals because they possessed the Platonic insight into the true Good, the immutable moral law that the institutions of society ought to implement.[68]

Although the spokesmen of the prophetic minority were usually cast in the role of dissenters, from their ranks also came, at occasional moments of crisis, the seminal legislators, whom Thoreau conceived in a more or less Rousseauvian sense, whose moral insights shaped the constitution of the state for generations. (Thoreau did not share in the national idolatry of the Founding Fathers; he felt that America had not yet seen any such archetypal legislators.)[69] In the long run, a democratic government will be responsive to its wise minority, its collective conscience. This is why civil disobedience can work as a practical matter: "If the alternative is to keep all just men in prison, or give up war and slavery, the State will not hesitate which to choose."[70] Ultimately, right would make might. In this sense, resistance to government was useful, although Thoreau subordinated his argument for its usefulness to his argument for its rightness in absolute terms. For him to calculate too carefully exactly when civil disobedience would make a politically effective tactic would have been uncharacteristic and an exercise in mere utilitarianism.

Although Thoreau's use of liberalism was satirical, it was also serious, in the sense that he carried the principles of liberal individualism to Romantic individualist extremes. He expanded the Lockean notion of a right of revolution in several directions. (1) The moral individual has a right of revolution without waiting on the will of the majority; (2) there is a right to resist the state selectively, on a law-by-law basis; (3) and, most importantly, not only do people have a right to resist state actions that conflict with their *interests,* they also have a right to resist state actions that conflict with their *principles,* their *consciences.* Thoreau did not bother to defend the familiar right to resist the government in self-defense, which even Paley acknowledged. After all, he was not addressing slaves, Mexicans, or Native Americans, but northern whites, for whom the evils he protested were moral issues rather than matters of their own survival.

The distinction between rights and duties, emphasized in the title of Thoreau's lecture version of his essay, is important for understanding his argument. When Thoreau was talking about *duties,* he treated liberalism satirically, but he also held a conception of *rights* that accepted liberal premises. Thoreau believed a right to resist the government existed whenever the government had forfeited, by immoral actions, its claim to the general allegiance of the subject. The American government, Thoreau believed, had forfeited its claim by perpetuating slavery and perpetrating aggressive war on behalf of slavery. "I cannot for an instant recognize that political organization as *my* government, which is the *slave's* government also."[71] The citizen had a right to resist such government injustice whether or not the overthrow of the government was presently feasible. But the right to resist from moral principle was not necessarily a duty, Thoreau was careful to specify. A person was not obliged to go seeking a confrontation with the government, even when its injustices were clear and grave.[72] The right of conscientious resistance only became a duty when the individual was called upon to abet the wrong personally.

Because he regarded selective resistance to government as a special case of the right of revolution, Thoreau did not rule out the possibility of violence. "Suppose blood should flow," he asked. "Is there not a sort of blood shed when the conscience is wounded?"[73] The important thing for Thoreau was that a person should take *direct action* out of principle, regardless of what form that action took. His northern neighbors should not profess to believe in freedom while acquiescing in a law of slavery. "Cast your whole vote, not a strip of paper merely, but your whole influence."[74]

As time went by, Thoreau, like other antislavery northerners, became more extreme in his methods of resistance. He helped at least one fugitive slave, possibly more, and also one of John Brown's antislavery raiders, to escape to freedom in Canada in defiance of existing law.[75] Taken in themselves, these actions were more significant than the tax protest, but they could not be made public in his lifetime lest the network of the underground railway be jeopardized. Thoreau's lecture-essay "Slavery in Massachusetts," delivered in 1854 in reaction against the notorious return of the escaped slave Anthony Burns, defended the antislavery crowds who had confronted the federal military in Boston. Rather than acquiesce in more such renditions, he declared: "I need not say what match I would touch, what system endeavor to blow up. . . . My thoughts are murder to the State."[76]

Thoreau's endorsement of violence became even stronger in his 1859 essays on John Brown. There, he took the position that slavery was large-scale institutionalized immoral violence, which could legitimately be resisted by violence, on the basis of either self-defense or altruistic principle. John Brown, about to be executed for leading an unsuccessful military raid to free the slaves, typified for Thoreau, as for Frederick Douglass, the heroism of the conscientious man.[77] Thoreau celebrated Brown as Carlyle had celebrated Cromwell: "an old Hebrew warrior, indeed, and last right-hand man of the Lord of Hosts, that has blown his ram's horn about Jericho."[78] He praised Brown as a reincarnation of the courageous spirit of Cromwell, one who rose above the trivialities of ordinary existence to act out of principle, one who by his martyrdom hastened the ultimate triumph of justice. But while Thoreau clearly believed that resort to violence in a just cause could be a right, he never went so far as to declare it actually a duty.

Though I have called Henry David Thoreau a prophet, he was a prophet who did not believe in the God of Abraham and Sarah, Isaac and Rebecca, Jacob and Rachel. He might even have approved of Friedrich Nietzsche's truculent dictum, "God is dead." The revelation Thoreau invoked was transcribed nowhere but in the book of nature and the human heart ("the starry heavens above and the moral law within," in Goethe's phrase). Thoreau was under no illusions that many would heed his prophetic message, but—like Isaiah and Ezekiel —defiantly proclaimed it anyway. Thoreau's belief in a transcendent moral order set him apart from any form of nihilism; his admiration for John Brown was therefore different from Nietzsche's celebration of heroic militancy.[79]

✌ PROPHECY AND POLITICS

In summary, Thoreau's essay presents no fewer than three justifications for resistance to civil government: (1) the duty to disobey immoral commands; (2) the right to resist an immoral government, either selectively or by general revolution; (3) the exercise of moral leadership by a prophetic minority. What all three have in common is the object of strengthening conscience over prudential considerations and the individual's value judgments against those of society. The three lines of argument do not seem necessarily incompatible, but Thoreau neither clearly differentiates them nor logically integrates them.

Distinguishing the three lines of Thoreau's argument enables us to understand that refusing to pay the poll tax was an example of the second and third principles, not the first. By his own reasoning, Thoreau was exercising the right to disobey an immoral government, and in making his challenge public was setting an example for the instruction and inspiration of others; but he was not defying an intrinsically immoral command. So far as we can tell, the poll tax itself was not a particularly unjust law in Thoreau's eyes: he never criticized it (as he might have done) for being economically regressive, or for discouraging voting by poor people.

Of the three lines of argument by which Thoreau justifies resistance to government immorality, the most important, and the one that best explains his own behavior, is the third. "Resistance to Civil Government" is the work of a prophetic critic of society and spiritual mentor of the individual. The message of the essay is existential rather than philosophical; it is congruent with the message of his other writings. Be clear about your priorities in life, he always challenges his audience. Set these priorities for yourself. Simplify your life by sticking to what you really believe in; refuse to be distracted by other people's standards. The essay on "Resistance to Civil Government" is a special case of this general challenge.

Like his contemporaries Carlyle and Marx, Thoreau was concerned about the problem of alienation in modern life. "The mass of men lead lives of quiet desperation," he wrote in *Walden;* they find their work boring and stifling but don't know how to escape their lot.[80] "Resistance to Civil Government" is about the problem of *political alienation* that exists even in a democracy. The citizens can vote, but they still feel powerless, and tend to become passive and apathetic. Concerned as he was with the issues of slavery and the Mexican War, Thoreau also felt that he had a more general point to make, and this must be why he thought it worthwhile to publish his essay even after the war was over, and he was (perhaps) resuming payment of his poll tax. Thoreau wanted to awaken his audience to a sense of direct involvement in public affairs—through the participatory democracy of a town meeting such as he often addressed, or if necessary by defying the law.[81]

The pungency and arresting force of Thoreau's expression were his rhetorical means to this evangelical goal. He turned the trivial experience of a night in the county jail for refusing a pay a small tax into a symbol of the possibilities for authenticity that are presented in the ordinary course of daily life. Any contact with government can be made the occasion, if one so wishes, for the affirmation of independence and human moral priorities. Thoreau thus implemented a precept of Carlyle's that he admired: "Do the duty which lies nearest thee."[82] Thoreau made a similar point in his move to Walden, where his act of symbolic withdrawal from society only required moving a couple of miles, not all the way out to the frontier.

In asserting his independence against the middle-class majority of his own time and place, Thoreau was doing the duty that lay nearest him. He didn't hate the tyranny of the majority *more* than he hated other tyrannies, but it was the closest to him. The strength of his affirmation of individual principle is that it can be used to challenge *any* immoral authority.

The essay on "Resistance to Civil Government," though almost ignored in the author's lifetime, has proved a remarkably durable and effective piece of evangelical rhetoric since his death. Despite frequent misunderstandings of its contents, the essay has been invoked across time and space and varied circumstances. It has helped empower the powerless, engage the marginalized, and nurture a sense of moral integrity. Henry David Thoreau, if he could see how his essay has been used, might permit himself a brief smile of satisfaction.

Conclusion

We approach the end of this book without having come near to exhausting its theme, the construction of the self in American thought. By focusing attention in the final section on a single group, New England intellectuals, we have been able to develop a certain depth of evidence and richness of interpretation, though other important social groups engaged in self-fashioning, including both the southern plantation aristocracy and their slaves, remain for other investigations.[1] I am particularly aware that I have not treated any charlatans or confidence tricksters. These were important figures on the American scene and often pointed out as counterexamples by the advocates of honest self-construction.[2] But while more remains to be done, I feel that there is enough here to indicate the main outlines of an approach to a major theme in American history.

Charles Taylor, in his wide-ranging account of what he calls "the making of modern identity," identifies three fundamental approaches to the construction of the self. The first is the tribal ideal of the warrior self, celebrating masculine courage and leadership. The second is the ideal, advanced by the Greek philosophers and the Christian monastics, of the philosophical self, which honors the life of contemplation. Lastly, he identifies the modern ideal of selfhood, which values the ordinary lives of ordinary people and seeks to promote the realization of their potential. Economic activity and family life, both of which are subordinated in the first two visions of the good life, are much more highly esteemed in the modern version of self-construction.[3] This book has been about the partial realization of that modern concept of selfhood in a portion of American history.

The attitude toward the self we have been examining ultimately implies a form of equality. This has been summarized by Jerome Huyler: "Let every individual live for *his or her own sake*—neither sacrificing (i.e. politically exploiting) others nor depriving oneself for the benefit of others."[4] Beyond that, the attitude we have studied also assumes that the nature of the self is something voluntarily chosen. The capacity to choose is at the heart of political freedom as Americans have conceived of it, and the capacity to choose or revise one's own identity is perhaps the ultimate exercise of that capacity.

?◉ THE IDEAL OF SELF-CONSTRUCTION IN VICTORIAN AMERICA

Before undertaking to summarize the contents of this book, let us take a look at a contemporary work that was in itself a summary of the ideal of self-construction as generally understood in Victorian America: *Self-Culture: Physical, Intellectual, Moral, Spiritual,* by James Freeman Clarke (1810–1888). As we have seen, Clarke was a Transcendentalist and a confidant of Margaret Fuller. But in this book he obtained a much wider audience than Concord intellectuals. Bridging what would later be thought of as high and popular cultures, this masterpiece of inspirational Arminianism reached a broad public in its time. The book originated as a lecture series; published in 1880, it went through at least twenty-one editions to the end of the century.[5] It shows how the democratic and Romantic impulses of Transcendentalism could be expressed within the framework of traditional Enlightenment faculty psychology in a Victorian ideology of self-improvement.

Clarke postulates that God has created individual human beings with a duty to fulfill their nature, that is, to develop and use their faculties and talents. This he terms "man's duty to grow." If powers are not "improved" in both senses of the word (that is, used and developed) they are lost.[6] The wise person does not seek to construct a self chosen arbitrarily or whimsically, Clarke declares. In reality, a person's innate qualities—physical, temperamental, intellectual—define a possible range of choices. Wisdom consists in enough self-understanding to see where one's potential lies, and then in working to realize it.[7] Clarke's project of self-culture could be termed, in our own language, self-realization.

Formal education is but one small part of the development of the faculties as Clarke envisions it. The unimaginative pedagogy of most schools compares very unfavorably with the methods by which we learn from nature or from the society of other people. For the most part, formal education confines itself to what is properly but the first stage of self-culture, "instruction." The second stage, "training," represents the exercise of the faculties; the third stage, "development," is the balanced "unfolding of the whole nature."[8]

Is self-culture "a selfish aim?" Clarke asks. Not if it is pursued in a balanced way, he answers, with regard for both public and private virtues. In a balanced self-culture, the self is developed with an eye to serving God and neighbor, but to be concerned to some extent with the private self and our immediate circle is by no means wrong. There is, after all, a danger in being too altruistic—in becoming a certain kind of notorious reformer, devoted entirely to "large abstractions" and impossible to live with as a human being.[9] As examples of self-fulfillment ("heroes," in his terminology and that of his age) Clarke cited people with contrasting personalities: Franklin, Voltaire, Swedenborg, and John Wesley, as well as his friend Margaret Fuller. But his favorite examples were obscure, small-town people, whose range of influence was small but who were recognized by their communities as warm, responsive human beings.[10]

The body is not the enemy of the soul, as medieval ascetics thought, Clarke insists. After all, "the Son of Man came eating and drinking."[11] On the other hand, the body is not a mere reflection of the soul or mind either; Clarke rejects the position of his contemporary New England philosophical idealist, Mary Baker Eddy, that the mental can entirely control the physical, and that illness is a form of sin. Clarke praises the ancient Greeks for their devotion to physical exercise. Like the English Victorians, this American Victorian has become persuaded that sports and games can be a wholesome moral influence, a training in the balanced development of the faculties.[12]

Within the mind, Clarke recognizes a variety of faculties, each of which requires a certain amount of use and development to function properly. The conscience is no exception; it too needs to be educated and exercised. The conscience may become diseased, as it is in the case of fanatics and persecutors, but more commonly it atrophies through "stupor and ignorance."[13] Most people will educate their consciences no farther than the prevailing state of public opinion; this is why such care must be taken to keep public opinion "right in its standard of duty." Clarke is worried that the popular media do not accept their responsibility to maintain moral standards, but welcomes novelists like Charles Dickens and Sir Walter Scott who do.[14] Where antebellum American writers like Channing, Emerson, and Thoreau had looked to the individual to redeem society, Clarke's generation fears that society may corrupt the individual.

Among the faculties, Clarke espouses the conventional ideal: the "harmonious and well balanced working of the different moral powers."[15] He interprets this traditional ideal in ways typical of his own generation. He wants to encourage the faculty of "hope," because he sees it as a spur to the kind of social progress in which his age believed.[16] He welcomes the industrial and technological revolutions: they provide "more of the necessaries and comforts of life—not for the rich only, but for all persons." Furthermore, they multiply the number of occupations, thereby providing a wider range of choices appropriate to different personality types.[17] But people need to be educated in their responsibilites if they are to take proper advantage of the opportunities provided by economic progress. For example, they need to be educated in the proper use of money: how to save it, how to invest it, how to give it to charity, what to spend it on. Not all ways of earning money are socially beneficial and therefore morally legitimate: among the illegitimate sources of income are gambling, selling shoddy goods that deceive the consumer, and "speculation."[18]

One of the faculties most in need of education is "the will." There are two kinds of will power, Clarke declares, and they are typified by Andrew Jackson and Abraham Lincoln. The two leaders represent the "natural force of will" and the "educated force of will," respectively. (Since neither man had significant formal schooling, it is clear that Clarke does not mean this in speaking of an "educated will.") Jackson "was a great general but a dangerous President. His strong will was often willful and guided by passion and prejudice more than by reason." Lincoln, on the other hand, moved slowly and hesitatingly at first, but having finally made up his mind, "he was firm as a rock in mid-ocean." Both were honest, but Jackson was "like a wild storm,

violent and destructive, though sublime." Lincoln's self-educated will
was "like the shining auroral light of a near morning, which shines
more and more unto the perfect day."[19] Lincoln's will represented a
truer model of self-construction, one that looks beyond itself toward a
transcendent goal and fulfillment. The proper construction of the self,
as Americans understood it from the Enlightenment through the Victorian era, was based on belief in absolute moral standards.

?⊷ SUMMARY

The ideal of self-construction in eighteenth-century America evolved
at a time of encounter between two great intellectual traditions, Protestantism and the Enlightenment. Protestantism taught that the natural self was corrupt and in need of redemption; the Enlightenment
taught that human beings were capable of self-direction and self-
definition. In America, these two seemingly antithetical visions of
human nature and human capacity came to a kind of distinctive synthesis. Enlightenment thinkers such as Benjamin Franklin agreed with
Protestant theologians like Jonathan Edwards that there was much in
human nature that needed changing, even if they refused to call it by
the name "original sin." For their part, the evangelical Christians,
beginning with Princeton Presbyterian academics but soon including
popular preachers like the Methodists, came to embrace the Enlightenment goal of self-improvement. Many Christian groups adopted versions of Arminianism (the theology of self-help) in practice and often
in theory as well. Less well recognized but of considerable importance
is the extent to which American Christians came to accept polite
culture as defining some of the goals of self-improvement. For the most
part, Protestantism and the Enlightenment worked as allies in the
American context, alike endorsing free institutions, as well as promoting social reform and the individual reform we have been calling
self-improvement.

Out of the synthesis of Protestantism and the Enlightenment
expressed in faculty psychology came a powerful normative model for
what a properly constructed self should be like: the balanced character.
A person with a properly balanced character expressed and developed
all aspects of human nature—intellectual, spiritual, emotional, physical—but did so within an overarching rational pattern that prevented

any one faculty from usurping control. In the shorthand of the time, a balanced character subordinated passion to reason. Such a person could be trusted with political freedom because he (and originally the model was fully applicable only to males) could be trusted to be responsible. Such a person would make a good citizen in a republic, whether one defined that republic in communitarian terms or liberal ones. Thus reassured that liberty would not lead to anarchy, American Protestantism and the Enlightenment embraced the goal of the balanced character, and even supported similar techniques for developing that character through education and self-discipline.

The framers of the American Constitution clearly intended that the system of government they created should provide a framework for constructive self-development. On the individual level they took a liberal approach, that is, they believed in leaving individuals free to develop their faculties in their own ways. But in their construction of institutions they took a more prescriptive approach, favoring reason over passion. They predicated this approach upon a powerful analogy they drew between the construction of a balanced polity and the construction of a balanced personality. A recent scholar has described Publius's doctrine thus: "a democratic citizenry will submit itself voluntarily to enforceable restrictions on its own whim in order to ensure that its reason will outweigh its passion in the public realm."[20]

Both the framers of the Constitution and the religious leaders of the young republic found the faculty psychology expounded by the Scottish moral philosophers a convenient and lucid model of improvable human nature. These intellectual borrowings were perfectly logical in view of all that the American and Scottish Enlightenments had in common. Both were designed to promote commerce and civilization, economic and intellectual freedom, rational religion, social and individual progress.

The individual whose thinking illustrates most vividly both the aspirations and the limitations of the American Enlightenment was Thomas Jefferson. He concerns us, therefore, not only because of the actual influence he exerted as a powerful statesman, but even more as representative man. At its most sublime, Jefferson's vision of his country's future is truly inspirational: economically and psychologically secure individuals, their rational and affective faculties appropriately balanced, liberated from superstition and fear, working at healthful occupations on their own property, repaying with public-spirited involvement the commonwealth that has educated them, freely choosing the wisest and most virtuous as their leaders. Yet, despite his assurance in the Declaration of Independence that natural rights belonged to "all men," in practice the human nature Jefferson trusted and wanted to develop to its fullest potential was that of white males only. Other human beings he assumed existed for the benefit of that group, and he accordingly regarded them as means, not as ends in themselves. Women he valued as men always had, as mothers and wives. Native Americans, for all his interest in their languages and ethnography, he valued primarily for their lands, the expropriation of which by the whites was a goal of the highest priority. And while he admitted that African-Americans had natural rights, Jefferson actually valued them only as slave labor, and since he did not consider that labor on balance worth having, he hoped to get rid of them through a giant colonization program.[21]

In calling attention to the limitations on Jefferson's vision, we should not forget to contextualize it historically: in its time, the vision was much more notable for its sweeping inclusiveness than for its exclusions. Indeed, the exclusions were manifestly anomalous, and this proved a lever of critical importance to excluded groups later, when they were struggling for full participation. The generation after the death of Jefferson would prove a time for the implementation of parts of his vision of self-determination, most rapidly by white males, with much greater difficulty by others. Of course, the utopian aspects of the Jeffersonian vision never came close to realization; Jefferson had been overly optimistic about both human nature and the American future, as he himself began to fear in old age.[22] But the ideal of the autonomous and balanced, that is, self-governing, character spread throughout the society. And Jefferson's vision of the American nation as the example *par excellence* of a country where individuals were free to make themselves persisted, to be reinvigorated by Lincoln.

The next stage in our account dealt with the democratization of the ideal of self-construction. The period viewed was one of extraordinary social fluidity in the United States. In this amorphous and expanding environment, many ordinary people were suddenly freer than ever before to choose and even create new identities for themselves. Among these identities were new occupations, consumption patterns, membership in voluntary societies, and an amazing variety of religious movements. In this society a remarkably large number of people accepted as a goal what we could call the ultimate identity of choice, that is, the full development of their human potential, to be achieved through the work of self-improvement. While this enterprise is not uncommon in societies undergoing modernization, and was especially similar to what was happening simultaneously in Victorian Britain, it was particularly typical of and widely celebrated in the United States.

The writers on moral philosophy of this middle period of American history contrast in some respects with Publius and the other framers of the Constitution. Since they acknowledged that the work of shaping American political institutions had been accomplished, they tended to look beyond politics to other means for the promotion of virtue in society. Among these means were education, religion, manners, and culture. Where the framers had accepted a diversity of interests in the American nation and sought to turn it into a source of strength, the moralists of a later era were more likely to look for the possibility of consensus, seeking to overcome diversity through common schools and other forces of cultural assimilation. While the nineteenth-century moralists continued to believe in the supremacy of reason, they were more indulgent of the emotions than Publius had been, hoping to enlist them, along with prudence, in the service of virtue. And, finally, they sought to be ever more inclusive in applying the principles of autonomy and self-construction to various groups in the population. Despite all these changes, however, the ideal of constructing a balanced character remained essentially continuous across the generations. Likewise the interpretation of American political institutions by analogy with psychological faculties remained standard throughout the antebellum period.[23]

"The nature of cultural development specifically depends for its forms on the existing vision of self," the historian Warren Susman has written.[24] Understanding the program of self-construction, the normative model of the balanced character, and the theory of faculty psychology on which they rested will help us understand many aspects of the history of American culture. In what is perhaps the largest and most general sense, this understanding enables us to see that the opportunity promised by America consisted of something larger than simply the opportunity to make money. The pursuit of happiness as Jefferson defined it and Americans generally accepted it entailed the opportunity to shape one's own destiny. It entailed the right to become the kind of person one wished (as humanist liberals would see it) or to fulfill one's potential (as reform liberals would define it).

More specifically, an understanding of the ideal of balanced character helps us see how it was possible for liberalism and classical republicanism to coexist so easily for so long in American political language. A citizen with a balanced character would make responsible political choices. In his actions the rational dictates of enlightened prudence would reinforce those of a virtuous dedication to community welfare, so that the practical consequences of liberal behavior would be equivalent to those of classical republicanism. As a safeguard against the problem that all citizens would not have balanced characters, the political institutions themselves would have a balanced character.

In antebellum America, the social and cultural consequences of the practice of self-improvement and the pursuit of balanced character were multiform. They fostered the spread among Christians of the Arminian theology of free will. They encouraged the spread of educational institutions as well as reform movements that sought to redeem the characters of prison inmates, drunkards, and the insane. They provided the antislavery movement with one of its most effective arguments—namely, that slavery corrupted the character of master and slave alike. They found literary exponents in didactic writers like Harriet Beecher Stowe and Henry Wadsworth Longfellow as well as in popular self-help manuals. They encouraged humane child-rearing practices such as those advocated by Horace Bushnell. Furthermore, belief in self-improvement set the stage for some of the most prolonged controversies in American history, as groups excluded from full participation in self-improvement began to demand inclusion.

Recognizing the importance of the ideology of self-improvement also helps us understand antebellum party politics. I suggested in an earlier chapter that the Jacksonian Democrats believed in the *right* of self-improvement, the Whigs in the *right and duty* of self-improvement. But there is also another way of distinguising the two political parties' approaches to the subject. Each party chose to put primary emphasis on one half of the idea of self-improvement. The Democrats emphasized self and the Whigs emphasized improvement. For the Democrats, it was important to leave individuals alone, so that their characters would develop in accordance with their own wishes, and they could be held unreservedly accountable. For the Whigs, however, the improvement of character was so important that intervention to assist others was amply justified. Although the Democrats won most of the national elections, the Whig emphasis on the redemption of human character had at least as large a cultural influence in the long run.

Someone who had conspicuously succeeded in the process of character-building, one who could be held up as an encouraging example, was referred to by contemporaries as "self-made." To be recognized as self-made was to enjoy one of the major rewards of self-improvement, that is, the esteem of others. In Abraham Lincoln and the myth that came after him, we have a classic statement of the conventional American Victorian ideal of self-improvement and the self-made man. According to the legend that his admirers created, Lincoln's self-improvement was appropriately rewarded by political success, and once he was in a position of political power, his moral character showed itself in his statesmanship. In Frederick Douglass we found the ideal of the self-made man at once affirmed and challenged by the demand that it be expanded to include African-Americans. Douglass demonstrates how faculty psychology and the ideal of autonomous self-construction were invoked against both slavery and racism. He also shows how a commitment to the ideal of self-construction is by no means a narrowly selfish, self-absorbed, or narcissistic goal indifferent to the autonomy of others.

Our study of the construction of character has necessarily included not only self-construction but also the construction of the characters of others. In the period we have treated, the goal of such construction was typically to create characters that would be, in the long run, autonomous and responsible. Hence the concern with the education of children and newly emancipated slaves, the reform of alcoholics and criminals, the curing of the insane. Helping others to become autonomous necessarily entails a risk of compromising the very autonomy that is sought. While this problem did not seem pressing in the work of Horace Mann and Dorothea Dix, in the case of Horace Bushnell it led to a logical paradox.

Bushnell's sense of the malleability of human nature in early youth carried out an insight earlier adumbrated by Franklin and anticipated the later work of Sigmund Freud. Its potential was actually far more wide-ranging than the program of Christian nurture Bushnell himself was seeking to implement. Bushnell extended the autonomy of parents to control not only their own characters but also those of their children. His goal in doing so was the creation of offspring with autonomous characters, but his method compromised his intended result. If children's characters were formed by the age of three as a result of parental determination, in what sense was the resulting adult autonomous and responsible? And if character was created by emotional conditioning, what hope could there be that reason could ever prevail over passion? Although Bushnell was a deep thinker, he did not fully appreciate the implications of his own analysis. He supposed that he was undergirding moral responsibility by insisting on the importance of family values. In the long run, however (and in the hands of others), his approach led to the conclusion that individual characters were the product of their early environment rather than self-constructed.

In the concluding section of the book, we investigated the celebration of individual self-construction in the literature of the American Renaissance. To appreciate the literary achievement of Emerson and other Transcendentalists it is necessary to understand their context, religious and philosophical. Such a context was identified in a version of Neoplatonic self-culture practiced by the New England Unitarians of the antebellum era. This peculiarly American kind of mysticism—a life-affirming, rather than a life-denying, mysticism—found inspiration in the writings of the seventeenth-century group of Christian humanists called the Cambridge Platonists. Their Platonism made use of a model of faculty psychology much like that of Scottish moral philosophy, one that could complement it if thinkers were so inclined. Being absolutists and rationalists in their ethical teachings, the Cambridge Platonists could readily be used to reinforce the ethical theory of Scots like Thomas Reid and Dugald Stewart. The Cambridge Platonists' quest for communion with the divine was taken over by their nineteenth-century American followers as a religious form of self-development. Their metaphysical speculations about the priority of mind over matter became understood in America as poetic exhortations to impose rational order on whatever was physical, including the human passions.

The use to which American thinkers were able to put such imported ideologies as Platonism, classical republicanism, German Romanticism, or Scottish moral philosophy, synthesizing or adapting them as needed, provides a new meaning to the notion of American practicality: a practicality not *opposed* to theory or foreign ideas, but *open* to them and able to turn them to account.

No thinker illustrates American syncretistic originality better than Margaret Fuller. Drawing upon a range of Platonisms and Romanticisms for inspiration and making use of classical mythology for illustrative archetypes, she pursued the endeavor of self-culture in both theory and practice. In Margaret Fuller we found not only a call to extend the opportunity for self-improvement to women but a profound rethinking of the ideal self-made character itself. In the course of adapting self-culture to make it applicable to both sexes, she drastically transformed the ideal of the balanced character. Instead of emphasizing the hierarchy of the faculties, she emphasized their symmetry and complementarity. She brought to fulfillment the process of accepting the affective side of human personality, a process we have followed from its beginnings in Jefferson's sensibility through nineteenth-century thinkers like William Ellery Channing and Catharine Beecher. Because she teaches that a commitment to self-construction does not require denying our feelings but calls for nurturing them properly, Fuller remains perhaps the most enduringly relevant of all the thinkers we have examined.

Finally, we come to the most radical of our exemplars of self-construction, Henry David Thoreau. Thoreau subordinates the demands of society, even when most urgently expressed as law, to the individual's pursuit of moral perfection. Thoreau also wants to make each individual the judge of what kind of character he wishes to pursue. "If a man does not keep pace with his companions, perhaps it is because he hears a different drummer. Let him step to the music which he hears, however measured or far away."[25] The lesson Thoreau imparts is that self-determination and self-construction are not the privilege of a few heroes only (although such can be useful examplars); these projects are both the right and the duty of everyone, in even the most commonplace of situations. Everyone has a conscience and the chance to use it. "Every man is potentially his own hero."[26]

But Thoreau was no moral relativist. Like the other self-improvers, he continued to accept the covential model of the faculties of human nature, with the necessity, somehow, to empower conscience over self-interest. The moral faculty, he believed, puts us in touch with an objective moral order. At the last, the different drums that good people hear will all be synchronized. When this millennial day dawns, the state will have become superfluous, as will all social conventions, including politeness.

To allude to Thoreau's millennial vision is to underscore the difference between his outlook and our own. We live in a world that has become much more cynical than that of the nineteenth century about progress, both social and individual. Today the prevailing orthodoxies teach us to discount the chances for self-improvement and the opportunity to be self-made. They teach that our identities are determined by the social matrix in which all are embedded, often defined at birth by race, class, and gender. They also cast doubt on the hope of collective improvement, such as the nineteenth century saw in the growth of personal freedom, democratic politics, politeness, commerce, and technology. It is not fashionable today to believe in progress, either social or individual.

Our own age seems to have lost a normative rationale for self-construction, such as the balanced character provided in earlier generations. In the early twentieth century people still believed in the ideals of a cultivated self and a liberal culture that such a self would embrace, and they made an effort to democratize these ideals.[27] How these ideals gradually declined over the decades would be the subject for another book. First, moral philosophy and the classics were displaced from their centrality in the educational system. New intellectual movements took their place, including literary modernism and popularized forms of psychoanalysis, both of which celebrated the expression of the passions rather than their subordination to reason. The rise of cultural anthropology encouraged a cultural relativism that, while originally intended as broadening, undermined faith in absolute values. So did Marxism, with its project of demystifying conventional ideals, although its influence in the United States was limited. Probably most important of all the forces destroying the old practice and theory of self-improvement was the emergence of a culture of hedonism and the eventual widespread breakdown of respect for moral values.[28] Finally, the proliferation of various postmodern ideologies in the academy undertook the deliberate elimination of normative standards there.

At the mid-point of the twentieth century, American society still felt a sense of loss over the demise of the old model of faculty psychology, with its rational moral sense acting as a gyroscope to give direction to a person's character. This seems apparent both in David Riesman's 1950 book *The Lonely Crowd: A Study of the Changing American Character* and in the widespread popular reaction to it.[29] By the last years of the century, however, even the memory of such a self seems to be fading rapidly, especially in Los Angeles, the new cultural capital of America and the vantage point from which these words are written. There is no longer any accepted normative model for what kind of selves we should construct.

Yet the need for human autonomy is still present and recognized. Ironically, existing opportunities for self-construction have never been more widely available, or more highly prized by ordinary people, than they are now.[30] More and more often, historians and political scientists are finding that they must recognize that people—even ordinary people—can resist manipulation, exercise a measure of autonomy, behave rationally, and define their own identities. In response to this recognition, the political scientist Stephen Macedo has turned around the analogy Publius employed: where Publius analyzed the Constitution of the United States in terms drawn from the individual personality, Macedo analyzes individual personality in terms borrowed from the Constitution and prescribes accordingly. "We can distinguish liberal virtues of private life that are judicial, legislative, and executive in character," he writes. "Judicial" virtues include impartiality and "attachment to principle." The "legislative" virtues are those of broad sympathy and respect for the rights of others. The "executive" virtues "empower one, having judged and reflected, to resolve, act, and persevere rather than drift, dither, and crumble." All of these virtues are not only useful to the citizen but actually fostered by the exercise of free citizenship. What is more, Macedo argues, these virtues need to be "balanced" within the commonwealth of the mind.[31]

I share Stephen Macedo's sense that the old faculty psychology and the principles of self-construction that it fostered still address our situation. There is still a need to justify education as a form of self-fulfillment, not only as vocational training. Even in our own day, it is considered important for the young to have exemplars ("role models") to help them define themselves. The control of the passions is hardly irrelevant to a society increasingly afflicted with violent crime, the abuse of drugs and alcohol, and the abuse of women and children by men. Most urgently felt is the need to rebuild a functioning democracy on habits of personal responsibility, civility, and self-discipline. Can we recover a model to help guide us in our quest for self-definition? While I have been writing this book, some thoughtful social commentators have begun to reexamine and reaffirm the place of morality and the "moral sense" in the process of character-formation.[32] Despite the unfashionable quality of their principles, the American advocates and exemplars of self-construction do, I think, speak to our times if we choose to listen.

Notes

Introduction

1. David A. Hollinger, *In the American Province: Studies in the History and Historiography of Ideas* (Bloomington, Ind., 1985), 130–51.

2. See T. W. Heyck, *The Transformation of Intellectual Life in Victorian England* (London, 1982), 15; and Peter Allen, "The Meanings of 'an Intellectual': Nineteenth- and Twentieth-Century English Usage," *University of Toronto Quarterly* 55 (Summer 1986), 342–58.

3. Stephen Greenblatt, *Renaissance Self-Fashioning* (Chicago, 1980), 1.

4. Charles Taylor, *Sources of the Self: The Making of the Modern Identity* (Cambridge, Mass., 1989).

5. This school of thought derives to a large extent from French postmodernism. For a recent example, see Kenneth Lockridge, *On the Sources of Patriarchal Rage: The Commonplace Books of William Byrd and Thomas Jefferson and the Gendering of Power in the Eighteenth Century* (New York, 1992).

6. Robert H. Frank, *Passions within Reason: The Strategic Role of the Emotions* (New York, 1988).

7. Quotations from Alexander H. Stephens, "Address at Emory College, Georgia" (1852), printed in Henry Cleveland, *Alexander H. Stephens* (Philadelphia, 1866), 368; and Lyman Beecher, *Instructions for Young Christians* (Cincinnati, 1833), 16.

8. See Merle Curti, *Human Nature in American Thought: A History* (Madison, 1980), esp. chap. 4, "Searching for Balance," pp. 105–46.

9. George Bancroft, *A History of the United States* (Boston, 1858), VII, 396–97.

10. Stephen Holmes, *Passions and Constraint: On the Theory of Liberal Democracy* (Chicago, 1995); quotations from pp. 24 and 4.

11. Recent work emphasizing the international quality of the great revival includes: W. R. Ward, *The Protestant Evangelical Awakening* (Cambridge, Eng., 1992); Michael J. Crawford, *Seasons of Grace: Colonial New England's Revival Tradition in Its British Context* (New York, 1991); and Mark Noll, David Bebbington, and George Rawlick, eds., *Evangelicalism: Comparative Studies of Popular Protestantism in North America, the British Isles, and Beyond, 1700–1990* (New York, 1994).

12. See Christopher Clark, *The Roots of Rural Capitalism: Western Massachusetts, 1780–1860* (Ithaca, 1990).

13. See Joyce Appleby, "The Radical *Double-Entendre* in the Right to Self-Government," in Margaret Jacob and James Jacob, eds., *Origins of Anglo-American Radicalism* (London, 1984), 304–12.

14. See, for example, Dickson D. Bruce, *Violence and Culture in the Antebellum South* (Austin, 1979).

15. On liberty *versus* license, see Barry Shain, *The Myth of American Individualism: The Protestant Origins of American Political Thought* (Princeton, 1994), 201–03, 232, 279, 313–17.

16. This large literature has been the subject of repeated historiographical surveys. Among them, see Dorothy Ross, "The Liberal Tradition Revisited and the Republican Tradition Addressed," in John Higham and Paul Conkin, eds., *New Directions in American Intellectual History* (Baltimore, 1979); Robert E. Shalhope, "Republicanism and Early American Historiography," *William and Mary Quarterly* 39 (April 1982), 334–56; Isaac Kramnick, "Republican Revisionism Revisited," *American Historical Review* 87 (June 1982), 629–64; Daniel Walker Howe, "European Sources of Political Ideas in Jeffersonian America," *Reviews in American History* 10 (December 1982), 28–44; James Kloppenberg, "The Virtues of Liberalism: Christianity, Republicanism, and Ethics in Early American Political Discourse," *Journal of American History* 74 (June 1987), 9–33; and Daniel T. Rodgers, "Republicanism: The Career of a Concept," *Journal of American History* 79 (June 1992), 11–38.

17. On the classical republican tradition, see J. G. A. Pocock, *The Machiavellian Moment: Florentine Political Thought and the Atlantic Republican Tradition* (Princeton, 1975); and—for some important corrections—Paul Rahe, *Republics Ancient and Modern: Classical Republicanism and the American Revolution* (Chapel Hill, N.C., 1992).

18. Recent reassessments of the liberal tradition in America include Thomas L. Pangle, *The Spirit of Modern Republicanism: The Moral Vision of the American Founders* (Chicago, 1988); Steven M. Dworitz, *The Unvarnished Doctrine: Locke, Liberalism, and the American Revolution* (Durham, N.C., 1990); and Joyce Appleby, *Liberalism and Republicanism in the Historical Imagination* (Cambridge, Mass., 1992).

19. On the eclecticism of Americans in drawing upon both classical and liberal ideas of politics, see also Michael Lienesch, *New Order of the Ages: Time, the*

Constitution, and the Making of Modern American Political Thought (Princeton, 1988); and Carl J. Richard, *The Founders and the Classics: Greece, Rome, and the American Enlightenment* (Cambridge, Mass., 1994), 1–11.

20. See Dorothy Ross, "Liberalism," in Jack P. Greene, ed., *Encyclopedia of American Political History* (New York, 1984), II, 750–63; and John Gray, *Liberalism,* 2d ed. (Buckingham, Eng., 1995).

21. Stephen Macedo, *Liberal Virtues: Citizenship, Virtue, and Community in Liberal Constitutionalism* (Oxford, 1991); quotations from pp. 214, 216, and 251.

22. See Jack P. Greene, "The Concept of Virtue in Late Colonial America," in *Virtue, Corruption, and Self-Interest: Political Values in the Late Eighteenth Century,* ed. Richard K. Matthews (Bethlehem, Penn., 1994), 27–54.

23. On *Cato's Letters* and their influence, see Ronald Hamowy, "Cato's Letters, John Locke, and the Republican Paradigm," *History of Political Thought,* 11 (Summer 1990), 279–94; Shelley Burtt, *Virtue Transformed: Political Argument in England, 1688–1740* (Cambridge, Eng., 1992); Bernard Bailyn, *Ideological Origins of the American Revolution,* rev. ed. (Cambridge, Mass., 1992); and Caroline Robbins, *The Eighteenth-Century Commonwealthman* (Cambridge, Mass., 1959).

24. [John Trenchard and Thomas Gordon] *Cato's Letters* (London, 1724), 4 vols., I, 7, 116, 254; II, 172.

25. *Ibid.,* I, 15, 25, 83–84, 116.

26. *Ibid.,* I, 219; II, 186; III, 121.

27. *Ibid.,* I, 200–07, 296.

28. *Ibid.,* II, 41–44.

29. *Ibid.,* II, 45–54.

30. *Ibid.,* I, 309–10.

31. *Ibid.,* II, 234–35.

32. *Ibid.,* I, 245–70; quotation from p. 266.

33. *Ibid.,* III, 69; II, 90..

34. *Ibid.,* I, 25–26, 182–83.

35. *Ibid.,* I, 97, 270; II, 236; III, 79; IV, 4.

36. *Ibid.,* III, 326.

37. *Ibid.,* II, 95.

38. *Ibid.,* II, 189.

39. After writing this section, I came upon the excellent discussions of *Cato's Letters* in Michael P. Zuckert, *Natural Rights and the New Republicanism* (Princeton, 1994), 297–319; and Jerome Huyler, *Locke in America: The Moral Philosophy of the Founding Era* (Lawrence, Kan., 1995), 210–30. Both clearly demonstrate the way Cato put classical republican principles into the service of a Lockean outlook, but neither emphasizes the role of faculty psychology.

40. Gertrude Himmelfarb, *Victorian Values and Twentieth-Century Condescension* (London, 1987), 15.

41. *Cato's Letters,* IV, 35.

42. OED, s.v. "politeness," definition 2.

43. Daniel Boorstin, *The Genius of American Politics* (Chicago, 1953). To see

how much the Americans discussed here had in common with their European, especially British, contemporaries, cf., for example, J. W. Burrow, *Whigs and Liberals: Continuity and Change in English Political Thought* (Oxford, 1988), esp. chap. 4, "Autonomy and Self-Realization" and chap. 5, "Balance and Diversity."

1. Benjamin Franklin, Jonathan Edwards, and the Problem of Human Nature

1. *The Spectator,* no. 6 (March 8, 1711) and no. 408 (June 18, 1712), ed. Donald F. Bond (Oxford, 1965), I, 29; III, 524; Norman Fiering, "Will and Intellect in the New England Mind," *William and Mary Quarterly* 29 (Oct. 1972), 515–58; Daniel W. Howe, *The Unitarian Conscience,* rev. ed. (Middletown, Ct., 1988), 56–64; Arthur O. Lovejoy, *The Great Chain of Being* (Cambridge, Mass., 1936), chap. VI; Arthur O. Lovejoy, *Reflections on Human Nature* (Baltimore, 1961).

2. On Franklin, see Albert Furtwangler, *American Silhouettes: Rhetorical Identities of the Founders* (New Haven, 1987), 20–34; and Jeanette S. Lewis, " 'A Turn of Thinking': The Long Shadow of *The Spectator* in Franklin's *Autobiography,*" *Early American Literature* 13 (Winter 1978–79), 268–77. On Edwards, see Norman Fiering, "The Transatlantic Republic of Letters," *William and Mary Quarterly* 33 (Oct. 1976), 642–60.

3. Jonathan Edwards, "Charity and Its Fruits" in *Ethical Writings,* ed. Paul Ramsay, *The Works of Jonathan Edwards* (New Haven, 1959–), VIII, 277. Benjamin Franklin, "Poor Richard's Almanac" (1749 and 1750), in *The Papers of Benjamin Franklin,* ed. Leonard W. Labaree et al. (New Haven, 1959–), III, 340, 441. (I have modernized the spelling.)

4. See Robert Middlekauff, *Benjamin Franklin and His Enemies* (Berkeley, 1995).

5. A famous indictment of Franklin was handed down by D. H. Lawrence, *Studies in Classic American Literature* (London, 1924). More recent assessments of the problem of Franklin's identity are Mitchell R. Breitwieser, *Cotton Mather and Benjamin Franklin: The Price of Representative Personality* (Cambridge, Eng., 1984); and Ormond Seavey, *Becoming Benjamin Franklin: The Autobiography and the Life* (University Park, Penn., 1988).

6. Franklin to Joseph Priestley, June 7, 1782, *Works,* ed. Jared Sparks (Chicago, 1882), IX, 226. (I use Sparks's edition for the years that the Yale edition has not yet reached.) Franklin to James Logan [1737?], *Papers,* II, 185.

7. See David Larson, "Franklin on the Nature of Man and the Possibility of Virtue," *Early American Literature* 10 (Fall 1975), 111–20; and Ronald A. Bosco, " 'He That Best Understands the World, Least Likes It': The Dark Side of Benjamin Franklin," *Pennsylvania Magazine of History and Biography* 111 (Oct. 1987), 525–54.

8. *Papers,* III, 481. Franklin repeated this passage *verbatim* when he revised his Will in 1757: *Papers,* VII, 204.

9. *Papers,* I, 105.

10. Franklin to Samuel Johnson, Aug. 23, 1750, *Papers,* IV, 41. "Poor Richard's Almanac" (1745), *Papers,* III, 6.

11. Francis Hutcheson, *An Inquiry into the Original of Our Ideas of Beauty and Virtue* (London, 1729), 180. On Franklin as a proto-utilitarian, see also Norman Fiering, "Benjamin Franklin and the Way to Virtue," *American Quarterly* 30 (Summer 1978), 199–223. The political dimension of Franklin's concept of virtue is discussed in Paul W. Conner, *Poor Richard's Politicks: Benjamin Franklin and His New American Order* (New York, 1965); and Drew R. McCoy, "Benjamin Franklin's Vision of a Republican Political Economy for America," *William and Mary Quarterly* 35 (Oct. 1978), 605–28.

12. "Poor Richard's Almanac" (1739), *Papers,* II, 223; cf. *ibid.,* IV, 86. See also Paul Conkin, "Benjamin Franklin: Science and Morals," in his *Puritans and Pragmatists* (Bloomington, 1976), esp. 87–89.

13. *The Autobiography of Benjamin Franklin,* ed. Leonard W. Labaree et al. (New Haven, 1964). An example of Franklin's early interest in deism, "A Dissertation on Liberty and Necessity" (1725), *Papers,* I, 57–71, expounded a system which, although internally logical, was not in the slightest useful to mankind.

14. Franklin to George Whitefield, Sept. 2, 1769, *Papers,* XVI, 192.

15. For Franklin's interest in liturgics, see his revision of the Lord's Prayer (1768) and of the Anglican Book of Common Prayer (1773), *Papers,* XV, 299–303, and XX, 343–52. On prayer, see his "Articles of Belief and Acts of Religion" (1728), *Papers,* I, 101–09.

16. "On the Providence of God in the Government of the World" (1732), *Papers,* I, 264.

17. In a letter to his Calvinist sister Jane Mecom, Franklin invoked (for tactical reasons) the authority of Jonathan Edwards to score a point; *Papers,* II, 384f. "The Education of Youth" (1749), *Papers,* III, 413.

18. Franklin to unknown addressee [Dec. 13, 1757], *Papers,* VII, 294.

19. "Poor Richard's Almanac" (1758); *Papers,* VII, 353.

20. Franklin to Samuel Mather, May 12, 1784, *Writings,* IX, 208; Franklin to Josiah and Abiah Franklin, April 13, 1738, *Papers,* II, 203; *Papers,* III, 125.

21. On Franklin's religion, see Elizabeth Dunn, "From Bold Youth to Reflective Sage: A Re-evaluation of Benjamin Franklin's Religion," *Pennsylvania Magazine of History and Biography* 111 (Oct. 1987), 501–24; D. H. Meyer, "Franklin's Religion," in *Critical Essays on Benjamin Franklin,* ed. Melvin Buxbaum (Boston, 1987), 147–67; and Alfred O. Aldridge, *Benjamin Franklin and Nature's God* (Durham, N.C., 1967).

22. See Alfred Owen Aldridge, *Benjamin Franklin: Philosopher and Man* (Philadelphia, 1965), 39–46. On the Societies for the Reformation of Manners, see Shelley Burtt, *Virtue Transformed: Political Argument in England, 1688–1740* (Cambridge, Eng., 1992), 22–24. Franklin's own account of the Junto is given in his *Autobiography,* 162f.

23. Alexander Hamilton, in *The Federalist,* no. 72, ed. Jacob Cooke (Middletown, Ct., 1961), 488.

24. W. E. Gladstone, ed., *The Works of Joseph Butler* (Oxford, 1896), I, 97–98.

25. On the relationship between happiness and virtue in Franklin's thought, see Lorraine Smith Pangle and Thomas L. Pangle, *The Learning of Liberty: The Educational Ideals of the American Founders* (Lawrence, Kan., 1993), 265f.

26. On this process, see Albert O. Hirschman, *The Passions and the Interests: Political Arguments for Capitalism Before Its Triumph* (Princeton, 1977).

27. See, e.g., "Poor Richard's Almanac" (1744), *Papers,* II, 397; *Autobiography,* 160.

28. See *Papers,* VII, 89.

29. "Wealth" was a relative term for Franklin: "Who is rich? He that rejoices in his portion." "Poor Richard's Almanac" (1744), *Papers,* II, 395.

30. Since Jared Sparks supposed Franklin the author of the dialogues, he printed them in his edition of the *Works,* II, 46–57. Alfred Owen Aldridge, "Franklin's 'Shaftesburian' Dialogues Not Franklin's," *American Literature* 21 (May 1949), 151–59.

31. See Wilbur Samuel Howell, *Eighteenth-Century British Logic and Rhetoric* (Princeton, 1971); William Charvat, *Origins of American Critical Thought* (Philadelphia, 1936, reprinted 1961).

32. David M. Larson, "Benevolent Persuasion: The Art of Benjamin Franklin's Philanthropic Papers," *Pennsylvania Magazine of History and Biography* 110 (April 1986), 195–218, quotation from p. 216. See also Edward J. Gallagher, "The Rhetorical Strategy of Franklin's 'Way to Wealth,' " *Eighteenth-Century Studies* 6 (June 1973), 475–85.

33. "Poor Richard's Almanac" (1755 and 1758), *Papers,* V, 473 and VII, 350. See also Cameron Nickels, "Franklin's Poor Richard's Almanacs," in *The Oldest Revolutionary: Essays on Benjamin Franklin,* ed. J. A. Leo Lemay (Philadelphia, 1976), 77–89.

34. Franklin? "Letter from Father Abraham to His Beloved Son" (1758), *Papers,* VIII, 123f; Franklin, *Autobiography,* 148.

35. Franklin, "A Man of Sense," (1735), *Papers,* II, 15–19.

36. Franklin to Lord Kames, May 3, 1760, *Papers,* IX, 105. Franklin's famous description of the regimen and his practice of it is in *Autobiography,* 148–60.

37. David L. Parker, "From Sound Believer to Practical Preparationist: Some Puritan Harmonics in Franklin's *Autobiography,*" in Lemay, ed., *Oldest Revolutionary,* 67–75.

38. See Fiering, "Franklin and the Way to Virtue."

39. Franklin? "Letter from Father Abraham" (1758), *Papers,* VIII, 127; *Autobiography,* 148.

40. The first part of the definition follows Locke. Franklin, *Papers,* I, 262.

41. Franklin, "Self-Denial Not the Essence of Virtue," (1735), *Papers,* II, 19–21; quotations from p. 21. Franklin was probably arguing against Bernard

Mandeville, though the position that virtue implies self-denial is also associated with Kant.

42. Franklin to Samuel Johnson, Aug. 23, 1750, *Papers,* IV, 41.

43. Franklin, "Proposals Relating to the Education of Youth in Pennsylvania" (1749), *Papers,* III, 419. The Scottish moral philosopher Francis Hutcheson defined the "moral importance of any agent" as M = B x A, where B = benevolence and A = abilities. See his *Inquiry* (cited in n. 11), 185.

44. Franklin's position resembles that attributed to the English "Court Whigs" in Shelley Burtt, *Virtue Transformed,* 112.

45. See Albert J. Wurth, Jr., "The Franklin Persona: The Virtue of Practicality and the Practicality of Virtue," in *Virtue, Corruption, and Self-Interest: Political Values in the Eighteenth Century,* ed. Richard K. Matthews (Bethlehem, Penn., 1994), 76–102.

46. "Proposals and Queries to Be Asked the Junto" (1732), *Papers,* I, 263.

47. Norman Fiering, *Jonathan Edwards's Moral Thought and Its British Context* (Chapel Hill, N.C., 1981), 7. For Edwards's participation in transatlantic religious dialogue, see Harold P. Simonson, "Jonathan Edwards and his Scottish Connections" [British] *Journal of American Studies* 21 (Dec. 1987), 353–76.

48. Perry Miller, *Jonathan Edwards* (New York, 1949), pp. 180–84, 237, 252. Miller seems to have thought that if one rejected the existence of innate *ideas,* one had to reject the existence of innate *powers,* which is what the faculties were.

49. Jonathan Edwards, *The Freedom of the Will,* ed. Paul Ramsay, in *Works,* I, 133. On Edwards's use of faculty psychology, see William J. Scheick, *The Writings of Jonathan Edwards: Theme, Motif, and Style* (College Station: Texas, 1975).

50. *The Republic* IV.434D–441C.

51. Jonathan Edwards, *A Treatise Concerning Religious Affections,* ed. John Smith, in *Works,* II, 122. On Edwards's Platonism, see Paul Conkin, "Jonathan Edwards: Theology," in *Puritans and Pragmatists.*

52. Edwards, "A Divine and Supernatural Light" (1734), in Jonathan Edwards, *Representative Selections,* ed. Clarence Faust and Thomas Johnson (New York, 1935), 103.

53. Edwards, "Charity and Its Fruits," in Jonathan Edwards, *Ethical Writings,* ed. Paul Ramsay, in *Works,* VIII, 286f.

54. *Ibid.,* 252; Edwards, "Divine and Supernatural Light," *Selections,* 103.

55. Benjamin Franklin, "Defence of Rev. Mr. Hemphill" (1735), *Papers,* II, 114.

56. Edwards, *Religious Affections,* 206–07. See also Clyde Holbrook, *The Ethics of Jonathan Edwards: Morality and Aesthetics* (Ann Arbor, 1973), esp. pp. 56–71.

57. See Fiering, "Will and Intellect," and Fiering, *Edwards's Moral Thought,* 263–69.

58. "All acts of the will are acts of the affections." Edwards, "Some Thoughts

Concerning the Revival of Religion in New England" (1742), in Jonathan
Edwards, *The Great Awakening,* ed. C. C. Goen, in *Works* IV, 297. Cf. Edwards,
"The Mind," in Jonathan Edwards, *Scientific and Philosophical Writings,* ed. Wallace Anderson, in *Works,* VI, 388, which equates the affections with "lively
exercises of the will."

59. Edwards, "Charity and Its Fruits," in *Ethical Writings,* 277.

60. Edwards, *Religious Affections,* 98, 350; "Charity and Its Fruits," in *Ethical
Writings,* 277.

61. Edwards, *True Grace, Distinguished from the Experience of Devils* (1753),
quoted in Fiering, *Edwards's Moral Thought,* p. 61.

62. Edwards, "Charity and Its Fruits," *Ethical Writings,* 278; Fiering, *Edwards's
Moral Thought,* 92.

63. James Madison, in *The Federalist,* no. 72, p. 349.

64. These "Resolutions" are among many printed in Edwards, *Representative
Selections,* 38.

65. "Natural Philosophy," in *Scientific and Philosophical Writings,* 193.

66. Edwards, "Journal" (1723), quoted in Fiering, *Edwards's Moral Thought,*
151.

67. Franklin, *Autobiography,* 159–60.

68. "Diary" in *Selections,* 51.

69. See Holbrook, *Ethics of Edwards,* 91.

70. Edwards, "Charity and Its Fruits," *Ethical Writings,* 254.

71. Edwards, *Ethical Writings,* 176.

72. *Ibid.,* 271. In Puritan moral theology, it was important to "wean" one's
affections away from selfish and wordly things.

73. These quotations are from "Charity and Its Fruits," *ibid.,* 260, 276, and
269.

74. *Ibid.,* 260.

75. *Ibid.,* 271; Richard Bushman, ed., *The Great Awakening: Documents on the
Revival of Religion 1740–1745* (New York, 1970), 166–68.

76. Mark Valeri, "The Economic Thought of Jonathan Edwards," *Church
History* 60 (March 1991), 37–54. Patricia Tracy calls Edwards's outlook "Tory"
(*Jonathan Edwards, Pastor* [New York, 1980], p. 149); perhaps a more accurate
term would be "patriarchal."

77. See Barry Shain, *The Myth of American Individualism: The Protestant Origins
of American Political Thought* (Princeton, 1994).

78. "Charity and Its Fruits," *Ethical Writings,* 242–79; quotations from
pp. 261 and 242.

79. See Paul Ramsey's commentary, *ibid.,* 105–06 and 242n.

80. Edwards, "Some Thoughts," in *The Great Awakening,* 522. This was the
passage that Franklin cited approvingly; see n. 17 above.

81. See "Introduction" to Jonathan Edwards, *The Life of David Brainerd,* ed.
Norman Pettit, in *Works,* VII.

82. E.g., *ibid.*, 261. An interesting exception is Brainerd's encounter with an Indian medicine man who explained a little of the native religion to him (*ibid.*, 329–30).

83. The two quotations are from Edwards, "Charity and Its Fruits," *Ethical Writings*, 393–94.

84. *Ibid.*, 252–53; "Divine and Supernatural Light," 103.

85. Edwards, "The Nature of True Virtue," in *Ethical Writings*, 540.

86. Edwards, "Miscellanies," no. 116, in *The Philosophy of Jonathan Edwards*, Harvey G. Townsend, ed. (Eugene, Or., 1955), 109–110.

87. Edwards, "A Divine and Supernatural Light," *Representative Selections*, 102–11.

88. "Charity and Its Fruits," *Ethical Writings*, 396.

89. Edwards, "The Nature of True Virtue," *Ethical Writings*, 596.

90. Edwards, "Divine and Supernatural Light," *Representative Selections*, 108.

91. Fiering, *Edwards's Moral Thought*, 64–66, 87, 103–04, 119, 143.

92. Edwards, *A Treatise Concerning Religious Affections, Works*, II, 283.

93. Edwards, *Miscellanies*, no. 141, quoted in Fiering, *Edwards's Moral Thought*, 351.

94. Many writers have commented on Edwards's aesthetics. Besides Holbrook, *The Ethics of Edwards*, chap. 6, see esp. Roland DeLattre, *Beauty and Sensibility in the Thought of Jonathan Edwards* (New Haven, 1968).

95. Paul Conkin, "Jonathan Edwards," in *Puritans and Pragmatists* (cited in n. 12 above), 46. See also Wallace Anderson's superb introduction to Edwards's *Scientific and Philosophical Writings* (cited in n. 58), pp. 1–142.

96. "Some Thoughts Concerning the Present Revival of Religion," *The Great Awakening*, 344–45.

97. See David T. Morgan, "A Most Unlikely Friendship: Benjamin Franklin and George Whitefield," *The Historian* 47 (Feb. 1985), 208–18.

98. Edwards, *Ethical Writings*, 271n.

99. See James D. German, "The Social Utility of Wicked Self-Love: Calvinism, Capitalism, and Public Policy in Revolutionary New England," *Journal of American History* 82 (Dec. 1995), 965–98.

100. See Joseph Conforti, *Samuel Hopkins and the New Divinity Movement* (Grand Rapids, Mich., 1981). Still very useful is Alexander Allen, "The Transition in New England Theology," *Atlantic Monthly* 68 (Dec. 1891), 767–80.

101. Joseph Tracy, *The Great Awakening: A History of the Revival of Religion in the Time of Edwards and Whitefield* (Edinburgh, 1976; first published in 1842). I am here using the term Second Great Awakening, as historians sometimes do, to refer to the entire era of evangelical activity from 1800 to the Civil War.

102. See Joseph Conforti, *Jonathan Edwards, Religious Tradition, and American Culture* (Chapel Hill, N.C., 1995); Nathan Hatch and Harry Stout, eds., *Jonathan Edwards and the American Experience* (New York, 1988); Mark Noll, "The Con-

tested Legacy of Jonathan Edwards in Antebellum Calvinism," *Canadian Review of American Studies* 19 (Summer 1988), 149–64; and Daniel B. Shea, "Jonathan Edwards: The First Two Hundred Years," [British] *Journal of American Studies* 14 (August 1980), 181–98.

103. James Moorhead, "Social Reform and the Divided Conscience of Antebellum Protestantism," *Church History* 48 (Dec. 1979), 416–30.

2. The American Founders and the Scottish Enlightenment

1. Garry Wills, *Inventing America: Jefferson's Declaration of Independence* (Garden City, N.J., 1978). For convincing critiques of it, see Gilman M. Ostrander, "New Lost Worlds of Thomas Jefferson," *Reviews in American History* 7 (1979), 183–88; Ronald Hamowy, "Jefferson and the Scottish Enlightenment," *William and Mary Quarterly* 36 (1979), 503–23; and Ralph E. Luker, "Garry Wills and the New Debate Over the Declaration of Independence," *Virginia Quarterly Review* 56 (Spring 1980), 244–61.

2. I. Woodbridge Riley, *American Philosophy: The Early Schools* (New York, 1907); Herbert W. Schneider, *History of American Philosophy* (New York, 1947); Donald Harvey Meyer, *Democratic Enlightenment* (New York, 1976); Henry F. May, *The Enlightenment in America* (New York, 1976).

3. Among many works, see especially Richard B. Sher and Jeffrey R. Smitten, *Scotland and America in the Age of the Enlightenment* (Edinburgh, 1990); William R. Brock, *Scotus Americanus: A Survey of the Sources for Links between Scotland and America in the 18th Century* (Edinburgh, 1982); Andrew Hook, *Scotland and America: A Study of Cultural Relations, 1750–1835* (Glasgow, 1975); Douglas Sloan, *The Scottish Enlightenment and the American College Ideal* (New York, 1971); Ned Landsman, *Scotland and Its First American Colony, 1683–1765* (Princeton, 1985).

4. See Douglass Adair, *Fame and the Founding Fathers,* ed. Trevor Colbourn (New York, 1974); David Lundberg and Henry F. May, "The Enlightened Reader in America," *American Quarterly* 28 (1976), 262–83; James Conniff, "The Enlightenment and American Political Thought," *Political Theory* 8 (1980), 381–402; Roy Branson, "James Madison and the Scottish Enlightenment," *Journal of the History of Ideas* 42 (1979), 235–50; John M. Warner, "David Hume and America," *Journal of the History of Ideas* 33 (1972), 439–56; Forrest McDonald, *Novus Ordo Seclorum: The Intellectual Origins of the Constitution* (Lawrence, Kan., 1985).

5. T. C. Smout, *A History of the Scottish People, 1560–1830* (London, 1969), is a masterpiece. See too Jane Rendall, *The Origins of the Scottish Enlightenment* (London, 1978); Anand C. Chitnis, *The Scottish Enlightenment: A Social History* (London, 1976); E. J. Hobsbawm, "Scottish Reformers of the Eighteenth Century and Capitalist Agriculture," in *Peasants in History,* E. J. Hobsbawm et al., eds. (Calcutta, 1980), 3–29; Richard Teichgraeber, "Politics and Morals in the Scot-

tish Enlightenment," Ph.D. diss., Stanford University, 1978; Davis D. McElroy, *Scotland's Age of Improvement* (Pullman, Wash., 1969).

6. On the influence of Dugald Stewart, see Stefan Collini, Donald Winch, and John Burrow, *That Noble Science of Politics: A Study in Nineteenth-Century Intellectual History* (Cambridge, Eng., 1983), 1–62.

7. Hugh Trevor-Roper, "The Scottish Enlightenment," *Studies on Voltaire and the 18th Century* 58 (1967), 1650. See also Henry Grey Graham, *The Social Life of Scotland in the Eighteenth Century* (New York, 1971, first published in 1899).

8. Richard Sher, *Church and University in the Scottish Enlightenment* (Edinburgh, 1985); Andrew Drummond and James Bulloch, *The Scottish Church, 1688–1843: The Age of the Moderates* (Edinburgh, 1973); Norman Macdougall, ed. *Church, Politics, and Society: Scotland, 1408–1929* (Edinburgh, 1983).

9. Ernest Campbell Mossner, *The Life of David Hume,* 2d ed. (Oxford, 1980), 272–85, 336–55.

10. See Nicholas Phillipson, "The Scottish Enlightenment," in *The Enlightenment in National Context,* Roy Porter and Mikulas Teich, eds. (Cambridge, Eng., 1983), 19–40; idem, "Culture and Society in the Eighteenth-century Provinces: The Case of Edinburgh and the Scottish Enlightenment," in *The University and Society,* Lawrence Stone, ed. (Princeton, 1974), II, 407–48; Charles Camic, *Experience and Enlightenment: Socialization for Cultural Change in Eighteenth-Century Scotland* (Chicago, 1983).

11. Gladys Bryson, *Man and Society: The Scottish Inquiry of the Eighteenth Century* (Princeton, 1945), remains the major study; see also Louis Schneider, ed., *The Scottish Moralists on Human Nature and Society* (Chicago, 1967); Alan Swingewood, "Origins of Sociology: The Case of the Scottish Enlightenment," *British Journal of Sociology* 17 (1978), 19–40; and Salim Rashid, "Dugald Stewart, 'Baconian' Methodology, and Political Economy," *Journal of the History of Ideas* 46 (1985), 245–57.

12. See Caroline Robbins, *The Eighteenth-Century Commonwealthman* (Cambridge, Mass., 1959); J. G. A. Pocock, *The Machiavellian Moment: Florentine Political Thought and the Atlantic Republican Tradition* (Princeton, 1975); and Zera S. Fink, *The Classical Republicans: An Essay in the Recovery of a Pattern of Thought in Seventeenth-Century England* (Evanston, Ill., 1945).

13. Phillipson, "The Scottish Enlightenment"; James Moore, "Hume's Political Science and the Classical Republican Tradition," *Canadian Journal of Political Science* 10 (1977), 809–39.

14. There were variations, and some analyses show only three stages. See Ronald Meek, *Social Science and the Ignoble Savage* (Cambridge, Eng., 1976); and George Stocking, "Scotland as the Model for Mankind: Lord Kames's Philosophical View of Civilization," in *Towards a Science of Man: Essays in the History of Anthropology* (The Hague, 1975), 65–89.

15. David Hume, *History of England* (London, 1822), VI, 46.

16. See Leonard Billet, "Justice, Liberty and Economy," in *Adam Smith and the*

Wealth of Nations, ed. Fred Glahe (Boulder, Colo., 1978), 83–109; David A. Reisman, *Adam Smith's Sociological Economics* (London, 1976); and *Essays on Adam Smith,* eds. Andrew Skinner and Thomas Wilson (Oxford, 1975).

17. Edmund Burke, "Letters on a Regicide Peace" (1796), in his *Works* (Boston, 1871), V, 208.

18. See Phillipson, "Scottish Enlightenment."

19. The secondary literature on *The Spectator* and its program of polite culture is enormous, but see especially Peter France, *Politeness and Its Discontents* (Cambridge, Eng., 1992). Quotations from pp. 76 and 65.

20. Cf. Susan Manning, *The Puritan-Provincial Vision: Scottish and American Literature in the Nineteenth Century* (Cambridge, Eng., 1990), 108.

21. Dugald Stewart, *Lectures on Political Economy,* quoted in Collini et al., *That Noble Science of Politics,* 27.

22. See Biancamaria Fontana, *Rethinking the Politics of Commercial Society: the Edinburgh Review, 1802–1832* (Cambridge, Eng., 1985).

23. See Stephen A. Conrad, "Citizenship and Common Sense: The Problem of Authority in the Social Background and Social Philosophy of the Wise Club of Aberdeen," Ph.D. diss. Harvard University, 1980.

24. The liberal or radical implications of their ideas are stressed in Caroline Robbins, *Eighteenth-Century Commonwealthman;* and Sher and Smitten, *Scotland and America in the Age of the Enlightenment.*

25. T. D. Campbell, "Francis Hutcheson: 'Father' of the Scottish Enlightenment," in *The Origins and Nature of the Scottish Enlightenment,* ed. R. H. Campbell and Andrew Skinner (Edinburgh, 1982), 167–85.

26. Sir John Dalrymple, *Essay Towards a General History of Feudal Property in Great Britain* (first published in 1757).

27. Norman Kemp Smith, *The Philosophy of David Hume* (London, 1941), is still authoritative.

28. See Peter Gay, *The Enlightenment: An Interpretation.* Volume I: *The Rise of Modern Paganism* (New York, 1967), Book One, "The Appeal to Antiquity."

29. On the continuities between civic humanism and the Scottish Enlightenment, see Istvan Hont and Michael Ignatieff, eds., *Wealth and Virtue: The Shaping of Political Economy in the Scottish Enlightenment* (Cambridge, Eng., 1983) and Donald Winch, *Adam Smith's Politics* (Cambridge, Eng., 1978). Edwin J. Harpham, "Liberalism, Civic Humanism, and the Case of Adam Smith," *American Political Science Review* 78 (1984), 764–74, reaffirms the essential opposition between Smith and civic humanism.

30. In the course of emphasizing the American debt to Scottish writers, scholars have sometimes created the misleading impression that all Scottish philosophers thought alike. For a corrective see Daniel Walker Howe, "European Sources of Political Ideas in Jeffersonian America," *Reviews in American History* 10 (Dec. 1982), 28–44.

31. See Edmund S. Morgan, "The American Revolution Considered as an

Intellectual Movement," in *Paths of American Thought,* ed. Arthur M. Schlesinger, Jr., and Morton White (Boston, 1963), 11–33.

32. Bernard Bailyn, *The Peopling of British North America: An Introduction* (New York, 1986).

33. *Ibid.,* p. 131.

34. See Tamara Thornton, *Cultivating Gentlemen: The Meaning of Country Life Among the Boston Elite, 1785–1860* (New Haven, 1989).

35. See also Steven A. Marini, "Religion, Politics, and Ratification," in *Religion in a Revolutionary Age,* ed. Ronald Hoffman and Peter Albert (Charlottesville, Va., 1994), 184–217. For a comparative perspective on eighteenth-century American religion, see Daniel Walker Howe, "The Decline of Calvinism: An Approach to Its Study," *Comparative Studies in Society and History* 14 (1972), 306–27.

36. See Ann Fairfax Withington, *Toward a More Perfect Union: Virtue and the Formation of the American Republic* (New York, 1991), 13 et passim.

37. [James Wilson and William White] "The Visitant," [Philadelphia] *Pennsylvania Chronicle,* April 4–11 and April 18–25, 1768.

38. Stephen A. Conrad, "Polite Foundation: Citizenship and Common Sense in James Wilson's Republican Theory," *Supreme Court Review: 1984,* ed. Philip Kurland et al. (Chicago, 1985), 359–88; quotations from pp. 375 and 383. See also Shannon C. Stimson, "Common Sense Philosophy and the Jurisprudence of James Wilson," in Sher and Smitten, *Scotland and America,* 193–208.

39. See John Clive and Bernard Bailyn, "England's Cultural Provinces: Scotland and America," *William and Mary Quarterly* 11 (1954), 200–13; Nicholas Phillipson, "Towards a Definition of the Scottish Enlightenment," in *City and Society in the 18th Century,* eds. Paul Fritz and David Williams (Toronto, 1973), 125–47; and Susan Manning, *The Puritan-Provincial Vision.*

40. See Gordon Wood, *The Creation of the American Republic* (Chapel Hill, N.C., 1969); Jennifer Nedelsky, "Confining Democratic Politics: Antifederalists, Federalists, and the Constitution," *Harvard Law Review* 96 (1982), 340–60; Michael Lienesch, "Interpreting Experience: History, Philosophy, and Science in the American Constitutional Debates," *American Politics Quarterly* 11 (1983), 379–401.

41. See Michael J. Crawford, *Seasons of Grace: Colonial New England's Revival Tradition in Its British Context* (New York, 1991); and Marilyn Westercamp, *The Triumph of the Laity: Scots-Irish Piety and the Great Awakening* (New York, 1988).

42. Robert Davidson, *An Oration on the Independence of the United States of America* (Carlyle, Pa., 1787), 15, quoted in Lienesch, 397.

43. Richard D. Brown, "Modernization: A Victorian Climax," *American Quarterly* 27 (1975), 537.

44. *The Federalist* 10:9. There are so many editions of *The Federalist* in circulation that I have chosen to cite it by number and paragraph, separated by a colon. I use the edition by Jacob E. Cooke (Middletown, Conn., 1961), which has the

most complete scholarly apparatus, along with Thomas S. Engeman et al., eds., *The Federalist Concordance* (Middletown, Conn., 1980), which is keyed to it. I have modernized spelling and punctuation.

45. Besides Moore, "Hume's Political Science," see J. G. A. Pocock, "Hume and the American Revolution," in *McGill Hume Studies,* ed. David F. Norton et al. (San Diego, 1979), 325–43.

46. See Thomas L. Pangle, "The *Federalist Papers'* Vision of Civic Health and the Tradition Out of Which That Vision Emerges," *Western Political Quarterly* 39 (1986), 577–602.

47. For more observations on the reconciliation of Enlightenment and civic humanist strands in the thought of the American Founders, see James Kloppenberg, "The Virtues of Liberalism," *Journal of American History* 74 (June 1987), 9–33.

48. Isaac Kramnick illuminates this in "The Discourse of Politics in 1787: The Constitution and Its Critics on Individualism, Community, and the State," a paper delivered at the Constitution Bicentennial Conference of the United States Capitol Association, Washington, D.C., May 1987.

49. Morton White's recent study, *Philosophy, The Federalist, and the Constitution* (New York, 1987), confirms that Publius did not follow Hume's moral philosophy, despite his other borrowings from Hume.

50. See Theodore Draper, "Hume and Madison: The Secrets of Federalist Paper No. 10," *Encounter* 58 (February 1982), 34–47. Unlike Madison's Publius, Hamilton's Publius openly acknowledged his use of Hume (*The Federalist,* 85:14).

51. *The Federalist* 33:3.

52. See H. M. Gardiner et al., *Feeling and Emotion: A History of Theories* (New York, 1937), 89–118; Perry Miller, *The New England Mind: The Seventeenth Century* (Cambridge, Mass., 1939), 239–279; William T. Costello, *The Scholastic Curriculum at Early Seventeenth-Century Cambridge* (Cambridge, Mass., 1958), 94–97; and Norman Fiering, *Moral Philosophy at Seventeenth-Century Harvard: A Discipline in Transition* (Chapel Hill, N.C., 1981), chaps. 3 and 4. For the application of faculty psychology to literature and philosophy see Arthur O. Lovejoy, *The Great Chain of Being: A Study of the History of an Idea* (Cambridge, Mass., 1936), and E. M. W. Tillyard, *The Elizabethan World Picture* (New York, 1944). The concept of psychological "faculties" does not lack defenders even today: see Jerry A. Fodor, *The Modularity of Mind: An Essay on Faculty Psychology* (Cambridge, Mass., 1983).

53. Francis Hutcheson, *An Essay on the Nature and Conduct of the Passions and Affections . . .* (1742), ed. Paul McReynolds (Gainesville, Fla., 1969), 183 (emphasis deleted and capitalization modernized).

54. *The Book of Common Prayer* (1549), "Litany and Suffrages"; *Paradise Lost,* Bk. 12, lines 86–90. See J. Rodney Fulcher, "Puritans and the Passions: The Faculty Psychology in American Puritanism," *Journal of the Behavioral Sciences* 9 (1973), 123–139.

55. See Barry Shain, *The Myth of American Individualism: The Protestant Origins of American Thought* (Princeton, 1994), 301–19.

56. Thomas Reid, "Essays on the Active Powers of Man" (1788), in William Hamilton, ed., *The Works of Thomas Reid,* 6th ed. (Edinburgh, 1863), II, 543, 551, 572, 579.

57. John Witherspoon, "The Dominion of Providence over the Passions of Man," in *The Selected Writings of John Witherspoon,* ed. Thomas Miller (Carbondale, Ill., 1990), 126–147. See also Richard B. Sher, "Witherspoon's *Dominion of Providence* and the Scottish Jeremiad Tradition," in Sher and Smitten, *Scotland and America,* 46–64.

58. *The Federalist* 71:1; Albert O. Hirschman, *The Passions and the Interests: Political Arguments for Capitalism Before Its Triumph* (Princeton, 1977).

59. Jefferson to Benjamin Rush, April 21, 1803, in *The Writings of Thomas Jefferson,* ed. Paul Leicester Ford (New York, 1892–99), VIII, 225–6. Thomas Jefferson, "A Bill for Proportioning Crimes and Punishments in Cases Heretofore Capital" (1779) in *The Papers of Thomas Jefferson,* ed. Julian P. Boyd (Princeton, 1950–), II, 492. Since Boyd's definitive edition is not yet complete, I have had to cite other collections of Jefferson's works as well.

60. Thomas Jefferson to David Ross, May 8, 1786, in Boyd, ed., *Papers,* IX, 474. Later he complained that British policy toward the United States had been dictated, "nine times out of ten," by "passion, and not reason." Jefferson to John Jay, October 8, 1787, *ibid.,* XII, 216.

61. There is a good presentation of Jefferson's faculty psychology in Lee Quinby, "Thomas Jefferson: The Virtue of Aesthetics and the Aesthetics of Virtue," *American Historical Review* 87 (April 1982), 337–56. However, Quimby claims that Jefferson followed Shaftesbury in defining ethics as a form of aesthetics, though Jefferson explicitly rejected this position in his letter to Thomas Law, June 13, 1814, *The Writings of Thomas Jefferson,* ed. Andrew Lipscomb and Albert E. Bergh (Washington, D.C., 1904), XIV, 140.

62. Jefferson to John Adams, April 8, 1816, in Lester J. Cappon, *The Adams-Jefferson Letters* (Chapel Hill, N.C., 1959, reprinted 1988), 467.

63. On Jefferson's integration of Lockean liberalism with classical republicanism, see Garrett Ward Sheldon, *The Political Philosophy of Thomas Jefferson* (Baltimore, 1991).

64. See David N. Mayer, *The Constitutional Thought of Thomas Jefferson* (Charlottesville, Va., 1994).

65. Thomas Jefferson, "First Inaugural Address" (March 4, 1801), in Lipscomb and Bergh, eds., *Writings,* III, 320.

66. Boyd, ed., *Papers,* I, 213; "Draft of the Kentucky Resolutions" (October 1798), Ford, ed., *Writings,* VII, 303.

67. See Gilman Ostrander, "Jefferson and Scottish Culture," *Historical Reflections/Reflexions Historiques* 5 (Winter 1978), 233–49, and the works cited in notes 1, 2, and 3 of this chapter.

68. A virtual identity of outlook between the two friends is the thesis of Adrienne Koch, *Jefferson and Madison: The Great Collaboration* (New York, 1950). More recently the differences have been emphasized—perhaps overemphasized—in Richard K. Matthews, *If Men Were Angels: James Madison and the Heartless Empire of Reason* (Lawrence, Kan., 1995). In my opinion the chief difference between Jefferson and Madison lay in the degree of confidence they felt in human nature.

69. Jefferson to William Green Munford, June 18, 1799, in *Thomas Jefferson: Writings,* ed. Merrill D. Peterson (New York, 1984), 1064. Cf. Thomas Reid, writing in 1788: "Man is evidently made for living in society. His social affections shew this as evidently as that the eye was made for seeing." *Works,* II, 666.

70. See Jefferson to Francis W. Gilmer, June 7, 1816, Lipscomb and Bergh, *Writings,* XV, 24; Jefferson to John Adams, April 8 and October 14, 1816, Cappon, ed., *Letters,* 467 and 492.

71. Jefferson to P. S. Dupont de Nemours, April 24, 1816, Ford, ed., *Writings,* X, 22; see also Charles A. Miller, *Jefferson and Nature* (Baltimore, 1988), 56–87. Adam Smith's *Theory of Moral Sentiments* (1759), explaining human social affections, helps to justify the laissez-faire principles of his *Wealth of Nations* (1776).

72. Morton White, *The Philosophy of the American Revolution* (New York, 1978), 113–27. Earlier, White had taken a view of Jefferson's moral philosophy closer to that of Wills (see Morton White, *Science and Sentiment in America* [New York, 1972], 67–70), but he changed his mind after further study.

73. See Gilman M. Ostrander, "Lord Kames and American Revolutionary Culture," *Essays in Honor of Russel B. Nye,* ed. Joseph Waldmeir (East Lansing, Mich., 1978), 168–79. One of the few books that survived the burning of Jefferson's library in 1770 was Kames's *Essays on the Principles of Morality and Religion* (1751); on the improvement of the moral sense, see pp. 140–46.

74. This is the essence of Ronald Hamowy's argument cited above, n. 1. In the comprehensive bibliography that Jefferson drew up for Robert Skipwith (August 3, 1771), he listed "Locke on government" as well as Locke's writings on religion and education; Boyd, ed. *Papers,* I, 79–80.

75. Jefferson to William Short, October 31, 1819, Ford, ed. *Writings,* X, 146.

76. Jefferson to Peter Carr, August 10, 1787, Boyd, ed., *Papers,* XII, 14–18. See also Jefferson to John Adams, October 14, 1816, Cappon, ed., *Letters,* 492.

77. Jefferson to Thomas Law, June 13, 1814, Lipscomb and Bergh, eds., *Writings,* XIV, 138–44; Thomas Law, whose views Jefferson here endorses, expressed himself on the moral feelings and their social utility in his *Thoughts on Instinctive Impulses* (Philadelphia, 1810); and *Second Thoughts on Instinctive Impulses* (Philadelphia, 1813). Cf. Kames, *Essays on the Principles of Morality,* 67f.

78. See John Witherspoon, *Selected Writings,* 157–59; Kames, *Essays on the Principles of Morality,* 76–91; Dugald Stewart, *Philosophy of the Active and Moral Powers,* ed. James Walker (Cambridge, Mass., 1849).

79. Jefferson to Peter Carr, August 10, 1787, Boyd, ed., *Papers*, XII, 14–18; Jefferson to Richard Price, July 11, 1788, *ibid.*, XIII, 345.

80. Contrast Wills, *Inventing America*, 181–92, with Daniel Walker Howe, *The Unitarian Conscience: Harvard Moral Philosophy, 1805–1861*, rev. ed. (Middletown, Ct., 1988), 45–49. White sought to connect the term "self-evident" specifically with Locke and Wills specifically with Reid (mistakenly assuming Reid shared Hutcheson's emotive doctrine of morality); for a better understanding of the term as expressing general philosophical rationalism see Michael P. Zuckert, "Self-Evident Truth and the Declaration of Independence," *Review of Politics* 49 (1987), 319–39.

81. Jefferson to Maria Cosway, October 12, 1786, Boyd, ed. *Papers*, X, 443–54, quotation from p. 450. Whether the two ever consummated their mutual attraction is a matter of inference and a subject of disagreement among historians. In any case, the comment of Noble Cunningham, Jr., is apt: "the outcome of the relationship demonstrated that reason ultimately prevailed in ordering Jefferson's life" (*In Pursuit of Reason: The Life of Thomas Jefferson* [Baton Rouge, La., 1987], 105).

82. See Andrew Burstein, "Jefferson and the Familiar Letter," *Journal of the Early Republic* 14 (Summer 1994), 195–220.

83. Jefferson to Peter Carr, August 10, 1787, Boyd, ed., *Papers*, XII, 14–18.

84. Jefferson to Robert Skipwith, August 3, 1771, *ibid.* I, 76–77; Jefferson to Peter Carr, August 19, 1785, *ibid.*, VIII, 405–08; and Jefferson to Martha Jefferson, May 21, 1787, *ibid.*, XI, 369–70 ("a mind always employed is always happy," p. 370).

85. On the relationship of happiness and virtue in Jefferson's thought, see Lorraine Smith Pangle and Thomas L. Pangle, *The Learning of Liberty: The Educational Ideals of the American Founders* (Lawrence, Kan., 1993), 250–64.

86. Jefferson to Adams, January 22, 1821, Cappon, ed. *Letters*, 570; Jefferson to Joseph Priestley, June 19, 1802, Ford, ed., *Writings*, IX, 158.

87. Thomas Jefferson, "Report of the Commisioners for the University of Virginia" (August 4, 1818), Peterson, ed., *Writings*, 461. See also Sheldon, *Political Philosophy*, pp. 63–67 and 146.

88. Thomas Jefferson, "Bill for the More General Diffusion of Knowledge" (drafted 1776, introduced into the Virginia legislature 1779), Boyd, ed. *Papers*, II, 526–33; quotations from p. 527.

89. Jefferson to John Adams, October 28, 1813, Cappon, ed. *Letters*, 388.

90. Jefferson to Nathaniel Burwell, March 14, 1818, Ford, ed. *Writings*, X, 104–06; Thomas Jefferson, *Notes on the State of Virginia* (1787), Query VI (3d American ed., New York, 1801), 90ff.

91. See especially Winthrop Jordan, *White Over Black: American Attitudes Toward the Negro, 1550–1812* (Chapel Hill, N.C., 1968), 429–81; John Chester Miller, *The Wolf by the Ears: Thomas Jefferson and Slavery* (New York, 1977), 46–103; and Paul Finkelman, "Jefferson and Slavery: Treason Against the Hopes

of the World," in *Jeffersonian Legacies,* ed. Peter S. Onuf (Charlottesville, Va., 1993), 181–221.

92. Jefferson, *Notes on the State of Virginia,* Query XIV, 203–14; quotations from p. 206.

93. Jefferson's attitudes toward black intellectuals are discussed in Miller, *Wolf by the Ears,* 74–78.

94. *Notes on the State of Virginia,* Query VI, 88ff; Jefferson to the Marquis de Chastellux, June 7, 1785, Boyd, ed., *Papers,* VIII, 184–86; Jefferson to Benjamin Hawkins, February 18, 1803, Ford, ed., *Writings,* VIII, 211–16; Jefferson to Governor William Henry Harrison, February 27, 1803, Lipscomb and Bergh, eds., *Writings,* X, 368–73.

95. Jefferson to Henri Gregoire, February 26, 1809, Ford, ed., *Writings,* IX, 246–47.

96. *Notes on the State of Virginia,* Query XVIII, 240–42; Query VIII, 133. The evil effects of slavery on the self-construction of the master class are portrayed in Kenneth S. Greenberg, *Honor and Slavery* (Princeton, 1996).

97. *Notes on the State of Virginia,* Query XIX; Jefferson to George Wythe, August 13, 1786, Boyd, ed., *Papers,* X, 244; Jefferson to Charles Bellini, September 30, 1785, *ibid.,* VIII, 569.

98. Jefferson to John Adams, October 28, 1813, Cappon, ed., *Letters,* 391.

99. See Jefferson to Philip Mazzei, November [ ], 1785, Boyd, ed., *Papers,* IX, 68. Jefferson expressed doubt that the Latin Americans, even after independence, were culturally ready for free government, though he was confident that in the long run they would come up to the mark: Jefferson to Adams, May 17, 1818, and August 1, 1816, Cappon, ed., *Letters,* 524 and 485.

100. Jefferson to Robert Skipwith, August 3, 1771, Boyd, ed., *Papers,* I, 79.

101. Jefferson to Charles Bellini, September 30, 1785, Boyd, ed., *Papers,* VIII, 569; Jefferson to Thomas Jefferson Randolph, November 24, 1808, Ford, ed., *Writings,* IX, 231–32.

102. Gordon S. Wood, "The Trials and Tribulations of Thomas Jefferson," in *Jeffersonian Legacies,* 405; Jefferson to Thomas Jefferson Randolph, November 24, 1808, Ford, ed., *Writings,* IX, 231–32.

103. Thomas Jefferson, *Autobiography* (1821) (New York, 1959), 55.

104. E.g., Jefferson to the Marquis de Chastellux, June 7, 1785, Boyd, ed., *Papers,* VIII, 184–86; Jefferson to Edward Coles, August 25, 1814, Ford, ed., *Writings,* IX, 477–79.

105. Jefferson to John Holmes, April 22, 1820, *Ford,* X, 157–58.

106. Jefferson to William Green Munford, June 18, 1798, Peterson, ed., *Writings,* 1065–66.

3. *The Political Psychology of* The Federalist

1. See Martin Diamond, "The Federalist, 1787–1788," in Leo Strauss and Joseph Cropsey, eds., *The History of Political Philosophy* (Chicago, 1972), 631–51; Gottfried Dietze, *The Federalist: A Classic on Federalism and Free Government* (Baltimore, 1960); Robert A. Dahl, *A Preface to Democratic Theory* (Chicago, 1956); Morton White, *The Philosophy of the American Revolution* (New York, 1978); and Morton White, *Philosophy, The Federalist, and the Constitution* (New York, 1987).

2. A recent work emphasizing how close Madison and Hamilton were in outlook is Richard K. Matthews, *If Men Were Angels: James Madison and the Heartless Empire of Reason* (Lawrence, Kan., 1995). Even those who have thought they detected differences between Madison's Publius and Hamilton's have not claimed that these extended to his psychology. See Alpheus Thomas Mason, "The Federalist—A Split Personality," *American Historical Review* 57 (1952), 625–43.

3. J. G. A. Pocock, *Politics, Language, and Time: Essays on Political Thought and History* (New York, 1971), 19. For sophisticated applications of this approach, see Anthony Pagden, ed., *The Languages of Political Theory in Early-Modern Europe* (Cambridge, 1987).

4. For examples of reasoning by analogy in eighteenth-century America, see Robert H. Wiebe, *The Opening of American Society: From the Adoption of the Constitution to the Eve of Disunion* (New York, 1984), 9.

5. *The Federalist* 16:1, 22:13, and *passim*. See also Merle Curti, *Human Nature in American Thought* (Madison, Wis., 1980), esp. 5–7, 88–91, 107–12; and H. Trevor Colbourn, *The Lamp of Experience: Whig History and the Intellectual Origins of the American Revolution* (Chapel Hill, N.C., 1965).

6. See Barry Shain, *The Myth of American Individualism: The Protestant Origins of American Thought* (Princeton, 1994), 155–92.

7. For more on the rhetoric of Publius, see Albert Furtwangler, *The Authority of Publius: A Reading of the Federalist Papers* (Ithaca, N.Y., 1984); and Forrest McDonald, "The Rhetoric of Alexander Hamilton," *Modern Age* 25 (1981), 114–24.

8. See Wilbur Samuel Howell, *Eighteenth-Century British Logic and Rhetoric* (Princeton, 1971).

9. For example, Benjamin F. Wright, "*The Federalist* on the Nature of Political Man," *Ethics* 59 (1949), 1–31; and Richard Hofstadter, *The American Political Tradition and the Men Who Made It* (New York, 1948), 3–17. For arguments that Publius is in the tradition of Hobbes, see George Mace, *Locke, Hobbes, and the Federalist Papers* (Carbondale, Ill., 1979); for Publius in the tradition of Calvin, see John Patrick Diggins, *The Lost Soul of American Politics: Virtue, Self-Interest, and the Foundations of Liberalism* (New York, 1984).

10. The scholarly literature (stemming from Charles Beard and Harold Laski) treating Publius as a proto-liberal pluralist is so large that it has a historiography

of its own; see Paul F. Bourke, "The Pluralist Reading of James Madison's Tenth *Federalist*," *Perspectives in American History* 9 (1975), 271–95.

11. Gordon S. Wood argues that Publius retained a concern with virtue in government even while transcending classical political theory in other ways (*The Creation of the American Republic, 1776–1787* [Chapel Hill, N.C., 1969], 505, 606–15). Garry Wills emphasizes Publius's concern for virtue even more (*Explaining America: The Federalist* [Garden City, N.Y., 1981]). See also two articles by Jean Yarbrough: "Representation and Republicanism: Two Views," *Publius* 9 (1979), 77–98, and "Republicanism Reconsidered: Some Thoughts on the Foundation and Preservation of the American Republic," *Review of Politics* 41 (1979), 61–95.

12. On Witherspoon, see Mark A. Noll, *Princeton and the Republic: 1768–1822* (Princeton, 1989); and Richard B. Sher and Jeffrey R. Smitten, eds., *Scotland and America in the Age of the Enlightenment* (Edinburgh, 1990), esp. Part I, "Religion and Revolution: The Two Worlds of John Witherspoon," pp. 29–132.

13. On this context, see Peter J. Diamond, "Witherspoon, William Smith, and the Scottish Philosophy in Revolutionary America," in Sher and Smitten, *Scotland and America,* 115–32.

14. James P. Scanlan first sorted out Publius's treatment of human motives into these three groupings, though he did not connect them with faculty psychology or eighteenth-century rhetorical theory ("*The Federalist* and Human Nature," *Review of Politics* 21 [1959], 657–77).

15. John Locke, *The Reasonableness of Christianity* (1695), ed. Ian T. Ramsay (Stanford, 1958), 61; John Adams, quoted in Curti, *Human Nature in American Thought,* 105; Alexander Pope, *Moral Essays,* Epistle III, line 153.

16. *The Federalist* 15:12 and 51:4.

17. For example, *The Federalist* 2:10.

18. Joseph Butler, *Five Sermons Preached at the Rolls Chapel and a Dissertation upon the Nature of Virtue* (1726), ed. Stephen Darwall (Indianapolis, Ind., 1983), 40. *The Federalist* 73:1.

19. See Albert O. Hirschman, *The Passions and the Interests: Political Arguments for Capitalism before Its Triumph* (Princeton, 1977).

20. *The Federalist* 37:6; 20:21; *et passim.*

21. *Ibid.,* 6:9; 42:9.

22. *Ibid.,* 17:4; 34:4.

23. *Ibid.,* 34:4; 23:7–8.

24. Hugh Blair, *Lectures on Rhetoric and Belles Lettres* (Philadelphia, 1866), 234–64. First published in 1783, this textbook was reprinted many times in America, beginning in Philadelphia in 1784.

25. *The Federalist* 49:10.

26. *Ibid.,* 61:1.

27. Norman Fiering, *Moral Philosophy at Seventeenth-Century Harvard: A Discipline in Transition* (Chapel Hill, N.C., 1981), 148.

28. *The Federalist* 1:5, 46:3, 83:18.

29. Henry F. May, *The Enlightenment in America* (New York, 1976), 42–65. *The Federalist* 49:10; 50:6.

30. Francis Hutcheson, *An Essay on the Nature and Conduct of the Passions and Affections . . .* (1742), ed. Paul McReynolds (Gainesville, Fla., 1969), 183. See also Hirschman, *Passions and Interests,* 20–31.

31. *The Federalist* 51:5; 51:4; 72:5.

32. See Maynard Smith, "Reason, Passion and Political Freedom in *The Federalist,*" *Journal of Politics* 22 (1960), 525–44.

33. *The Federalist* 29:13; 4:11; 49:7.

34. *Ibid.,* 1:1; 1:2.

35. *The Tempest,* act V, scene i.

36. *The Federalist* 71:2.

37. *Ibid.,* 55:9.

38. Quotation from Thomas Reid, "Essays on the Active Powers of Man" (1788) in William Hamilton, ed., *The Works of Thomas Reid,* 6th ed. (Edinburgh, 1863), II, 573, discussing Pythagoras. This analogy had also been prominent in Aristotelian, Thomistic, Renaissance, and Reformation thought.

39. *The Federalist* 55:3; 58:14; 55:3.

40. For example, *ibid.,* 10:6; 10:8.

41. *Ibid.,* 10:17; 57:3.

42. See David F. Epstein, *The Political Theory of the Federalist* (Chicago, 1984); Yarbrough, "Representation and Republicanism," 77–98; and Paul Carson Peterson, "The Political Science of *The Federalist*" (Ph.D. diss., Claremont Graduate School, 1980), 96–99.

43. Gordon Wood, *Creation of the Republic,* 471–508. By contrast, Garry Wills is inclined to admire Publius's dedication to virtuous leadership (*Explaining America,* 268–70).

44. *The Federalist* 2:10; 37:9.

45. *Ibid.,* 38:1–4; 20:21.

46. *Ibid.,* 35:10; 35:6.

47. *Ibid.,* 36:1. See J. R. Pole, "Historians and the Problem of Early American Democracy," *American Historical Review* 67 (1962), 626–46. Locke, too, believed in the "differential rationality" of the social classes, according to C. B. Macpherson, *The Political Theory of Possessive Individualism* (Oxford, 1962), 230–38. However, Locke held out the promise of upward social mobility to those who applied reason and industry; see Neal Wood, *The Politics of Locke's Philosophy* (Berkeley, 1983), 177.

48. *The Federalist* 35:6–11; 35:7.

49. *Ibid.,* 71:2; 10:22.

50. *Ibid.,* 17:8; 36:5; cf. 35:5, 35:10.

51. *Ibid.,* 36:17.

52. *The Federalist* 12:2; 37:5.

53. *Ibid.,* 36:1; Wiebe, *Opening of American Society,* 40. Clinton Rossiter comments that *The Federalist* served as "a kind of debater's handbook in Virginia and New York" during the ratification campaign ("Introduction" to *The Federalist Papers* [New York, 1961], xi).

54. See Cecelia M. Kenyon, "Men of Little Faith: The Anti-Federalists on the Nature of Representative Government," *William and Mary Quarterly,* 3d ser., 12 (1955), 3–43; and Lois J. Einhorn, "Basic Assumptions in the Virginia Ratification Debates: Patrick Henry vs. James Madison on the Nature of Man and Reason," *Southern Speech Communication Journal* 46 (1981), 237–340.

55. *The Federalist* 24:8; 76:10; 49:6.

56. *Ibid.,* 14:4. See, for example, Diamond, "The Federalist, 1787–1788," 642–43; and George W. Carey, "Separation of Powers and the Madisonian Model," *American Political Science Review* 72 (1978), 151–64. The European theorists of mixed government who were most relevant to the Americans are described in Z. S. Fink, *The Classical Republicans* (Evanston, Ill., 1945); Caroline Robbins, *The Eighteenth-Century Commonwealthman* (Cambridge, Mass., 1959); and J. G. A. Pocock, *The Machiavellian Moment: Florentine Political Thought and the Atlantic Republican Tradition* (Princeton, 1975).

57. *The Federalist* 63:9–12. See also Gilbert Chinard, "Polybius and the American Constitution," *Journal of the History of Ideas* 1 (1940), 38–58; Paul Eidelberg, *The Philosophy of the American Constitution* (New York, 1968); and Paul Peterson, "The Meaning of Republicanism in *The Federalist,*" *Publius* 9 (1979), 43–75.

58. *The Federalist* 9:3.

59. *Ibid.,* 73:8; 63:7.

60. James Harrington, *The Commonwealth of Oceana,* ed. J. G. A. Pocock (Cambridge, Eng., 1992), 10, 19–20.

61. Reid, "Essays," in Hamilton, ed., *Works,* II, 533–36 (reason v. passion), 537–41 (understanding and will), 589–92 (conscience).

62. *The Federalist* 84:4; 78:10–12; 78:19; 78:7.

63. *Ibid.,* 70:1; 70:7.

64. *Ibid.,* 56:1; 48:5.

65. Fiering, *Moral Philosophy,* 147.

66. *The Federalist* 71:2; 62:9; 27:2.

67. *Ibid.,* 15:14; 3:14, 16.

68. *Ibid.,* 71:2 and 63:7 ("deliberate sense"); 48:8 ("elective despotism").

69. *Ibid.,* 63:7.

70. *Ibid.,* 62:6; 73:9.

71. [John Trenchard and Thomas Gordon] *Cato's Letters* (London, 1724), II, 235.

72. *Ibid.,* 10:2; 10:7.

73. *The Federalist* 10:6–7. Hume, whom Madison-Publius was following here, made it clearer that factions could derive from "principle," that is, reason, as well as from "interest" and "affection." See Douglass Adair, "That Politics May Be

Reduced to a Science: David Hume, James Madison, and the Tenth Federalist," *Huntington Library Quarterly* 20 (1957), 343–60.

74. *The Federalist* 15:12.

75. *Ibid.,* 10:7; 10:6.

76. See Stephen Holmes, *Passions and Constraint: On the Theory of Liberal Democracy* (Chicago, 1995), 48–53; Epstein, *Political Theory of the Federalist,* 68–72.

77. *The Federalist* 71:2; see also 49:10, 50:6.

78. *Ibid.,* 1:5; 85:15. Madison may well have intended the figure of the demagogue to correspond to his rival Patrick Henry, who was opposing the Constitution.

79. E.g., *ibid.,* 3:15, 42:11.

80. *Ibid.,* 10:1, 10:8.

81. *Ibid.,* 10:21; 10:20.

82. Thomas Jefferson, "Second Inaugural Address" (March 4, 1805), in *Writings of Thomas Jefferson,* ed. Paul Leicester Ford (New York, 1892–99), VIII, 344.

83. *The Federalist* 10:20; 26:10.

84. *Ibid.,* 51:5; 10:20; 51:10.

85. Thanks to Adair and Wills, Publius's indebtedness to David Hume is well recognized. However, the principle of countervailing passions was widely accepted among eighteenth-century moral philosophers, and its application to factions was not peculiar to Hume; Adam Ferguson, for example, endorsed it in *An Essay on the History of Civil Society* (Edinburgh, 1767). See also Arthur O. Lovejoy, *Reflections on Human Nature* (Baltimore, 1961), 37–66.

86. *The Federalist* 10:11.

87. *Ibid.,* 39:4; 10:16.

88. *Ibid.,* 10:17; 27:2; 3:8.

89. See Yarbrough, "Representation and Republicanism," 77–98.

90. *The Federalist* 64:4; 68:8.

91. *Ibid.,* 53:9; 58:14.

92. For example, *ibid.,* 10:6.

93. For example, Ralph Ketcham, "Party and Leadership in Madison's Conception of the Presidency," *Quarterly Journal of the Library of Congress* 37 (1980), 258. Martin Diamond addressed this question in a series of articles; see esp. "Ethics and Politics: The American Way," in Robert H. Horwitz, ed., *The Moral Foundations of the American Republic* (Charlottesville, Va., 1977), 39–72.

94. Colleen Shehan, "The Politics of Public Opinion: James Madison's 'Notes on Government'," *William and Mary Quarterly* 49 (Oct. 1992), 609–29; quotation from p. 627.

95. *Politics,* bk. I, chap. 2.

96. For an extended comparison between the American Founders and the political philosophers of antiquity, see Paul A. Rahe, *Republics Ancient and Modern: Classical Republicanism and the American Revolution* (Chapel Hill, N.C., 1992). Also

useful are Carl J. Richard, *The Founders and the Classics: Greece, Rome, and the American Enlightenment* (Cambridge, Mass., 1994); and M. N. S. Sellers, *American Republicanism: Roman Ideology in the United States Constitution* (London, 1994).

97. Besides Pocock, *Machiavellian Moment,* see also Yarbrough, "Republicanism Reconsidered," esp. 70–75; Anne Cohler, *Montesquieu's Comparative Politics and the Spirit of American Constitutionalism* (Manhattan, Kan., 1988); and Herbert J. Storing, "Introduction," in *The Complete Anti-Federalist* (Chicago, 1981), I, 15–23, 46–47, 73.

98. Wills treats Publius as an ethical sentimentalist but presents scarcely any evidence to justify this (*Explaining America,* 185–92). Presumably his treatment rests on the same basis as his argument that Thomas Jefferson was an ethical sentimentalist, presented in *Inventing America: Jefferson's Declaration of Independence* (Garden City, N.Y., 1978), which has been convincingly refuted (see above, chap. 2, note 1).

99. *The Federalist* 2:10; 17:4.

100. *Ibid.,* 27:4; 49:6.

101. For a careful consideration of the differences between Publius and both the classical and neoclassical conceptions of civic virtue, see also Thomas L. Pangle, *The Spirit of Modern Republicanism: The Moral Vision of the American Founders* (Chicago, 1988).

102. *The Federalist* 85:4; 85:14.

103. *Ibid.,* 10:9; 72:4. See also Lovejoy, *Reflections on Human Nature,* 153–193, and Gerald Stourzh, *Alexander Hamilton and the Idea of Republican Government* (Stanford, 1970), 95–106.

104. Bernard Mandeville, *The Fable of the Bees; or, Private Vices, Public Benefits,* ed. Douglas Garman (London, 1934), 230; Nathan Rosenberg, "Mandeville and Laissez-Faire," *Journal of the History of Ideas* 24 (1963), 183–96; A. L. Macfie, *The Individual in Society: Papers on Adam Smith* (London, 1967), 53–54, 75–81; Joseph Cropsey, "Adam Smith and Political Philosophy," in Andrew W. Skinner and Thomas Wilson, eds., *Essays on Adam Smith* (Oxford, 1975), 132–53.

105. James Madison to George Washington, April 16, 1787, in *The Writings of James Madison,* ed. Gaillard Hunt (New York, 1900), II, 346; *The Federalist* 43:19. The concept of government as umpire was conventional in Lockean and Scottish thought; see James Conniff, "The Enlightenment and American Political Thought," *Political Theory* 8 (1980), 401.

106. *The Federalist* 63:7; 85:5; 77:11.

4. The Emerging Ideal of Self-Improvement

1. *The Journals and Miscellaneous Notebooks of Ralph Waldo Emerson,* ed. William H. Gilman et al. (Cambridge, Mass., 1960–82); III, 70; entry written betweeen January 31 and February 2, 1827. See also Louis P. Masur, " 'Age of the First Person Singular': The Vocabulary of the Self in New England, 1780–1850," *Journal of American Studies* 25:2 (1991), 189–211.

2. "Life Without Principle" [delivered as a lecture in 1854], in Henry David Thoreau, *Reform Papers,* ed. Wendell Glick (Princeton, 1973), 174.

3. For two recent reassessments of antebellum individualism, see Wilfred M. McClay, *The Masterless: Self and Society in Modern America* (Chapel Hill, N.C., 1994), 40–73; and Robert H. Wiebe, *Self-Rule: A Cultural History of American Democracy* (Chicago, 1995), 13–111.

4. See Barry Shain, *The Myth of American Individualism: The Protestant Origins of American Political Thought* (Princeton, 1994); John O. Lyons, *The Invention of the Self: The Hinge of Consciousness in the 18th Century* (Carbondale, Ill., 1978).

5. Still valuable on these and related themes are the essays collected in C. Vann Woodward, ed., *The Comparative Approach to American History* (New York, 1968).

6. See, e.g., the autobiographical accounts discussed in Robert M. Calhoon, *Evangelicals and Conservatives in the Early South, 1740–1861* (Columbia, S.C., 1988), chap. 5. See also Donald Yacovone, "The Transformation of the Black Temperance Movement," *Journal of the Early Republic* 8 (Fall 1988), 281–98; C. Eric Lincoln and Lawrence H. Mamiya, *The Black Church in the African American Experience* (Durham, N.C., 1990), pp. 50–55, 92, 116, 240–44; Nancy A. Hardesty, *Your Daughters Shall Prophesy: Revivalism and Feminism in the Age of Finney* (Brooklyn, 1991); Nancy A. Hewitt, *Women's Activism and Social Change: Rochester, New York, 1822–1872* (Ithaca, N.Y., 1984).

7. Alexis de Tocqueville, *Democracy in America,* ed. Phillips Bradley (New York, 1945; first pub. in French in 1835); I, 191–98, 301–18; II, 20–32, 106–20; more recently, Stuart Blumin, *The Emergence of the Middle Class: Social Experience in the American City, 1760–1900* (Cambridge, Eng., 1989).

8. Richard T. Hughes and C. Leonard Allen, *Illusions of Innocence: Protestant Primitivism in America, 1630–1875* (Chicago, 1988); cf. Theodore Dwight Bozeman, *To Live Ancient Lives: The Primitivist Dimension in Puritantism* (Chapel Hill, N.C., 1988).

9. Christopher Clark, *The Roots of Rural Capitalism: Western Massachusetts, 1780–1860* (Ithaca, 1990).

10. As I have argued elsewhere, I believe that a misleading picture of these cultural conflicts is painted in Charles Sellers, *The Market Revolution: Jacksonian America, 1815–1846* (New York, 1991). Sellers portrays market participation as an imposition forced upon an unwilling population, disregarding the benefits of the personal autonomy it brought.

11. See Richard D. Brown, *Modernization: The Transformation of American Life, 1600–1865* (New York, 1976); Richard R. John, *Spreading the News: The American Postal System from Franklin to Morse* (Cambridge, Mass., 1995).

12. The literature on the culture of consumerism is substantial and growing; two wide-ranging accounts that include the antebellum period are James Lincoln Collier, *The Rise of Selfishness in America* (New York, 1991); and Richard D. Bushman, *The Refinement of America: Persons, Houses, Cities* (New York, 1992).

13. See R. Laurence Moore, *Selling God: American Religion in the Marketplace of*

Culture (New York, 1994); and Frank Lambert, *"Pedlar in Divinity": George Whitefield and the Transatlantic Revivals* (Princeton, 1994).

14. See Marvin S. Hill, *Quest for Refuge: The Mormon Flight from American Pluralism* (Salt Lake City, 1989).

15. Paul Boyer, *Urban Masses and Moral Order in America, 1820–1920* (Cambridge, Mass., 1978), p. 61.

16. Martin J. Wiener, "Market Culture, Passion, and Victorian Punishment," in *The Culture of the Market,* ed. Thomas Haskell and Richard Teichgraeber (Cambridge, Eng., 1993), 136–60.

17. On the ethnoreligious interpretation of antebellum politics, see Daniel Feller, "Politics and Society: Toward a Jacksonian Synthesis," *Journal of the Early Republic* 10 (Summer 1990), 135–62; and Robert P. Swierenga, "Ethnoreligious Political Behavior in the Mid-Nineteenth Century," in *Religion and American Politics,* ed. Mark Noll (New York, 1990).

18. See Linda Kerber, *Women of the Republic* (Chapel Hill, 1980); Kathryn Kish Sklar, "The Founding of Mount Holyoke College," in *Women of America: A History,* ed. Carol Berkin and Mary Beth Norton (Boston, 1979), 177–201.

19. Paul Langford, *A Polite and Commercial People: England, 1727–1783* (Oxford, 1992), chap. 3; see also Neil McKendrick, John Brewer, and J. H. Plumb, *The Birth of a Consumer Society: The Commercialization of Eighteenth Century England* (London, 1982).

20. Bushman, *The Refinement of America.*

21. See John F. Kasson, *Rudeness and Civility: Manners in Nineteenth-century Urban America* (New York, 1990).

22. See Mary Reed Bobbitt, *A Bibliography of Etiquette Books Published in America Before 1900* (New York, 1947).

23. Karen Halttunen, *Confidence Men and Painted Women: A Study of Middle-Class Culture in America, 1830–1870* (New Haven, 1982).

24. The visitors' reports are surveyed in Wiebe, *Self-Rule,* 41–60.

25. See, e.g., William R. Sutton, "Benevolent Calvinism and the Moral Government of God: The Influence of Nathaniel W. Taylor on Revivalism in the Second Great Awakening," *Religion in American Culture* 2 (Winter 1992), 23–47; George M. Marsden, *The Evangelical Mind and the New School Presbyterian Experience: A Case Study of Thought and Theology in Nineteenth-Century America* (New Haven, 1970); Glenn Hewitt, *Regeneration and Morality: A Study of Charles Finney, Charles Hodge, John W. Nevin, and Horace Bushnell* (Brooklyn, 1991).

26. On the colonial period, see Charles Hambrick-Stowe, *The Practice of Piety: Puritan Devotional Disciplines in Seventeenth-Century New England* (Chapel Hill, N.C., 1982); and Charles Lloyd Cohen, *God's Caress: The Psychology of Puritan Religious Experience* (New York, 1986). On the antebellum period, see Richard Rabinowitz, *The Spiritual Self in Everyday Life: The Transformation of Personal Religious Experience in Nineteenth-Century New England* (Boston, 1989).

27. The social control/displaced elite theory of the nature of reform was first formulated in Frank T. Carlton, "Humanitarianism, Past and Present," *International Journal of Ethics* 17 (July 1907), 48–55; see also Lois Banner, "Religious

Benevolence as Social Control: A Critique of an Interpretation," *Journal of American History* 60 (1973), 34–41; and Martin J. Wiener, ed., "Humanitarianism or Control? A Symposium," *Rice University Studies* 67 (1981), 1–84.

28. The tiny bands of supporters of free love and anarchy carried this logic to drastic extremes, rejecting the institutions of marriage and government as coercing behavior that should come from inner discipline.

29. Sophisticated analyses of the quest for identity among evangelical reformers include Robert Abzug, *Cosmos Crumbling: American Reform and the Religious Imagination* (New York, 1994); Lawrence J. Friedman, *Gregarious Saints: Self and Community in American Abolitionism, 1830–1870* (Cambridge, Eng., 1982); Lewis Perry, *Radical Abolitionism: Anarchy and the Government of God in Antislavery Thought* (Ithaca, 1973); and Martin Duberman, ed., *The Antislavery Vanguard* (Princeton, 1965).

30. See Whitney R. Cross, *The Burned-Over District: The Social and Intellectual History of Enthusiastic Religion in Western New York, 1800–1850* (Ithaca, 1950); Timothy Smith, *Revivalism and Social Reform in Mid-Nineteenth Century America* (New York, 1957); William G. McLoughlin, *Revivals, Awakenings, and Reform* (Chicago, 1978); Paul E. Johnson, *A Shopkeeper's Millennium: Society and Revivals in Rochester, New York, 1815–1837* (New York, 1978); Nathan O. Hatch, *The Democratization of American Christianity* (New Haven, 1989).

31. Randolph A. Roth, *The Democratic Dilemma: Religion, Reform, and the Social Order in the Connecticut River Valley of Vermont, 1791–1850* (Cambridge, Eng., 1987); quotation from p. 6.

32. David G. Hackett, *The Rude Hand of Innovation: Religion and Social Order in Albany, New York, 1652–1836* (New York, 1991).

33. See Edward A. Bloom and Lillian D. Bloom, *Joseph Addison's Sociable Animal in the Marketplace, on the Hustings, in the Pulpit* (Providence, R.I., 1971). Still of interest is Hoxie N. Fairchild, *Religious Trends in English Poetry* (New York, 1948), I, 535–76. Brief but suggestive is J. G. A. Pocock, "Virtue, Rights, and Manners," in his *Virtue, Commerce, and History* (Cambridge, Eng., 1985), 35–50.

34. On the eighteenth century, see Harry S. Stout, "Religion, Communication, and the Ideological Origins of the American Revolution," *William and Mary Quarterly* 34 (Oct. 1977), 519–41; on the nineteenth, see Hatch, *Democratization of American Christianity*, pp. 3–11 and 146–61.

35. On the Southern synthesis of evangelical Christianity with politeness, see Brooks Holifield, *The Gentlemen Theologians: American Theology in Southern Culture, 1795–1860* (Durham, N.C., 1978), esp. pp. 36–49.

36. See, e.g., Dickson D. Bruce, *Violence and Culture in the Antebellum South* (Austin, 1979).

37. Aspects of this process are treated in Jane Tompkins, *Sensational Designs: The Cultural Work of American Fiction, 1790–1860* (New York, 1985).

38. Kathryn Kish Sklar, *Catharine Beecher: A Study in American Domesticity* (New Haven, 1973); quotations from p. 83. On the Beecher family, see Marie Caskey [Morgan], *Chariot of Fire: Religion and the Beecher Family* (New Haven, 1972).

39. [Catharine Beecher,] *Elements of Mental and Moral Philosophy* (Hartford, 1831), 412. Italics in original.

40. See Catharine Beecher, *The Moral Instructor for Schools and Families: Containing Lessons on the Duties of Life, Arranged for Study and Recitation* (Cincinnati, 1838); Sklar, *Catharine Beecher*, 125–29.

41. Catharine Beecher, *The Duty of American Women to Their Country* (New York, 1845).

42. *Ibid.*

43. Sklar, *Catharine Beecher*, 135–37.

44. See Walter Houghton, *The Victorian Frame of Mind, 1830–1870* (New Haven, 1957), esp. pp. 233–34.

45. On the difference between the nineteenth-century concept of "character" and the twentieth-century concept of "personality," see Warren I. Susman, " 'Personality' and the Making of 20th-Century Culture," in *New Directions in American Intellectual History*, ed. John Higham and Paul Conkin (Baltimore, 1979), 212–26.

46. Stefan Collini, *Public Moralists: Political Thought and Intellectual Life in Britain, 1850–1930* (Oxford, 1991), 95.

47. The information in this paragraph comes from the OED, VII, s.v. "improve" and "improvement"; the quotation is of James Fordyce, Scottish divine.

48. Isaac Watts, *Divine Songs for Children* (1715), reprinted in his *Poems* (Chiswick, 1822), I, 125.

49. Lewis Carroll, *The Annotated Alice: Alice's Adventures in Wonderland and Through the Looking Glass,* ed. Martin Gardner (New York, 1960), 38.

50. Samuel Smiles, *Self-Help: With Illustrations of Conduct and Perseverance*, with an intro. by Asa Briggs (London, 1958; first pub. 1859 and revised, 1866).

51. John Cawelti, *Apostles of the Self-Made Man* (Chicago, 1965), esp. 52–55 and 95.

52. Joseph Kett, *The Pursuit of Knowledge Under Difficulties: From Self-Improvement to Adult Education in America, 1750–1990* (Stanford, 1994). See also Paul Faler, "Cultural Aspects of the Industrial Revolution," *Labor History* 15 (Summer 1974), 367–94; Thomas Laqueur, *Religion and Respectability: Sunday Schools and Working-Class Culture, 1780–1850* (New Haven, 1976).

53. See Gertrude Himmelfarb, *Victorian Values and Twentieth-Century Condescension* (London, 1987), 13–15.

54. Collini, *Public Moralists*, 93.

55. Richard D. Brown, *Knowledge Is Power: The Diffusion of Information in Early America, 1700–1865* (New York, 1989), 218–44.

56. Samuel Hoar, "Speech to the Middlesex County Association for the Improvement of Common Schools," *Common School Journal*, I, no. 4 (February 15, 1839), 57.

57. For a statement of mainstream northern opinion, see "Education of Women," *American Review* 4 (October 1846), 416–26.

58. On the rationale for education in antebellum America, see Carl F. Kaestle, *Pillars of the Republic: Common Schools and American Society, 1780–1860* (New York, 1983); and Frederick J. Antczak, *Thought and Character: The Rhetoric of Democratic Education* (Ames, Iowa, 1985).

59. Such institutions are richly described in Kett, *Pursuit of Knowledge Under Difficulties.*

60. Education is treated in a broad cultural context, involving many kinds of institutions, in Lawrence Cremin, *American Education: The National Experience, 1783–1876* (New York, 1980).

61. John L. Hart, *In the School-Room* (Philadelphia, 1868), 274.

62. Horace Mann, "Baccalaureate Address Delivered at Antioch College, 1859," in *The Life and Writings of Horace Mann*, ed. Mary Peabody Mann (Boston, 1891), V, 516, 518.

63. See Mark A. Noll, *Princeton and the Republic: 1768–1822* (Princeton, 1989); Ned C. Landsman, "Witherspoon and the Problem of Provincial Identity in Scottish Evangelical Culture," in Richard B. Sher and Jeffrey R. Smitten, eds., *Scotland and America in the Age of the Enlightenment* (Edinburgh, 1990), 29–45; and Donald R. Come, "The Influence of Princeton on Higher Education in the South Before 1825," *William and Mary Quarterly*, 3d ser., 2 (1945), 359–96.

64. See George Schmidt, *The Old Time College President* (New York, 1930); Wilson Smith, *Professors and Public Ethics: Studies of Northern Moral Philosophers Before the Civil War* (Ithaca, 1956); Donald Harvey Meyer, *The Instructed Conscience: The Shaping of the American National Ethic* (Philadelphia, 1972); Daniel Walker Howe, *The Unitarian Conscience: Harvard Moral Philosophy, 1805–1861*, rev. ed. (Middletown, Ct., 1988).

65. E.g., see Hughes and Allen, *Illusions of Innocence: Protestant Primitivism*, 153–58.

66. See, for example, John Witherspoon, *Lectures on Moral Philosophy* [1800], annotated and edited by Jack Scott (Newark, 1982); Levi Frisbie, *Miscellaneous Writings* (Boston, 1823); Francis Wayland, *Elements of Moral Science* [1832], ed. Joseph Blau (Cambridge, Mass., 1973); Archibald Alexander, *Outlines of Moral Science* (New York, 1852); Mark Hopkins, *Lectures on Moral Science, Delivered Before the Lowell Institute* (Boston, 1862).

67. See, for example, Laurens P. Hickok, *A System of Moral Science* (Schenectady, N.Y., 1853); Eliphalet Nott, *Counsels to Young Men on the Formation of Character and the Principles Which Lead to Success and Happiness in Life* (New York, 1841).

68. Yale Faculty, "Original Papers in Relation to a Course of Liberal Education," *American Journal of Science and Art* 15 (1829), 299–320. Among countless other endorsements of mental discipline, see also Lyman Beecher, *A Plea for Colleges* (Cincinnati, 1836), 29, 43; Lewis Cass, *Address Delivered Before the Alumni of Hamilton College* (Utica, N.Y., 1830), 30–39; Daniel Webster, "Remarks on Education," *Writings and Speeches* (Boston, 1903), XIII, 106–07.

69. See Conrad Wright, *The Beginnings of Unitarianism in America* (Boston,

1955); David Robinson, *The Unitarians and the Universalists* (Westport, Ct., 1985).

70. Literary scholars who have dealt with the liberal/Unitarian religious tradition include Perry Miller, Alan Heimert, Ann Douglas, Andrew Delbanco, and David Robinson. See especially Lawrence Buell, *New England Literary Culture from Revolution through Renaissance* (Cambridge, Eng., 1986).

71. See Jack Mendelsohn, *Channing: The Reluctant Radical* (Boston, 1971); and Madeline Hooke Rice, *Federal Street Pastor* (New York, 1961).

72. Some of the uncompleted manuscript is printed in William Ellery Channing, *Dr. Channing's Notebook: Passages from Unpublished Manuscripts*, ed. Grace Ellery Channing (Boston, 1887).

73. See Conrad Edick Wright, *The Transformation of Charity in Postrevolutionary New England* (Boston, 1992).

74. "Self-Culture" (1838), *The Complete Works of William Ellery Channing, D.D., with an Introduction* (London, [1873]), 10–30; quotations from pp. 10–12.

75. *Ibid.,* 11–13.

76. See Tamara Thornton, *Cultivating Gentlemen: The Meaning of Country Life Among the Boston Elite, 1785–1860* (New Haven, 1989). The title of the book is, of course, a pun.

77. For his ethical rationalism, see William Ellery Channing, *The Perfect Life*, ed. William Henry Channing (Boston, 1873), 943; and Howe, *The Unitarian Conscience,* 50–54.

78. "Self-Culture," 13.

79. *Ibid.,* 13–14.

80. William Ellery Channing, "Spiritual Freedom: A Discourse Preached at the Annual Election, May 26, 1830," *Complete Works,* 143–55; quotation from p. 153.

81. "Self-Culture," *Complete Works,* 15.

82. *Ibid.,* 16.

83. *Ibid.,* 26.

84. *Ibid.,* 21, 29; see chapter 1 above.

85. Kett, *Pursuit of Knowledge Under Difficulties,* 81–87.

5. Self-Made Men: Abraham Lincoln and Frederick Douglass

1. William Craigie and James Hurlburt, *A Dictionary of American English on Historical Principles* (Chicago, 1938–44), IV, 2065; Henry Clay, "The American System" (1832), *Works,* ed. Calvin Colton (New York, 1904), VII, 464.

2. Charles C. B. Seymour, *Self-Made Men* (New York, 1858).

3. Harriet Beecher Stowe, *The Lives and Deeds of Our Self-Made Men . . .* (Hartford, Ct., 1872). Stowe explained that her "self-made" men were chosen because of their characters as exemplified in public life, regardless of whether or not they were self-educated (pp. vii and 601).

4. For one perspective on how "self-made" came to mean "capitalist," see Gary J. Kornblith, "Self-Made Men: The Development of Middling-Class Consciousness in New England," *Massachusetts Review* 26 (Summer-Autumn 1985), 461–74. Also see Irvin G. Wyllie, *The Self-Made Man in America: The Myth of Rags to Riches* (New Brunswick, N.J., 1954); Isadore Barmash, *The Self-Made Man: Success and Stress—American Style* (New York, 1969); and Moses Rischin, ed., *The American Gospel of Success: Individualism and Beyond* (Chicago, 1965).

5. For example, an antebellum speaker could describe master mechanics as "self-made men, the architects of their own fortunes" (James L. Homer, *An Address Delivered Before the Massachusetts Charitable Mechanics Association* (Boston, 1836), 24.

6. Richard Weiss, *The American Myth of Success: From Horatio Alger to Norman Vincent Peale* (New York, 1969), esp. pp. 48–63. See also Richard M. Huber, *The American Idea of Success* (New York, 1971).

7. Ralph Waldo Emerson, *Representative Men: Seven Lectures* (Boston, 1850).

8. Quoted in William H. Herndon and Jesse Weik, *Abraham Lincoln* (Chicago, 1889, reprinted 1921), 2.

9. See Merrill D. Peterson, *Lincoln in American Memory* (New York, 1994).

10. William E. Barton, *The Lineage of Lincoln* (Indianapolis, 1929), established that Lincoln's parents were legally married.

11. Abraham Lincoln to John D. Johnston, Jan. 12, 1851, *The Collected Works of Abraham Lincoln,* ed. Roy P. Basler, 9 vols. (New Brunswick, N.J., 1953–55), II, 96f.

12. David Herbert Donald, *Lincoln* (New York, 1995), 33. Some historians conclude that relations between Abraham and Thomas Lincoln were positively hostile; see Michael Burlingame, *The Inner World of Abraham Lincoln* (Urbana, Ill., 1994), esp. pp. 37–42.

13. Abraham Lincoln to Jesse Fell, Dec. 20, 1859, *Collected Works,* III, 511.

14. Jean H. Baker, *"Not Much of Me": Abraham Lincoln as a Typical American* (Fort Wayne, Ind., 1988), 7.

15. Eleanor Gridley, *The Story of Abraham Lincoln* (n.p. 1902), 84; quoting interview with John J. Hall (1891).

16. See Jean H. Baker, *Mary Todd Lincoln: A Biography* (New York, 1987); and James Hurt, "All the Living and the Dead: Lincoln's Imagery," *American Literature* 52 (November 1980), 351–80.

17. Joyce Appleby, "New Cultural Heroes in the Early National Period," in *The Culture of the Market,* ed. Thomas Haskell and Richard Teichgraeber (Cambridge, Eng., 1993), 163–88; quotations from pp. 187 and 176.

18. Gabor S. Boritt, "The Right to Rise," in *The Public and the Private Lincoln,* ed. Cullom Davis et al. (Carbondale, Ill., 1979), 57–70.

19. Harry Watson, *Liberty and Power: The Politics of Jacksonian America* (New York, 1990), 186.

20. See Lewis Perry, *Boats Against the Current: American Culture Between Revolution and Modernity, 1820–1860* (New York, 1993), 25–38.

21. Louise Stevenson, *Scholarly Means to Evangelical Ends: The New Haven Scholars and the Transformation of Higher Learning in America* (Baltimore, 1986), 5–6.

22. The double meaning of "internal improvements" was often invoked by contemporaries; see *Common School Journal* 2 (July 1, 1840), 208, quoting the *Iowa Sun.*

23. Lawrence Frederick Kohl, *The Politics of Individualism: Parties and the American Character in the Jacksonian Era* (New York, 1989).

24. J. David Greenstone, *The Lincoln Persuasion: Remaking American Liberalism* (Princeton, 1993), 50–62. Greenstone's distinction between two kinds of liberalism is related to the distinction between "negative" and "positive" liberty made by Sir Isaiah Berlin, "Two Concepts of Liberty," in his *Four Essays on Liberty* (New York, 1969), 118–72.

25. Thomas B. Stevenson to Henry Clay, August 10, 1848; quoted in Peter B. Knupfer, *The Union as It Is: Constitutional Unionism and Sectional Compromise, 1787–1861* (Chapel Hill, N.C., 1991), 156.

26. John William Ward, *Andrew Jackson, Symbol for an Age* (New York, 1955).

27. See above, chapter 4, n. 2.

28. Abraham Lincoln to Edward Piper, November 8, 1861, *Collected Works,* V, 18.

29. Abraham Lincoln, "Address Before the Young Men's Lyceum" (1838), *Collected Works,* I, 108–15; quotation on p. 109. There is a psychoanalytic interpretation of this speech in George B. Forgie, *Patricide in the House Divided: A Psychological Interpretation of Lincoln and His Age* (New York, 1979), chap. 2. A more comprehensive examination is provided by Major L. Wilson, "Lincoln and Van Buren in the Steps of the Fathers: Another Look at the Lyceum Address," *Civil War History* 29 (Sept. 1983), 197–211.

30. "Address Before the Young Men's Lyceum," *Collected Works,* I, 115, 113; italics in original.

31. See Ian R. Tyrrell, *Sobering Up: From Temperance to Prohibition in Antebellum America, 1800–1860* (Westport, Ct., 1979); on the problem of intemperance, see W. J. Rorabaugh, *The Alcoholic Republic: An American Tradition* (New York, 1979).

32. Abraham Lincoln, "Temperance Address" (1842), *Collected Works,* I, 271–79; quotations on 276 and 279.

33. Abraham Lincoln, "First Debate with Stephen A. Douglas at Ottawa, Illinois" (1858), *Collected Works,* III, 29.

34. Lincoln's decision to give the eulogy may have been influenced by feelings of guilt toward his hero: he had supported Zachary Taylor in preference to Clay for the Whig presidential nomination in 1848.

35. Mark E. Neely, Jr., "American Nationalism in the Image of Henry Clay:

Abraham Lincoln's Eulogy on Henry Clay in Context," *Register of the Kentucky Historical Society* 73 (1975), 31–60.

36. Abraham Lincoln, "Eulogy on Henry Clay" (1852), *Collected Works,* II, 121–32; quotation from p. 126.

37. See Knupfer, *The Union as It Is,* chap. 4.

38. Lincoln, "Eulogy on Clay," *Collected Works,* II, 126.

39. Abraham Lincoln, "Address Before the Wisconsin State Agricultural Society, Milwaukee, Wisconsin" (1859), *Collected Works,* III, 471–82.

40. *Ibid.,* 471–2, 476.

41. Both expressions ("free labor" and "mudsill") are Lincoln's (p. 480). On the ideology of free labor, see Eric Foner, *Free Soil, Free Labor, Free Men* (New York, 1970). On the mud-sill theory, see Drew Faust, *James Henry Hammond and the Old South* (Baton Rouge: Louisiana State University Press, 1982).

42. "Address Before the Wisconsin Agricultural Society," *Complete Works,* III, 478–79.

43. Thomas Jefferson, *Notes on the State of Virginia,* Query XIX.

44. Lincoln, *Complete Works,* III, 480, 481.

45. *Ibid.,* 482.

46. See Garry Wills, *Lincoln at Gettysburg: The Words That Remade America* (New York, 1992). The text of the speech and the problems in establishing it are presented on pp. 191–204 and 261–63.

47. Abraham Lincoln, "Speech at Peoria, Illinois" (1854), *Collected Works,* II, 276.

48. Wills emphasizes that the Emancipation Proclamation is not specifically mentioned, but (as he also observes), it does not need to be (*Lincoln at Gettysburg,* 120, 145).

49. "If every drop of blood drawn with the lash, shall be paid by another drawn with the sword, as was said three thousaand years ago, so still it must be said, 'the judgments of the Lord, are true and righteous altogether.' " "Second Inaugural Address," *Collected Works,* VIII, 333. (Lincoln is quoting Psalm 19:19.)

50. See William Clebsch and Sydney Ahlstrom, "Christian Interpretations of the Civil War," *Church History* 30 (June 1961), 1–19; Elton Trueblood, *Abraham Lincoln: Theologian of American Anguish* (New York, 1973), chap. 6; Glen E. Thurow, *Abraham Lincoln and American Political Religion* (Albany, N.Y., 1976).

51. *Narrative of the Life of Frederick Douglass, an American Slave, Written by Himself* (1845); *My Bondage and My Freedom* (1855); *Life and Times of Frederick Douglass* (1881 and 1893). The three have at last been published together: Frederick Douglass, *Autobiographies,* with notes by Henry Louis Gates, Jr. (New York, 1994). The quotation from the *Narrative* appears in *Autobiographies,* p. 60. Generally, I cite the *Life and Times* in accordance with the principle that an author's final revision constitutes his preferred text.

52. William L. Andrews, "*My Bondage and My Freedom* and the American

Literary Renaissance of the 1850s" in *Critical Essays on Frederick Douglass,* ed. William L. Andrews (Boston, 1991), 146.

53. *Autobiographies,* 913.

54. *Ibid.,* 663.

55. For a recent example, see William S. McFeely, *Frederick Douglass* (New York, 1991), 216. For all his merits as a biographer, McFeely never fully believes in the authenticity of the man Frederick Douglass became; he only believes in Frederick Bailey (the name Douglass bore as a slave).

56. Douglass to James Redpath, July 29, 1871, in Joseph A. Borome, ed., "Some Additional Light on Frederick Douglass," *Journal of Negro History* 38 (April 1953), 217.

57. For this context, see Wilbur Howell, *Eighteenth-Century British Logic and Rhetoric* (Princeton, 1971); and Hugh Blair, *Lectures on Rhetoric and Oratory* (1783), ed. Harold Harding (Carbondale, Ill., 1965).

58. Caleb Bingham, *The Columbian Orator: Containing a Variety of Original and Selected Pieces, Together with Rules; Calculated to Improve Youth and Others in the Ornamental and Useful Art of Eloquence* (Boston, 1832; first published 1797). Most relevant of all the "pieces" to Douglass was the "Dialogue between a Master and Slave" (pp. 240–42).

59. *Autobiographies,* 835. Douglass makes reference to *Hamlet,* act III, scene ii.

60. *Ibid.,* 536.

61. *Ibid.,* 591.

62. McFeely, *Frederick Douglass,* pp. 47f.

63. *Autobiographies,* 96.

64. *Ibid.,* 364, 660.

65. See further Ann Kibbey and Michele Stepto, "The Antilanguage of Slavery: Frederick Douglass's 1845 *Narrative,*" in Andrews, *Critical Essays on Frederick Douglass,* 166–91.

66. For literary treatments of this subject, see Kenneth W. Warren, "Frederick Douglass's *Life and Times:* Progressive Rhetoric and the Problem of Constituency," in Eric J. Sundquist, ed., *Frederick Douglass: New Literary and Historical Essays* (Cambridge, Eng., 1990), 253–70; and Thad Ziolkowski, "Antitheses: The Dialectic of Violence and Literacy in Frederick Douglass's *Narrative* of 1845," in Andrews, *Critical Essays,* 148–65.

67. *Autobiographies,* 937. According to Douglass in his *Life and Times,* these words were part of the speech he gave in Elmira, N.Y., on August 1, 1880; but the authoritative edition of his *Papers* uses a very different text without these words, and dates the speech August 3. John Blassingame et al., eds., *The Frederick Douglass Papers: Series One: Speeches, Debates, and Interviews* (New Haven, 1979–92), IV, 562–81.

68. *Autobiographies,* 994.

69. "An Address Delivered in Belfast, Ireland, on 5 December 1845," *Papers: Series One,* I, 93.

70. *Autobiographies,* 572; "Barbarism Against Civilization" (1871), *The Life and Writings of Frederick Douglass,* ed. Philip S. Foner (New York, 1955), IV, 243.

71. *Autobiographies,* 493.

72. "A Few Words to Our Own People," *North Star* (January 19, 1849), reprinted in *Life and Writings,* I, 347.

73. Blassingame et al., *Papers: Series One,* I, 56, n. 3.

74. "Intemperance and Slavery: An Address Delivered in Cork, Ireland, on 20 October 1845," *Papers: Series One,* I, 58.

75. "An Address Delivered in Glasgow, Scotland, on 15 January 1846," *Papers: Series One,* I, 136. Like many nineteenth-century reports of speeches, this one was printed in the third person, which I have changed to the first.

76. See, e.g., Frederick Cooper, "Elevating the Race," *American Quarterly* 24 (December 1972), 604–25.

77. The review of Armistead appeared in the *North Star* (April 7, 1849); that of Brown in *Douglass's Monthly* (January 1863); they are reprinted in *Life and Writings,* I, 379–84; and III, 312–13.

78. Waldo E. Martin, Jr., *The Mind of Frederick Douglass* (Chapel Hill, N.C., 1984), 256–65. Philip Foner did not include the speech (though it was Douglass's most popular) in the four-volume *Life and Writings;* William S. McFeely mentions it only in passing (*Frederick Douglass,* pp. 197, 298, 363).

79. The first version for which we have a text was delivered in Halifax, Yorkshire, in 1860, *Papers, Series One,* III, 289–300; the last known was delivered to an Indian Industrial School in Carlyle, Pennsylvania, in 1893, *ibid.* V, 545–75. The latter shows the benefit of many revisions, and it is the one I quote.

80. "Self-Made Men: An Address Delivered in Carlisle, Pennsylvania, in March 1893," *Papers: Series One,* V, 546–47.

81. *Ibid.,* 550.

82. *Ibid.,* 552–56.

83. "Did John Brown Fail? An Address Delivered in Harper's Ferry, West Virginia, on 30 May 1881," *Papers: Series One,* V, 7–35.

84. E.g., "The Constitution and Slavery," *North Star* (March 16, 1849), reprinted in *Life and Writings,* I, 361–67.

85. Greenstone had intended to include a chapter on Douglass as an example of "reform liberalism" in his book, but died before writing it. See *The Lincoln Persuasion,* p. xxiii.

86. "Self-Made Men," *Papers: Series One,* V, 561.

87. *Ibid.,* 574.

88. "The Douglass Institute: An Address Delivered in Baltimore, Maryland, on 29 September 1865," *Papers: Series One,* IV, 88.

89. "The Nation's Problem: An Address Delivered in Washington, D.C. on 16 April 1889," *Papers: Series One,* V, 411.

90. On the "protean" nature of Douglass's writing, which has been invoked by such divergent writers as Booker T. Washington and Philip S. Foner, see Peter

Walker, *Moral Choices: Memory, Desire and Imagination in Nineteenth-Century American Abolitionism* (Baton Rouge, La., 1978), 212–13. Two of the most judicious biographies are Benjamin Quarles, *Frederick Douglass,* preface by James M. McPherson (New York, 1968; first published 1948); and Nathan Irvin Huggins, *Slave and Citizen: The Life of Frederick Douglass* (Boston, 1980).

91. "Self-Made Men," *Papers: Series One,* V, 557.

6. *Shaping the Selves of Others*

1. William Ellery Channing, "The Perfect Life," in *Works, to Which Is Added The Perfect Life* (Boston, 1890), 1005.

2. On Mann's foreign influence, see Mathieu Jules Gaufres, *Horace Mann: son oeuvre, ses écrits* (Paris, 1888 and subsequent eds.); Donald K. Jones, "Horace Mann, the American Common School and English Provincial Radicals in the Nineteenth Century," *History of Education* 15 (1986), 235–46; Bruce Curtis, *Building the Educational State: Canada West, 1836–1871* (London, Ont., 1988).

3. See Jonathan Messerli, *Horace Mann: A Biography* (New York, 1972), 22–23, 68, 159–62, 176–80, 228–30; Barbara Finkelstein, "Perfecting Childhood: Horace Mann and the Origins of Public Education in the United States," *Biography* 13 (1990), 6–19. Harriet Beecher Stowe satirized Nathaneal Emmons in her novel *Oldtown Folks.*

4. Horace Mann, "Introduction to the Third Volume," *Common School Journal* 3 (January 1, 1841), 1–16. Quotation from George B. Emerson, "Moral Education," *Common School Journal* 4 (September 15, 1842), 284. See also Messerli, *Horace Mann,* 350–52, 361–62.

5. Horace Mann, "Second Annual Report of the Board of Education" (1838), *Life and Works of Horace Mann,* ed. Mary Peabody Mann (Boston, 1891), II, 494.

6. Horace Mann, "Prospectus of the *Common School Journal*" (1839) and "Special Training a Prerequisite to Teaching" (1838), *Life and Works,* II, 20 and 112–16.

7. See Horace Mann, "Sixth Annual Report" (1842), *Life and Works,* III, 129–229; Horace Mann, *A Few Thoughts for a Young Man* (Boston, 1850), 15–27; "The Importance of Physical Education," *Common School Journal* 3 (April 1, 1841), 108–110.

8. See "Human Powers," *Common School Journal* 2 (July 15, 1840), 212–15; "The Motives to Be Addressed in the Instruction of Children," *ibid.,* 2 (Jan. 15, 1840), 17–19; "The Supremacy of the Moral Sentiments," *ibid.,* 3 (Jan. 1, 1841), 9–15.

9. See Peter J. Wosh, "Sound Minds and Unsound Bodies: Massachusetts Schools and Mandatory Physical Training," *New England Quarterly* 55 (March 1982), 39–60.

10. Horace Mann, "Introduction to Volume VII," *Common School Journal* 7 (Jan. 1, 1845), 28; "Ninth Annual Report" (1845), *Life and Works,* IV, 36.

11. Horace Mann, "Prospectus of the *Common School Journal*" (1839); "Eighth Annual Report" (1848), *Life and Works,* II, 1–32; III, 463–66.

12. Horace Mann, "The Necessity of Education in a Republican Government" (1838), *Life and Works,* II, 143–88; quotation from 177.

13. Horace Mann, "Oration Delivered Before the Authorites of the City of Boston, July 4, 1842," *Life and Works,* IV, 341–403; quotations from pp. 345–46 and 403. The peroration made such an impression that James Henry, Jr., the Superintendent of common schools for Herkimer County, New York, copied it as the conclusion for his own *Address upon Education in the Common Schools* (Albany, 1843).

14. Horace Mann, "Introduction" to *Common School Journal* 9 (Jan. 1847), 6.

15. Horace Mann, "Seventh Annual Report" (1843), *Life and Works,* III, 230–418; "Ninth Annual Report" (1845), *ibid.,* 36; "What God Does and What He Leaves for Man to Do, in the Work of Education" (1840), *ibid.,* II, 191, 195.

16. *The Educational Writings of John Locke,* ed. James L. Axtell (Cambridge, Eng., 1968), quotation on p. 114. See also Lorraine Smith Pangle and Thomas L. Pangle, *The Learning of Liberty: The Educational Ideas of the American Founders* (Lawrence, Kan., 1993).

17. See John Locke, *The Reasonableness of Christianity, with a Discourse of Miracles and Part of a Third Letter Concerning Toleration,* ed. I. T. Ramsey (Stanford, 1958).

18. Michael Katz, *The Irony of Early School Reform: Educational Innovation in Mid-Nineteenth-Century Massachusetts* (Cambridge, Mass., 1968); Horace Mann, "Fifth Annual Report" (1841), *Life and Works,* III, 96; "Twelfth Annual Report" (1848), *ibid.,* IV, 251; David Hogan, "Modes of Discipline: Affective Individualism and Pedagogical Reform in New England, 1820–1850," *American Journal of Education* 99 (1990), 1–56, esp. 6–7. There is a Marxist interpretation similar to Katz's in Samuel Bowles and Herbert Gintis, *Schooling in Capitalist America: Educational Reform and the Contradictions of Economic Life* (New York, 1976), 164–79.

19. Horace Mann, "Ninth Annual Report" (1845), *Life and Works,* IV, 37; "The Condition of the Children of Laborers on Public Works," (1840), *ibid.,* V, 193–96.

20. Messerli, *Horace Mann,* 326–31; Carl F. Kaestle and Maris A. Vinovskis, *Education and Social Change in Nineteenth-Century Massachusetts* (Cambridge, Mass., 1980), 221–28.

21. See Horace Mann, "Twelfth Annual Report" (1848), *Life and Works,* IV, 292.

22. Raymond B. Culver, *Horace Mann and Religion in the Massachusetts Public Schools* (New Haven, 1929). For an account by an evangelical Protestant sympathetic to Mann's critics, see Charles Leslie Glenn, Jr., *The Myth of the Common School* (Amherst, 1988), 115–45. A good contemporary collection of primary documents on both sides is *The Common School Controversy* (Boston, 1844).

23. Horace Mann, "Seventh Annual Report" (1843), *Life and Works,* III,

310–19 (on reading); "Eighth Report" (1844), *ibid.*, III, 445–66 (on music); "On School Punishments" (1840), *ibid.*, II, 333–68; "The Substitute for Premiums and the Rod," *Common School Journal* 6 (1844), 283–87.

24. Association of Masters of the Boston Public Schools, *Remarks on the Seventh Annual Report of the Hon. Horace Mann* . . . (Boston, 1844); Horace Mann, *Reply to the "Remarks" of Thirty-One Boston Schoolmasters* . . . (Boston, 1844); Association of Masters of the Boston Public Schools, *Rejoinder to the "Reply" of the Hon. Horace Mann* . . . (Boston, 1845); Horace Mann, *Answer to the "Rejoinder" of Twenty-Nine Schoolmasters* . . . (Boston, 1845).

25. Association of Masters, *Remarks,* 125, 48.

26. For analyses of the controversy between Mann and the Boston schoolmasters, see Katz, *Irony of Early School Reform,* 139–53; and Hogan, "Modes of Discipline"; for the outcome, which was a victory for Mann, see Messerli, *Horace Mann,* 412–21.

27. On women as teachers, see Horace Mann, "Eighth Annual Report," *Life and Works,* III, 428–33; Henry Barnard, *First Annual Report as Secretary to the Board of Commissioners of Common Schools in Connecticut* (Hartford, 1839); and Jo Anne Preston, "Domestic Ideology, School Reformers, and Female Teachers: Schoolteaching Becomes Women's Work in Nineteenth-Century New England," *New England Quarterly* 66 (December 1993), 531–51.

28. On the case of Daniel Drayton and Edward Sayres, see Messerli, *Horace Mann,* 462–68, 481–86, 494, 500–01, and 530. Mann's opening argument in U.S. v. Drayton et al. is reprinted in Horace Mann, *Slavery: Letters and Speeches* (Boston, 1851), 84–118.

29. Horace Mann, "Speech in the United States House of Representatives, June 30, 1848," in Mann, *Slavery,* 10–83; quotation from p. 33.

30. Horace Mann, "Dedication" to *Slavery,* pp. v–x.

31. *Common School Journal* 4 (July 15, 1842), 218–19; Horace Mann, "Special Preparation a Prerequisite to Teaching" (1838), *Life and Works,* II, 73–79, 98–101; "Dedicatory and Inaugural Address" (Antioch College, 1853), *ibid.,* V, 362, 389–95.

32. Horace Mann, *A Few Thoughts on the Powers and Duties of Women* (Syracuse, 1853), 66–67. In practice, Mann found it difficult to reconcile coeducation with his strict views of propriety; see John Rury and Glenn Harper, "The Trouble with Coeducation: Mann and Women at Antioch, 1853–1860," *History of Education Quarterly* 26 (Winter 1986), 481–502.

33. Horace Mann, "Eleventh Annual Report" (1847), *Life and Works,* IV, 219–20; "Twelfth Report" (1848), *ibid.,* IV, 289–90.

34. There is a review of Catharine Beecher's *Treatise on Domestic Economy* in Horace Mann's *Common School Journal* 5 (Nov. 15, 1843), 340–47.

35. Nancy Cott, "Passionlessness: An Interpretation of Victorian Sexual Ideology, 1790–1850," *Signs* 4 (Winter 1978), 219–36; quotation from p. 233.

36. Horace Mann, *Powers and Duties of Women,* 25–26.

37. See Lawrence Kramer, "Dorothea Lynd Dix and the Care of the Insane: A Psychobiographical Study," Ph.D. diss., UCLA, forthcoming.

38. There are two fine new biographies: David Gollaher, *Voice for the Mad: The Life of Dorothea Dix* (New York, 1995); and Thomas Brown, *Dorothea Dix: Portrait of a Reformer* (forthcoming). They supersede Francis Tiffany, *Life of Dorothea Lynde Dix* (Cambridge, Mass., 1891); and Helen E. Marshall, *Dorothea Dix* (Chapel Hill, N.C., 1937).

39. William Lincoln, quoted in Marshall, *Dix,* 16.

40. The letters are in the Dorothea Dix Papers, Harvard College Library; and *Letters of Elizabeth Palmer Peabody: American Renaissance Woman,* ed. Bruce Ronda (Middletown, Ct., 1984). On women's correspondence, see Carroll Smith-Rosenberg, "The Female World of Love and Ritual," *Signs* 1 (Autumn 1975), 1–29.

41. See David L. Gollaher, "Dorothea Dix and the English Origins of the American Asylum Movement," *Canadian Review of American Studies* 23 (Spring 1993), 149–75.

42. Messerli, *Horace Mann,* 367.

43. On the psychobiography of Dix, see Kramer's dissertation, cited above. Kramer relates Dix's psychological struggles to the broader social issues of her time along the lines suggested by Erik Erikson, *Young Man Luther: A Study in Psychoanalysis and Society* (New York, 1958).

44. Dorothea Lynde Dix, *Memorial to the Legislature of Massachusetts* (Boston, 1843).

45. [John Trenchard and Thomas Gordon,] *Cato's Letters* (London, 1724), IV, 215–38; Thomas Cogswell Upham, *Outlines of Imperfect and Disordered Mental Action* (New York, 1840).

46. Dorothea Dix, manuscript "Commonplace Book" (1839), quoted in Kramer. See also Eric T. Carlson and Norman Dain, "The Meaning of Moral Insanity," *Bulletin of the History of Medicine* 36 (Jan.–Feb. 1962), 130–40.

47. See Dorothea L. Dix, *Memorial on the Use of Tobacco* (Montgomery, Ala. 1850).

48. *Memorial of D. L. Dix, Praying a Grant of Land for the Relief and Support of the Indigent Curable and Incurable Insane in the United States* (Washington, D.C., 1848), 1–5; cf. Amariah Brigham, M.D., *Observations on the Influence of Religion Upon the Health and Physical Welfare of Mankind* (Boston, 1835), 275. Dix was probably influenced in her opinion by the census of 1840, which presented flawed statistics on mental illness among African-Americans, slave and free.

49. *Memorial of D. L. Dix,* 3–4; cf. Alexis de Tocqueville, *Democracy in America,* ed. Phillips Bradley (New York, 1945; first published 1835), II, 142.

50. *Report of the Board of Managers of the Eastern Lunatic Asylum, at Lexington, for the Years 1856–7* (Frankfort, Ky., 1858), 8.

51. See Eric T. Carlson and Norman Dain, "The Psychotherapy That Was Moral Treatment," *American Journal of Psychiatry* 117 (Dec. 1960), 519–24;

Andrew T. Scull, "Moral Treatment Reconsidered," *Psychological Medicine* 9 (1979), 421–28.

52. Vieda Skultans, *English Madness: Ideas on Insanity, 1580–1890* (London, 1979), 52–62; Evelyn A. Woods and Eric T. Carlson, "The Psychiatry of Philippe Pinel," *Bulletin of the History of Medicine* 35 (Jan.–Feb. 1961), 14–25; Kathleen M. Grange, "Pinel and Eighteenth-Century Psychiatry," *ibid.*, 35 (Sept.–Oct. 1961), 442–53.

53. Psychiatrists in that period were called alienists because they treated mental alienation, that is, derangement of the faculties. *OED*, s.v. "alienist" and "alienation."

54. See, e.g., Dorothea L. Dix, *Memorial Soliciting a State Hospital for the Insane, Submitted to the Legislature of New Jersey* (Trenton, 1845), 29–32.

55. Michel Foucault, *Madness and Civilization: A History of Insanity in the Age of Reason* (New York, 1965; first published in French in 1961), 254–55; Charles L. Cherry, *A Quiet Haven: Quakers, Moral Treatment, and Asylum Reform* (Rutherford, N.J., 1989); William F. Bynum, "Rationales for Therapy in British Psychiatry, 1780–1835," *Medical History* 18 (September 1964), 317–34.

56. On the "domestication of madness," see Andrew Scull, *Social Order/Mental Disorder: Anglo-American Psychiatry in Historical Perspective* (Berkeley, 1989), 54–79, and Nancy Tomes, *A Generous Confidence: Thomas Story Kirkbride and the Art of Asylum-Keeping, 1840–1883* (Cambridge, Eng., 1984).

57. Dorothea L. Dix, *Memorial Soliciting a State Hospital for the Protection and Cure of the Insane, Submitted to the General Assembly of North Carolina* (Raleigh, 1848), 43.

58. Vieda Skultans, *Madness and Morals: Ideas on Insanity in the Nineteenth Century* (London, 1975), 17.

59. David J. Rothman, *The Discovery of the Asylum: Social Order and Disorder in the New Republic*, revised ed. (Boston, 1971, 1990); Mary Ann Jimenez, *Changing Faces of Madness: Early American Attitudes and Treatment of the Insane* (Hanover, N.H., 1987); Gollaher, "Dorothea Dix and English Origins." See also Gerald N. Grob, *Mental Institutions in America: Social Policy to 1875* (New York, 1973); and Scull, *Social Order/Mental Disorder*, 31–53.

60. Ralph Waldo Emerson, *Journals and Miscellaneous Notebooks*, ed. W. H. Gilman and J. E. Parsons (Cambridge, Mass., 1960–75), VIII, 87.

61. D. L. Dix, *A Review of the Present Condition of the State Penitentiary of Kentucky, with Brief Notices and Remarks upon the Jails and Poor-Houses in Some of the Most Populous Counties, Written by Request. Printed by Order of the Legislature* (Frankfort, Ky., 1846), 36.

62. A dozen of her memorials have been reprinted in Dorothea L. Dix, *On Behalf of the Insane Poor: Selected Reports* (New York, 1971).

63. *Memorial of D. L. Dix*, cited above, n. 48.

64. Thomas Brown's forthcoming biography is particularly thorough in reconstructing the years of political maneuvering in Congress that lay behind the eventual passage of Dix's bill in 1854.

65. Dorothea Dix, *Remarks on Prison and Prison Discipline* (Boston, 1845), 72.

66. Franklin Pierce, Veto Message, May 3, 1854, *Messages and Papers of the Presidents*, ed. James D. Richardson, IV, 2782; Dorothea Dix to Millard Fillmore, May 20, 1854, *The Lady and the President: The Letters of Dorothea Dix & Millard Fillmore*, ed. Charles M. Snyder (Lexington, Ky., 1975), 196.

67. D. L. Dix, Circular no. 8 (July 14, 1862), *Records of the Surgeon General's Office, Record Group 112.*

68. "Testimony of Miss D. L. Dix, Taken at Baltimore, Maryland, June 1st, 1864," *Narrative of Privations and Sufferings of United States Officers and Soldiers While Prisoners of War in the Hands of the Rebel Authorities* (Philadelphia, 1864), 184–86.

69. David J. Rothman, "Dorothea Lynde Dix," *Encylopedia of American Biography*, ed. John Garraty (New York, 1974), 283.

70. For assessments of the nineteenth-century asylums and their shortcomings, see Scull, *Social Order/Mental Disorder*, 213–38; and Gerald Grob, *The Mad Among Us: A History of the Care of America's Mentally Ill* (Cambridge, Mass., 1994), 79–102.

71. Barbara Cross, *Horace Bushnell, Minister to a Changing America* (Chicago, 1958), is mainly concerned with social context. For Bushnell's life itself, see Robert L. Edwards, *Of Singular Genius, Of Singular Grace: A Biography of Horace Bushnell* (Cleveland, Ohio, 1992); for an overview of his thought, Howard A. Barnes, *Horace Bushnell and the Virtuous Republic* (Methuchen, N.J., 1991). Theological scholarship on Bushnell is extensive and specialized; a good example is James O. Duke, *Horace Bushnell on the Vitality of Biblical Language* (Chico, Calif., 1984).

72. Bushnell supported Mann's program for public education, including the teaching of nonsectarian Protestantism in the public schools; see Horace Bushnell, "Christianity and Common Schools," *Common School Journal* 2 (Feb. 15, 1840), 57–60.

73. Horace Bushnell, *Christ and His Salvation* (New York, 1865), 25; idem., *Views of Christian Nurture*, ed. Philip B. Eppard (Delmar, N.Y., 1975; first published 1847), 68.

74. Horace Bushnell, *Christian Nurture*, intro. Luther Weigle (New Haven, 1947; first published 1861), 4. This version of *Christian Nurture* is a revision of the 1847 one cited in the previous note; it is less polemical and contains more advice to parents on practical matters of child-rearing.

75. *Common School Journal* 2 (Nov. 2, 1840), 329–31.

76. Horace Bushnell, "Regeneration," *Sermons for the New Life* (New York, 1858), 106–26.

77. *Ibid.*, 211.

78. Samuel Taylor Coleridge, *Aids to Reflection in the Formation of a Manly Character, on the Several Grounds of Prudence, Morality, and Religion*, with a preliminary essay by James Marsh (Burlington, Vt., 1829).

79. Horace Bushnell, *God in Christ: Three Discourses Delivered at New Haven, Cambridge, and Andover, with a Preliminary Dissertation on Language* (Hartford, Ct., 1849).

80. *Christian Nurture* (1861), 212.

81. Horace Bushnell, "Unconscious Influence," in *Sermons for the New Life* (New York, 1869), 186–205.

82. The many books treating aspects of this subject include Peter Gregg Slater, *Children in the New England Mind: In Death and in Life* (Hamden, Ct., 1977); Daniel Calhoun, *The Intelligence of a People* (Princeton, 1973); Bernard Wishy, *The Child and the Republic: The Dawn of Modern American Child Nurture* (Philadelphia, 1968); Anne L. Kuhn, *The Mother's Role in Childhood Education* (New Haven, 1947); and Monica Keefer, *American Children Through Their Books, 1700–1835* (Philadelphia, 1948).

83. *Christian Nurture* (1861), 76.

84. *Ibid.*, 17. Bushnell's child-rearing methods resembled in a general way those that Philip Greven, Jr., has classified as "moderate" in *The Protestant Temperament: Patterns of Child-Rearing, Religious Experience, and the Self in Early America* (New York, 1977).

85. *Christian Nurture* (1861), 272.

86. *Ibid.*, 40–44, 91–97, 102–35, 141.

87. See Horace Bushnell, *The Crisis of the Church* (Hartford, 1835); idem., *The Fathers of New England* (New York, 1850); idem., *Popular Government by Divine Right* (Hartford, 1864).

88. Quotation from *Views of Christian Nurture* (1847), 171; see also Horace Bushnell, "The True Wealth or Weal of Nations" (1837), in *Work and Play* (New York, 1864), 62; idem., "Growth, Not Conquest, the True Method of Christian Progress" (1844), in *Views of Christian Nurture* (1847), 147–81.

89. "Of Want and Waste," in Horace Bushnell, *The Moral Uses of Dark Things* (New York, 1868), 43; idem., *Our Obligations to the Dead* (New Haven, 1866).

90. Horace Bushnell, *Prosperity Our Duty* (Hartford, 1847), 6; idem., "The True Wealth or Weal of Nations," 52–53.

91. Horace Bushnell, *Barbarism the First Danger* (New York, 1847). See also idem., *A Discourse on the Moral Tendencies and Results of Human History* (New Haven, 1843).

92. Jean Matthews, *Rufus Choate: The Law and Civic Virtue* (Philadelphia, 1980).

93. Richard Bushman, *The Refinement of America: Persons, Houses, Cities* (New York, 1992), 348.

94. [Horace Bushnell,] "Taste and Fashion," *The New Englander*, 1 (April 1843), 153–68.

95. Horace Bushnell, *Women's Suffrage: The Reform Against Nature* (New York, 1869).

96. Christopher Lasch, *Haven in a Heartless World: The Family Besieged* (New York, 1977); see also William E. Bridges, "Family Patterns and Social Values in America, 1824–1875," *American Quarterly* 17 (Spring 1965), 3–11.

97. See Horace Bushnell, "American Politics," *American National Preacher* 14

(December 1840), 189–204; idem., *Politics under the Law of God* (Hartford, 1844).

98. Horace Bushnell, "Life, or the Lives" (n.d.) in *Work and Play* , 297–98; cf. "The True Wealth or Weal of Nations," 47; *Popular Government by Divine Right.*

99. See Horace Bushnell, *Reverses Needed: A Discourse Delivered on the Sunday after the Disaster at Bull Run* (Hartford, 1861). See also Howard A. Barnes, "The Idea That Caused a War: Horace Bushnell versus Thomas Jefferson," *Journal of Church and State* 16 (Winter 1974), 73–83.

100. Horace Bushnell, *The Northern Iron* (Hartford, 1854); Mary Bushnell Cheney, *The Life and Letters of Horace Bushnell* (New York, 1880), 482. Bushnell's views on slavery and race have been the subject of debate among historians: see Charles C. Cole, Jr. "Horace Bushnell and the Slavery Question," *New England Quarterly* 23 (March 1950), 19–30; and the convincing refutation of it by Ralph E. Luker, "Bushnell in Black and White: Evidences of the 'Racism' of Horace Bushnell," *ibid.* 45 (September 1972), 408–16.

101. Henry Home, Lord Kames, *Essays on the Principles of Morality and Natural Religion* (Edinburgh, 1751), 139–46, 151–218.

102. "American Politics," 198. On the ideal character Bushnell wished to create, see Bushnell, *Reverses Needed,* 19.

103. Cf. Elizabeth B. Clark, "The Sacred Rights of the Weak: Pain, Sympathy, and the Culture of Individual Rights in Antebellum America," *Journal of American History* 82 (September 1995), 463–93.

104. See Bruce Kuklick, *Churchmen and Philosophers from Jonathan Edwards to John Dewey* (New Haven, 1985); Steven C. Rockefeller, *John Dewey: Religious Faith and Democratic Humanism.* (New York, 1991).

105. Recent scholarship attaches importance to Jefferson's self-image as a rational Christian; see Garrett Ward Sheldon, *The Political Philosophy of Thomas Jefferson* (Baltimore, 1991), 103–11; Paul Conkin, "The Religous Pilgrimage of Thomas Jefferson," *Jeffersonian Legacies,* ed. Peter S. Onuf (Charlottesville, Va., 1993), 19–49.

106. See Arthur C. McGiffert, "Protestant Liberalism," in *Liberal Theology: An Appraisal,* ed. David E. Roberts and Henry Pitney Van Dusen (New York, 1942), 106–20.

7. The Platonic Quest in New England

1. F. O. Matthiessen, *American Renaissance: Art and Expression in the Age of Emerson and Whitman* (New York, 1941), 1.

2. "The American Scholar: An Oration Delivered Before the Phi Beta Kappa Society at Cambridge" (1837), *Complete Works of Ralph Waldo Emerson* (Boston, 1904), I, 79–116.

3. Timothy Smith, *Revivalism and Social Reform in Mid-Nineteenth-Century America* (New York, 1957), 95–102; Daniel Walker Howe, *The Unitarian Conscience: Harvard Moral Philosophy, 1805–1861,* rev. ed. (Middletown, Ct., 1988),

151–73; Anne C. Rose, *Transcendentalism as a Social Movement, 1830–1850* (New Haven, 1981), 28–37.

4. See Lawrence Buell, *Literary Transcendentalism* (Ithaca, 1973), 1–139; William R. Hutchison, *The Transcendentalist Ministers: Church Reform in the New England Renaissance* (New Haven, 1959).

5. For background, William Ralph Inge, *The Platonic Tradition in English Religious Thought* (New York, 1926), and John H. Muirhead, *The Platonic Tradition in Anglo-Saxon Philosophy* (New York, 1931), are still helpful.

6. Henry Wilder Foote, *The Wisdom from Above. Sermon Occasioned by the Death of James Walker* (Boston, 1875), 13. Although the Cambridge Platonists were originally called Latitudinarians, their school should be distinguished from the Lockean Latitudinarianism of Archbishop Tillotson.

7. There are many books on the Cambridge Platonists; among the most useful are Rosalie Colie, *Light and Enlightenment: A Study of the Cambridge Platonists and the Dutch Arminians* (Cambridge, Eng., 1957); James D. Roberts, *From Puritanism to Platonism in Seventeenth Century England* (The Hague, 1968); Gerald R. Cragg, *From Puritanism to the Age of Reason* (Cambridge, Eng., 1950, reprinted 1966); and Frederick J. Powicke, *The Cambridge Platonists* (Cambridge, Mass., 1926).

8. On the relationship of the Cambridge Platonists to Locke, see Jerome Huyler, *Locke in America: The Moral Philosophy of the Founding Era* (Lawrence, Kan., 1995), 63–78, 93–95, as well as John Gascoigne, *Cambridge in the Age of the Enlightenment* (Cambridge, Eng., 1989).

9. Benjamin Whichcote, *Aphorism* no. 121, quoted in Cragg, *From Puritanism to the Age of Reason,* 42.

10. See Daniel Walker Howe, "Classical Education and Political Culture in Nineteenth-Century America," *Intellectual History Newsletter* 5 (1983), 9–14.

11. See David Tyack, *George Ticknor and the Boston Brahmins* (Cambridge, Mass., 1967); and Hugh Hawkins, *Between Harvard and America: The Educational Leadership of Charles W. Eliot* (New York, 1972).

12. For example, see Andrew Preston Peabody, "A Liberal Education," *The New Englander and Yale Review* 9 (1886), 193–207. For a statement on the relationship between classical studies and the new elective system, see Peabody, *The Elective System in Colleges. A Paper Read Before the National Education Association* (Worcester, 1874). Ralph Cudworth set forth his views on the education of the faculties in his defense of rational religion before the House of Commons, March 31, 1647, reprinted in Gerald R. Cragg, ed., *The Cambridge Platonists* (New York, 1968), 369–406.

13. The best general introductions to Plotinus are William Ralph Inge, *The Philosophy of Plotinus,* 2 vols. (New York, 1918), and Emile Brehier, *The Philosophy of Plotinus* (Chicago, 1958). Inge translates *Nous* as Spirit; Brehier as Intelligence.

14. For distinctions among different kinds of Unitarianism, see Conrad Wright, *Three Prophets of Religious Liberalism: Channing, Emerson, Parker* (Boston, 1961).

15. Thomas Reid, founder of the branch of the Scottish school followed by the

Unitarians, explains his purposes in the introduction to his *Inquiry into the Human Mind* (1764), reprinted in his *Works,* ed. Sir William Hamilton (Edinburgh, 1863), I, 97–104.

16. Reid, *Works,* I, 438; cf. Cragg, *Cambridge Platonists,* 295 (Cudworth), 300 (More), 330–31 (Smith), 410 (Whichcote). As indicated in Chapter 2 above, Hume was the exception to the Scottish philosophers' endorsement of faculty psychology.

17. See Howe, *The Unitarian Conscience,* 27–44.

18. William Ellery Channing, *The Perfect Life: In Twelve Discourses,* ed. William Henry Channing (Boston, 1901; first published 1872), 981.

19. Cragg, *Cambridge Platonists,* 189 (More); 245–49 (Cudworth); 334 (Smith). In my opinion, Bruce Kuklick errs in characterizing the Cambridge Platonists as "anti-dualistic" (*Churchmen and Philosophers From Jonathan Edwards to John Dewey* [New Haven, 1985], 18); they believed in a dualism of mind and matter parallel to a dualism of activity and passivity. Contrary to the Cartesian dualists, however, they believed that mind and matter can readily interact.

20. See Eugene Austin, *The Ethics of the Cambridge Platonists* (Philadelphia, 1935), 12–13; J. A. Passmore, *Ralph Cudworth* (Cambridge, Eng.,1951), 9–12, 19–28; John De Boer, *The Theory of Knowledge of the Cambridge Platonists* (Madras, India, 1931), esp. 140–41, 148–49.

21. See Genevieve Lloyd, *The Man of Reason: "Male" and "Female" in Western Philosophy,* 2d ed. (Minneapolis, 1993). The relationship between ideas about the supremacy of reason over passion and ideas about the supremacy of men over women will be explored in the next chapter.

22. Abraham Lincoln, "Temperance Address" (1842), *Collected Works of Abraham Lincoln,* ed. Roy Basler (New Brunswick, N.J., 1953), I, 279.

23. James Walker, "Man's Competency to Know God" (1858), *Reason, Faith, and Duty: Sermons Preached Chiefly in the College Chapel* (Boston, 1877), 18–36.

24. *Ibid.,* 36.

25. Henry W. Bellows, *Restatements of Christian Doctrine: In Twenty-Five Sermons* (New York, 1860), 93–94.

26. E.g., Cragg, ed., *Cambridge Platonists,* 102–117 (Smith); 263–68 (More).

27. C.P. [Cazneau Palfrey?], "The Personality of God," *Monthly Religious Magazine* 38 (1867), 26–42.

28. *The Connection Between Science and Religion* (Boston, 1845), 12.

29. See Henry Ware, Jr., *On the Formation of the Christian Character: Addressed to Those Who are Seeking to Lead a Religious Life* (Boston, 1831).

30. Orville Dewey, *Works, with a Biographical Sketch* (Boston, 1893), 176; Whichcote, Sermon on Philippians 4:8, in Cragg, ed., *Cambridge Platonists,* 68.

31. Convers Francis, *Grace, as Connected with Salvation: A Sermon Preached at the Installation of Rev. Rufus A. Johnson, in Grafton* (Boston, 1833), 20–21.

32. Delivered as a sermon in 1834 and printed that year as a tract by the American Unitarian Association, it may also be found in the *Christian Examiner* 17 (1835), 1–17; and in James Walker, *Reason, Faith, and Duty,* 37–61.

33. On the connection with James, see Gerald E. Myers, *William James: His*

Life and Thought (New Haven, 1986), 461–462 and 473. The Unitarian religious philosopher Frederic Henry Hedge attributed the argument from religious experience to the Cambridge Platonist John Norris; see Hedge, *Ways of the Spirit and Other Essays* (Boston, 1878), 187.

34. William Ellery Channing, *The Perfect Life,* 931.

35. William Henry Channing, "Title and Character of This Book," *ibid.,* 928–29.

36. *Ibid.,* 929.

37. The technical name for the Christological doctrine that the classic Unitarians embraced is Arianism.

38. William Ellery Channing, "Likeness to God" (1828), *Works,* 230–39; quotations from pp. 232, 236, 230.

39. E.g., Robert L. Patterson in *The Philosophy of William Ellery Channing* (New York, 1952), 63–65.

40. See, e.g., Henry W. Bellows, *Religious Education, from Within and from Above* (Boston, 1857).

41. Channing, *The Perfect Life,* 929.

42. Abiel Abbot Livermore, *Union with God and Man* (Boston, 1848), 3, 5.

43. *Ibid.,* 4, 8, 11.

44. *Ibid.,* 12, 13–16.

45. Dewey, *Works,* 28–35; quotation from p. 29. Elsewhere, Dewey declared that "all true moral beauty is a part of religion." ("On the Identity of Religion with Goodness and with the Good Life," *Works,* 151.)

46. See Lawrence Buell, *Literary Transcendentalism: Style and Vision in the American Renaissance* (Ithaca, N.Y., 1973), 23–54.

47. John Smith, "The True Way or Method of Attaining Divine Knowledge" (1660), in Cragg, ed., *Cambridge Platonists,* 90.

48. Frederick Henry Hedge, *Ways of the Spirit,* 140.

49. "Introduction," in Sydney E. Ahlstrom and Jonathan S. Carey, eds., *An American Reformation: A Documentary History of Unitarian Christianity* (Middletown, Ct., 1985), 28. Matthiessen, *American Renaissance,* 103–07.

50. *The Journals and Miscellaneous Notebooks of Ralph Waldo Emerson,* William H. Gilman et al., eds. (Cambridge, Mass., 1960–73); quotations from V, 343 (1837) and VI, 507 (1841). For his interest in Pythagorean idealism, see III, 366–67 (1830).

51. Ralph Waldo Emerson, *Two Unpublished Essays,* ed. Edward Everett Hale (Boston, 1896), 57. Emerson owned at least two editions of Cudworth. Surviving records of his library use confirm his obvious interest in Platonism. See Kenneth Walter Cameron, *Emerson and Thoreau as Readers* (Hartford, Ct., 1972), passim.

52. Ralph Waldo Emerson, "A Letter to Plato" (unpublished), *Journals,* ed. Gilman et al., II, 250.

53. *Young Emerson Speaks: Unpublished Discourses on Many Subjects by Ralph*

Waldo Emerson, ed. Arthur Cushman McGiffert, Jr. (Boston, 1938), 99–104; quotation from p. 101.

54. A beautiful example of the self-conscious perpetuation of this tradition by a Christian Unitarian strongly influenced by Transcendentalism is William Rounseville Alger, *The Divine Life and Its Way* (Boston, 1866).

55. For Emerson's strong attraction to Plotinus, see especially Stanley Brodwin, "Emerson's Version of Plotinus: The Flight to Beauty," *Journal of the History of Ideas* 35: 465–483 (1974).

56. "Journal Y" (1845) *Journals,* IX, 265. On Emerson's use of Cudworth, including the reservations he held about him, see also Vivian C. Hopkins, "Emerson and Cudworth: Plastic Nature and Transcendental Art," *American Literature* 23 (1951), 80–98.

57. See Robert D. Richardson, *Henry Thoreau: A Life of the Mind* (Berkeley, 1986), 78.

58. See Conrad Wright, *The Beginnings of Unitarianism in America,* (Boston, 1955), 3–4, 135–138.

59. The debate was triggered by Emerson's "Divinity School Address" (1838). For two different interpretations of the issues, see Perry Miller, ed., *The Transcendentalists: An Anthology* (Cambridge, Mass., 1950), 157–246; and William R. Hutchison, *The Transcendentalist Ministers,* 52–97. Two major documents of the miracles controversy, Henry Ware, Jr.'s "The Personality of the Deity" (1839) and Andrews Norton's "The Latest Form of Infidelity" (1839), have recently been reprinted in Ahlstrom and Carey, eds., *An American Reformation,* 432–440 and 445–461.

60. Theodore Parker's "The Transient and the Permanent in Christianity" (1841) has been reprinted in Wright, *Three Prophets of Religious Liberalism,* 113–49. Quotation from p. 117.

61. Theodore Parker, "Cudworth's *Intellectual System,*" *Christian Examiner* 27 (1840), 289–319.

62. See, e.g., George Moore, "Exercises with Dr. [Henry] Ware in Natural and Revealed Religion," an undergraduate notebook for the academic year 1836–37, ms. in Harvard University Archives.

63. Parker, "Cudworth," 293–94, 297.

64. *Ibid.,* 310 and 314–16.

65. Plotinus, *Enneads,* iii.2.3.

66. "The Over-Soul," in *Essays: First Series* (1841); reprinted in *The Selected Writings of Ralph Waldo Emerson,* ed. Brooks Atkinson (New York, 1940), 262.

67. "Naught cares he for number or proportion," says the poet of the snow storm.

68. "Plato; or, The Philosopher" in *Representative Men* (1850); reprinted in *Selected Writings,* 474, 482, 483, and 479.

69. Octavius B. Frothingham, *Transcendentalism in New England,* intro. by Sydney Ahlstrom (New York, 1959; first published 1876), 110.

70. Perry Miller, "From Edwards to Emerson" (first published 1940), in *Errand into the Wilderness* (Cambridge, Mass., 1956), 184–203; quotation from p. 196.

71. Arthur O. Lovejoy, "Kant and the English Platonists," in *Essays Philosophical and Religious in Honor of William James. By His Colleagues at Columbia University* (New York, 1908), 301–02.

72. The best work on Marsh is Peter Carafiol, *Transcendent Reason: James Marsh and the Forms of Romantic Thought* (Tallahassee, Fla. 1982). The reaction of New England Transcendentalists to Coleridge was mixed, since despite their admiration for his poetry and his Neoplatonism, they found his turn toward political and theological conservatism distasteful. Particularly galling, of course, was his repudiation of earlier Unitarian views. See [Frederic Henry Hedge,] "Coleridge's Literary Character," *Christian Examiner* 14 (1833), 108–29.

73. The most concrete evidence of links between Emerson and the New Lights is supplied by Phyllis Blum Cole in "From the Edwardses to the Emersons: Four Generations of Evangelical Family Culture," which I read in manuscript. Mary Moody Emerson transmitted the family's ancestral New Light piety to her young nephew. However—as Dr. Cole shows—Mary Moody Emerson also participated in the intellectual tradition of liberal pietism: see, e.g., her writings in the *Monthly Anthology* (under the pen-name Cornelia) during 1804–05. She was, therefore, a conduit through which New England pietism in *both* its Calvinist and liberal forms reached her nephew.

74. See Chapter 1 above, and Emily Stipes Watts, "Jonathan Edwards and the Cambridge Platonists," Ph.D. diss., University of Illinois, 1963.

75. See note 59.

76. Edmund H. Sears, *The Fourth Gospel the Heart of Christ* (Boston, 1872); idem, *Foregleams and Foreshadows of Immortality,* 11th ed., revised and enlarged (Boston, 1873).

8. *Margaret Fuller's Heroic Ideal of Womanhood*

1. Margaret Fuller to the Marquis de Lafayette, undated 1824–25, *The Letters of Margaret Fuller,* ed. Robert N. Hudspeth (Ithaca, 1983), I, 150. Lafayette paid Boston two visits, and on the second one young Margaret did get to meet him; so did Dorothea Dix.

2. Margaret Fuller to William Henry Channing, Feb. 19, 1841, *Letters,* II, 202.

3. Margaret Fuller to Caroline Sturgis, May 25, 1844, *Letters,* III, 197.

4. See, e.g., Paula Blanchard, *Margaret Fuller: From Transcendentalism to Revolution* (New York, 1978), 342.

5. See Bell Gale Chevigny, "The Long Arm of Censorship: Myth-Making in Margaret Fuller's Time and Our Own," *Signs* 2 (Winter 1976), 450–60; Marie Mitchell Olesen Urbanski, *Margaret Fuller's Woman in the Nineteenth Century: A*

Literary Study (Greenwood, Ct., 1980), 3–46; and the exchange between Urbanski and David M. Robinson in *PMLA* 97 (Oct. 1982), 873–75.

6. Her friend Emerson quoted an unidentified correspondent as having told him, "Margaret was one of the few persons who looked upon life as an art, and every person not merely as an artist, but as a work of art." [Ralph Waldo Emerson, James Freeman Clarke, and William Henry Channing,] *Memoirs of Margaret Fuller Ossoli* (Boston, 1852), I, 238. Because these *Memoirs* are known to be unreliable as texts for Fuller's writings, I employ them only as a source for the opinions of others, or (cautiously) when no more authoritative source exists.

7. Quoted in Urbanski, *Margaret Fuller's Woman,* 14.

8. Much of her literary criticism was biographical in nature. See William R. Ebbit, "Margaret Fuller's Ideas on Criticism," *Boston Public Library Quarterly* 3 (July 1951), 171–87; and Richard N. Hudspeth, "'A Higher Standard in Thought and Action': Margaret Fuller and the Idea of Criticism," in *American Unitarianism, 1805–1865,* ed. Conrad Edick Wright (Boston, 1989), 145–62.

9. See Elizabeth Hardwick, "The Genius of Margaret Fuller," *New York Review of Books* (April 10, 1986), 14–22; Joan von Mehren, *Minerva and the Muse: The Life of Margaret Fuller* (Amherst, Mass., 1994). The definitive biography for the years it covers is now Charles Capper, *Margaret Fuller: An American Romantic Life.* Volume I: *The Private Years* (New York, 1992); the best account by a contemporary is Thomas Wentworth Higginson, *Margaret Fuller Ossoli* (Boston, 1885).

10. Margaret Fuller to James Nathan, May? 4? 1845, *Letters,* IV, 94.

11. See Chapter 2 above.

12. Margaret Fuller to Timothy Fuller, various dates, 1822–25, *Letters,* I, 124, 127, 139, 146, 151; Timothy Fuller to Margaret Fuller, Jan. 25, 1820, quoted in Capper, *Margaret Fuller,* I, 50.

13. See Daniel Walker Howe, *The Unitarian Conscience: Harvard Moral Philosophy, 1805–1861,* rev. ed. (Middletown, Ct., 1987), chap. 7.

14. See Linda Kerber, *Women of the Republic: Intellect and Ideology in Revolutionary America* (Chapel Hill, N.C., 1980), chaps. 7 and 9; Rosemary Zagarri, "Morals, Manners, and the Republican Mother," *American Quarterly* 44 (June 1992), 192–215.

15. See Capper, *Margaret Fuller,* I, 8–15. Timothy Fuller to (his wife) Margarett [sic] Crane Fuller, Jan. 22, 1820, discusses the education of their daughter in relation to the ideas of Mary Wollstonecraft (*ibid.* I, 30, 365 n.10).

16. Margaret Fuller, autobiographical fragment, *Memoirs,* I, 17–18, 22. There is no surviving original text of this reminiscence of Fuller's childhood, which the editors of the *Memoirs* dated 1840.

17. See Ruth Bloch, "The Gendered Meaning of Virtue in Revolutionary America," *Signs* 13 (1987), 37–58.

18. Quoted in Eve Kornfeld and Melissa Merks, "Margaret Fuller: Minerva and the Muse," *American Culture* 13 (1990), 47.

19. Capper, *Margaret Fuller,* I, 133.

20. Margaret Fuller, *Woman in the Nineteenth Century,* intro. Madeleine B. Stern (Columbia, S.C., 1980; facsimile of the 1845 ed.), 20 and 128–31.

21. [George Bancroft,] "Slavery in Rome," *North American Review* 39 (1834), 413–37; J. [Margaret Fuller], "Brutus," *Boston Daily Advertiser* (Nov. 27, 1834), 2; H., "The Character of Brutus," *Boston Daily Advertiser* (Dec. 4, 1834), 2. It has been speculated that "H." was Nathaniel Hawthorne, who was an ardent supporter of the Democratic party. Margaret Fuller recurred to Brutus as a model, this time with his wife Portia, in *Woman in the Nineteenth Century,* 40–41.

22. See Robert D. Richardson, "Margaret Fuller and Myth," *Prospects* 4 (1979), 169–84; and Jeffrey Steele, *The Representation of the Self in the American Renaissance* (Chapel Hill, 1987), 105–21.

23. Margaret Fuller to Caroline Sturgis, Jan. 27, 1839, *Letters,* II, 40.

24. *Woman in the Nineteenth Century,* 154.

25. Margaret Fuller, "Swedenborgianism" (1845), in her *Art, Literature, and the Drama,* ed. Arthur B. Fuller (Boston, 1860), 336–41; Margaret Fuller, "The Two Herberts" (1844), *ibid.,* 25–44.

26. See Sydney Ahlstrom and Jonathan S. Carey, eds., *An American Reformation: A Documentary History of Unitarian Christianity* (Middletown, Ct., 1985); Elizabeth Palmer Peabody, *Reminiscences of William Ellery Channing* (Boston, 1880); and *Dr. Channing's Notebook,* ed. Grace Ellery Channing (Boston, 1887).

27. Edward Tyrell Channing, *Lectures Read to Seniors in Harvard College* (Boston, 1856); see pp. 31–32, 274. On Transcendentalist Platonism, besides the evidence presented in the previous chapter, see Barbara Harrell Carson, "Orpheus in New England: Alcott, Emerson, and Thoreau," Ph.D. diss., Johns Hopkins University, 1968.

28. Plato's treatment of women varies greatly: contrast *Republic,* 454–456, 460b, 540, and *Laws,* 805, with *Laws,* 772d–773c, 781a–b and *Timaeus,* 42a–d; see Susan Okin, *Women in Western Political Thought* (Princeton, 1979), 15–70; Margaret Fuller, *Woman in the Nineteenth Century,* 90.

29. Extensive and convincing evidence for Fuller's metaphysical dualism is marshalled in Jayne Sayler Devens, "The Education of Margaret Fuller," undergraduate honors essay, UCLA, 1991. For criticisms of the philosophical idealism of her friends, see Margaret Fuller to Caroline Sturgis, Jan. 29, 1839, and Oct. 25, 1840, *Letters,* II, 40 and 170.

30. See, e.g., Thomas Jefferson to John Adams, July 5, 1814, in Lester Cappon, ed., *The Adams-Jefferson Letters* (Chapel Hill, N.C., 1959, reprinted 1988), 431–34.

31. Margaret Fuller, *Summer on the Lakes in 1843,* intro. Madeleine B. Stern (Nieuwkoop, 1972, a facsimile of the Boston, 1844, ed.), 103.

32. See, e.g., Margaret Fuller to William Henry Channing, Aug. 29, 1841 (criticism of Frederic Henry Hedge), *Letters,* II, 227; Margaret Fuller to Samuel Ward, Dec. 29, 1844 (respect for Horace Greeley), *Letters,* III, 256. For her

negative judgment on a life she found did not successfully integrate thought and action, see "The Life of Sir James Mackintosh," in Margaret Fuller, *Papers on Literature and Art* (New York, 1846), I, 43–57.

33. Other treatments of the thought/action issue in Fuller's life include Bell Gale Chevigny, *The Woman and the Myth: Margaret Fuller's Life and Writings* (New York, 1976); and Ann Douglas, "Margaret Fuller and the Disavowal of Fiction," in *The Feminization of American Culture* (New York, 1977), 313–48.

34. David M. Robinson, "Margaret Fuller and the Transcendental Ethos," *PMLA* 97 (Jan. 1982), 83–98; see also idem., "The Legacy of Channing: Culture as a Religious Category in New England Thought," *Harvard Theological Review* 74 (April 1981), 221–39; and Susan Margaret Belasco Smith, "The Extension of Self-Culture: Margaret Fuller and Emily Dickinson," Ph.D. diss., Texas A & M University, 1987. [Clarke,] *Memoirs,* I, 132.

35. Cf. Elizabeth B. Keeney, *The Botanizers: Amateur Scientists in Nineteenth-Century America* (Chapel Hill, N.C., 1992), 38–46, which discusses botany as a metaphor for self-culture.

36. Margaret Fuller, "A Credo," printed in Frederick Augustus Braun, *Margaret Fuller and Goethe* (New York, 1910), 247–57. William Henry Channing bowdlerized the document in *Memoirs,* II, 88–92; he may have been responsible for rendering some of the original manuscript illegible as well.

37. Margaret Fuller to ?, c. winter 1829–30, *Letters,* I, 197; Margaret Fuller to William Henry Channing, Sept. 1? 1844, *Letters,* III, 224.

38. Though her perfectionist-heroic ideal exposed her to ridicule for arrogance, Fuller could be appropriately humble about the extent to which she attained it; see, e. g., Margaret Fuller to Charles Newcomb, Feb. 24, 1840, and Margaret Fuller to William Henry Channing, April 19, 1840, *Letters,* II, 123 and 131.

39. Margaret Fuller, *Woman in the Nineteenth Century,* pp. v, 84. The etymology of the word "educate" is the Latin "to draw out."

40. Margaret Fuller to Ralph Waldo Emerson, July 3, 1837, *Letters,* I, 288; Margaret Fuller, *Summer on the Lakes,* 159.

41. One could multiply examples indefinitely, but see Margaret Fuller to Ellen Fuller, Aug. 26, 1836, Margaret Fuller to Arthur Fuller, Dec. 31, 1837, and Margaret Fuller to Richard Fuller, May 12, 1842, *Letters,* I, 258 and 319, III, 64.

42. Quoted in *Memoirs,* I, 172; Capper accepts this as reliable (*Margaret Fuller,* I, 386, n.64).

43. See, e.g., Vernon Parrington, *Main Currents in American Thought* (New York, 1927, reprinted 1957), I, 418–26; and Margaret V. Allen, "The Political and Social Criticism of Margaret Fuller," *South Atlantic Quarterly* 72 (Autumn 1973), 560–73. But the commentator most hostile to Fuller's cultivation of the self was Nathaniel Hawthorne, who considered it the ultimate in pride and sensuality. See Paul John Eakin, *The New England Girl: Cultural Ideals in Hawthorne, Stowe, Howells, and James* (Athens, Ga., 1976), 49–70.

44. For this broader sense of the political, see Paula Baker, "The Domestica-

tion of Politics: Women and American Political Society, 1780–1920," *American Historical Review* 89 (June 1984), 620–47; and Daniel Walker Howe, "The Evangelical Movement and Political Culture in the North During the Second Party System," *Journal of American History* 76 (March 1991), 1216–39.

45. This is one of the meanings of the title metaphor of her article, "The Great Lawsuit: Man *versus* Men, Woman *versus* Women," *The Dial* 4 (July 1843), 1–47.

46. A "pilgrimage toward a common shrine" was her description of the ideal marriage; it applied equally well to her ideal of friendship. Margaret Fuller, *Woman in the Nineteenth Century,* 69.

47. For a sense of the tumult and complexities of Fuller's personal relationships, based on her writings and theirs, see Chevigny, *The Woman and the Myth,* 65–139.

48. Clarke, *Memoirs,* I, 132–34.

49. James Freeman Clarke, *Self-Culture: Physical, Intellectual, Moral, and Spiritual* (Boston, 1880), 31–32, 37. Clarke based his program on a mind-matter dualism like that of Fuller, but his invocation of Christian Scripture was quite unlike the thrust of her thinking.

50. Lawrence Buell, *Literary Transcendentalism: Style and Vision in the American Renaissance* (Ithaca, N.Y., 1973), 77–92.

51. Henry Ware, Jr., "Memoir of Nathan Appleton," *Works,* II, 27–84, quotation from p. 53. For other examples of Unitarian discussion groups, see William R. Hutchison, *The Transcendentalist Ministers* (New Haven, 1959), 147–48.

52. Charles Capper, "Margaret Fuller as Cultural Reformer: The Conversations in Boston," *American Quarterly* 39 (Winter 1987), 509–28, quotation from p. 515.

53. Caroline Wells Healey [Dall], *Margaret and Her Friends; or Ten Conversations with Margaret Fuller Upon the Mythology of the Greeks and Its Expression in Art,* (Boston, 1895), quotations from pp. 26 and 78. For portions of Dall's journal that she left out of the published version, see Joel Myerson, "Caroline Dall's Reminiscences of Margaret Fuller," *Harvard Library Bulletin* 22 (Oct. 1974), 414–28. Another first-hand account of the conversations is Elizabeth Peabody's, which exists in manuscript at the American Antiquarian Society.

54. See Capper, *Margaret Fuller,* I, 291–93.

55. See Margaret Fuller to Elizabeth Hoar, Oct. 20, 1844; and Margaret Fuller to Richard Fuller, Nov. 23, 1844, *Letters,* III, 237 and 247–48.

56. Margaret Fuller to Sophia Ripley? Aug. 27, 1839, *Letters,* 87.

57. "Margaret Fuller's Summer of 1844 Journal," quoted in Capper, *Margaret Fuller,* I, 297.

58. Margaret Fuller to ? c. Feb. 1835, *Letters,* I, 218; Margaret Fuller, *Woman in the Nineteenth Century,* 98–99.

59. Margaret Fuller to Ralph Waldo Emerson, Aug. 14, 1837, *Letters,* I, 295. For more of her Whig politics, see Margaret Fuller to James Nathan, June 24, 1845, *Letters,* IV, 121.

60. Margaret Fuller to William H. Channing? July 1842, *Letters,* III, 72–74.

The 1837 Whig caucus Fuller attended had been privotal in Dorr's break with the Whig party; George M. Dennison, *The Dorr War: Republicanism on Trial* (Lexington, Ky., 1976), 20–21 and 115. For another perspective on Fuller's reaction to the Dorr Rebellion, see Bell Gale Chevigny, "To the Edges of Ideology: Margaret Fuller's Centrifugal Evolution," *American Quarterly* 38 (Summer 1986), 173–201, esp. pp. 174–79.

61. *Woman in the Nineteenth Century,* 65.

62. See Margaret Fuller to Maria Weston Chapman, Dec. 26, 1840, 197–98; and Francis E. Kearns, "Margaret Fuller and the Abolition Movement," *Journal of the History of Ideas* 25 (Jan.–March 1964), 120–27.

63. For an eloquent example, see her "Fourth of July, 1845," reprinted from the *New York Tribune* in *Essays,* 297–99. For her practical, personal antislavery, see Margaret Fuller to Ellis and Louisa Loring, Aug. 22, 1845, *Letters,* IV, 150–53.

64. Margaret Fuller to Harriet Martineau, c. Nov. 1837, *Letters,* I, 307–10; Capper, *Margaret Fuller,* I, 223–24.

65. Harriet Martineau, *Autobiography,* ed. Maria Weston Chapman (Boston, 1877), I, 380–84.

66. E.g., Margaret Fuller to William Henry Channing? c. Oct. 31, 1840, *Letters,* II, 179–80. See Carl J. Guarneri, *The Utopian Alternative: Fourierism in Nineteenth-Century America* (Ithaca, N.Y., 1991).

67. See Margaret Fuller, *Woman in the Nineteenth Century,* 110–12. Her experiences in Italy made her more respectful than ever of Fourier's "associationism"; see Margaret Fuller to Mary Rotch, May 29, 1848, *Letters,* V, 71.

68. Margaret Fuller, "The Present State of German Literature," *American Monthly Magazine* 8 (July 1836), 1–13, esp. pp. 2–4.

69. On sculpture, see Albert J. von Frank, "Life as Art in America: The Case of Margaret Fuller," *Studies in the American Renaissance* (1981), 1–25, esp. 10–13. (In my opinion, von Frank overdoes his argument for America's "frontier" cultural primitivism.) On music, see, e.g., Margaret Fuller, "Lives of the Great Composers," *The Dial* 2 (Oct. 1841), 148–203.

70. Margaret Fuller, Nov. 25, 1843, ms in Houghton Library, printed in Chevigny, *The Woman and the Myth,* 61–62. The version printed in *Memoirs* is bowdlerized.

71. Margaret Fuller, "Entertainments of the Past Winter," *The Dial* 3 (July 1842), 46–72; quotation from p. 52.

72. Margaret Fuller, [review of] *Monaldi, a Tale* [by Washington Allston], *The Dial* 2 (Jan. 1842), 395–99; "Lives of the Great Composers," quotation from p. 203.

73. Margaret Fuller to James Freeman Clarke, May 4, 1830, *Letters,* I, 166–67. Although it was not available to the editor when Fuller's *Letters* were published, the full text of this letter survives in manuscript at the Massachusetts Historical Society; see Capper, *Margaret Fuller,* I, 106–07.

74. It has been argued that Fuller gave up her ambition to be a genius when she decided to become a literary critic instead of a novelist (Barbara Welter, *Dimity Convictions: The American Woman in the Nineteenth Century* [Athens, Ohio, 1976], 171–72). The evidence, however, does not bear this out; see, e.g., notes 2 and 10 above.

75. For the ramifications of the Reason/Understanding dichotomy, see Buell, *Literary Transcendentalism,* 1–74; still useful is Alexander Kern, "The Rise of Transcendentalism," in Harry Hayden Clark, ed., *Transitions in American Literary History* (Durham, N.C., 1953), 245–315.

76. See Howe, *Unitarian Conscience,* 45–64.

77. Margaret Fuller to William H. Channing?, 1840, *Letters,* II, 108.

78. Lawrence Buell, "Unitarian Aesthetics and Emerson's Poet-Priest," *American Quarterly* 20 (1968), 3–20.

79. Quoted in Perry Miller, "Foreword" to *Margaret Fuller: American Romantic* (Ithaca, N.Y., 1963), ix.

80. Thomas Carlyle to Ralph Waldo Emerson, May 7, 1852, *Correspondence of Thomas Carlyle and Ralph Waldo Emerson* (New York, 1884), II, 242.

81. See above, chapters 4 and 6.

82. Margaret Fuller, "The Great Lawsuit," esp. pp. 4–5.

83. See Virginia Sapiro, *A Vindication of Political Virtue: The Political Theory of Mary Wollstonecraft* (Chicago, 1992), esp. pp. 52–63.

84. David Robinson is undoubtedly right on this point, though many commentators have been unwilling to credit Fuller's radical feminism to the account of Transcendentalism; see his "Margaret Fuller and the Transcendental Ethos." See also Nancy M. Theriot, "Mary Wollstonecraft and Margaret Fuller: A Theoretical Comparison," *International Journal of Women's Studies* 2 (1979) 560–74.

85. Jeffrey Steele, *Representation of the Self,* p. 105. See also Urbanski, *Margaret Fuller's Woman,* chap. 5; and William J. Scheick, "The Angelic Artistry of Margaret Fuller's *Woman in the Nineteenth Century*," *Essays in Literature,* 11 (Spring 1984), 293–98.

86. Margaret Fuller, *Woman in the Nineteenth Century,* 7, 162. The influence of Plotinus is even more evident in Margaret Fuller, "Educate Men and Women as Souls," one of the "miscellanies" her brother appended to the work after Margaret's death (Margaret Fuller, *Woman in the Nineteenth Century and Kindred Papers,* ed. Arthur Fuller [Boston, 1855], 335–37).

87. Margaret Fuller, *Woman in the Nineteenth Century,* 22–23. For a survey of the belief that men have more of reason than women, see Genevieve Lloyd, *The Man of Reason: 'Male' and 'Female' in Western Philosophy* 2d ed. (Minneapolis, 1993).

88. Margaret Fuller, *Woman in the Nineteenth Century,* 84.

89. *Ibid.,* 159, 162.

90. *Ibid.,* 102. In identifying Minerva here as the Understanding and the Muse as Reason, I accept the argument of Robinson, "The Transcendental Ethos of

Margaret Fuller," 93–94. Elsewhere Fuller seems to me to use Minerva to represent the rational moral sense of eighteenth-century faculty psychology.

91. Margaret Fuller, *Woman in the Nineteenth Century,* 50, 106, 91.

92. *Ibid.,* 27.

93. On Franklinian prudence, see *Summer on the Lakes,* 104. For Fuller's ambivalence toward the passions, see *Woman in the Nineteenth Century,* 140; Margaret Fuller to Anna Ward, Nov. 16, 1845, *Letters,* IV, 167; Margaret Fuller, "Aglauron and Laurie," in *Kindred Papers,* ed. Arthur Fuller, 183–216.

94. Kornfeld and Merks, "Minerva and the Muse"; Elizabeth Ann Bartlett, "Liberty, Equality, Sorority: Frances Wright, Margaret Fuller, and Sarah Grimke," Ph.D. diss., University of Minnesota, 1981, esp. p. 125; and two papers presented to the meeting of the Organization of American Historians in April 1989: Jean Matthews, "Consciousness of Self and Consciousness of Sex in Antebellum Feminism;" and Charles Capper, "Between Culture and Ideology: The Romantic Feminism of Margaret Fuller."

95. Margaret Fuller, "Review of *Narrative of the Life of Frederick Douglass, an American Slave," New York Tribune,* June 10, 1845, p. 2; reprinted in *Critical Essays on Frederick Douglass,* ed. William L. Andrews (Boston, 1991), 21–23.

96. Margaret Fuller, *Woman in the Nineteenth Century,* 10, 22, 158, 161–62. See also Blanche Hersh, *The Slavery of Sex: Feminist Abolitionists in Nineteenth-Century America* (Urbana, Ill., 1978).

97. *Ibid.,* vi, 103–05, 154–55.

98. E.g., Parrington, *Main Currents,* and Allen, "Political and Social Criticism."

99. I am indebted to Charles Capper for instruction on the influence of Fuller on later generations. See also Sandra M. Gustafson, "Choosing a Medium: Margaret Fuller and the Forms of Sentiment," *American Quarterly* 47 (March 1995), 34–65.

100. Margaret Fuller, *Woman in the Nineteenth Century,* 163.

9. The Constructed Self Against the State

1. See Robert D. Richardson, *Henry Thoreau: A Life of the Mind* (Berkeley: 1986), 210–13; Marie Olesen Urbanski, "Henry David Thoreau and Margaret Fuller," *Thoreau Society Journal* 8 (October 1976), 24–30.

2. Among the few treatments of the essay on civil disobedience, see especially Sherman Paul, *The Shores of America: Thoreau's Inward Exploration* (Urbana, Ill., 1958, reprinted 1972), 239–45; and Richard Drinnon, "Thoreau's Politics of the Upright Man," *Massachusetts Review* 4 (Autumn 1962), 126–38.

3. See Michael Meyer, *Several More Lives to Live: Thoreau's Political Reputation in America* (Westport, Ct., 1977); supplement it with Walter Harding, Introduction to *The Variorum Civil Disobedience* (New York, 1967); Harpinder Kaur, *Gandhi's Concept of Civil Disobedience* (New Delhi, 1986); John H. Hicks, *Thoreau*

in Our Season (Amherst, Mass., 1962); and Eugene Timpe, ed., *Thoreau Abroad: Twelve Bibliographical Essays* (Hamden, Ct., 1971).

4. United States, Bureau of the Census, *Historical Statistics of the United States* (Washington, D.C., 1975), I, 163. Other information in this paragraph comes from John C. Broderick, "Thoreau, Alcott, and the Poll Tax," *Studies in Philology* 53 (1956), 612–26.

5. E.g., Angelina Grimke in 1836: "If a law commands me to *sin I will break it;* if it calls me to *suffer,* I will let it take its course *unresistingly.*" Quoted in Robert H. Abzug, *Cosmos Crumbling: American Reform and the Religious Imagination* (New York and Oxford, 1994), 211.

6. Henry David Thoreau to Ralph Waldo Emerson, 24 Jan. 1843, *Correspondence of Henry David Thoreau,* ed. Walter Harding and Carl Bode (New York, 1958), 77–78. Charles Lane explained the protest in *The Liberator* 13 (27 January 1843) 16. For more background, see Taylor Stoehr, *Nay-Saying in Concord: Emerson, Alcott, and Thoreau* (Hamden, Ct. 1979).

7. Dialogue as given in Walter Harding, *The Days of Henry Thoreau: A Biography* (New York, 1970), 199.

8. Walter Harding and Michael Meyer, *The New Thoreau Handbook* (New York, 1980), 41.

9. See "Resistance to Civil Government," in Henry David Thoreau, *Reform Papers,* ed. Wendell Glick (Princeton, 1973), 84.

10. Wendell Phillips, *The Constitution: A Pro-Slavery Compact* (Boston, 1844); Henry David Thoreau, "Wendell Phillips Before Concord Lyceum" (1845), in *Reform Papers,* 59–62. See also Thomas D. Morris, *Free Men All: The Personal Liberty Laws of the North, 1780–1861* (Baltimore, 1974), 109–115.

11. Thoreau, "Resistance," 79.

12. *The Boston Courier,* June 15, 1846, reprinted in Gary Scharnhorst, " 'Conflict of Laws': A Lost Essay by Henry Thoreau," *New England Quarterly* 61 (1988), 569–71.

13. "Resistance," 76.

14. Scharnhorst, " 'Conflict of Laws,' " 570.

15. On Garrisonian anarchism, see Lewis Perry, *Radical Abolitionism: Anarchy and the Government of God in Antislavery Thought* (Ithaca, N.Y., 1973). Other pacifists, led by William Ladd, supported international peace but did not renounce force against criminals. There were also other kinds of anarchists; see James J. Martin, *Men Against the State: The Expositors of Individualist Anarchism in America, 1827–1908* (DeKalb, Ill., 1953).

16. Raymond Adams, "Thoreau's Sources for 'Resistance to Civil Government,' " *Studies in Philology* 42 (1945), 640–53.

17. "Resistance," 63–64.

18. *Ibid.,* 74.

19. *Ibid.*

20. E.g., in Henry Seidel Canby, *Thoreau* (Boston, 1939), 235.

21. His explanation for why he left Walden Pond. Henry David Thoreau, *Walden,* ed. J. Lyndon Shanley (Princeton, 1971), 323.

22. See John Rawls, *A Theory of Justice* (Cambridge, Mass., 1971), 363–371; and Hugo Adam Bedau, ed., *Civil Disobedience: Theory and Practice* (New York, 1969).

23. "Resistance," 68.

24. In 1859, Thoreau complained that his own government was "effectively allied with France and Austria in oppressing mankind." ("A Plea for Captain John Brown," *Reform Papers,* p. 129.)

25. "Resistance," 65.

26. Amos Bronson Alcott, "Orphic Sayings," *The Dial* 1 (July, 1840), xvii.

27. "Resistance," 64. This is in fact Locke's justification for majority rule in *Two Treatises of Government,* II, 96.

28. "Resistance," 63.

29. There is a parallel with the opening section of Thoreau's *Walden,* where he parodies classical economics.

30. Carla M. Hess, "Introduction," to David Greenstone, *The Lincoln Persuasion: Remaking American Liberalism* (Princeton, 1993), p. xxv.

31. Walter Harding, ed., *Thoreau's Library* (Charlottesville, Va., 1957).

32. Kenneth W. Cameron, ed., *Thoreau's Harvard Years* (Hartford, Ct., 1967), is a collection of documents; Daniel W. Howe, *The Unitarian Conscience: Harvard Moral Philosophy, 1805–1861,* rev. ed. (Middletown, Ct., 1987), 64–67 and 332–33, describes Paley's treatment at Harvard.

33. William Paley, *Principles of Moral and Political Philosophy,* 19th edition (London, 1811), II, 140.

34. "Resistance," 68.

35. See above, chapter 1.

36. Ethel Seybold, *Thoreau: The Quest and the Classics* (New Haven, 1951), 16, 24, 66, 75.

37. "Resistance," 86. On Thoreau's attitude, see also George Kateb, "Democratic Individuality and the Claims of Politics," *Political Theory* (August 1984), 331–60.

38. *Ibid.,* 77–78. I am rejecting the argument that Thoreau was a classical republican presented in Leonard N. Neufeldt, "Henry David Thoreau's Political Economy," *New England Quarterly* 57 (1984), 359–83.

39. See above, chapter 4.

40. On the religious nature of Transcendentalism and its cultural background in Calvinism, see Lawrence Buell, *New England Literary Culture from Revolution Through Renaissance* (Cambridge, Eng., 1986).

41. See above, chapter 4.

42. See Sydney Ahlstrom and Jonathan S. Carey, eds., *An American Reformation: A Documentary History of Unitarian Christianity* (Middletown, Ct., 1985); and David M. Robinson, "The Legacy of Channing: Culture as a Religious Category

in New England Thought," *Harvard Theological Review* 74 (April 1981), 221–39.

43. "Resistance," 66.

44. See James Duban, "Thoreau, Garrison, and Dymond: Unbending Firmness of the Mind," *American Literature* 57 (1985), 309–17.

45. "Resistance," 76.

46. *Ibid.,* 70–71, 78.

47. Richardson, Jr., *Henry Thoreau,* 316.

48. Lewis Perry, *Boats Against the Current: American Culture Between Revolution and Modernity, 1820–1860* (New York, 1993).

49. *Walden,* 51.

50. See above, chapter 5.

51. See Christopher Johnstone, "Thoreau and Civil Disobedience: A Rhetorical Paradox," *Quarterly Journal of Speech* 60 (October 1974), 313–22.

52. Henry David Thoreau, "Reform and the Reformers," in *Reform Papers,* 181–97.

53. "Resistance," 70–71; Thoreau's italics.

54. *Ibid.,* 84.

55. Ralph Waldo Emerson, "Politics," in *Collected Works* (Cambridge, Mass., 1983), III, 115–29; quotation from p. 126. See also William A. Herr, "A More Perfect State: Thoreau's Concept of Civil Government," *Massachusetts Review,* 16 (Summer 1975), 470–87.

56. "Resistance," 89–90.

57. Thoreau's lecture-essay,"Thomas Carlyle and His Works" (1847), reprinted in his *Early Essays and Miscellanies,* ed. J. J. Moldenhauer et al. (Princeton, 1975), 219–67, is his only comprehensive estimate of another writer. Later, Carlyle alienated his American antislavery admirers with his racist "Discourse on the Nigger Question" (1850) and the drift of his thinking toward authoritarianism.

58. "Resistance," 65.

59. *Ibid.,* 65.

60. *Ibid.,* 74.

61. For moral philosophy at Harvard, see Howe, *The Unitarian Conscience,* 56–64.

62. "Resistance," 72.

63. *Ibid.,* 66.

64. *Ibid.,* 86.

65. *Ibid.,* 87.

66. *Ibid.,* 73.

67. *Ibid.,* 69.

68. Edward Tyrell Channing, *Lectures Read to Seniors in Harvard College* (Boston, 1856), 160.

69. *Ibid.,* 88.

70. *Ibid.,* 76.

71. *Ibid.*, 67.

72. *Ibid.*, 71.

73. *Ibid.*, 77. In *Walden* Thoreau gives a very brief explanation for why he did not choose to resist his arrest for nonpayment of the poll tax; in the essay, he does not address the issue at all. "I might have resisted forcibly with more or less effect, might have run 'amok' against society; but I preferred that society should run 'amok' against me, it being the desperate party." *Walden,* 171.

74. *Ibid.*, 76. See Staughton Lynd, "Henry Thoreau: The Admirable Radical," *Liberation* 7 (February 1963), 21–26.

75. Thoreau, *Journal,* ed. B. Torrey and F. H. Allen (Boston, 1906), III (Sept. 1851), 37–38; Richardson, *Henry Thoreau,* 372.

76. Henry David Thoreau, "Slavery in Massachusetts," in *Reform Papers,* 91–109, quotations from pp. 102 and 108.

77. Henry David Thoreau, "A Plea for Captain John Brown," "The Martyrdom of John Brown," and "The Last Days of John Brown," in *Reform Papers,* 111–38, 139–44, and 145–54. See also James Goodwin, "Thoreau and John Brown: Transcendental Politics," *Emerson Society Quarterly,* 25 (3d quarter, 1979), 156–68.

78. Thoreau's description of Carlyle's portrait of Cromwell. "Thomas Carlyle and His Works," *Early Essays,* 260.

79. I dissent from the interpretation of Thoreau as a Nietzschean in Nancy Rosenblum, "Thoreau's Militant Conscience," *Political Theory* 9 (February 1981), 81–110; repeated in *Another Liberalism: Romanticism and the Reconstruction of Liberal Thought* (Cambridge, Mass., 1987), 103–24.

80. *Walden,* 8.

81. Thoreau praised "an obscure country town" meeting as "the true Congress." "Slavery in Massachusetts," *Reform Papers,* 99.

82. Quoted by Thoreau in "Thomas Carlyle and His Works," *Early Essays,* 254.

Conclusion

1. As we have seen, both Thomas Jefferson and Frederick Douglass deplored the way slavery warped the practice of self-construction among the master class. Vivid illustrations of this are provided in Kenneth S. Greenberg, *Honor and Slavery* (Princeton, 1996).

2. See Karen Halttunen, *Confidence Men and Painted Women: A Study of Middle-Class Culture in America, 1830–1870* (New Haven, 1982).

3. Charles Taylor, *Sources of the Self: The Making of the Modern Identity* (Cambridge, Mass., 1989), esp. pp. 211–14.

4. Jerome Huyler, *Locke in America: The Moral Philosophy of the Founding Era* (Lawrence, Kan., 1995), 148.

5. James Freeman Clarke, *Self-Culture: Physical, Intellectual, Moral, and Spiritual* (Boston, 1880).

6. *Ibid.,* 31–33.

7. *Ibid.,* 39–42.

8. *Ibid.,* 3–8.

9. *Ibid.,* 44–47.

10. *Ibid.,* 37, 43–44, 71.

11. *Ibid.,* 54. Clarke is quoting Matthew 11:19.

12. *Ibid.,* 62.

13. *Ibid.,* 104, 195, quotation from 207.

14. *Ibid.,* 203–04, 311–15.

15. *Ibid.,* 290.

16. *Ibid.,* 410.

17. *Ibid.,* 267 and 415.

18. *Ibid.,* 263–78.

19. *Ibid.,* 368–71.

20. Stephen Holmes, *Passions and Constraint: On the Theory of Liberal Democracy* (Chicago, 1995), 272.

21. For his calculations of the value of the African-Americans, see Thomas Jefferson to Jared Sparks, February 4, 1824, in *The Writings of Thomas Jefferson,* ed. Paul Leicester Ford (New York, 1892–99), X, 289–93.

22. Thomas Jefferson to John Holmes, April 22, 1820, *ibid.,* X, 157–58.

23. See, e.g., Arthur Wrobel, "Phrenology as Political Science," in *Pseudo-Science and Society in Nineteenth-Century America,* ed. Arthur Wrobel (Lexington, Ky., 1987), 122–43.

24. Warren Susman, " 'Personality' and the Making of Twentieth-Century Culture," in *New Directions in American Intellectual History,* ed. John Higham and Paul Conkin (Baltimore, 1977), 224.

25. Henry David Thoreau, *Walden,* ed. J. Lyndon Shanley (Princeton, 1971), 326.

26. Richard Teichgraeber III, " 'A Yankee Diogenes': Thoreau and the Market," in *The Culture of the Market,* ed. Thomas Haskell and Richard Teichgraeber III (Cambridge, Eng., 1993), 319.

27. See Joan Shelly Rubin, *The Making of Middlebrow Culture* (Chapel Hill, N.C., 1992), esp. pp. 1–34; and Henry F. May, *The End of American Innocence: A Study of the First Years of Our Own Time, 1912–1917* (New York, 1959).

28. On the loss of moral values, see Robert Bellah et al., *Habits of the Heart: Individualism and Commitment in American Life* (Berkeley, 1985); idem., *The Good Society* (New York, 1992); and, from a different ideological perspective, Gertrude Himmelfarb, *The De-Moralization of Society: From Victorian Virtues to Modern Values* (New York, 1995).

29. David Riesman, *The Lonely Crowd: A Study of the Changing American Character* (New Haven, 1950, revised 1961 and 1969); Wilfred M. McClay, "The

Strange Career of *The Lonely Crowd:* or the Antinomies of Autonomy," in *The Culture of the Market,* ed. Haskell and Teichgraeber, 397–440.

30. For example, the demand for voluntary adult education is stronger than ever: "each advance in educational opportunity is accompanied by a new wave of learners eager to pursue knowledge under difficulties," Joseph Kett, *The Pursuit of Knowledge Under Difficulties: From Self-Improvement to Adult Education in America, 1750–1990* (Stanford, 1994).

31. Stephen Macedo, *Liberal Virtues: Citizenship., Virtue, and Community in Liberal Constitutionalism* (Oxford, 1991), 275–77.

32. The quest cuts across political lines. See James Q. Wilson, *The Moral Sense* (New York, 1993); and Robert Wright, *The Moral Animal* (New York, 1994). Also attempting to reconstruct ideals of public morality and civility is the journal called *The Responsive Community: Rights and Responsibilities* (1990–).

Acknowledgments

This book has been a long time in the making, and during that time I have run up many debts. Both UCLA, where I taught for nineteen happy years, and Oxford University, where I have taught for five happy years so far, have generously provided sabbatical leave and research funds that I devoted to this project. I have been further helped by research fellowships from the John Simon Guggenheim Memorial Foundation and the Henry E. Huntington Library. At Cornell University the History Department was hospitable to me for a beautiful fall week in 1994, when I delivered versions of chapters 5, 8, and 9 as the Carl Becker Lectures. I am grateful to Aida Donald of Harvard University Press for (among other things) her patience.

Many kind friends have helped me along the way, especially Joyce Appleby, Ruth Bloch, and Steven Novak, all of whom read an earlier version of the entire manuscript and gave me the benefit of their criticisms; this version is much the better for them, though no doubt it has its shortcomings too, for which I alone am responsible. Among the other generous scholars who have helped in various ways are Terence Ball, Rachelle Friedman, David Hall, Lawrence Kramer, Marc Kruman, Katherine Lloyd, the late Angus Macintyre, Gary Nash, Mark Noll, Barbara Oberg, John Pocock, Jack Pole, Donald Ratcliffe, Robert Richardson, John Rowett, Harry Stout, William Thomas, Conrad E. Wright, and C. Conrad Wright. To all go my thanks.

Sandra, my wife of thirty-three years who makes it all possible, has had to wait much too long to have a book dedicated to her.

The overall thesis of this book is new and has not been previously published. However, while working on the subject I have from time to time published some of my thoughts as I went along. As a result, some portions of this book make use of earlier publications of mine, although in every case they have been substantially revised. I wish to acknowledge here the respective permissions of the publishers to reuse material from: "Franklin, Edwards, and the Problem of Human Nature," in *Benjamin Franklin, Jonathan Edwards, and the Representation of American Culture,* ed. Barbara B. Oberg and Harry S. Stout (New York: Oxford University Press, 1993); "Why the Scottish Enlightenment Was Useful to the Framers of the American Constitution," *Comparative Studies in Society and History* 31 (July 1989); "The Political Psychology of *The Federalist*," *William and Mary Quarterly* 44 (July 1987); "The Language of Faculty Psychology in *The Federalist Papers*," in *Conceptual Change and the Constitution,* ed. Terence Ball and J. G. A. Pocock (Lawrence: University Press of Kansas, 1988); "The Evangelical Movement and Political Culture in the North During the Second Party System," *Journal of American History* 77 (March, 1991); "Why Abraham Lincoln Was a Whig," *Journal of the Abraham Lincoln Association* 16 (Winter 1995); "The Social Science of Horace Bushnell," *Journal of American History* 60 (September, 1983); "The Cambridge Platonists of Old England and the Cambridge Platonists of New England," in *American Unitarianism, 1805–1865,* ed. Conrad E. Wright (Boston: Massachusetts Historical Society and Northeastern University Press, 1989); and *Henry David Thoreau on the Duty of Civil Disobedience: An Inaugural Lecture Delivered before the University of Oxford on 21 May 1990* (Clarendon Press of Oxford University Press, 1991).

Daniel Walker Howe
St. Catherine's College, Oxford, and Sherman Oaks, California
October 1995

Index